2015 YEARBOOK

OF THE GENERAL ASSEMBLY

CUMBERLAND PRESBYTERIAN CHURCH

Office of the General Assembly

Cumberland Presbyterian Church

July 2015

8207 Traditional Place
Cordova (Memphis), Tennessee 38016

Published and distributed exclusively by The Discipleship Ministry Team, CPC, Memphis, Tennessee. Additional copies may be acquired through Cumberland Presbyterian Resources.

The Discipleship Ministry Team of the Ministry Council of the Cumberland Presbyterian Church is the successor organization to the Board of Christian Education of the Cumberland Presbyterian Church.

Funded, in part, by your contributions to Our United Outreach.

First Edition 2015

ISBN-13: 978-0692425527
ISBN-10: 0692425527

OUR UNITED OUTREACH
Made Possible In Part By Your Tithe To Our United Outreach

CUMBERLAND PRESBYTERIAN CENTER OFFICES
8207 TRADITIONAL PLACE
CORDOVA, TENNESSEE 38016

Central Telephone for Center Offices: (901)276-4572, Historical Foundation Telephone: (901)276-8602

BOARD OF STEWARDSHIP, FOUNDATION AND BENEFITS
Phone (901)276-4572   FAX (901)272-3913
Robert Heflin, Executive Secretary
  rah@cumberland.org   Ext-207
Mark Duck, Coordinator of Benefits
  rmd@cumberland.org   Ext-204
Kathryn Gilbert Craig, Administrative Assistant
  kgc@cumberland.org   Ext-206

CENTRAL SERVICES
Phone (901)276-4572   FAX (901)272-3913
Dan Scherf, Accounting Supervisor
  dscherf@cumberland.org   Ext-233
Matthew Gore, Computer Services
  mhg@cumberland.org   Ext-252

GENERAL ASSEMBLY OFFICE
Phone (901)276-4572   FAX (901)272-3913
Michael Sharpe, Stated Clerk
  msharpe@cumberland.org   Ext-225
Elizabeth Vaughn, Assistant to the Stated Clerk
  eav@cumberland.org   Ext-226

HISTORICAL FOUNDATION OF THE CPC & CPCA
Phone (901)276-8602   FAX (901)272-3913
Susan Knight Gore, Archivist
  skg@cumberland.org
Lauren Gam Gilliland, Archival Assistant
  lgilliland@cumberland.org

MINISTRY COUNCIL
Phone (901)276-4572   FAX (901)276-4578
Edith Old, Director of Ministries
  eold@cumberland.org   Ext-228
Executive Assistant to the Director of Ministries
     Ext-217

PASTORAL DEVELOPMENT MINISTRY TEAM
Phone (901)276-4572   FAX (901)276-4578
Chuck, Brown, Team Leader
  crb@cumberland.org   Ext-235

COMMUNICATIONS MINISTRY TEAM
Phone (901)276-4572   FAX (901)276-4578
Mark J. Davis, Team Leader/Editor
  mdavis@cumberland.org   Ext-216
Sowgand Sheikholeslami, Senior Art Director
  sowgand@cumberland.org   Ext-211

CP RESOURCES
resources@cumberland.org   (901)276-4581

DISCIPLESHIP MINISTRY TEAM
Phone (901)276-4572   FAX (901)276-4578
Elinor Brown, Team Leader
  esb@cumberland.org   Ext-205
Matthew Gore, Resources Development
  & Distribution
  mhg@cumberland.org   Ext-252
Nathan Wheeler, Youth & Young Adult Ministry
  nwheeler@cumberland.org   Ext-218
Cindy Martin, Adult & Third Age Ministry
  chm@cumberland.org   Ext-219
Jodi Rush, Children & Family Ministry
  jhr@cumberland.org   Ext-223

MISSIONS MINISTRY TEAM
Phone (901)276-4572   FAX (901)276-4578
Milton Ortiz, Team Leader
  mortiz@cumberland.org   Ext-234
Jinger Ellis, Manager, Finance and Administration
  jellis@cumberland.org   Ext-230
Pam Phillips-Burk, Congregational/Women's Ministry
  pam@cumberland.org   Ext-203
Johan Daza, Cross Culture Immigrant Ministries USA
  jdaza@cumberland.org   Ext-202
T.J. Malinoski, Evangelism & New Church Development
  tmalinoski@cumberland.org   Ext-232
Lynn Thomas, Global Cross Culture Missions
  4833 Caldwell Mill Lane, Birmingham, AL 35242   Ext-261
  lynndont@gmail.com   (205)601-5770

OTHER CHURCH OFFICES

BETHEL UNIVERSITY
325 Cherry Avenue, McKenzie, TN 38201
Phone (731)352-4000   FAX (731)352-6387
Walter Butler, President
Dale Henry, Vice President for Development
Steve Perryman, Vice President for Finance
Nancy Bean, Vice President for College of Arts & Sciences
Roland Colson, Vice President for College of Public Service
Joe Hames, Vice President for College of Health Sciences
Kelly Kelley, Vice President for College of Professional Studies

CHILDREN'S HOME
909 Greenlee Street, Denton, TX 76201
  Mail Address: Drawer G, Denton, TX 76202
Phone (940)382-5112   FAX (940)387-0821
    cpch@cpch.org   www.cpch.org
Richard Brown, President, CEO & General Counsel   (817)360-6874
  rbrown@cpch.org
Larry Brown, Vice President, Development   (817)341-1235
  lbrown@cpch.org

MEMPHIS THEOLOGICAL SEMINARY
168 East Parkway South, Memphis, TN 38104-4395
Phone (901)458-8232   FAX (901)452-4051
    www.MemphisSeminary.edu
Daniel J. Earheart-Brown, President
Cassandra Price-Perry, Vice-President of Operations/CFO
Stan Wood, Interim Vice-President of Academic Affairs/Dean
Keith Gaskin, Vice President of Advancement
Cory Williams, Chief Information Officer
Laurie Sharpe, Executive Assistant to the President

OUR UNITED OUTREACH
4782 Waverly Court, Ooltewah, TN 37363
Cliff Hudson, Development Director   Phone (901)276-4572 Ext-210
  gchudson3@gmail.com

PROGRAM OF ALTERNATE STUDIES
168 East Parkway South, Memphis, TN 38104-4395
Phone (901)334-5853   FAX (901)452-4051
Michael Qualls, Director
  mqualls@memphisseminary.edu
Karen Patten, Administrative Assistant
  kpatten@memphisseminary.edu

2015 YEARBOOK

General Assembly
Cumberland Presbyterian Church

Vision of Ministry

Biblically-based and Christ-centered
    born out of a specific sense of mission,
    the Cumberland Presbyterian Church strives to be true to its heritage:
    to be open to God's reforming spirit,
    to work cooperatively with the larger Body of Christ,
    and to nurture the connectional bonds that make us one.
The Cumberland Presbyterian Church seeks—to be the hands and feet of Christ in witness and service to the world and, above all, the Cumberland Presbyterian Church lives out the love of God to the glory of Jesus Christ.

Containing Statistics for the Year 2014

Changes Made to Other Data Through Print Time

(The Yearbook is updated periodically on our website www.cumberland.org/gao)

Compiled & Edited by

Elizabeth Vaughn

TABLE OF CONTENTS

Directory of Board and Agency Offices..C
Vision of Ministry and Priority Goals...i
General Assembly Officers and Members of Boards and Agencies 1
Living General Assembly Moderators 9
Abbreviations of Synods and Presbyteries 10
Stated Clerks of Synods and Presbyteries..10
Ministers Gained and Lost 14
Chaplains, Alphabetical Roll 15
Memorial Roll of Ministers 16
Surviving Spouses of Ministers 17
Cumberland Presbyterians Serving Outside the United States 21
New Church Developments & Mission Probes 22
Provisional Churches 23
Mission Churches/Pastors under care of Missions Ministry Team......................................24
Camp Grounds 26
Explanation of Symbols...27
Summary of Statistics of Presbyteries by Synods for 2013 28
Directories of Churches by Presbyteries
    Andes Presbytery (MSAN)..29
    Arkansas Presbytery (GRAR)..32
    Cauca Valley Presbytery (MSCA) 38
    Choctaw (MSCH) 41
    Columbia Presbytery (TNCO) 42
    Covenant Presbytery (MICO)...46
    Cumberland Presbytery (MICU)...51
    Cumberland East Coast Presbytery (SEEC) 58
    Presbytery del Cristo (MSDC)..59
    Presbytery of East Tennessee (SEET)...62
    Grace Presbytery (SEGR) 67
    Hong Kong Presbytery (MSHK) 72
    Hope Presbytery (SEHO)..74
    Japan Presbytery (MSJA) 76
    Missouri Presbytery (GRMI)..79
    Murfreesboro Presbytery (TNMU)..82
    Nashville Presbytery (TNNA) 87
    North Central Presbytery (MINC) 92
    Red River Presbytery (MSRR) 96
    Robert Donnell Presbytery (SERD)...100
    Tennessee-Georgia Presbytery (SETG) 103
    Trinity Presbytery (MSTR)..106
    West Tennessee Presbytery (GRWT)..109
Alphabetical Roll of Ministers..120
Alphabetical Index of Churches..146
Location Index of Churches..153
Directory of Cumberland Presbyterian Church in America..159

GENERAL ASSEMBLY OFFICERS

MODERATOR
THE REVEREND LISA HALL ANDERSON
1790 FAXON AVENUE
MEMPHIS, TN 38112
(901)246-8052
anderli60@gmail.com

VICE MODERATOR
THE REVEREND PAULA LOUDER
98 GALLANT COURT
CLARKSVILLE, TN 37043
(615)804-4809
paula.louder@cmcss.net

STATED CLERK AND TREASURER
THE REVEREND MICHAEL SHARPE
8207 Traditional Place
Cordova, TN 38016
(901)276-4572
FAX (901)272-3913
msharpe@cumberland.org

ENGROSSING CLERK
THE REVEREND VERNON SANSOM
7810 Shiloh Road
Midlothian, TX 76065
(972)825-6887
vernon@sansom.us

THE BOARD OF DIRECTORS OF THE GENERAL ASSEMBLY CORPORATION

(Members whose terms expire in 2015)
(3)REV. MELISSA MALINOSKI, 9087 Fenmore Cove, Cordova, TN 38016
    mmalinoski@memphisseminary.edu
(3)MR. JERRY WEATHERSBY, 119 County Road 743, Cullman, AL 35055
    jerryw@cullmanelectric.com
(Members whose terms expire in 2016)
(1)MR. TIM GARRETT, 150 Third Avenue South, Suite 2800, Nashville, TN 37201
    tgarrett@bassberry.com
(1)REV. BOBBY COLEMAN, 704 E Webb Street, Mountain View, AR 72560
    bobby.coleman@gmail.com
(Members whose terms expire in 2017)
(1)REV. JOHN BUTLER, PO Box 257, Sacramento, KY 42372
    jbutler@iccable.com
(1)MS. BETTY JACOB, PO Box 158, Broken Bow, OK 74728
    chocpres@pine-net.com

*Ecumenical Partners
+Cumberland Presbyterians in America
Numbers in parenthesis denote number of terms.

MINISTRY COUNCIL

(Members whose terms expire in 2015)
(2)MS. SALLY ALLEN, 1035 Stonewall Street N, McKenzie, TN 38201
(1)MR. KENNETH BEAN, 3510 Clubhouse Road, Somerset, KY 42503
(1)MS. MARY ANN COLE, 620 Plum Springs Road, Bowling Green, KY 42101
(3)REV. CARLTON HARPER, 255 Glenview Circle, Lenoir City, TN 37771
(1)REV. RON MCMILLAN, 675 Kimberly Drive, Atoka, TN 38004
(Members whose terms expire in 2016)
(3)MS. JILL CARR, PO Box 1547, Lebanon, MO 65536
(2)REV. TROY GREEN, 105 Cobb Hollow Lane, Petersburg, TN 37144
(3)MS. ELIZABETH HORSLEY, 1200 Imperial Drive, Denton, TX 76201
(3)MS. GWEN RODDYE, 3728 Wittenham Drive, Knoxville, TN 37921
(3)REV. SAM ROMINES, PO Box 127, Lewisburg, KY 42256
(Members whose terms expire in 2017)
(2)REV. DONNY ACTON, 1413 Oakridge Drive, Birmingham, AL 35242
(3)REV. MICHELE GENTRY DE CORREAL, Urb San Jorge casa 28, Km 8 via a La Tebaida
    Armenia, Quinido, COLOMBIA, SOUTH AMERICA
(2)REV. LANNY JOHNSON, 120 S Mill Street, Morrison, TN 37357
(1)MR. ADAM MCREYNOLDS, PO Box 162, Bethany, IL 61914
(2)REV. TOM SANDERS, 4201 W Kent Street, Broken Arrow, OK 74012

YOUTH ADVISORY MEMBERS
(2)MR. EDDIE MONTOYA, JR, 270 Windsor Drive, Roselle, IL 60172
(1)MS. CAROLINA GILLIS, 6243 Sioux Lane, Birmingham, AL 35242
(1)MS. EMILY MAHONEY, 31 Barbara Circle, McMinnville, TN 37110

ADVISORY MEMBERS
REV. LISA ANDERSON, 1790 Faxon Avenue, Memphis, TN 38112
REV. FOREST PROSSER, 1157 Mountain Creek Road, Chattanooga, TN 37405
REV. MICHAEL SHARPE, 8207 Traditional Place, Cordova, TN 38016

COMMUNICATIONS MINISTRY TEAM

(Members whose terms expire in 2015)
(2)REV. MICHAEL CLARK, 80 Bryan Drive, Winchester, TN 37398
(2)REV. JAMES D. MCGUIRE, 220-2 Southwind Circle, Greeneville, TN 37743
(Members whose terms expire in 2016)
(1)REV. NICHOLAS CHAMBERS, 11300 Road 101, Union, MS 39365
(1)REV. STEVEN SHELTON, 7886 Farmhill Cove, Bartlett, TN 38135
(Members whose terms expire in 2017)
(3)MS. B. DENISE ADAMS, 126 Ray, Monticello, AR 71655
(2)MRS. DUSTY SHULL, 110 Windmere Cove, Paducah, KY 42001

*Ecumenical Partners
+Cumberland Presbyterians in America
Numbers in parenthesis denote number of terms.

DISCIPLESHIP MINISTRY TEAM

(Members whose terms expire in 2015)
(2)MS. JOANNA WILKINSON, 403 Enclave Circle, Nashville, TN 37217
(1)MS. RACHEL COOK, 210 Bynum Street, Scottsboro, AL 35768
(1)REV. CHRISTIAN SMITH, 475 State Street, Cookeville, TN 38501
(Members whose terms expire in 2016)
(3)REV. MINDY ACTON, 1413 Oak Ridge Drive, Birmingham, AL 35242
(1)REV. NANCY MCSPADDEN, 120 Roberta Drive, Memphis, TN 38112
(1)REV. JOSEFINA SANCHEZ, 7 Hancock Street, Melrose, MA 02176
(Members whose terms expire in 2017)
(2)MS. LE ILA DIXON, 4406 John Reagan Street, Marshall, TX 75672
(2)REV. AARON FERRY, 122 Crimson Drive, Winchester, TN 37398
(3)MS. SAMANTHA HASSELL, 510 N Main Street, Sturgis, KY 42459

MISSIONS MINISTRY TEAM

(Members whose terms expire in 2015)
(2)REV. JIM BARRY, 1405 Anna Street, Hixson, TN 37343
(1)MR. TIM CRAIG, 8958 Carriage Creek Road, Arlington, TN 38002
(1)REV. CARDELIA HOWELL-DIAMOND, 1580 Jeff Road NW, Huntsville, AL 35806
(2)MS. SHERRY POTEET, P.O. Box 313, Gilmer, TX 75644
(1)MS. MELINDA REAMS, 10 W Azalea Lane, Russellville, AR 72802
(Members whose terms expire in 2016)
(2)REV. MAKIHIKO ARASE, 3-355-4 Kamikitadai Higashiyamato-Shi, Tokyo, 207-0023 JAPAN
(1)REV. VICTOR HASSELL, 510 N Main Street, Sturgis, KY 42459
(1)MR. DOMINIC LAU, 3820 Anza Street, San Francisco, CA
(1)MS. BRITTANY MEEKS, 1340 Tutwiler Avenue, Memphis, TN 38107
(1)REV. CHRIS WARREN, 906 Prince Lane, Murfreesboro, TN 37129
(Members whose terms expire in 2017)
(2)REV. JAMES BUTTRAM, 103 Golfcrest Lane, Oak Ridge, TN 37830
(3)REV. JIMMY BYRD, 176 E Valley Road, Whitwell, TN 37397
(1)MS. DONNA CHRISTIE, 3221 Whitehall Road, Birmingham, AL 35209
(3)REV. RICARDO FRANCO, 7 Hancock Street, Melrose, MA 02176
(1)MRS. MS. KAREN TOLEN, 6859 A East County Road 000N, Trilla, IL 62469

PASTORAL DEVELOPMENT MINISTRY TEAM

(Members whose terms expire in 2015)
(1)REV. DUAWN MEARNS, 107 Westoak Place, Hot Springs, AR 71913
(2)REV. LINDA SNELLING, 15791 State Highway W, Ada, OK 74820
(Members whose terms expire in 2016)
(2)MS. MICAIAH THOMAS, PO Box 5204 SBN 499, Princeton, NJ 08543 (resigned)
(1)REV. PATRICK WILKERSON, 7719 S Whispering Oak Circle, Powell, TN 37849
(Members whose terms expire in 2017)
(2)REV. AMBER CLARK, 80 Bryan Drive, Winchester, TN 37398
(2)REV. DREW HAYES, 6322 Labor Lane, Louisville, KY 40291

*Ecumenical Partners
+Cumberland Presbyterians in America
Numbers in parenthesis denote number of terms.

GENERAL ASSEMBLY BOARD OF:

I. TRUSTEES OF BETHEL UNIVERSITY

(Members whose terms expire in 2015)
(3)*MR. MICHAEL (MIKE) CARY, 181 Angel Cove, Huntingdon, TN 38344
(2)MR. CHARLIE GARRETT, 107 Willow Green Drive, Jackson, TN 38305
(1)+REV. ELTON C. HALL, SR., 305 Tiffton Circle, Hewitt, TX 76643
(1)REV. MARK S. HESTER, 763 Finn Long Road, Friendsville, TN 37737
(3)*MS. CHARLENE P. JONES, 137 Moore Avenue W, McKenzie, TN 38201
(1)MS. DEWANNA LATIMER, 1077 Jr. Jones Road, Humboldt, TN 38343
(2)REV. EUGENE LESLIE, 13155 Center Hill Road, Olive Branch, MS 38654 (deceased)

(Members whose terms expire in 2016)
(1)MR. JEFF AMREIN, 11711 Paramont Way, Prospect, KY 40059
(3)DR. LARRY A. BLAKEBURN, 230 Heathridge Drive, Dyersburg, TN 38024
(2)*JUDGE BEN CANTRELL, 415 Church Street #2513, Nashville, TN 37219
(2)+DR. ARMY DANIEL, 3125 Searcy Drive, Huntsville, AL 35810
(3)MR. LAWRENCE (LADD) DANIEL, 13023 Taylorcrest, Houston, TX 77079
(1)MR. BILL DOBBINS 5716 Quest Ridge Road, Franklin, TN 37064
(2)DR. ROBERT LOW, c/o New Prime, Inc., 2740 W Mayfair Avenue, Springfield, MO 65803
(3)MR. BEN T. SURBER, 1145 Hico Road, McKenzie, TN 38201

(Members whose terms expire in 2017)
(2)*MS. LISA COLE, PO Box 198615, Nashville, TN 37219
(2)MR. CHESTER (CHET) DICKSON, 24 W Rivercrest Drive, Houston, TX 77042
(2)*MR. ARTHUR (ART) LAFFER, JR., 410 Wilsonia Avenue, Nashville, TN 37205
(1)REV. NANCY MCSPADDEN, 2011 Woodridge Drive, St. Peters, MO 63376
(3)MR. BOBBY OWEN, 1625 Cabot Drive, Franklin, TN 37064
(2)DR. ED PERKINS, 721 Paris Street, McKenzie, TN 38201
(1)MR. KENNETH (KEN) D. QUINTON, 2912 Waller Omer Road, Sturgis, KY 42459
(3)REV. ROBERT (ROB) TRUITT, 1238 Old East Side Road, Burns, TN 37029
(1)REV. ROBERT (BOB) WATKINS, 10950 West Union Hills Drive #1356, Sun City, AZ 85373

Trustee Emeritus – Dr. Vera Low, 3653 Prestwick Court, Springfield, MO 65809 (deceased)

II. TRUSTEES OF CUMBERLAND PRESBYTERIAN CHILDREN'S HOME

(Members whose terms expire in 2015)
(2)*MS. KAY GOODMAN, 1042 Bobcat Road, Sanger, TX 76266
(3)MS. PAT HUFF, 249 Rancho Drive, Saginaw, TX 76179
(2)REV. MELISSA KNIGHT, 5730 Haley Road, Meridian, MS 39305
(3)MS. RUBY LETSON, 2921 Alexander, Florence, AL 35633
(2)*MR. BARON H. SMITH, 3401 Hasland Drive, Flower Mound, TX 75022

(Members whose terms expire in 2016)
(2)*MR. RICHARD DEAN, 2140 Cove Circle North, Gadsden, AL 35903
(2)MS. PATRICIA LONG, 525 E Oak Street, Aledo, TX 76008
(3)REV. ALFONSO MARQUEZ, 389 Bethel Drive, Lenoir City, TN 37772
(3)MR. MICKEY SHELL, 2143 Griderfield-Ladd Road, Pine Bluff, AR 71601

(Members whose terms expire in 2017)
(1)REV. LISA ANDERSON, 1790 Faxon Street, Memphis, TN 38112
(1)MS. CAROLINE BOOTH, 2200 Westview Trail, Denton, TX 76207
(3)+MS. MAMIE HALL, 305 Tiffton Circle, Hewitt, TX 76643
(1)MR. CHARLES HARRIS, 3293 Birch Avenue, Grapevine, TX 76051
(1)MR. KNIGHT MILLER, 1035 Garden Creek Circle, Louisville, KY 40223
(1)MR. JOHN O'CARROLL, 1701 Live Oak Lane, Southlake, TX 76092
(2)*MS. TIFFANY SMITH, 2901 Corporate Circle, Flower Mound, TX 75028
(3)REV. DON TABOR, 9611 Mitchell Place, Brentwood, TN 37027

*Ecumenical Partners
+Cumberland Presbyterians in America
Numbers in parenthesis denote number of terms.

III. TRUSTEES OF HISTORICAL FOUNDATION

(Members whose terms expire in 2015)
(3)REV. TOMMY JOBE, 807 Rockwood Drive, Nolensville, TN 37135
(2)DR. SIDNEY L. SWINDLE, 4407 Swann Avenue, Tampa, FL 33609
(Members whose terms expire in 2016)
(3)+MS. VANESSA BARNHILL, 819 King Street, Sturgis, KY 42459
(3)MS. PAMELA DAVIS, 5111 County Road 7545, Lubbock, TX 79424
(3)+MS. NAOMI KING, 3850 Millsfield Highway, Dyersburg, TN 38024 (resigned)
(2)REV. MARY KATHRYN KIRKPATRICK, 401 1/2 Henley-Perry Drive, Marshall, TX 75670
(3)MS. SIDNEY MILTON, 27 Kalee Lane, Calvert City, KY 42029
(Members whose terms expire in 2017)
(3)+MS. EDNA BARNETT, 7 Breezewood Cove, Jackson, TN 38305
(3)MR. MICHAEL FARE, 401 E Deanna Lane, Nixa, MO 65714
(2)*MS. DOROTHY HAYDEN, 3103 Carolina Avenue, Bessemer, AL 35020
(3)+REV. RICK WHITE, 124 Towne West, Lorena, TX 76655

IV. TRUSTEES OF MEMPHIS THEOLOGICAL SEMINARY OF THE CUMBERLAND PRESBYTERIAN CHURCH

(Members whose terms expire in 2015)
(2)REV. KEVIN BRANTLEY, 729 Old Hodgenville Road, Greensburg, KY 42743
(3)REV. JODY HILL, 4030 St Andrew Circle, Corinth, MS 38834
(3)MS. JAN HOLMES, 5209 87th Street, Lubbock, TX 79424
(2)MR. MARK MADDOX, 225 Oak Drive, Dresden, TN 38225
(1)MS. SONDRA RODDY, 2583 Hedgerow Lane, Clarksville, TN 37043
(2)MR. TAKAYOSHI SHIRAI, 25 Minami Kibogaoka Asahi-ku, Yokohama, Kanagawa-ken 241-0824 JAPAN
(1)*REV. MELVIN CHARLES SMITH, 1263 Haynes Street, Memphis, TN 38114
(1)*MS. LATISHA TOWNS, The Med, 877 Jefferson Avenue, Memphis, TN 38103
(Members whose terms expire in 2016)
(2)MR. MICHAEL R. ALLEN, 149 Windwood Circle, Alabaster, AL 35007
(1)*MR. JOHNNIE COOMBS, PO Box 127, Blue Mountain, MS 38610
(2)MS. DIANE DICKSON, 24 West Rivercrest, Houston, TX 77042
(2)*MR. HARVEY G. FERGUSON, 630 Gaines Road, Hernando, MS 38682
(3)*MR. DAN HATZENBUEHLER, 1544 Carr Avenue, Memphis, TN 38104
(1)*DR. RICK KIRCHOFF, 2044 Thorncroft Drive, Germantown, TN 38138
(3)MR. TIM ORR, 1591 Laura Lane, Dyersburg, TN 38024
(2)*DR. INETTA RODGERS, 1824 S Parkway E, Memphis, TN 38114
(3)*MRS. K.C. WARREN, 215 Buena Vista Place, Memphis, TN 38112
(Members whose terms expire in 2017)
(2)REV. DOY DANIELS Jr., 6083 S First Street, Milan, TN 38358
(2)*REV. ROBERT MARBLE, 515 Shamrock Drive, Little Rock, AR 72205
(3)MS. PAT MEEKS, 8540 Edney Ridge Drive, Cordova, TN 38016
(2)REV. JENNIFER NEWELL, 2322 Marco Circle, Chattanooga, TN 37421
(3)REV. ROBERT M. SHELTON, 7128 Lakehurst Avenue, Dallas, TX 75230
(3)+DR. JOE WARD, 2620 Rabbit Lane, Madison, AL 35758
(3)*MS. RUBY WHARTON, 1183 E Parkway South, Memphis, TN 38114

V. STEWARDSHIP, FOUNDATION AND BENEFITS

(Members whose terms expire in 2015)
(2)MR. ANDREW B. FRAZIER, JR., 107 Doris Street, Camden, TN 38320
(3)MR. ROBERT LATIMER, RR 1 Box 123, Miami, MO 65344
(1)MR. MICHAEL ST. JOHN, 324 Carriage Place, Lebanon, MO 65536

*Ecumenical Partners
+Cumberland Presbyterians in America
Numbers in parenthesis denote number of terms.

(Members whose terms expire in 2016)

(3)MR. CHARLES G. FLOYD, 1617 Championship Drive, Franklin, TN 37064

(1)REV. CHARLES (BUDDY) POPE, 2391 Fairfield Pike, Shelbyville, TN 37160

(2)MS. SUE RICE, 1301 Brooker Road, Brandon, FL 33511

(2)MS. DEBBIE SHELTON, 1255 MG England Road, Manchester, TN 37355

(Members whose terms expire in 2017)

(1)REV. RANDY DAVIDSON, PO Box 880, Ada, OK 74821

(3)MR. CHARLES DAY, 9312 Owensboro Road, Falls of Rough, KY 40119

(3)MS. SYLVIA HALL, 930 Sherry Circle, Hixson, TN 37343

(3)MR. JACKIE SATTERFIELD, 2303 County Road 730, Cullman, AL 35055

GENERAL ASSEMBLY COMMISSIONS:

I. MILITARY CHAPLAINS AND PERSONNEL

(2) Term Expires in 2015–REV. LOWELL RODDY, 2583 Hedgerow Lane, Clarksville, TN 37043, lgroddy@yahoo.com

(1) Term Expires in 2016–REV. CASSANDRA THOMAS, 1920 Dancy Street, Fayetteville, NC 28301, chcothomas@yahoo.com

(2) Term Expires in 2017–REV. MARY MCCASKEY BENEDICT, 892 Pen Oak Drive, Cookeville, TN 38501, marykat_61@hotmail.com

These three persons and the Stated Clerk represent the denomination as members of the Presbyterian Council for Chaplains and Military Personnel, 4125 Nebraska Avenue NW, Washington, DC 20016

GENERAL ASSEMBLY COMMITTEES

I. JUDICIARY

(Members whose terms expire in 2015)

(1)REV. ANNETTA CAMP, 2263 Mill Creek Road, Halls, TN 38040
anetta@cumberlandchurch.com

(3)MR. CHARLES DAWSON, PO Box 904, Scottsboro, AL 35768
rdpfcd@scottsboro.org

(2)MS. KIMBERLY SILVUS, 1128 Madison Street, Clarksville, TN 37040
kgsilvus@gmail.com

(Members whose terms expire in 2016)

(3)REV. SHERRY LADD, 4521 Turkey Creek Road, Williamsport, TN 38487
revsherryladd@gmail.com

(2)REV. ANDY MCCLUNG, 919 Dickinson Street, Memphis, TN 38107
scubarev@att.net

(3)MS. FELICIA WALKUP, 179 Mary Anne Lane, Manchester, TN 37355
fbwalkup@gmail.com

(Members whose terms expire in 2017)

(1)REV. HARRY CHAPMAN, 4908 El Picador Court SE, Rio Rancho, NM 87124
wrightrev2gmail.com

(2)REV. ROBERT D. RUSH, 12935 Quail Park Drive, Cypress, TX 77429
rushrd74@comcast.net

(3)MR. WENDELL THOMAS, JR., 1200 Paradise Drive, Powell, TN 37849
volbaby@comcast.net

*Ecumenical Partners
+Cumberland Presbyterians in America
Numbers in parenthesis denote number of terms.

II. JOINT COMMITTEE ON AMENDMENTS

The committee consists of five members of the Judiciary Committee of the Cumberland Presbyterian Church in America and the Cumberland Presbyterian Church.

III. NOMINATING

(Members whose terms expire in 2015)
(1)MR. RICK GAMBLE, 2430 Mount View Road, Manchester, TN 37355
  gamble-ra@charter.net
(1)REV. ALAN MEINZER, 25 Rosewood Road, Batesville, AR 72501
  brotheralan@suddenlink.net
(Members whose terms expire in 2016)
(1)MS. NANCY BEAN, 3510 Clubhouse Road, Somerset, KY 42503
  beann@bethelu.edu
(1)REV. CHARLES MCCASKEY, 679 Canter Lane, Cookeville, TN 38501
  charles@cookevillecpchurch.org
(1)REV. JIMMY PEYTON, 1455 County Road 643, Cullman, AL 35055
  jakjpeyton@att.net
(1)MS. MARJORIE SHANNON, 2307 Littlemore Drive, Cordova, TN 38016
  margieshannon@att.net
(Members whose terms expire in 2017)
(1)REV. TOBY DAVIS, 502 S Alley Street, Jefferson, TX 75657
  pastortobydavis@gmail.com
(1)MS. CAROLYN HARMON, 4435 Newport Highway, Greeneville, TN 37743
  richardharmon09@comcast.net
(1)MS. ELLIE SCRUDDER, 29688 S 535 Road, Park Hill, OK 74451
  escrudder@gmail.com
(1)REV. KEVIN SMALL, 6492 E 400th Road, Martinsville, IL 62442
  revkev61@gmail.com

IV. OUR UNITED OUTREACH COMMITTEE

(Members whose terms expire in 2015)
(1)MR. RANDY WEATHERSBY, 1502 Pinecrest Street NW, Cullman, AL 35055
(1)MS. ROBIN WILLS, 4607 E Richmond Shop Road, Lebanon, TN 37090
(Members whose terms expire in 2016)
(3)MR. RON D. GARDNER, 8668 Wood Mills Drive W, Cordova, TN 38016
(Members whose terms expire in 2017)
(3)MS. SHARON RESCH, PO Box 383, Dongola, IL 62926
(3)REV. WILLIAM RUSTENHAVEN III, PO Box 1303, Marshall, TX 75671

V. PLACE OF MEETING

THE STATED CLERK OF THE GENERAL ASSEMBLY
THE MODERATOR OF THE GENERAL ASSEMBLY
A REPRESENTATIVE OF WOMEN'S MINISTRIES OF THE MISSIONS MINISTRY TEAM

*Ecumenical Partners
+Cumberland Presbyterians in America
Numbers in parenthesis denote number of terms.

VI. UNIFIED COMMITTEE ON THEOLOGY AND SOCIAL CONCERNS

(Members whose terms expire in 2015)

(1)MR. DAVID PHILLIPS-BURK, 3325 Bailey Creek Cove N, Collierville, TN 38017
    dlphillipsburk@aol.com; (256)520-1380
(1)REV. GEORGE ESTES, 7910 Cloverbrook Lane, Germantown, TN 38138
    geoestes@gmail.com; (901)755-6673
(1)REV. SHELIA O'MARA, 533 Loughton Lane, Arnold, MD 21012
    chaplainshelia@aol.com; (410)757-5713; (443)370-7218 cell

(Members whose terms expire in 2016)

(3)MS. LEZLIE P. DANIEL, 13023 Taylorcrest Road, Houston, TX 77079
    lululoop@me.com
(2)+MRS. JIMMIE DODD, c/o Hopewell CPCA, 4100 Millsfield Highway, Dyersburg, TN 38024
    dodd125@gmail.com
(2)REV. BYRON FORESTER, 2376 Eastwood Place, Memphis, TN 38112
    bforester@bellsouth.net; (901)246-1242
(1)REV. JOHN A. SMITH, 916 Allen Road, Nashville, TN 37214
    john.a.smith.81@gmail.com; (573)453-8455
(2)+ELDER JOY WALLACE, 6940 Marvin D Love Freeway, Dallas, TX 75237
    jwallace@wlgllc.net

(Members whose terms expire in 2017)

(2)+DR. NANCY FUQUA, 1963 County Road 406, Towncreek, AL 35672
    fuq23@bellsouth.net; (256)566-1226
(2)REV. RANDY JACOB, PO Box 158, Broken Bow, OK 74728
    chocpres@pine-net.com; (580)584-3770; (580)236-2469 cell
(3)+REV. NOVALENE SITGRAVES, 3345 Grand Avenue, Louisville, KY 40211

President of Memphis Theological Seminary - Ex-officio Member
    REV. JAY EARHEART-BROWN, 866 N McLean Boulevard, Memphis, TN 38107
    jebrown@memphisseminary.edu; (901)278-0367

OTHER DENOMINATIONAL PERSONNEL

REPRESENTATIVES TO:
American Bible Society: REV. MICHAEL SHARPE, 8207 Traditional Place, Cordova, TN 38016

Caribbean and North American Area Council, World Communion of Reformed Churches:
STATED CLERK MICHAEL SHARPE, 8207 Traditional Place, Cordova, TN 38016

(Member whose terms expire in 2017)
(2)MS. LAURIE SHARPE, 3423 Summerdale Drive, Bartlett, TN 38133

*Ecumenical Partners
+Cumberland Presbyterians in America
Numbers in parenthesis denote number of terms.

LIVING GENERAL ASSEMBLY MODERATORS

2014—REV. LISA HALL ANDERSON, 1790 Faxon Avenue, Memphis, TN 38112
2013—REV. FOREST PROSSER, 1157 Mountain Creek Road, Chattanooga, TN 37405
2012—REV. ROBERT D. RUSH, 12935 Quail Park Drive, Cypress, TX 77429
2011—REV. DON M. TABOR, 9611 Mitchell Place, Brentwood, TN 37027
2010—REV. BOYCE WALLACE, Cra 101 No 15-93, Cali, Colombia, South America
2009—ELDER SAM SUDDARTH, 206 Ha Le Koa Court, Smyrna, TN 37167
2008—REV. JONATHAN CLARK, 88 Woodcrest Drive, Winchester, TN 37398
2007—REV. FRANK WARD, 8207 Traditional Place, Cordova, TN 38016
2006—REV. DONALD HUBBARD, 2128 Campbell Station Road, Knoxville, TN 37932
2005—REV. LINDA H. GLENN, 49 Mason Road, Threeway, TN 38343
2004—REV. EDWARD G. SIMS, 2161 N. Meadows Drive, Clarksville, TN 37043
2003—REV. CHARLES MCCASKEY, 679 Canter Lane, Cookeville, TN 38501
2001—REV. RANDOLPH JACOB, 610 W. Adams Street, Broken Bow, OK 74728
1999—ELDER GWENDOLYN G. RODDYE, 3728 Wittenham Drive, Knoxville, TN 37921
1998—REV. MASAHARU ASAYAMA, 3-15-9 Higashi, Kunitachi-shi, Tokyo, JAPAN
1996—REV. MERLYN A. ALEXANDER, 80 N. Hampton Lane, Jackson, TN 38305
1995—REV. CLINTON O. BUCK, PO Box 770068, Memphis, TN 38117
1993—REV. ROBERT M. SHELTON, 7128 Lakehurst Avenue, Dallas, TX 75230
1992—REV. JOHN DAVID HALL, 109 Oddo Lane SE, Huntsville, AL 35802
1990—REV. THOMAS D. CAMPBELL, PO Box 315, Calico Rock, AR 72519
1989—REV. WILLIAM RUSTENHAVEN, Jr., 703 W. Burleson, Marshall, TX 75670
1988—ELDER BEVERLY ST. JOHN, 806 Evansdale Drive, Nashville, TN 37220
1982—REV. WILLIAM A. RAWLINS, 3100 Cook Lane, Longview, TX 75604
1981—REV. W. JEAN RICHARDSON, 7533 Lancashire, Powell, TN 37849
1975—REV. ROY E. BLAKEBURN, 111 Park Place, Greeneville, TN 37743

IN MEMORY OF:

Moderator of the139th General Assembly
REV. J. DAVID HESTER
Died July 31, 2014

Moderator of the148th General Assembly
REV. JOSE FAJARDO
Died February 21, 2015

Moderator of the155th General Assembly
REV. VIRGIL H. TODD
Died October 21, 2014

Moderator of the157th General Assembly
ELDER WILBUR S. WOOD
Died October 26, 2014

---

*Ecumenical Partners
+Cumberland Presbyterians in America
Numbers in parenthesis denote number of terms.

SYNOD AND PRESBYTERY CLERKS

SYNOD OF GREAT RIVERS

The Reverend Andy McClung
919 Dickinson Street
Memphis, TN 38107
(901)606-6615
scubarev@att.net

Arkansas Presbytery (GRAR)

Janie Stamps
4008 Logan Lane
Fort Smith, AR 72903
(479)478-0161 (Home)
(479)883-5633 (Cell)
(479)782-0454 FAX
bjstamps@msn.com (Home)

Missouri Presbytery (GRMI)

Larry Nottingham
PO Box 281
Stockton, MO 65785
(417)276-3792
mopresbyterycpc@yahoo.com

West Tennessee Presbytery (GRWT)

The Reverend C. William Jones, Jr.
109 Lakewood Drive
Lexington, TN 38351
(731)967-7618 (Home)
(731)968-7176 (Church)
patfreelandjones@yahoo.com

**SYNOD OF MIDWEST
(MI)**

The Reverend Carroll Richards
210 Allison Drive
Lincoln, IL 62656
(217)732-7894
(217)732-7894 (FAX)
midwestsynod@comcast.net

Covenant Presbytery (MICO)

Reese Baker
1175 Rowland Cemetery Road
Fredonia, KY 42411
(270)545-3483
rbaker@kynet.biz

Cumberland Presbytery (MICU)

The Reverend Darrell Pickett
113 Woods Drive
Glasgow, KY 42141
(270)834-6102
dpickett@glasgow-ky.com

North Central Presbytery (MINC)

The Reverend Ralph Blevins
1623 County Road 2375 E
Geff, IL 62842
(618)854-2494
statedclerk@ncpwebsite.com

SYNOD AND PRESBYTERY CLERKS

MISSION SYNOD
(MS)

Joseph Owen Smith
119 Pine Island Drive
Marshall, TX 75672
(903)928-9887
otsmith@gmx.com

Andes Presbytery (MSAN)

The Reverend Diana Valdez
Calle 65 #98-45, interior 174
Altos de la Macarena
(Robledo-LaCampina)
Medellin, Antioquia
Colombia, South America
(57)313-826-3153
dianamariavaldezduque@gmail.com

Cauca Valley Presbytery (MSCA)

Jairo Lopez
Paraiso la Morada
5ta Etapa, Casa 36, Jamundi
Colombia, South America
011-5726-615410

Choctaw Presbytery (MSCH)

The Reverend Virginia Espinoza
PO Box 132
Boswell, OK 74727
(580)434-7971
vespinoza@choctawnation.com

Presbytery del Cristo (MSDC)

Karen Avery
9420 Layton Court NE
Albuquerque, NM 87111
(505)821-7668
kavery5@comcast.com

Hong Kong Presbytery (MSHK)

Eliza Yl Chui
2/F Welland Plaza
188 Nam Chong Street
Sham Shui Po, Hong Kong
(011)852-2783-8923
(011)852-2771-2726 FAX
elizaylyau@yahoo.com.hk

Japan Presbytery (MSJA)

Takoyoshi Shirai
25 Minami Kobogaoka
Asahi-ku Yokohama
Kanagawa-ken
241-0824 JAPAN
(011)81-45-361-0059
cpc_japan@ybb.ne.jp

Red River Presbytery (MSRR)

The Reverend Vernon Sansom
7810 Shiloh Road
Midlothian, TX 76065
(972)825-6887
vernon@sansom.us

SYNOD AND PRESBYTERY CLERKS

Trinity Presbytery (MSTR)

Paula Hayes
PO Box 5449
Longview, TX 75608
(903)759-1896 (Home)
(903)759-0092 (Work)
phayes7442@aol.com

SYNOD OF SOUTHEAST
(SE)

The Reverend Forest Prosser
1157 Mountain Creek Road
Chattanooga, TN 37405
(423)877-4114
forestprosser@comcast.net

Cumberland East Coast Presbytery (SEEC)

The Reverend Forest Prosser
1157 Mountain Creek Road
Chattanooga, TN 37405
(423)877-4114
forestprosser@comcast.net

Presbytery of East Tennessee (SEET)

The Reverend Ronald L. Longmire
2041 Eckles Drive
Maryville, TN 37804
(865)984-1647
ronaldlongmire@charter.net

Grace Presbytery (SEGR)

Jessie Dunnaway
New Hope CP Church
5521 Double Oak Lane
Birmingham, AL 35242
(205)991-5252
jessie@newhopecpc.org

Hope Presbytery (SEHO)

Mr. Gerald McGee
9491 Highway 101
Lexington, AL 35648
(256)229-5613
nebo9491@gmail.com

Robert Donnell Presbytery (SERD)

Frances Dawson
PO Box 904, 221 S Market St.
Scottsboro, AL 35768
(256)244-0554 (Cell)
(256)259-0904 (Business)(FAX)
rdpfcd@scottsboro.org

Tennessee-Georgia Presbytery (SETG)

Tracey Gann
475 Sequachee Drive
Whitwell, TN 37397
(423)309-1497
tngastatedclerk@gmail.com

SYNOD AND PRESBYTERY CLERKS

TENNESSEE SYNOD
(TN)

The Reverend Charles McCaskey
565 East Tenth Street
Cookeville, TN 38501
(931)526-6585 (Office)
(931)372-2620 FAX
charles@cookevillecpchurch.org

Columbia Presbytery (TNCO)

The Reverend Charles (Buddy) Pope
2391 Fiarfield Pike
Shelbyville, TN 37160
(931)680-4334
pope6897@yahoo.com

Murfreesboro Presbytery (TNMU)

The Reverend Charles McCaskey
565 East Tenth Street
Cookeville, TN 38501
(931)526-6585 (Office)
(931)528-2273 FAX
charles@cookevillecpchurch.org

Nashville Presbytery (TNNA)

The Reverend Fred Polacek
907 Graham Drive
Old Hickory, TN 37138
(615)754-5328 (Home)
revfredp@gmail.com

MINISTERS GAINED AND LOST IN 2014

MINISTERS RECEIVED BY ORDINATION

NAME	PRESBYTERY	DATE
Burns, Garrett Alan	Arkansas	06/08/14
Choi, Sun Man (Ezra)	East Tennessee	01/26/14
Fell, Ron	North Central	10/26/14
Gonzales, Miguel	East Tennessee	05/18/14
Hung, Ella Siu Kei Hung	Hong Kong	04/06/14
Lee, Ted Shuk Tak	Hong Kong	04/06/14
Mars, Stan	Arkansas	09/13/14
Mata, Elizabeth	del Cristo	10/19/14
Prenshaw, Rebecca	East Tennessee	04/27/14
Saldana, Manuel (Alex)	del Cristo	10/19/14
Terrell, Elizabeth	Arkansas	10/12/14
Tucker, Nathan Paul	Columbia	08/17/14
Warren, Glenn	Nashville	01/04/15
Wong, So Li	Hong Kong	04/06/14

MINISTERS REINSTATED OR RECEIVED FROM OTHER DENOMINATIONS

NAME	PRESBYTERY	CHURCH	DATE
Hamilton, Bruce	Arkansas	Church of God	03/20/14

MINISTERS WHO HAVE MOVED TO OTHER DENOMINATIONS

NAME	DENOMINATION	DATE
Insley, Michael	Baptist	2014
Smith, Charles D	Order of John the Baptist	2014

MINISTERS DROPPED FROM MINISTRY BY PRESBYTERY

NAME	PRESBYTERY	DATE
McBeth, David	East Tennessee	10/04/14

MILITARY CHAPLAINS

Acuff, David   (M8)
4969 Quail Lane
Columbia, SC 29206
david.acuff@us.army.mil
(803)790-9151   TNNA#7300

Baranoski, Timothy   (M8)
8040 Starz Loop
Killeen, TX 76544
(615)440-3499
timothy.i.baranoski@us.army.mil

Headrick, Anthony   (M8)
3327 N Eagle Road Ste 110-132
Meridian, ID 83646
chaps2a@yahoo.com
(619)435-0825   SEGR#0100

LeFavor, David E   (M8)
4100 W 3rd Street
Dayton, OH 45428
david.lefavor@med.va.gov
(813)613-4133   SEGR#0100

Logan, Jason B   (M8)
4895 Diggins Drive
Fort Meade, ND 20755
jason.b.logan@us.army.mil
(410)305-8494   TNMU#7200

Nash, Zachary   (M8)
(on file in General Assembly Office)
zachary.nash@us.af.mil
( )   GRWT#9100

O'Mara, Shelia   (M8)
533 Loughton Lane
Arnold, MD 21012
chaplainshelia@aol.com
(410)757-5713   MSDC#8700

Prewitt, Curtis   (M8)
3712 Carmel Lane
Paducah, KY 42003
prewitt@apex.net
(270)554-9779   MICO#3400

Santillano, Ray Paul   (M8)
1270 Polo Road Apt 618
Columbia, SC 29223
ramon.santillano@us.army.mil
(915)500-4928   MSTR#8704

Sumrall, Phil   (M9)
107 Barnhardt Circle
Fort Oglethorpe, GA 30742
phil.sumrall@gmail.com
(423)903-1938   SETG#2100

NON-MILITARY CHAPLAINS

Aden, Marty   (M9)
202 Bennington Place
Wilmington, NC 28412
maden@ec.rr.com
(910)274-8465   MSRR#8400

Anderson, Lisa   (M9)
1790 Faxon Avenue
Memphis, TN 38112
anderli60@gmail.com
(901)246-8052   GRWT#9305

Bone, Leslie   (M9)
16504 George Franklyn Drive
Independence, MO 64055
lesliebone@comcast.net
(816)373-6625   GRMI#4100

Bowers, Sharon G   (M9)
1011 Barbara Drive
San Marcos, TX 78666
sharon.bowers@gmail.com
(512)230-7078   MSTR#8100

Brown, Mark   (M9)
752 Hawthorne Street
Memphis, TN 38107
dmbrown@utmem.edu
(901)274-1474   GRWT#9100

Carter, Patricia   (M9)
2509 Decatur Stratton Road
Decatur, MS 39327
revtree@yahoo.com
(601)635-4120   SEGR#0100

Cook, Lisa   (M9)
4101 Dalemere Court
Nashville, TN 37207
tgoose@comcast.net
(615)868-4118   TNNA#7300

Diamond, James   (M9)
PO Box 1220
Smyrna, TN 37167
FAX: (615)220-1077
jameswdiamond@yahoo.com
(615)220-2341   TNMU#7200

Ferrol, Ruben   (M9)
1823 Straford Court
Allentown, PA 18103
rubeferrol@msn.com
(610)966-7289   MSRR#8400

Gentry, Michele   (M9)
Urb San Jorge casa 28
Km 8 via a La Tebaida
Armenia, Quindio, Colombia
South America
gentry.andes@yahoo.com
(318)285-1161   MSAN#8900

Hames, Anne   (M9)
118 Paris Street
Mc Kenzie, TN 38201
FAX: (731)352-4069
hamesa@bethel-college.edu
(731)352-4066   GRWT#9100

Hartung, J Thomas   (M9)
2291 Americus Boulevard W Apt 1
Clearwater, FL 33763
revtom6@aol.com
(727)797-2882   SEGR#0100

Jackson, Terry   (M9)
1461 Mt Pleasant Road
Hernando, MS 38632
tjackson48@comcast.net
(662)429-9741   GRWT#9100

Kelly, Patrick L   (M9)
1449 Rainbow Road
Mountain City, TN 37683-2110
(423)727-4067   SEET#2200

Kennemer, Darren   (M9)
8828 Highway 119
Alabaster, AL 35007
(205)663-3152
darren.kennemer@va.gov   SERD#0107

Knight, Melissa   (M9)
5730 Haley Road
Meridian, MS 39305
(530)632-6472
revlissa@gmail.com   MSDC#8700

Lain, Judy   (M9)
1928 Pine Ridge Drive
Bedford, TX 76021-4650
(817)660-8020   MSRR#8400

Lounsbury-Lombard, Kristi   (M9)
902 Clearview
Krum, TX 76249
kristilounsbury@gmail.com
(940)435-5077   MSRR#8400

McCarty, John   (M9)
305 W Martindale Drive
Marshall, TX 75672
mtsjohn@gmail.com
(423)650-8788   SETG#2100

McClung, Tiffany   (M9)
919 Dickinson Street
Memphis, TN 38107
tmcclung@memphisseminary.edu
(901)606-6604   GRWT#9100

McSpadden, Nancy   (M9)
120 Roberta Drive
Memphis, TN 38112
revnancy77@gmail.com
(870)612-0067   GRAR#1100

Melson, Glenda   (M9)
331 Tickle Weed Road
Swansea, SC 29160
glendamelson@fidnet.com
(417)588-2758   SEET#2200

Messer, James C   (M9)
3653 Old Madisonville Road
Henderson, KY 42420
jcmess@hotmail.com
(270)827-0711   MINC#5304

Mills, David M   (M9)
528 County Road 322
Bertram, TX 78605
(512)355-3511   MSTR#8100

Oliver, Lisa   (M9)
110 Allen Drive
Hendersonville, TN 37075
( )   TNMU#7200

Pickett, Patricia   (M9)
1460 Cheatham Dam Road
Ashland City, TN 37015
tovahtoo@aol.com
(615)792-4973   TNNA#7300

Rice, Keith   (M9)
PO Box 100
Itasca, TX 76055
rsvkeith@yahoo.com
(254)087-2418   MSRR#8400

Richards, Carroll   (M9)
210 Allison Drive
Lincoln, IL 62656
FAX: (217)732-7894
dr_cr@comcast.net
(217)732-7894   MINC#5200

Ruggia, Mario (Bud)   (M9)
603 Rumsey Street
Kiowa, KS 67070
ruggia@aol.com
(620)825-4509   MSRR#8400

Scott, Lisa   (M9)
lascott1979@att.net
(816)332-0604   GRMI#4100

Scott, Jerry   (M9)
2310 Sentell Drive
Maryville, TN 37803
dmjlscott@yahoo.com
(865)809-2621   SEET#2200

Smith, John Adam   (M9)
916 Allen Road
Nashville, TN 37214
john.a.smith.81@gmail.com
(573)453-8455

Travis, Kermit   (M9)
3220 Sharon Highway
Dresden, TN 38225
(731)364-2315   GRWT#9415

Truax, Robert Lee, Jr   (M9)
2989 Champions Drive Apt 204
Lakeland, TN 38002
revtruax@yahoo.com
(901)266-5927   GRWT#9100

Varner, Susan   (M9)
1502 Green Mountain Drive Apt 187
Little Rock, AR 72211
smvarner76@yahoo.com
(901)371-1249   TNNA#7300

West, David   (M9)
2027 Lucille Street
Lebanon, TN 37087
(217)732-7568   MINC#5405

Wilson, Don   <M1 M9>
7300 Calle Montana NE
Albuquerque, NM 87113
(505)823-2594
don-wilson07@comcast.net

Winslett, Don   (M9)
Baptist Hospital Pastoral Care
1000 W Moreno Street
Pensacola, FL 32521
(217)732-7568   MINC#5405

MEMORIAL ROLL OF MINISTERS

IN MEMORY OF
MINISTERS LOST BY DEATH

NAME	PRESBYTERY	AGE	DATE
Brodeur, Evelyn M	Robert Donnell	91	12/02/14
Chang, John	del Cristo		03/08/14
Chesnut, Walter	Cumberland	98	12/26/14
Cravens, Marvin	Missouri	86	08/02/14
Denton, Clyde M	Columbia	72	06/27/14
Drylie, James T	West Tennessee	75	02/14/15
Fajardo, Jose	Red River	101	02/21/15
Gerard, Eugene "Stan"	Covenant	82	04/26/15
Hester, J. David	East Tennessee	83	07/31/14
Leslie, Eugene	West Tennessee	83	03/10/15
Matlock, Joe	del Cristo		02/26/15
McGregor, David	Columbia	86	01/23/14
McKee, Margaret	West Tennessee	87	11/06/14
Morgan, Jerry	Red River		09/19/14
Palmer, Walter (Pete)	Red River	87	07/26/14
Powell, Omer Thomas	Cumberland	90	01/30/15
Rapson, Tim <Candidate>	Tennessee-Georgia		03/30/14
Rodriguez, Paul	Cauca Valley		03/10/14
Todd, Virgil	Nashville	93	10/20/14
Wilkins, Marvin E	Columbia	65	04/01/14

SURVIVING SPOUSES OF MINISTERS BY PRESBYTERY
(Deceased spouse in parenthesis.)

ARKANSAS

Batholomew, Maudline
(Harold Bartholomew)
 13395 Highway 265
 Prairie Grove, AR 72753
 (479)846-2850

DuBose, Sandra
(Paul DuBose)
 207 7th Street
 Cotter, AR 72626
 (870) 373-1021

Elkins, Patsy
(Robert Harold Elkins)
 525 Elkins Road
 Magazine, AR 72943
 (479)637-3723
 robtelkins@cej.net

Faith, Jeannine
(Charles Faith)
 4710 Mount Olive Road
 Melbourne, AR 72556
 (870)368-4069

Hollenbeck, Linda
(Edward B. Hollenbeck)
 409 Carson Drive
 Benton, AR 72015
 (501)315-9737

Kinslow, Jean
(Alfred Kinslow)
 29209 Perdido Beach Blvd
 Vista Bella #701
 Orange Beach, AL 36561
 (251)981-8385

Wynne, Glenna
(W. J. Wynne)
 1501 W Block
 El Dorado, AR 71730
 (870)863-9444

CAUCA VALLEY

Munoz, Aliria Correal de
(Gerardo Munoz)
 5405 Robelene Drive
 Metaire, LA 70003
 gwilson54@cox.net

Yepez, Mrs. (??)
(Juan Yepez)
 Colombia, South America

COLUMBIA

Bates, Betty Ruth
(Harold Bates)
 204 Apache Trail
 Columbia, TN 38401
 (931)381-6737

Burns, Angela C.
(Bobby G. Burns)
 328 Dunnaway Road
 Shelbyville, TN 37160
 (931)294-5105

Denton, Virgie
(Clyde Denton)
 2538 County Club Lane
 Columbia, TN 38401
 (931)388-7154

Gibson, Ernestine
(Charles Gibson)
 33 Hilldale Church Road
 Fayetteville, TN 37334
 (931)433-2666

Green, Marie
(Odis Green)
 18 Oakwood Street NW
 Rome, GA 30165
 (706)291-1738

Nugent, Sue
(Samuel Ellis Nugent)
 2124 Carrie Court
 Columbia, TN 38401
 (931)490-7571
 sue@cadprodinc.com

Sain, Sally
(Edwin Sain)
 27 Hilltop Road
 Fayetteville, TN 37334
 (931)433-8708
 ssain@fayelectric.com

Seaton, Whitney
(Charlie Seaton)
 111 W Hardin Drive
 Columbia, TN 38401
 (931)388-0319

Smith, Patricia
(Cordell Smith)
 5808 Robertson Avenue
 Nashville, TN 37209
 (615)731-0938

Walker, Lilly Mae
(James Finis Walker)
 704 Woods Drive
 Columbia, TN 38401

Wilkins, Dianne S
(Marvin Edward Wilkins)
 209 Mackey Street
 Rogersville, AL 35652
 (256)247-5557
 marvinwilkins@msn.com

COVENANT

Atchison, Cheryl
(Dean Atchison)
 206 Marsha Drive
 Ledbetter, KY 42058

Cannon, Joyce
(Chester Cannon)
 1026 W Center Street
 Madisonville, KY 42431

Clark, Eileen
(Morris Clark)
 8720 State Route 132 W
 Clay, KY 42404

Dixon, Sonja
(Robert Dixon)
 8550 Lafayette Road
 Hopkinsville, KY 42240
 (270)886-7647
 sonjadixon@earthlink.net

Gerard, Vanda
(Eugene "Stan" Gerard
 615 N 42nd Street
 Paducah, KY 42001
 (270)443-2889

Lindsey, Pearl
(Eugene Lindsey)
 311 Oak Hurst Circle
 Cadiz, KY 42211
 (270)522-3398

Lively, Louella
(James Lively)
 196 Vicksburg Estate Road
 Benton, KY 42025
 (270)527-3776

Marsiglio, June
(Roger Marsiglio)
 505 Logan
 Providence, KY 42450)

Moreland, Eva
(James Moreland)
 9158 Tom Counce Road
 South Fulton, TN 38257

Murphy, Robbie
(Vernon Murphy)
 128 New Liberty Church Road
 Kevil, KY 42053
 (270)522-3398

Owen, Pat
(Bert Owen)
 7906 Manner Pointe Drive
 Louisville, KY 40220
 (502)749-1940
 bertorpatowen@insightbb.com

SURVIVING SPOUSES OF MINISTERS BY PRESBYTERY CONTINUED
(Deceased spouse in parenthesis.)

Pettit, Jennie
(William H. Pettit)
248 Skyline Drive
Princeton, KY 42245
(270)365-9076

CULLMAN

Kimbrell, Glenda
(Bobby Kimbrell)
9479 Cumberland Oaks Drive
Pinson, AL 35126
(205)680-1743

Weathersby, Dorothy
(E.W. Weathersby)
1203 2nd Avenue NE
Cullman, AL 35055
(256)734-2886

CUMBERLAND

Graham, Mary
(Harold Graham)
103 Freeman Green Drive
Elizabethtown, KY 42701
(270)360-1191

Johnson, Genevie
(Robert Johnson)
351 Bacon Court
Harrodsburg, KY 40330
(859)734-3789

Milam, Dona
(Robert Milam)
9294 Owensboro Road
Falls of Rough, KY 40119
(270)879-8985

Mouser, Wynemia Despain
(Calvin Mouser)
204 Sunrise Drive
Greensburg, KY 42743
(270)932-7377

Phelps, Diann
(John Phelps)
4743 Happy Hollow Road
Hawesville, KY 42348
(270)927-9835
haor@juno.com

Renner, Wallace
(Patricia Renner)
1648 Griffith Avenue
Owensboro, KY 42301
(270)685-4359
pwrenner@adelphia.com

Sprague, Rose
(George Sprague)
101 Clyde Morris Hall #242
Ormond Beach, FL 32174

DEL CRISTO

Appleby, Judy
(Bob Appleby)
3265 16th Street
San Francisco, CA 94103
(415)703-6090
gfcc@gum.org

Chang, Grace
(John Chang)
1753 Castro Drive
San Jose, CA 95130
(408)370-0643

Ellis, Ernestine
(John Ellis)
1432 Cape Verde Place
Tucson, AZ 85748
(520)296-9027

Freeman, ??
(Jack Freeman)
3559 Cody Way
Sacramento, CA 95864
(916)489-2567

Kennedy, Louise
(John F Kennedy)
4916 44th Street
Lubbock, TX 79414
(806)796-0738

Matlock, Bettye
(Joe Matlock)
5905 Hickory Grove Lane
Bartlett, TN 38134
(901)937-8457

Moss, Beth
(Greg Moss)

EAST TENNESSEE

Alexander, Carolyn Roberts
(Don Charles Alexander)
2520 107 Cutoff
Greeneville, TN 37743
(423)638-8453
alexandercda@msn.com

Broyles, Elizabeth
(Lon Broyles)
753 Snapp Bridge Road
Limestone, TN 37681
(865)483-8433

Broyles, Minnie
(Raymond Broyles)
4944 Kilaminajaro
Old Hickory, TN 37138-4102
(615)428-8640

Johnson, Rebecca
(Scott Johnson)
512 Rolling Creek Circle
Knoxville, TN 37922
(865)966-3699

Scott, Betty
(Lee Scott)
319 Lavista Drive
Maryville, TN 37804
(731)415-2936

GRACE

Baker, Ola
(L. G. Baker)
7208 12th Street
Tampa, FL 33604
(813)5239-3356

Brown, Marye
(Richard C Brown)
2100 NE 140th Street Apt 510E
Edmond, OK 73013
(205)663-5486

Buerhaus, Charity
(Chuck Buerhaus)
313 S Main Street
Piedmont, AL 36272
(256)447-6195

Hegwood, Clara
(James "Pete" Hegwood)
125 Pinewood Lane
Montevallo, AL 35115
(205)665-2134

Mims, Martha Jo
(Howell "Gay" Mims)
3011 Wolfe Road
Columbus, MS 39705
(662)328-3778
mjmims@muw.edu

Phillips, Edna
(Troy Phillips)
2024 Hilltop Road
Rock Hill, SC 29732
(803)325-1416

Tant, Becky
(Robert H Tant)
516 Davis Drive
Glencoe, AL 35905
(256)494-9450
rtant82091@aol.com

HOPE

Bright, Mildred
(J. P. Bright)
1716 Broadway Boulevard
Florence, AL 35630
(256)766-8361

Copeland, Frances S.
(Bill Copeland)
142 Thornton Terrace Drive
Rogersville, AL 35652
(256)247-1688

SURVIVING SPOUSES OF MINISTERS BY PRESBYTERY CONTINUED
(Deceased spouse in parenthesis.)

Hyden, Mae
(Lee Hyden)
    2195 Allsboro Road
    Cherokee, AL 35616
    (256)360-2896

MISSOURI

Bornert, Paughnee
(Robert D. Bornert)
    932 E Snider Street
    Springfield, MO 65803
    (417)833-2627

Cantrell, Mary
(Ernest Cantrell)
    7047 N Garnet Lane
    Strafford, MO 65757
    (417)736-9017

Cravens, Doris
(Marvin L Cravens)
    604 N Hovis Street
    Mountain Grove, MO 65711
    (417)926-5778

Cravens, Hallie
(Ellis Cravens)
    9566 Highway Z
    Hartville, MO 65667
    (417)668-5954

Cravens, Thelma
(Wilbur Cravens)
    2144 Wilbur Road
    Mansfield, MO 65704
    417-924-8553

Dailey, Sarah
(Larry Dailey)
    656 Grand Point Boulevard
    Sunrise Beach, MO 65079
    (573)374-9537

Fleming, Betty
(Ronald Fleming)
    657 S Main Avenue Apt 1
    Springfield, MO 65806
    (417)873-2222

Gardner, Dossie
(Don Gardner)
    26 W Pearl
    Aurora, MO 65605
    (417)678-3278

Gould, Marjorie
(Robert Gould)
    204 W Pleasant
    Aurora, MO 65605
    (417)678-5422

Hensley, Jean Ann
(Howard Hensley)
    537 Piperpoint
    Rogersville, Mo 65742
    (414)753-1108

McCloud, Johnnie
(Theron McCloud)
    419 Magnolia Court
    Lebanon, MO 65536
    (417)532-3388
    jmccloud@advertisenet.com

Scobey, Darlis
(James Scobey)
    105 Oak Hill Downs Street
    Farmington, MO 63640
    (573)756-1683

MURFREESBORO

Basham, Earline
(Willard Basham)
    335 Myers Road
    Winchester, TN 37398

Breeding, Karen
(Gordon Breeding)
    1907 Susan Drive
    Murfreesboro, TN 37129
    (615)867-3660
    zanylady1000@yahoo.com

Denman, Susie
(E. H. Denman)
    525 Golf Club Drive
    Smithville, TN 37166
    (615)597-7122

Dickerson, Helen
(Andrew Mizel Dickerson, Jr.)
    914 Dogwood Drive
    Murfreesboro, TN 37129

Martindale, Dana
(J. Craig Martindale)
    2913 Pellas Place
    Murfreesboro, TN 37127
    (615)653-0858
    w5bu@hotmail.com

Salisbury, Helen Margaret
(A.D. Salisbury)
    1927 Memorial Boulevard
    Murfreesboro, TN 37129

Salisbury, Rebecca
(Loyce Estes)
    1033 Twin Oaks Drive
    Murfreesboro, TN 37130
    (615)410-7801
    rebsalisbury@yahoo.com

Watson, Mary Leota
(David E Watson)
    804 W Main Street
    McMinnville, TN 37110
    (931)473-7561
    leotaw@blomand.net

NASHVILLE

Allen, Hester
(Paul Allen)
    300 Bantam Court
    LaVerne, TN 37086

Burnett, Mary Lee
(Cecil Burnett)
    321 Raindrop Lane
    Hendersonville, TN 37075

Maxedon, Chris
(Julian Maxedon)
    2260 Highway 31
    White House, TN 37188

Stiles, Peggy
(John Stiles)
    300 Bantam Court
    Clarksville, TN 37043

Wilkins, Connie
(Tom Wilkins)
    109 Annalise Drive
    Clarksville, TN 37043
    (931)358-2892

NORTH CENTRAL

McCain, Violet
(Terence McCain)
    15804 Camden Avenue
    Eastpointe, MI 48021
    (586)774-4861

Springer, Eileen
(Robert Springer)
    403 Prairie Ridge Court
    Eureka, IL 61530
    (309)467-5030

RED RIVER

Brown, Beth
(LaRoyce Brown)
    311 S 8th Street
    Marlow, OK 73055
    (580)658-3989

Fajardo, Fanny
(Jose Fajardo)
    101 Vanderbilt Lane
    Waxahachie, TX 75165
    (972)923-2955
    fannyfajardo123@sbcglobal.net

Gilbert, Freda M
(James C. Gilbert)
    c/o Elizabeth G. Horsley
    1200 Imperial Drive
    Denton, TX 76209
    (940)387-2272

SURVIVING SPOUSES OF MINISTERS BY PRESBYTERY CONTINUED
(Deceased spouse in parenthesis.)

Morgan, Sharon
(Jerome Morgan)
8420 Baumgarten Drive
Dallas, TX 75228

ROBERT DONNELL

Hunter, Jean
(James E. Hunter)
1905 Delynn
Hazel Green, AL 35750
(256)838-3902

TENNESSEE-GEORGIA

Galloway, Katherine
(Cliff Galloway)
7127 White Oak Valley Road
McDonald, TN 37353

Kapperman, Linda
(Glenn Kapperman)
2719 Rio Grande Road
Chattanooga, TN 37421
(423)894-7924

Naugher, Catherine
(Doyce Naugher)
985 Mt Pleasant Road
Rydal, GA 30171
(770)382-1982

TRINITY

Allen, Ann M
(Paul Allen)
1814 Swan
Longview, TX 75604
(903)759-5508

Johnson, Clyde
(Dave Johnson)
2801 E Travis Apt 108
Marshall, TX 75672
(903)938-9953

Leslie, Jenann
(Marvin E. Leslie)
300 Henley Perry Drive
Marshall, TX 75670
(903)938-6642
jenann.leslie@gmail.com

Ward, Suzie
(Kevin Ward)
216 E Caroline
Marshall, TX 75672

WEST TENNESSEE

Brown, Beverly
(Paul B. Brown)
406 N McNeil Street
Memphis, TN 38112
(901)278-6909

Brown, Phyllis
(David Brown)
1930 Mignon
Memphis, TN 38107
(901)274-1513

Cook, Marcine
(Paul V. Cook)
144 Big John Drive
Martin, TN 38237
(731)587-0787
marcine175@aol.com

Davis, Willene
(Harold Davis)
7820 Walking Horse Circle #311
Germantown, TN 38138
(901)757-1394

Drylie, Linda
(James Drylie)
512 JE Blaydes Parkway
Atoka, TN 38004
(901)837-1627

Forester, Willie Mae
(J. C. Forester)
833 Main Street
McKenzie, TN 38201
(731)352-3107

Hall, Patsy
(Charles R. Hall)
4341 Pebble Garden Court
Birmingham, AL 35235
(205)538-7993

Hicks, Ruby
(Willam D. Hicks)
3938 Cardinal Drive
Union City, TN 38261
(731)885-5887

Knight, Helen
(James Knight)
8081 Jills Creek Drive
Bartlett, TN 38133
(901)387-0675

Laurence, Brenda
(G. Larry Laurence)
2823 Nine Mile Road
Enville, TN 38332
(731)687-2022
southernmoma@hotmail.com

Leslie, Cheryl
(Randall Leslie)
3374 Walnut Grove Road
Memphis, TN 38111
(901)458-4413

Leslie, Marilyn
(Eugene Leslie)
13155 Center Hill Road
Olive Branch, MS 38654
(731)613-0425
eleslie1@bellsouth.net

Lynch, Van
(Jerry Lynch)
73 Baseline Road
Dyer, TN 38330

McMahen, Sandra
(Rowe Gene McMahen)
92 Stonewall Circle
McKenzie, TN 38201
(731)352-3067

Stott, Beverly
(Melvin Buddy Stott)
200 E Main Street
Dresden, TN 38225
(731)364-5863
bevstott@frontiernet.net

CUMBERLAND PRESBYTERIANS
SERVING OUTSIDE THE UNITED STATES

Please e-mail missionaries before mailing anything to them to determine the best way to send them letters or packages. If you want to communicate with missionaries in closed countries, first e-mail the Missions Ministry Team (Lthomas@cumberland.org) and we will forward your e-mail to the missionary.

N B—China
email: Lthomas@cumberland.org

Boyce & Beth Wallace—Colombia
e-mail: hbwcali@yahoo.com
oovoo and facetime: Boyce Wallace

Anay Ortega—Guatemala
e-mail: anayortegamonroy@hotmail.com
skype: Anay Ortega Monroy
oovoo: Anay Ortega

Fhanor & Socorro Pejendino—Guatemala
email: pastorfhanor@gmail.com
skype: Fhanor Pejendino Arcos
oovoo: pastorestulua

Glenn Watts—Hong Kong
email: hongkongbrother@hotmail.com
skype: HongKongBROTHER

T T G—Kyrgyzstan
email: Lthomas@cumberland.org

D S L—Laos and Cambodia
email: Lthomas@cumberland.org

Carlos & Luz Dary Rivera—Mexico
email: caralrifra@une.lnet.co
oovoo: Carlos Rivera

Daniel & Kay Jang—Philippines
Ilollo Cumberland Mission Church
email: goingup129@hanmail.net

John & Joy Park—deputation, Philippines

Kenneth & Delight Hopson—Uganda
e-mail: ken.hopson@wgm.org
skype: Delight Hopson
oovoo: Kenneth Hopson

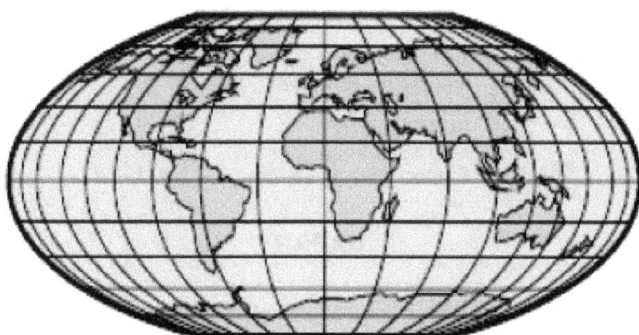

The Cumberland Presbyterian Church
has five families working in closed countries as
humanitarian workers.

NEW CHURCH DEVELOPMENTS & MISSION PROBES

ANDES

Aguadas
Cra 3 #7-14
Aguadas, Caldas
Colombia, SA
(576)851-4773
jeob40@hotmail.com
Pastor: Joaquin Orozco   (M2)
Began: 1996 (as re-development)

Amaga
Cra San Fernando #48-56
Amaga, Antioquia
Colombia, SA
(574)847-3250
rebcaldas@une.net.co
Pastor: Jhon Jairo Arias   (M3)
Began: 1997

Chinchina
Mz 2 Casa 21, Urb. Milan
Dosquebradas, Ris
Colombia, SA
(476)322-2177
oikoninonia@gmail.com
Pastor: Rodrigo Martinez   (M1)

Quimbaya
Cra 6 #25-54
Quimbaya, Quindio
Colombia, SA
(576)752-3570
joenjimu@yahoo.es
Pastor: Jorge Enrique Jimenez
                                (M3)
Began: 04/02

Senda de Libertad
Cra 120 #39 F-91
Medellin, Antioquia
Colombia, SA
(574)496-1681
ipcsaladomedellin@gmail.com
Pastor: Cruzana Guerrero
        & Libardo Gutierrez   (M2)
Began: 1998

ARKANSAS

Bryant-Benton CP Mission
Fellowship
16904 Old Mill Road
Little Rock, AR 72206
(501)888-4190
Pastor: Dwight Shanley   (M1)
Began: 2005

CAUCA VALLEY

Casa de Oracion

Dia de Salvacion
Pastor: Luis Cantor
(   )256-2835

Rios de Agua Viva
Pastor: Euripides Moreno   (M1)
(   )244-3557

COVENANT

Cadiz
Cadiz, KY
Pastor: Danny York   (M1)
Began: 2008

CUMBERLAND

Louisville Japanese Christian
Fellowship (3223)
c/o Reverend Iwao Satoh
8710 Hickory Falls Lane
Pewee Valley, KY 40056
(502)657-9643
iwaosatoh@gmail.com
Pastor: Iwao Satoh   (M1)
Began: 2010

DEL CRISTO

316 Christian Fellowship
2200 E Dartmouth Circle
Englewood, CO 80113
(303)504-0275
jeanhess@316denver.com
Pastor: Rick & Jean Hess   (M1)
Began: 08/10

Bethesda Korean Fellowship
139 Silverado Drive
Santa Teresa, NM 88008
(915)329-3451
pyongsanyu@hotmail.com
Pastor: Pyong San Yu   (M1)
Began: 03/10

Marantha East
12008 Fred Carter
El Paso, TX 79936
(915)857-1343
yaanaivitaly@yahoo.com
Pastor: Alfredo Rincon   (M1)
Began: 2012

GRACE

Naples Fellowship (0309)
842 Bent Creek Way
Naples, FL 34114
(931)273-0768
revga@hotmail.com
Pastor: Ramon Garcia   (M1

JAPAN

Ichikawa Grace Mission Point (8314)
3-19-5 Sugano
Ichikawa-shi, Chiba-ken
272-0824 JAPAN
(047)326-8675
(047)326-8675 FAX
fwgc6854@mb.infoweb.ne.jp
Pastor: Yasuo Masuda   (M2)

RED RIVER

Church of St. Giles
3500 S Peoria Avenue
Tulsa, OK 74105
(918)760-6145
Pastor: William G. Webb, Jr. (M1)

TRINITY

Kardia Fellowship
16637 FM 293 Unit D
Tyler, TX 75703
hoginbama@yahoo.com
Pastor: Mark Davenport   (M1)

WEST TENNESSEE

Grace Fellowship (9323)
9160 Tchulahoma Road
Southaven, MS 38671
(662)393-2552
tthompson393@aol.com
Pastor: Tommy Thompson   (M1)

Hope Fellowship
440 Blackmon Road
Medina, TN 38355
(731)738-0308
Pastor: Steven Rogers   (M1)

Iona Community of Faith
1790 Faxon Avenue
Memphis, TN 38112
website: www.iona.gutensite.com
(901)283-8062
wa4mff@aol.com
Pastor: Barry Anderson   (M1)

PROVISIONAL CHURCHES AND PROVISIONAL FELLOWSHIPS

"A provisional fellowship is a pre-existing non-English congregation that is being received into the Cumberland Presbyterian Church through an authorized assimilation process.

ARKANSAS

_____ (2135)
Arkansas Korean Loving Church
8201 Frenchmans Lane
Little Rock, AR 72209
Pastor: Sun Wan Cho   (M1)

COVENANT

_____ (3420)
Zion CP Fellowship
1347 S 6th Street
Paducah, KY 42003
(270)442-6414
zioncpcinfo@gmail.com
Pastor: Steve/Teresa Shauf (M1)
Began: 10/2012

CUMBERLAND EAST COAST

_____ (2446)
Comeback Church
316 Prospect Avenue Apt 6D
Hackensack, NJ 07601
Pastor: Rev. Ji Woo Park
(201)694-3005
jwoos@gmail.com
_____ (2444)
Gil Community Church
139 A Grove Street
Tenafly, NJ 07670
Pastor: Sichun Ryu
(201)410-3445
isaac9191@hotmail.com
_____ (2445)
Immanuel Presbyterian Church
67-17 215th
Oakland Gardens, NY 11364
Pastor: Soo Yeol Park
(646)599-4941
shwbpark@naver.com
_____ (2443)
True Love Church of New York
42-40 208th Street
Bayside, NY 11361
(347)308-4333
ingodswill@gmail.com
Pastor: Taeho Oh   (M1)

EAST TENNESSEE

_____ (2321)
Iloilo Cumberland Mission Church
PO Box #5, Aduana Street
Iloilo City 5000, Philippine
Pastor: WonJeon (Daniel) Jang
                              (M1)
_____ (2322)
Mok-Yang Presbyterian Church
#304-28 Sinlim-Dong
Kwanak-Gu
Seoul, Korea
02-884-3474
Pastor: Bo-Seong Park   (M1)
_____ (2323)
Sae-Sam Presbyterian Church
#325-1 DongHyen-Dong
Jenchen-city
Choongbuk, Korea
043-652-0540
lifeyu@hanmail.net
Pastor: Wn-Young Yu   (M1)

_____
Walkertown
6885 Kingsport Highway
Afton, TN 37616
(423)639-1333
Pastor: Kevin McAmis   (M5)

_____ (2324)
Ye-Il Presbyterian Church
#1304 Kakyeng-Dong
Sangdang-Gu
Cheongju-City
Choongbuk, Korea
043-235-0219
Pastor: Da-Wit (David) Ahn
_____ (2325)
Young-Kwang Presbyterian Church
#1342 Seocho-2dong
Seocho-Gu
Seoul, Korea
02-3474-8405
Pastor: Sango-Do Lee

MISSOURI

_____
First CPC Korean Mission
4216 Charleston Avenue
Springfield, MO 65408
(417)883-4248
Pastor: Sang H Park   (M1)

RED RIVER

_____
Casa del Alfarero
Calle Norte 12 Aesquino Oriente 53
Colonia Union de Guadalupe Chaico
MEXICO
54-4-627-5570
alaprep28@hotmail.com
Pastor: Alejandro Alejo   (M1)

_____
Iglesia Presbiterana Marantha
Calle 21 Lote 22 Mzn Dll
Colonoa Guadalupe Proleteria
C P 07670 Mexico City
MEXICO
54-53-67-9103
jessevega69@gmail.com
Pastor: Jedidiah Vega   (M1)

_____
Restauracion de Vida
Calle C numero 24
Cononia San Marcos
Delegacion Azcapotzalco C P 02020
MEXICO
54-5-318-7622
castro_dan@hotmail.com
Pastor: Jose Dan Castro   (M1)

TENNESSEE GEORGIA

_____
Baek Seok Church
3075 Landington Way
Duluth, GA 30096
(404)398-8469
kpc0191@gmail.com
Pastor: Seung Chon Han   (M1)
_____ (2150)
Divinity Church
1 Clyde Orr Drive
Norcross, GA 3093
Pastor: Rev. Frederick Nah
Began: 2013
_____ (2130)
Korean Livingstone Presbyterian Church
3340 Bentbill xing
Cumming, GA 30041
(770)912-8477
barkmoksa@hanmail.net
Pastor: Rev Young Rae Park (M1)

_____
New York Chowon Mission Church
254-18 Northern Boulevard
Little Neck, NY 11362
(917)992-5200
lovedasol@gmail.com
Pastor: Si Hoon Park   (M1)

_____
Our Good Presbyterian Church
32132 Huntly Circle
Salisbury, MD 21804
(443)783-3809 (cell)
Pastor: Hyoung Sik Choi   (M1)
Began: 2001

_____
Phillipians Church
2310 His Way
Lawrenceville, GA 30044
(678)462-7526
agatopia@hanmail.net
Pastor: Jin Koo Kang   (M1)

_____
Trinity Church
1050 Grace Drive
Lawrenceville, GA 30043
(678)622-2717
Pastor: Rev. Min Soo Kim (M1)
_____ (2103)
The Cross Mission
5260 Coacoochee Ter
Alpharetta, GA 30022
(404)421-4262
Pastor: Jea Kwang Lee   (M1)
_____ (2125)
Walking with God Presbyterian Church
3299 Highway 120
Duluth, GA 30096
(678)600-2787
jaeyu117@yahoo.com
Pastor: Jae Hyung Yu   (M1)

_____
We Community Church
302 Satellite Boulevard
Suwanee, GA 30024
(678)908-9191
powerment@hotmail.com
Pastor: Hyang Koo Lee

TRINITY

_____
Ye Rang Korean Church (8602)
12320 Alameda Trail Circle #1309
Austin, TX 78727
(512)474-2646
preacherofgod@gmail.com
Pastor: Sung In Park   (M1)

WEST TENNESSEE

_____ (9436)
ACTS Church
6524 Summer Avenue
Memphis, TN 38134
(901)381-4790
usyoun61@hotmail.com
Pastor: Daniel Youn

_____
Redeemer Evangelical Church
7011 Poplar Avenue
Germantown, TN 38138
(901)737-3370
jimmylatimer@redeemerevangelical.com
Pastor: James M. Latimer

MISSION CHURCHES AND PASTORS
UNDER CARE OF MISSIONS MINISTRY TEAM
(General Assembly Ministry Council)

GUATEMALA
"Guatemala CP Council of Churches"

Iglesia Evangelica de Fe y Jubilo
(Provisional)
   6a avenida 3-56 Zona 19
   Colonia La Florida
   Guatemala City, Guatemala
   Pastor: Edgar Buni Avalos   (M1)

Casa de Fe y Oracion
(Provisional)
   31 calle 9-75 Colonia Miralvally
   Zona 6 de Mixco
   Guatemala

Comunidad de Fe
(Provisional)
   29 calle 14-41 Zona 12
   Coonia Santa Rosa II
   Guatemala City, Guatemala

MISSIONARIES:

Reverend Fhanor Pejendino
Reverend Socorro Pejendino
Ms Anay Ortega

PROVISIONAL PASTORS:

Avalos, Edgar Buni
   6a avenida 3-56 Zona 19
   Colonia La Florida
   Guatemala City, Guatemala

MEXICO
"Mexico CP Council of Churches"

PROVISIONAL CHURCHES:

Casa del Alfarero
   C Norte 12 A Esq OTE 53
   Chalco Edo
   Mexico

Iglesia Marantha
   Arroyo de Miumbre #1749
   Col Felipe Augeles
   Ciudad Juarez
   Mexico

Restauration de Vida
   Calle Benito Juarez #35
   Colonia Guadalupe Victoria
   Delegacion Gustavo A Madero
   Mexico

MISSIONS

Juan 3:16
   Calle Acelga 10011 Col
   Mezquital
   Ciudad Jarez

Fuente de Vida - Ajusco
   Calle Primera Cerrada de Hombres
   Ilustres 2B Colonia Santa Ceilia
   Tepetlapa Delebacion
   Xochimilco CP
   Ciudad Mexico

MISSIONARIES:

Reverend Carlos Rivera
Reverend Luz Dary Rivera

PROVISIONAL PASTORS:

Alejo, Alejandro (Robledo)
   Casa del Alfarero CP Church
   C Norte 12 Esq Ote 53 Col Union
   de GPE
   Chalco Mexico
   Phone: 46-27-5570
   aleprep28@hotmail.com
Castro, Jose Dan (Solis)
   Restauracion de Vida CP Church
   Calle C Col San Marcos
   Azcapotzalco C P 02020 Mexico
   Phone: 55-53-18-7622
   castro_dan@hotmail.com
Gallardo, Gabriel (Uzziel)
   NCD Mission Ajusco 1a Cda
   Hombres Ilustres 20B Sta Cecilia
   Tepetiapa Xochimilco Mexico
   DF CP 16880
   Phone: 55-48-1563
   pastoruzziel@hotmail.com
Mata, Jorge Fernando
   Marantha CP Church Towi 8127 Sta
   Fe Cd C Jaurez
   Chihuahua Mexico
   Phone: 656-62-59-975
   pastormata@hotmail.com

CANDIDATES:

Hernandez, Octavio
   c/o Iglesia Marantha
   Phone: 65-61-939157
Marroquin, Juan Carlos (Valencia)
   c/o Juan 3:16

PHILIPPINES
"Philippine CP Council of Churches"

Iloilo Cumberland Presbyterian
(Church)
  PO Box 5
  Aduana Street
  Iloilo City 5000, Philippines
  Pastor: Wond Jeon (Daniel) Jang
                        (M1)

Pavia Cumberland Presbyterian
(Mission)
  Jabonillo Street
  Pavia, Iloilo
  Pastor: Manual Job Baldevia   (M2)

Oton Cumberland Presbyterian
(Mission)
  Cabang
  Oton, Iloilo
  Pastor: Alexander Duyac, Jr.   (M1)

MISSIONARIES:

Reverend Daniel Yang
Mrs Kay Yang

FUTURE MISSIONARIES:

Reverend John Park
Mrs. Joy Park

PASTORS:

Duyac, Alexander, Jr.
  Brgy, Cabang, Oton, Iloilo

LICENTIATES:

Baldevia, Manuel Job
Saim, J Sean Espanueva
  c/o Iloilo CP Church
Tagurigan, Alpha Faith Singcuenco
  c/o Iloilo CP Church

CANDIDATES:

Agana, Rameo G, Jr.
  c/o Iloilo CP Church
Bonete, Harold Henry D
  c/o Iloilo CP Church
Dyuac, Aldrandreb D
  c/o Iloilo CP Church
Garnica, Darrel Von
  c/o Iloilo CP Church
Yutig, Lucelle E
  c/o Iloilo CP Church

SOUTH KOREA
"Korean CP Council of Churches"

_____(2221)
First Cumberland Presbyterian Church
of Korea
(Church)
  Hyundai I-park B-02
  Burim-dong 113
  Dongan-gu, Anyang-si
  Gyeonggi-do, Korea 431-787
  Phone: 82-70-8872-8033
  Pastor: Heungsoo Kang   (M2)
  Clerk: Yoon JinSub
  303-101 Raenian Ever heim Apt
  Naeson 2-dong, Uiwangsi
  Gyeonggi-do, Korea 437-761
  jinsyoon@gmail.com

Glory Church
(Mission)
  302 Si-Bum Building
  1342 Seocho 2-dong, Seocho-gu
  Seoul, Korea 137-861
  Phone: 82-2-3474-8405
  Pastor: Geumtaek Lim   (M1)

New Life Church
(Mission)
  325-1 Donghyeon-dong
  Jecheon-si
  Chungcheongbud-do, Korea 390-190
  Phone: 82-10-6655-9188
  Pastor: Woonyong Yu   (M1)

Ye-Il Church
(Mission)
  15 Seogyeong-ro, 28beong-gil
  Heungdeok-gu, Cheongiu-si
  Chungcheongbuk-do, Korea 361-803
  Phone: 82-42-232-6000
  Pastor: Dawie Ahn(M1)

PASTORS:

Ahn, Dawie
  606-304 Gapyeong Jugong Apt
  Jungnim-dong, Heungdeck-gu
  Cheongju-si
  Chungcheongbuk-do, Korea 361-850
  Phone: 82-10-2421-0219
  ankim91@hanmail.net
Lee, Sangdo
  507-1501 Samik Green Apt
  Myeongil 1-dong, Gngdong-gu
  Seoul, Korea 134-782
  Phone: 82-10-3353-2907
  humanolsd@hanmail.net
Lim, Geumtaek
  302-si-Bum Building
  1342 Seocho 2dong, Seccho-gu
  Seoul, Korea 137-861
  Phone: 82-11-9044-5250
  limkt114@hanmail.net
Yu, Woonyong
  325-1 Donghyeon-dong, Jecheon-si
  Chungcheongbuk-do, Korea 390-190
  Phone: 82-10-6655-9188
  lifeyu@hanmail.net

LICENTIATES:

Choi, Justin
  823-4 Naeson 1-dong, Uiwang-si
  Gyeonggi-do, Korea 437-838
  Phone: 82-10-2668-8795
  rev.choi@hotmail.com
Kang, Huengsoo
  Hyundai I-park B-02, Burim-dong 113
  Dongan-gu, Anyang-si
  Gyeonggi-do, Korea 431-787
  Phone: 82-10-8428-0084
  halieus@hanmail.net

CAMP GROUNDS

ARKANSAS PRESBYTERY

Camp Peniel
Robert Hill
797 Ferguson Valley Road
Booneville, AR 72927
(760)224-7396

CHOCTAW PRESBYTERY

Camp Israel Folsom
Box 158
Broken Bow, OK 74728
(580)584-2099

COLUMBIA PRESBYTERY

Crystal Springs Camp, Inc.
21 Crystal Springs Camp Road
Kelso, TN 37348
(931)937-8621
Medley@cafes.net
Camp Manager: Carol Medley

PRESBYTERY OF EAST TENNESSEE

Camp Chilhowee
c/o Bill & Traci Pressley
1920 Old Chilhowee Loop Road
Maryville, TN 37865
(865)983-7084

Camp John Speer
c/o Dennis Elwell
2154 Viking Mountain Road
Greeneville, TN 37743
(423)636-1366
dpelwell@gmail.com
www.campjohnspeer.com

GRACE PRESBYTERY

Camp Bailey
Route 1 Box 386
Union, MS 39365

Caretaker: Mr. Lynn Frederick
P. O. Box 574
Carthage, MS 39051

MISSOURI PRESBYTERY

Camp Cumberland
South Greenfield, Missouri
(417)637-2059
Renee Rogers, Business Manager

MURFREESBORO PRESBYTERY

Crystal Springs
21 Crystal Springs Camp Road
Kelso, TN 37348
(931)937-8621

NASHVILLE PRESBYTERY

Camp Crystal Springs
21 Crystal Springs Camp Road
Kelso, TN 37348
(931)937-8621
Carol Medley, Director

TENNESSEE-GEORGIA PRESBYTERY

Camp Glancy
1370 Coppinger Cove Road
Sequatchie, TN 37374

TRINITY PRESBYTERY

Camp Gilmont
Rt. 6, Box 254
Gilmer, TX 75644
(903)797-6400

WEST TENNESSEE PRESBYTERY

Camp Clark Williamson
390 Mason Road
Humboldt, TN 38343
(800)655-8204
(731)784-3221
Mike Hannaford, Administrator
www.campclarkwilliamson.com

Explanation of Symbols

MC=

Abbreviation for name of county or state if more than one church in the presbytery has the same name.

4= The number of Sundays each month the church engages in worship

M= Manse

E= Every Home Plan for The Cumberland Presbyterian

W= Organized women's ministry

P = Provisional Church
C = Church
F = Fellowship
U = Union Church

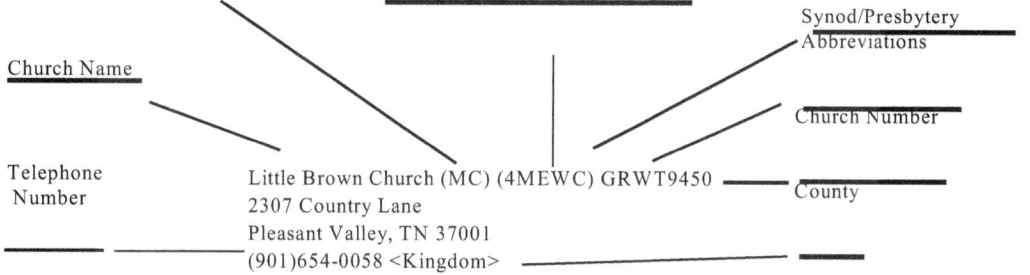

Synod/Presbytery Abbreviations

Church Name

Church Number

Telephone Number

Little Brown Church (MC) (4MEWC) GRWT9450

2307 Country Lane

Pleasant Valley, TN 37001

(901)654-0058 <Kingdom>

County

PA: John Doe   <M1>
        1 Church St.
        Pleasant Valley, TN 37001
        (901)654-3210

AP: Mary Smith   <M1>
        20 Serenity Lane
        Pleasant Valley, TN 37001
        (901)654-0123

CL: Jane Doe
        30 Charity Rd.
        Pleasant Valley, TN 37001
        (901)654-2345

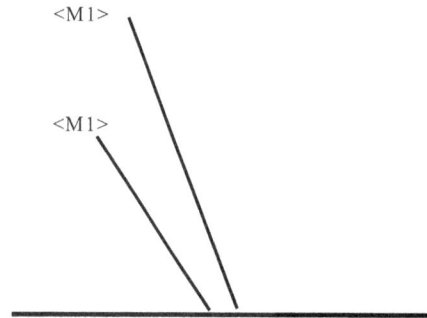

DE = Denominational Employee
ED = Editor
FM = Former Moderator
IT = In Transit to another Presbytery
M1 = Ordained Minister
M2 = Licentiate
M3 = Candidate
M4 = Minister of another denomination enrolled as a member through reciprocal agreement (Constitution 5.3)
M5 = Member of another denomination
M6 = Layperson serving church
M7 = Associate or Assistant Pastor
M8 = Military Chaplain
M9 = Non-Military Chaplain
M0 = Mentored Minister
MY = Missionary
OM = Other approved ministry
OP = Member of another presbytery
PR = Professor, Teacher
RT = Retired **or HR (honorably retired)**
ST = Student

CL= Clerk of Session
CO= Chair of commission appointed to govern church

AP = Associate/AssistantPastor
IP = Interim Pastor
LS = Layperson serving church
OD= Member of another denomination
PA = Installed Pastor
SS = Stated Supply

SUMMARY OF STATISTICS OF PRESBYTERIES BY SYNODS

(Number of Ministers)	1.Church Number	2.Active	3.Total	4.Church School	5.Prof. of Faith	6.Gains	7.Losses	8.Children Baptized	9. OUR UNITED OUT-REACH	10. Total Out-Reach Giving	11. All Other Expenses	12. Total Income Received	13. Value Church Prop. 1=1000
	1	2	3	4	5	6	7	8	9	10	11	12	13

GR: SYNOD OF GREAT RIVERS

Arkansas (42)	52	1,938	3,096	1,069	59	132	172	11	145,581	375,303	1,811,795	2,150,007	22,357
Missouri (19)	23	664	1,091	399	30	58	120	8	54,810	173,668	645,230	760,198	7,584
West Tennessee (111)	96	6,302	9,605	3,235	60	131	365	28	324,288	767,115	4,642,072	5,284,530	54,375
SYNOD (172)	170		13,792		149		657		524,679		7,099,097		84,316
TOTALS		8,904		4,703		321		47		1,316,086		8,194,735	

MI:SYNOD OF THE MIDWEST

Covenant (43)	45	2,666	5,269	1,626	47	83	127	18	130,619	434,824	2,518,514	2,885,033	26,500
Cumberland (60)	65	3,041	4,875	1,702	37	77	200	20	115,792	294,741	1,908,881	2,239,740	23,144
North Central (35)	32	1,119	1,968	922	27	19	146	2	81,907	230,579	908,632	1,135,108	11,442
SYNOD (138)	142		12,112		111		473		328,318		5,336,027		61,086
TOTALS		6,826		4,250		179		40		960,144		6,259,881	

MS:MISSION SYNOD

Andes (16)	10	1,813	1,912	916	136	153	137	0	7,000	0	1,041,881	1,100,903	1,526
Cauca Valley (16)	19	2,902	3,562	1,813	32	492	85	0	11,300	83,567	482,110	595,992	3,300
Choctaw (5)	7	74	138	84	0	3	3	0	0	2,541	9,991	11,304	230
del Cristo (53)	11	1,536	3,811	681	12	65	99	14	90,538	443,131	3,251,597	3,858,644	11,973
Hong Kong (10)	10	1,356	2,118	584	69	116	34	33	16,798	289,593	2,179,357	2,685,564	4,384
Japan (18)	14	1,164	2,278	727	29	36	67	1	37,115	215,029	1,309,159	1,460,889	3,129
Red River (60)	26	2,433	3,954	1,316	85	263	112	45	122,345	492,022	3,614,870	4,382,136	33,977
Trinity (44)	22	1,645	2,474	710	18	88	80	18	120,201	491,183	2,407,595	2,979,570	24,470
SYNOD (222)	119		20,247		381		617		405,297		14,296,560		82,989
TOTALS		12,923		6,831		1,216		111		2,017,066		17,075,002	

SE:SYNOD OF THE SOUTHEAST

Cum East Coast (??)	4	118	148	55	12	22	21	3	500	4,600	190,800	185,780	318
East Tennessee (60)	39	2,890	4,851	1,774	29	101	176	17	272,277	541,736	3,241,734	3,782,664	35,086
Grace (104)	37	2,717	3,737	1,498	91	209	149	27	157,412	431,423	2,769,810	3,242,275	30,814
Hope (10)	16	856	1,304	544	28	44	27	8	45,068	128,085	767,643	862,787	9,264
Robert Donnell (28)	16	1,031	1,726	374	6	26	36	6	62,128	194,761	1,041,303	1,264,847	13,191
Tennessee-Georgia (37)	25	1,822	2,310	765	18	54	98	7	62,089	175,930	1,467,671	1,813,068	19,561
SYNOD (239)	137		14,076		184		507		599,474		9,478,961		108,234
TOTALS		9,434		5,010		456		68		1,476,535		11,151,421	

TN:TENNESSEE SYNOD

Columbia (30)	38	1,503	2,510	929	31	81	183	8	76,118	256,001	1,879,214	2,029,176	19,737
Murfreesboro (53)	45	3,042	4,621	2,046	48	139	224	22	269,810	431,866	2,572,882	2,969,639	34,730
Nashville (52)	38	2,867	5,012	1,980	65	159	242	47	202,184	498,863	4,111,165	4,696,526	50,106
SYNOD (135)	121		12,143		144		649		548,112		8,563,261		104,573
TOTALS		7,412		4,955		379		77		1,186,730		9,695,341	

GRAND (906)	689		72,370		969		2,903		2,405,880		44,773,906		441,198
TOTALS		45,499		25,749		2,551		343		6,956,561		52,376,380	

Andes Presbytery
MISSION SYNOD

	1. Church Number	2. Active	3. Total	4. Church School	5. Prof. of Faith	6. Gains	7. Losses	8. Children Baptized	9. OUR UNITED OUT-REACH	10. Total Out-Reach Giving	11. All Other Expenses	12. Total Income Received	13. Value Church Prop. 1=1000
	1	2	3	4	5	6	7	8	9	10	11	12	13
Armenia*	8903	522	522	106	50	29	22	0			0	166,821	226,499	450
Cartago	8906	161	171	75	20	20	10	0			0	57,721	54,688	0
Dosquebradas	8907	219	219	285	40	24	18	0			0	115,245	115,768	112
El Rebano*	8905	273	273	60	0	16	25	0			0	100,922	107,947	161
Horeb-Central	8915	88	107	35	8	17	11	0			0	91,349	82,248	111
La Rosa*	8911	70	75	95	0	12	2	0			0	31,930	34,006	28
La Virginia Mis*	8913	30	30	20	18	13	13	0			0	15,357	15,357	21
Manizales*	8914	121	129	60	0	3	0	0			0	60,682	60,682	13
Pereira*	8916	232	282	130	0	19	26	0			0	346,151	347,582	500
Zamora	8918	97	104	50	0	0	10	0			0	55,703	56,126	130
Presbytery	8900								7,000					
TOTALS	10	1,813	1,912	916	136	153	137	0	7,000		0	1,041,881	1,100,903	1,526

*Math error corrected. **Purged roll..

CHURCHES, PASTORS, AND CLERKS:

Armenia   (4MWC)MSAN8903
   Cra 15 #16-39
   Armenia, Quindio
   Colombia, South America
   (574)745-4860   <S America>
   FAX: (574)745-4895
   ipc-armenia@hotmail.com
PA: John Jairo Correa   <M1>
   Calle 2 Norte #16-39
   Armenia, Quindio
   Colombia, South America
   (574)745-0496
   jjccdp07@hotmail.com
AP: Esperanza Diaz   <M1>
   Calle 2 Norte #16-19
   Armenia, Quindio
   Colombia, South America
   (576)745-0496
CL: Jose Leobardo Castro
   Calle 16 #14-43
   Armenia, Quindio
   Colombia, South America
   57(310)-389-2361

Cartago   (4MW C)MSAN8906
   Cra 12 #8-47
   Cartago, Valle
   Colombia, South America
   (572)214-5060   <S America>
   FAX: (572)214-5060
   presbicartago@gmail.com
PA: Cenobia Rivera   <M1>
   Cra 12 #8-47
   Cartago, Valle
   Colombia, South America
   57(310)500-1791
   zenobiadedaza@yahoo.com.mx
PA: Edilberto Daza   <M1>
   Cra 12 #8-47

Cartago, Valle
Colombia, South America
57(314)794-1905
presbicartago@gmail.com
CL: Verney Lopez
   Calle 25C #36-15
   Cartago, Valle
   Colombia, South America
   57(314)715-3075

Dosquebradas   (4MWC)MSAN8907
   Calle 51 #15-32 (mailing)
   Cra 15 A #50-31 (physical)
   barrio Los Naranjos
   Dosquebradas, Risaralda
   Colombia, South America
   (574)322-2938   <S America>
PA: Juan Esteban Blandon   <M1>
   Calle 51 #15-32
   barrio Los Naranjos
   Dosquebradas, Risaralda
   Colombia, South America
   (574)322-2938
   juanestebanblandon@yahoo.com
CL: Alba Rodriguez
   Cra 15 A #50-31
   barrio Los Naranjoa
   Dosquebradas, Risaralda
   Colombia, South America
   (574)322-4899

El Rebano-Caldas   (4WMCF)MSAN8905
   Calle 128 Sur #48-13
   barrio Central
   Caldas, Antioquia
   Colombia, South America
   (574)278-0787   <S America>
   FAX: (574)278-0787
   rebcaldas@une.net.co
SS: Juan Alexander Castano   <M3 ST>
   Calle 127 sur #42-38 Apto 301
   Caldas, Antioquia

Colombia, South America
(574)306-4435
FAX: (574)278-0787
juanalexandercastanovelez@yahoo.com
CL: Consuelo Pena
   Calle 130 Sur #57-09, Int 301
   Caldas, Antioquia
   Colombia, South America
   (574)338-6190
   FAX: (574)278-0787
   chelitopeco@hotmail.com

Horeb-Central   (4WMC)MSAN8915
   Carrera 50D #62-69, Prado Centro
   Medellin, Antioquia
   Colombia, South America
   (574)263-2154   <S America>
   ipchoreb@hotmail.com
PA: Ricardo Castaneda   <M1>
   Calle 65 #98-45 (Interior 174)
   Altos de la Macarena-Robledo La Campina
   Medellin, Antioquia
   Colombia, South America
   (574)577-0717
   rijcah@gmail.com
AP: Diana Valdez   <M1>
   Cra 50 D#62-69
   Medellin, Antioquia
   Colombia, South America
   (574)263-2154
   dianamariavaldezduque@gmail.com
CL: Lina Velasquez
   Calle 49E #83A91
   Recinto de La Arboleda, Calazans
   Medellin, Antioquia
   Colombia, South America
   (574)422-6698
   velasquezlina@yahoo.es

La Rosa de Saron   (4F)MSAN8911
   Calle 100 #50C-09
   Barrio Santa Cruz Sector La Rosa
   Medellin, Antioquia

ANDES PRESBYTERY CONTINUED

Colombia, South America
(574)236-6509   <S America>
SS: Andres Giraldo   <M2>
  Calle 76 #87-14 Apto 202
  Medellin, Antioquia
  Colombia, South America
  (574)422-6669
  andresgiraldo@une.net.co
CL: Claudia Cordoba
  Calle 100 #50C-35
  Barrio Santa Cruz Sector La Rosa
  Medellin, Antioquia
  Colombia, South America
  57(315)605-0011

La Virginia   (4WMF)MSAN8913
  Cra 4 bis #10-35
  La Virginia, Risalda
  Colombia, South America
  (576)368-3589   <S America>
CL: Nora Patricia Diaz
  Cra 4 bis #10-35
  LaVirginia, Risalda
  Colombia, South America
  (311)312-2349
  noris_1985@hotmail.com

Manizales   (4WMC)MSAN8914
  Calle 22 #25-33
  Manizales, Caldas
  Colombia, South America
  (576)883-0383   <S America>
  FAX: (576)833-0383
  manizales50ipc@hotmail.com
PA: William Diaz   <M1>
  Calle 42 #26B-68
  Manizales, Caldas
  Colombia, South America
  (574)890-2972
  manizales50ipc@hotmail.com
CL: Luz Dary Herrera
  Calle 5 #22-56
  Manizales, Caldas
  Colombia, South America
  (576)889-0994

Pereira   (4MWC)MSAN8916
  Cra 12 bis #11-69
  Pereira, Risaralda
  Colombia, South America
  (574)333-9295   <S America>
  FAX: (574)324-4110
  cumberlandpres@une.net.co
PA: David Montoya   <M1>
  Cra 12 bis #11-69
  Pereira, Risaralda
  Colombia, South America
  (574)324-4109
  FAX: (574)324-4110
  adamonva@gmail.com
AP: Luz Maria Heilbron   <M1>
  Cra 12 bis #11-51
  Pereira, Risaralda
  Colombia, South America
  (576)333-9295
  pastorapresbi@hotmail.com
AP: Rodrigo Martinez   <M1>
  Mz2 Casa 21 Urb Casas De Milan
  Dosquebradas, Risaralda
  Colombia, South America
  (576)322-2177

oikoinonia@gmail.com
CL: Shirley Murillo
  Cra 12 bis #11-69
  Pereira, Risaralda
  Colombia, South America

Zamora   (4WC)MSAN8918
  Calle 20D #42C-56 (physical)
  Cra 58 #32A-41 Apt 420 (mailing)
  Bello, Antioquia
  Colombia, South America
  (574)461-0069   <S America>
  ipczamora@gmail.com
PA: Alejandro Vasquez   <M1>
  Cra 58 #32A-41 Apt 420
  Bello, Antioquia
  Colombia, South America
  (574)451-4816
  almaesda@une.net.co
CL: Amparo Hoyos
  Calle 120D #42C-56
  Bello, Antioquia
  Colombia, South America
  57(315)424-4547
  chilalu1147@hotmail.com

OTHERS ON MINISTERIAL ROLL:

Daza, Johan   <M1>
  8148 Yellow Stone Drive
  Cordova, TN 38016
  (281)793-3869
  jdaza@cumberland.org
Gentry, Michele   <M1 M9>
  Urb San Jorge casa 28
  Km 8 via a La Tebaida
  Armenia, Quindio
  Colombia, South America
  (318)285-1161
  gentry.andes@yahoo.com
Guerrero, Luz Dary   <M1 MY>
  Calle 22 #25-33
  Manizales, Caldas
  Colombia, South America
  (576)888-4203
  clementinajacobo7@hotmail.com
Martinez, Dagoberto   <M1 RT>
  Cra 62D #71-113
  Bello, Antioquia
  Colombia, South America
  (574)452-3466
Ortiz, Jaime   <M1 RT>
  Cra 50D #62-69
  Medellin, Antioquia
  Colombia, South America
  (574)421-6339
Taborda, Arturo   <M1 RT>
  Cra 43 #20D-46
  Zamora, Medellin, Antioquia
  Colombia, South America
  (574)267-1351
  chilalu1147@hotmail.com
Valencia, Nulbel   <M1 RT>
  Diag 11D Casa 11 urbGemelas
  Dosquebradas, Risaralda
  Colombia, South America
  (576)330-7704
  nava1928@hotmail.com
Velez, Gabriel   <M1 RT>
  Calle 8A #16A-26, Villa Fanny
  Dosquebradas, Risaralda
  Colombia, South America
  (576)330-1168

OTHER LICENTIATES ON ROLL:

Guerrero, Cruzana   <M2>
  Calle 83 #74-179
  Medellin, Antioguia
  Colombia, South America
  (574)257-0613
Guerrero, Josue   <M2>
  Calle 76 #88-65
  Medellin, Antioquia
  Colombia, South America
  (574)412-3504
  josueggutierrez@yahoo.es
Gutierrez, Libardo   <M2>
  Calle 83 #74-179
  Medellin, Antioquia
  Colombia, South America
  (314)600-2020
  guzlibar@yahoo.es
Hoyos, Amparo   <M2>
  Cra 43 #20D-26
  Zamora, Antioquia
  Colombia, South America
  (574)278-0784
  chilalu1147@hotmail.com
Orozco, Joaquin   <M2>
  Cra 3 #7-14
  Aguadas, Caldas
  Colombia, South America
  (576)851-4773
  jeob40@hotmail.com

OTHER CANDIDATES ON ROLL:

Arias, John Jairo   <M3>
  Calle 144 sur #196-08 / Apto 202
  Caldas, Antioquia
  Colombia, South America
  (57)317-693-1162
  sajoarias@hotmail.com
Cardona, Nancy   <M3 ST>
  Calle 51 #15-32
  Dosquebradas, Risaralda
  Colombia, South America
  (576)322-2938
  nancycardona10@yahoo.com
Galvis, Alexander   <M3 ST>
  Calle 76 #87-63 Apto 211
  Medellin, Antioquia
  Colombia, South America
  (300)778-4354
  alexgt7@hotmail.com
Giraldo, Juan Pablo   <M3>
  Calle 51 #15-32
  barrio Los Naranjos
  Dosquebradas, Risaralda
  Colombia, South America
  (576)322-2938
Giraldo, Marcela   <M3>
  Calle 68 D #40-15
  Manizales, Caldas
  Colombia, South America
  (576)878-5412
Jimenez, Jorge Enrique   <M3>
  Urb Manantiales MzC Casa 6
  Armenia, Quindio
  Colombia, South America
  (321)643-0693
  joenjimu@yahoo.es
Laverde, Alina   <M3>
  Calle 100 #50C-09
  Barrio Santa Cruz Sector La Rosa

ANDES PRESBYTERY CONTINUED

Medellin, Antioquia
Colombia, South America
(574)236-6509
Lopez, Carlos Geovanny   <M3>
  Cra 12 bis #11-69
  Pereira, Risaralda
  Colombia, South America
  (576)333-9295
Morales, Juan Fernando   <M3>
  Calle 100 #50C-09
  Barrio Santa Cruz Sector La Rosa
  Medellin, Antioquia
  Colombia, South America
  (574)236-6509
Ortega, Juan   <M3>
  Colombia, South America
  (574)323-9305
Porras, Rene Wilgen   <M3>
  Cra 4 bis #10-51
  La Virginia, Risalda
  (576)367-9529

Vargas, Lida Patricia   <M3>
  Carrera 50D #62-69, Prado Centro
  Medellin, Antioquia
  Colombia, South America
  (574)263-2154
  lidapavargas@hotmail.com
Varilla, Adan Manuel   <M3>
  Calle 48 D E #96A-30
  Medellin, Antioquia
  Colombia, South America
  (57)313-691-1923
Velez, Gloria Patricia   <M3>
  Cra 4 bis #10-51
  LaVirginia, Risaralda
  Colombia, South America
  (576)385-4517
  renewilgen@hotmail.com

Arkansas Presbytery
GREAT RIVERS SYNOD

GENERAL		MEMBERSHIP			CHANGES				FINANCES				
	1.Church Number	2.Active	3.Total	4.Church School	5.Prof. of Faith	6.Gains	7.Losses	8.Children Baptized	9. OUR UNITED OUT-REACH	10. Total Out-Reach Giving	11. All Other Expenses	12. Total Income Received	13. Value Church Prop. |1=1000
	1	2	3	4	5	6	7	8	9	10	11	12	13
Appleton	1202	13	28	27	0	0	1	0	400	2,131	13,565	14,747	40
Arkansas Loving	2135	45	63	2	No Report Received			0	0	0	0	0	700
Barren Fork	1501	94	107	57	4	5	1	0	8,614	14,765	87,841	88,729	400
Ben Lomond	1301	17	17	17	0	12	0	0	0	5,526	32,939	34,126	80
Bethesda	1302	44	64	47	6	7	5	3	0	4,294	66,338	59,492	957
Booneville	1401	50	56	7	No Report Received			0	6,385	0	0	0	375
Byron	1508	11	11	12	0	0	0	0	300	2,399	4,463	7,982	287
Calico Rock	1503	101	117	55	6	18	10	5	15,167	46,426	76,883	134,792	1,276
Camden	1303	37	89	40	No Report Received			0	4,291	0	0	0	330
Camp Ground**	1101	47	92	20	0	0	31	0	6,355	12,751	44,849	68,093	600
Caulksville	1402	218	240	30	4	17	2	2	12,918	38,773	113,382	127,084	650
Dilworth	1304	7	13	8	1	0	0	0	0	1,645	20,835	21,815	125
Dover	1203	23	23	15	1	1	0	0	3,325	11,166	41,874	72,260	275
E. T. Allen	1307	17	17	12	No Report Received			0	0	0	0	0	225
Faith-Hopewell	1502	99	122	63	5	10	2	0	9,954	22,173	81,370	107,774	1,400
Falls Chapel	1308	39	39	30	0	7	0	0	0	4,102	76,418	57,804	n/a
Fellowship (BC)	1505	103	185	45	0	5	2	0	13,184	21,784	106,863	131,846	1,326
Fellowship (OC)	1309	45	52	43	12	17	1	0	3,265	5,847	33,303	36,014	117
Fomby	1310	5	31	8	0	0	0	0	0	4,654	11,788	18,794	138
Fort Smith	1406	47	173	14	0	0	3	0	2,717	2,400	55,298	24,000	800
Grace**	1405	22	22	9	0	0	34	0	4,105	8,119	35,191	43,310	272
Gum Springs (WC)	1205	9	9	11	0	0	0	0	0	627	7,500	8,300	n/a
Gum Springs (YC)	1206	6	10	3	0	0	13	0	0	800	16,960	27,702	250
Hector	1207	17	50	12	0	0	1	0	0	2,756	31,432	39,313	93
Lake Hamilton	1221	72	78	16	2	8	18	0	0	9,768	82,175	77,213	350
Lockesburg	1311	3	3	0	No Report Received			0	0	0	0	0	162
Lucas Community	1407				CLOSED 9/12/2014								65
Marietta	1408	47	47	47	1	1	2	0	0	3,508	39,018	38,894	350
Mars Hill	1211	15	35	0	No Report Received			0	1,000	0	0	0	200
Milligan C. G.	1516				CLOSED 9/12/2014								61
Mt. Carmel	1212	40	40	15	0	0	1	0	7,210	16,318	55,902	72,221	75
Mt. Olive	1517	26	35	8	4	4	8	0	1,775	31,616	17,250	50,366	230
New Hope	1510	11	11	9	0	0	7	0	2,811	4,642	14,520	29,174	350
Old Union	1409	27	51	27	4	3	0	0	3,100	5,598	17,575	36,996	119
Oxford	1511	27	27	30	0	0	1	0	300	7,012	7,990	13,717	175
Palestine	1103	82	130	53	0	13	4	0	3,850	12,963	101,785	131,144	1,575
Pilot Prairie	1411				CLOSED 9/12/2014								50
Pine Bluff, 1st	1104	13	103	0	No Report Received			0	0	0	0	0	766
Pine Ridge	1105	13	25	11	1	1	1	0	2,576	5,284	36,429	43,951	381
Pineville	1512	54	71	30	2	2	3	0	7,314	22,855	48,205	86,943	300
Pleasant Grove	1214	5	9	5	No Report Received			0	0	0	0	0	70
Prairie Grove	1412	8	14	6	No Report Received			0	0	0	0	0	530
Provo	1314	11	38	25	No Report Received			0	0	0	0	0	125
Rodney	1513	18	18	18	0	0	0	0	0	1,165	20,624	23,101	65
Rose Hill	1106	55	55	37	0	3	1	0	6,970	11,040	55,960	69,700	1,000
Russellville	1216	109	223	45	3	3	5	0	530	0	170,585	163,552	1,701
Salem (FC)	1514	28	29	15	No Report Received			0	1,500	0	0	0	250
Searcy	1218	30	56	22	0	0	0	0	1,200	3,410	16,847	18,124	240
Shaver	1413	1	1	0	No Report Received			0	0	0	0	0	10
Shell Chapel	1108	8	31	4	0	0	0	0	1,059	2,011	17,854	13,885	500
Sherwood	1220	20	183	7	0	0	1	0	99	990	36,894	38,969	777
Sidney	1515	9	18	9	No Report Received			0	0	0	0	0	200
Sulphur Springs	1315	16	48	11	0	1	0	0	0	2,773	23,981	32,245	29
Trimble Camp G**	1504	35	20	33	No Report Received			0	5,196	0	0	0	365
Trinity	1219	14	34	0	0	0	1	0	0	1,457	26,271	24,665	220
Walkerville	1317	12	26	12	0	0	1	0	8,111	16,005	26,048	24,913	150
Walnut Grove	1414	32	59	18	3	6	0	0	0	3,750	36,610	36,256	200
TOTALS	52	1,938	3,096	1,069	59	132	172	11	145,581	375,303	1,811,795	2,150,007	22,579

*Math error corrected. **Purged roll.

ARKANSAS PRESBYTERY CONTINUED

CHURCHES, PASTORS, AND CLERKS:

Appleton   (W4C)GRAR1202
171 Tate Street (mailing)
320 Tate Street (physical)
Atkins, AR 72823
( )   <Pope>
CL: Sue Bartlett
171 Tate Street
Atkins, AR 72823
(479)284-4357
msbart@thebartlettpage.com

Arkansas Loving   (P)GRAR2135
1603 Coolhurst Avenue
Sherwood, AR 72120
(501)247-5953   <Pulaski>
swcho100491@gmail.com
PA: Sung Wan Cho   <M1>
1603 Coolhurst Avenue
Sherwood, AR 72120
(501)247-5953
swcho100491@gmail.com
CL: Eun Hi Lee
110 Beaulieu Court
Maumelle, AR 72113
(501)247-4545

Barren Fork   (4MWC)GRAR1501
782 Barren Fork Road
Mount Pleasant, AR 72561
(870)346-5121   <Izard>
PA: Alan Meinzer   <M1>
25 Rosewood Road
Batesville, AR 72501
(870)793-3915
natsdad@suddenlink.net
CL: Connie Crafton
1275 Barren Fork Road
Mount Pleasant, AR 72561
(870)346-5349

Ben Lomond   (4C)GRAR1301
180 LR 39 (mailing)
Ogden, AR 71853
495 N Main Street (physical)
Ben Lomond, AR 71823
( )   <Sevier>
OD: Herman R Welch   <M5>
180 LR 39
Ogden, AR 71853
(903)748-2126
herawe@yahoo.com
CL: Cindy Mills
PO Box 55
Ben Lomond, AR 71823

Bethesda   (4MW C)GRAR1302
395 Ouachita 47
Camden, AR 71701
(870)231-4909   <Ouachita>
PA: Garrett Burns   <M1>
387 Forrest Avenue
McKenzie. TN 38201
(731)535-3126
gburns2888@gmail.com
CL: Ben Fields
451 Ouachita 47
Camden, AR 71701
(870)231-5080

bfields2011@hotmail.com

Booneville   (4MEW C)GRAR1401
PO Box 163 (mailing)
355 Sharp Street (physical)
Booneville, AR 72927
( )   <Logan>
church@boonevillecpc.com
PA: Henry Jenkins   <M1>
PO Box 148 (mailing)
90 W Grove (physical)
Magazine, AR 72943
(479)969-8351
henryj@magtel.com
CL: Janet Bedene
PO Box 7 (mailing)
113 Pine Street(physical)
Ratcliff, AR 72951
(479)847-6746
phaparis@magtel.com

Byron   (4WC)GRAR1508
PO Box 524 (mailing)
Byron Road, Viola, AR (physical)
Calico Rock, AR 72519
(870)291-8542   <Fulton>
calicowild@hotmail.com
PA: Victor Jones   <M1>
7017 Highway 177 S
Jordan, AR 72519
(870)499-5882
pam.jones@centurytel.net
CL: Session Clerk
PO Box 524
Calico Rock, AR 72519
(870)291-8542
calicowild@hotmail.com

Calico Rock   (4MEWC)GRAR1503
PO Box 315 (mailing)
692 AR 56 Highway E (physical)
Calico Rock, AR 72519
(870)297-3931   <Izard>
FAX: (870)297-3151
crcpc@centurytcl.net
PA: Thomas D Campbell   <M1>
PO Box 343
Calico Rock, AR 72519
(870)297-3931
FAX: (870)297-3151
tdcampbellar@gmail.com
CL: Carolyn Jeffery
PO Box 183
Calico Rock, AR 72519
(870)297-8530
cjeffery6@gmail.com

Camden   (4MEWC)GRAR1303
1545 California Avenue
Camden, AR 71701
(870)836-8712   <Ouachita>
CL: Deanie Tate
138 Ouachita 571
Camden, AR 71701
(870)403-4847
tdtate38@yahoo.com

Camp Ground   (4WMC)GRAR1101
1548 E AR 274 Highway
Hampton, AR 71744
(870)798-4302   <Calhoun>

PA: Garland Skidmore   <M1>
2083 US Highway 278 E
Hampton, AR 71744
(870)798-4634
CL: Shirley Strickland
1783 E AR 274 Highway
Hampton, AR 71744
(870)918-2344
strick6@sat-co.net

Caulksville   (4MWC)GRAR1402
PO Box 2 (mailing)
23 W Main, Caulksville, AR (physical)
Ratcliff, AR 72951
(479)635-4301   <Logan>
PA: Bill Van Meter   <M1>
10626 Highway 41
Charleston, AR 72933
(479)965-2998
revbill46@gmail.com
CL: Cherre Nietert
10201 Nietert Lane
Branch, AR 72928
(479)438-0673

Dilworth   (4C)GRAR1304
305 N 6th Street (mailing)
De Queen, AR 71832
2517 N Red Bridge Road (physical)
Horatio, AR 71842
(870)642-8051   <Sevier>
mtcarmel2@windstream.net
OD: Byron G Sullivan   <M5>
305 N 6th Street
De Queen, AR 71832
(870)642-8051
mtcarmel2@windstream.net
CL: Nita Sue Sullivan
305 N 6th Street
De Queen, AR 71832
(870)642-8051
mtcarmel2@windstream.net

Dover   (4MWC)GRAR1203
29 Maple Street (mailing)
Hector, AR 72843
96 Waters Street (physical)
Dover, AR 72837
(479)331-3130   <Pope>
markoe@centurytel.net
OD: Mike Galloway   <M5>
2821 Linker Mount Road
Dover, AR 72837
(479)331-0254
markoe@centurytel.net
CL: Beth McAlister
29 Maple Street
Hector, AR 72843
beth.ann56@hotmail.com

E T Allen   (4WC)GRAR1307
PO Box 822 (mailing)
153 Highway 71 N
Ashdown, AR 71822
( )   <Little Rive>
CL: Glen Ray Bowman
1050 Oak Place
Ashdown, AR 71822
(903)824-5000
botech64@aol.com

ARKANSAS PRESBYTERY CONTINUED

Faith-Hopewell (4WC)GRAR1502
3895 Harrison Street
Batesville, AR 72501
(870)612-5949 <Independence>
SS: Rian Puckett <M3 OP>
3784 Harrison Street
Batesville, AR 72501
(731)288-7742
rppuckett@memphisseminry.edu
CL: Ionna Hess
3075 O'Neal Road
Batesville, AR 72501
(870)793-5530
ionnahess@yahoo.com

_____

Falls Chapel (4MC)GRAR1308
182 Hunter Falls Loop (mailing)
127 LW Davis Road (physical)
Lockesburg, AR 71846
( ) <Sevier>
CL: Ann Keith
182 Hunter Falls Loop
Lockesburg, AR 71846
(870)289-6834
memaplayground@windstream.net

_____

Fellowship (BC) (4EWC)GRAR1505
PO Box 866 (mailing)
1206 E 9th Street (physical)
Mountain Home, AR 72653
(870)425-5419 <Baxter>
info@fellowshipcumberland.org
PA: Gary Robert Tubb <M1>
103 Forest Drive
Mountain Home, AR 72653
grtubb@yahoo.com
(870)424-0603
CL: Andy Marts
393 County Road 1085
Mountain Home, AR 72653
(870)481-6092
amarts@centurytel.net

_____

Fellowship (OC) (4WC)GRAR1309
478 Ouachita 54 (mailing)
2855 Ouachita 3 (physical)
Camden, AR 71701
( ) <Ouachita>
SS: Roberta Smith Johnson <M1>
397 Ouachita 54
Camden, AR 71701
(870)231-5827
CL: Charles T Jeffus
478 Ouachita 54
Camden, AR 71701
(870)231-9994
charlesjeffus@yahoo.com

_____

Fomby (4C)GRAR1310
704 Highway 317 (mailing)
1215 Highway 32 E (physical)
Ashdown, AR 71822
(870)898-2856 <Little Rive>
carole4485@att.net
CL: Carole C Booth
704 Highway 317
Ashdown, AR 71822
(870)898-2856
carole4485@att.net

_____

Fort Smith (4MEWC)GRAR1406

605 N 47th Street
Fort Smith, AR 72903
(479)782-0454 <Sebastian>
FAX: (479)782-0454
ksstamps@msn.com
OD: Randall Cross <M5>
608 N Crest Drive
Fayetteville, AR 72701
(870)917-9303
rkcross@cox.net
CL: Janie Stamps
4008 Logan Lane
Fort Smith, AR 72903
(479)478-0161
bjstamps@msn.com

_____

Grace (4C)GRAR1405
2451 Wedington Drive
Fayetteville, AR 72701
(479)442-6772 <Washington>
CL: Robin Thomas
1195 N White Rock Lane
Fayetteville, AR 72704
(479)521-0371
rthomas@mman.com

_____

Gum Springs(WC) (4C)GRAR1205
1717 W Arch Avenue (mailing)
Gum Springs Road (physical)
Searcy, AR 72143
(501)268-2615 <White>
SS: Jim Bradberry <M3>
120 Hummingbird Lane
Searcy, AR 72143
(501)278-9750
CL: J C Holleman
1717 W Arch Avenue
Searcy, AR 72143
(501)268-2615

_____

Gum Springs(YC) (4MC)GRAR1206
10146 Crescent Drive (mailing)
10048 Blessed Road (physical)
Dardanelle, AR 72834
(479)229-4140 <Yell>
wesides@centurytel.net
CL: Marilyn Roberts
10742 Gum Springs Road
Dardanelle, AR 72834
(479)229-3017

_____

Hector (4MWC)GRAR1207
PO Box 53 (mailing)
29 Maple (physical)
Hector, AR 72843
(479)747-7561 <Pope>
CL: Beth McAlister
PO Box 53
Hector, AR 72843
(479)747-7561

_____

Lake Hamilton (4 C)GRAR1221
2891 Airport Road
Hot Springs, AR 71913
(501)760-3800 <Garland>
lakehamiltoncpc@yahoo.com
PA: Duawn Mearns <M1>
107 Westoak Place
Hot Springs, AR 71913
(501)276-1266
lakehamiltoncpc@yahoo.com

CL: Phyllis Pipkin
197 Cobbleridge Trail
Hot Springs, AR 71913
(501)318-3462
sephpipkin@aol.com

_____

Lockesburg (1C)GRAR1311
279 N Park Avenue (mailing)
114 W Walnut (physical)
Lockesburg, AR 71846
( ) <Sevier>
CL: Joe E Bush
279 N Park Avenue
Lockesburg, AR 71846
(870)289-2433

_____

Lucas Community (4C)GRAR1407
Rt 1 Box 260
Booneville, AR 72927
( ) <Logan>
(CLOSED 9/12/2014)
(membership transferred to Booneville)

_____

Marietta (4C)GRAR1408
623 Church Street (mailing)
2604 West Main (physical)
Charleston, AR 72933
(479)965-0224 <Franklin>
SS: Vondal Davenport <M1>
PO Box 823
Lavaca, AR 72941
(479)965-2036
CL: Tim Aldridge
623 Church Street
Charleston, AR 72933
(479)965-7639
dcotim58@live.com

_____

Mars Hill (4WC)GRAR1211
172 Thompson Lane (mailing)
1224 State Route 363 (physical)
Pottsville, AR 72858
( ) <Pope>
PA: Jo Warren <M1>
811 Wall Street
Morrilton, AR 72110
(501)354-4139
pastorjo47@ymail.com
CL: Gary Thompson
172 Thompson Lane
Pottsville, AR 72858
(479)970-4652
thompgary@gmail.com
_____(no services 10/30/13)
Milligan C G (2C)GRAR1516
Strawberry, AR 72469
( ) <Sharp>
(CLOSED 9/21/2014)
(membership transferred to Faith-Hopewell)

_____

Mt Carmel (4C)GRAR1212
1470 Mt Carmel Road W
London, AR 72847
(479)293-4447 <Pope>
mtcarmel@centurylink.net
PA: Thomas (Tom) Deere <M1>
460 Yukon Drive
Russellville, AR 72811
(479)498-0318
tdeere@suddenlinkmail.com

ARKANSAS PRESBYTERY CONTINUED

CL: Jennifer Metz
276 Metz Lane
London, AR 72847
(479)293-4229
jmetz54@hotmail.com

Mt Olive (4EC)GRAR1517
214 Bear Trail Hollow (mailing)
5539 Mt Olive Road (physical)
Melbourne, AR 72556
(870)368-4923 <Izard>
bobeth@centurytel.net
SS: Stan Mars <M1>
PO Box 274
Mt Pleasant, AR 72561
(217)254-5120
smars2@liberty.edu
CL: Mary Beth Jeffery
214 Bear Trail Hollow
Melbourne, AR 72556
(870)368-4923
bobeth@centurytel.net

New Hope (2C)GRAR1510
25 Pine Hill Road (mailing)
3655 Bethesda Road (physical)
Batesville, AR 72501
( ) <Independence>
verenaherrin@yahoo.com
SS: Rian Puckett <M3 OP>
3784 Harrison Street
Batesville, AR 72501
(731)288-7742
rppuckett@memphisseminary.edu
CL: Verena Herrin
25 Pine Hill Road
Batesville, AR 72501
(870)793-6145
verenaherrin@yahoo.com

Old Union (4C)GRAR1409
PO Box 477 (mailing)
Old Union Road (physical)
Magazine, AR 72943
( ) <Logan>
PA: Henry Jenkins <M1>
PO Box 148
Magazine, AR 72943
(479)969-8352
henryj@magtel.com
CL: Lee Strickland
PO Box 477
Magazine, AR 72943
(479)849-0198
eljws1@live.com

Oxford (4U)GRAR1511
618 Camp Ground Road (mailing)
211 Main Street (physical)
Oxford, AR 72565
( ) <Izard>
SS: Bobby D Coleman <M1>
704 E Webb Street
Mountain View, AR 72560
(870)213-5410
bobbycoleman@gmail.com
CL: Willetta Everett
618 Camp Ground Road
Oxford, AR 72565
(870)258-7798
weverett@centurytel.net

Palestine (4MEWC)GRAR1103
PO Box 98 (mailing)
223 South Main Street (physical)
Palestine, AR 72372
(870)581-2600 <St. Francis>
FAX: (870)581-2600
PA: Jason Chambers <M1>
131 E Woods Street
Palestine, AR 72372
(870)807-1930
jmchambers@memphisseminary.edu
CL: Lisa Alldredge
PO Box 803
Palestine, AR 72372
(870)581-2913
lsatmall@yahoo.com

Pilot Prairie (4MC)GRAR1411
PO Box 1873
Waldron, AR 72958
(479)637-3938 <Scott>

Pine Bluff 1st (4W C)GRAR1104
2401 Camden Road
Pine Bluff, AR 71603
( ) <Jefferson>
CL: Catherine Currington
205 Moss Road
White Hall, AR 71602
(870)247-3839

Pine Ridge (4C)GRAR1105
4890 Grant 14
Grapevine, AR 72057
(870)942-1827 <Grant>
PA: James (Jim) Bradshaw <M1>
415 S Red Street
Sheridan, AR 72150
(870)942-2525
CL: Buren Walker
336 Grant 748
Sheridan, AR 72150
(870)942-4790

Pineville (4MWC)GRAR1512
PO Box 256 (mailing)
1229 AR 223 Highway (physical)
Pineville, AR 72566
(870)297-4104 <Izard>
CL: Janie Jenkins
PO Box 504
Calico Rock, AR 72519
(870)297-3991
djjenkins@centurytel.net

Pleasant Grove (2C)GRAR1214
1083 Highway 305 S
Searcy, AR 72143
(501)796-3466 <White>
CL: Robbie Stroud
1922 Highway 31 N
Beebe, AR 72012
(501)882-3262

Prairie Grove (4C)GRAR1412
200 West Buchanan
Prairie Grove, AR 72753
(479)846-3914 <Washington>
(CLOSED 9/12/2014)
(membership transferred to Grace CPC)

Provo (4C)GRAR1314
131 LR 47 (mailing)
Ashdown, AR 71822
125 Dooley Road (physical)
Lockesburg, AR 71846
( ) <Sevier>
CL: Mica Crow
131 LR 47
Ashdown, AR 71822
(870)898-8588

Rodney (2EC)GRAR1513
117 Flint Rock Trail (mailing)
1333 Rodney Road (physical)
Jordan, AR 72519
( ) <Baxter>
PA: Dave Williamson <M1>
PO Box 67
Dolph, AR 72528
(870)499-7448
CL: Carol Lee
1364 Rodney Road
Jordan, AR 72519
(870)499-3238
txgrany69@yahoo.com

Rose Hill (4MWC)GRAR1106
1031 Binns Drive (mailing)
2133 Highway 83 N (physical)
Monticello, AR 71655
(870)367-5114 <Drew>
gsaray@att.net
PA: Bruce Hamilton <M1>
1037 Binns Drive
Monticello, AR 71655
(870)224-5007
bruce@hamiltonnet.org
CL: Stephanie Ray
122 E Shelton Avenue
Monticello, AR 71655
(870)723-3785
gsaray@att.net

Russellville (4WC)GRAR1216
1200 N Arkansas Avenue
Russellville, AR 72801
(479)968-1061 <Pope>
FAX: (479)880-0071
fcpcrussellville@yahoo.com
PA: Steve Mosley <M1>
320 N Sherman Circle
Russellville, AR 72801
(479)968-1061
FAX: (479)880-0071
stevemosley@hotmail.com
CL: Deanna Boston
721 Kovel Court
Russellville, AR 72801
(479)890-3880
fcpcrussellville@yahoo.com

Salem (FC) (4MWC)GRAR1514
1003 Flint Springs Road (mailing)
Viola, AR 72583
Highway 5 S, Salem, AR (physical)
( ) <Fulton>
salemcumberlandchurch@gmail.com
SS: Bobby D Coleman <M1>
704 E Webb Street
Mountain View, AR 72560

ARKANSAS PRESBYTERY CONTINUED

(870)269-6010
bobby.coleman@gmail.com
CL: Bonnie Brown
1003 Flint Springs Road
Viola, AR 72583
(870)458-2657
bbrown325@centurytel.net

Searcy   (4MWC)GRAR1218
100 E Race Street
Searcy, AR 72143
(501)268-8278   <White>
SS: Jim Bradberry   <M3>
120 Hummingbird Lane
Searcy, AR 72143
(501)278-9750
CL:Howard Johnson
2180 Holmes Road
Searcy, AR 72143
(501)268-3071
howardwjohnson@gmail.com

Shaver   (1C)GRAR1413
(no longer has services 10/30/13)
401 Shaver Road (mailing)
1448 Shaver Road (physical)
Paris, AR 72855
(   )   <Logan>

Shell Chapel   (4WC)GRAR1108
2143 Grider Field Road (mailing)
3110 Highway 425 (physical)
Pine Bluff, AR 71601
(870)535-5408   <Jefferson>
PA: Barbara Jean Brewer   <M1>
1360 White Oak Bluff Road
Rison, AR 71665
(870)325-6449
CL: Joyce Shell
2143 Grider Field Road
Pine Bluff, AR 71601
(870)535-5408
mkshell@earthlink.net

Sherwood   (4WC)GRAR1220
1402 E Kiehl Avenue
Sherwood, AR 72120
(501)835-8889   <Pulaski>
SS: Elizabeth Terrell   <M1>
2073 Vinton Avenue
Memphis, TN 38104
(901)647-2788
CL: Olive Snow
5907 Woodview Drive S
Sherwood, AR 72120
(501)835-7819
ladysnow64@yahoo.com

Sidney   (2U)GRAR1515
Batesville, AR 72501
(   )   <Sharp>
PA: Alan Meinzer   <M1>
25 Rosewood Road
Batesville, AR 72501
(870)793-3915
natsdad@suddenlink.net
CL: Jodi Moody
127 Arkansas Highway 58
Sidney, AR 72577
(870)283-6766

Sulphur Springs   (4C)GRAR1315
3225 Ouachita 2 (mailing)
3086 Ouachita 2 (physical)
Louann, AR 71751
(870)689-3598   <Ouachita>
mdarden@oeccwildblue.com
CL:Paula G Darden
3225 Ouachita 2
Louann, AR 71751
(870)689-3598
mdarden@oeccwildblue.com

Trimble Camp G   (4WC)GRAR1504
PO Box 150 (mailing)
Trimble Camp Ground Road (physical)
Dolph, AR 72528
(870)297-8088   <Izard>
PA: Joel Snyder   <M1>
224 Lord Lane
Mountain View, AR 72560
(870)269-9743
synyder.joel@ymail.com
CL: Jana Cowgill
1037 Chriswood Drive
Clarkridge, AR 72623
(870)421-2106

Trinity   (4MEWC)GRAR1219
809 W Wall Street
Morrilton, AR 72110
(501)354-4139   <Conway>
PA: Gordon Warren   <M1>
811 Wall Street
Morrilton, AR 72110
(501)208-1120
jogordonwarren@suddenlink.net
CL: Jammie Bonds
809 Wall Street
Morrilton, AR 72110
(501)354-4139

Walkerville   (4MEWC)GRAR1317
10160 Highway 19 S
Magnolia, AR 71753
(   )   <Columbia>
CL: Jim Edwards
10570 S Highway 19
Emerson, AR 71740
(870)696-3973
jse10570@gmail.com

Walnut Grove   (4WC)GRAR1414
4724 N State Highway 23 (mailing)
1294 Six Mile Road (physical)
Magazine, AR 72943
(   )   <Logan>
danekas@centurytel.net
SS: Don Kennedy   <M3>
5335 Dizzy Dean Road
Booneville, AR 72927
(479)675-4418
donkennedy@centurytel.net
CL: Debbie Danekas
4724 N State Highway 23
Booneville, AR 72927
(479)675-5004
danekas@centurytel.net

OTHERS ON MINISTERIAL ROLL:

Blackburn, Samuel N   <M1 WC>
6706 S 6th Street
Fort Smith, AR 72908
(479)649-9436
Blanton, D B   <M1 RT>
ADDRESS UNKNOWN
Bowling, Andrew   <M1 WC>
20945 Highway 16 E
Siloam Springs, AR 72761
(479)524-6576
Chang, Leo   <M1 WC>
819 W Division SE
Springfield, MO 65803
(901)287-9901
Cook, Carl   <M1 WC>
475 Western Hills Loop
Mountain Home, AR 72653
(870)425-2570
carlc@suddenlink.net
Fisk, James R   <M1 WC>
1946 Lake Vernon Road
Leesville, LA 71446
jimfisk95@yahoo.com
(870)367-3086
Fleming, Patrick T   <M1 WC>
616 N Border Street
Benton, AR 72015
(501)944-4678
ptfleming@live.com
Guthrie, William   <M1 WC>
11130 Frenchmen Loop Apt B
Maumelle, AR 72113
(501)584-0019
billybarloe@yahoo.com
Halford, Angela   <M1 OM>
PO Box 191466
Little Rock, AR 72219
(501)407-0065
Hamlink, Ronald L   <M1 WC>
PO Box 923
Fairacres, NM 88033
(505)525-9867
hamronelink@yahoo.com
Holley, Ann   <M1 WC>
PO Box 345
Lockesburg, AR 71846
(870)289-3421
FAX: (870)289-2914
ladyrev1115@yahoo.com
Jeffrey, Sarah Ann   <M1 WC>
5271 Highway 202 E
Yellville, AR 72687
(870)453-7076
FAX: (870)715-9229
annjeffrey2001@yahoo.com
Jones, Michael   <M1 WC>
120 Jennifer Lane
Branson, MO 65616
(417)334-2058
Martin, William E, Jr   <M1 WC>
PO Box 98
131 E Wood Avenue
Palestine, AR 72372
(870)581-2530
juniormartin@yahoo.com
McSpadden, Nancy   <M1 M9>
120 Roberta Drive
Memphis, TN 38112

ARKANSAS PRESBYTERY CONTINUED

(870)612-0067
revnancy77@gmail.com
PA: Alan Meinzer <M1>
  25 Rosewood Road
  Batesville, AR 72501
  (870)793-3915
  natsdad@suddenlink.net
Moore, Angela <M1 WC>
  3756 Douglass Avenue
  Memphis, TN 38111
  (870)581-2509
Murray, Joshua <M1 WC>
  126 Ray Avenue
  Monticello, AR 71655
  (318)259-7828
  jdm4428@yahoo.com
SS: Richard Niswonger <M1>
  20941 Highway 16 E
  Siloam Springs, AR 72761
  (479)524-4081
  rniswonger@cox.net
O'Neal Danhof, Clair <M1 WC>
  301 Whispering Hills Street
  Hot Springs, AR 71901
  acglenn@aol.com
Pedigo, Russell <M1 WC>
  1002 Haney Avenue
  El Dorado, AR 71730
  (870)862-4689
  russell_pedigo@hotmail.com
Ryan, Jack <M1 WC>
  8806 Kennesaw Mountain Drive
  Mabelvale, AR 72103
  (501)749-8572
Shanley, Dwight <M1 WC>
  16904 Old Mill Road
  Little Rock, AR 72206
  (501)888-4190
  dwightshanley@att.net
Suttle, Michael <M1 WC>
  159 Ouachita 593
  Camden, AR 71701
  (870)836-0008
  m_s_suttle@msn.com
Sweigart, John M <M1 WC>
  PO Box 876
  Dover, AL 72837

(479)229-4041
Treadaway, Kenneth A <M1 WC>
  172 Miller County 494
  Texarkana, AR 71854
  treadaways@ark.net
  (870)574-1609
Wood, Wayne <M1 WC>
  HC 61 Box 600
  Calico Rock, AR 72519
  (870)297-2205
  FAX: (870)297-3151
  bexarwood@centurytel.net
Woodliff, George <M1 RT>
  310 W Cleveland Street Apt A3
  Prairie Grove, AR 72753
  (479)410-1933
  mwoodliff@kih.net
Wooten, Wallace <M1 WC>
  1152 Melrose Road
  Lockesburg, AR 71846
  (870)289-2224

OTHER LICENTIATES ON ROLL:

Anderson, Christopher <M2 ST>
  131 Roberta Drive
  Memphis, TN 38112
  (870)805-0886
  csanderson@memphisseminary.edu
Brown, Amy <M2>
  679 Freeze Bend Road
  Newport, AR 72112
Harbour, Ethan <M2>
  77 Burton Road
  Booneville, AR 72927
  (479)849-6329
  ethanharbour@gmail.com
Washburn, Gloria <M2>
  PO Box 2484
  Jordan, AR 72519
  (870)321-4596
  grwashburn07@gmail.com

OTHER CANDIDATES ON ROLL:

Anderson, Kyle <M3>
  828 E Main Street
  Batesville, AR 72501
  (870)834-5799
  kanderson@memphisseminary.edu
Walsh, Devin <M3>
  801 East "M" Street
  Russellville, AR 72801
  (479)890-6716
Warren, Elizabeth
  811 W Wall Street
  Morrilton, AR 72110
  (501)354-4139

Cauca Valley Presbytery
MISSION SYNOD

GENERAL		MEMBERSHIP			CHANGES				FINANCES				
	1.Church Number	2.Active	3.Total	4.Church School	5.Prof. of Faith	6.Gains	7.Losses	8.Children Baptized	9. OUR UNITED OUT-REACH	10. Total Out-Reach Giving	11. All Other Expenses	12. Total Income Received	13. Value Church Prop. 1=1000
	1	2	3	4	5	6	7	8	9	10	11	12	13
Betania Mission	8204	38	38	20	No Report Received			0	0	0	0	0	110
Bethel	8205	163	163	230	0	11	0	0	0	860	22,500	23,281	135
Caleb Mission	8223	85	98	60	10	6	2	0	0	1,969	12,500	14,860	90
Central	8208	238	240	138	0	1	0	0	0	14,320	34,200	67,500	350
Divino Redentor	8206	169	192	100	0	34	1	0	0	8,929	46,960	56,019	200
Emaus	8219	65	70	60	0	35	3	0	0	1,054	5,500	7,873	95
Filipos	8211	72	72	50	No Report Received			0	0	0	0	0	100
Getsemani	8210	31	34	15	No Report Received			0	0	0	0	0	90
Maranatha	8220	93	137	30	15	15	1	0	0	1,855	34,200	33,760	150
Nueva Esperanza	8221	119	109	20	7	40	8	0	0	4,321	19,300	25,207	200
Nueva Jerusalen	8222	26	79	45	0	8	1	0	0	1,600	9,750	11,600	150
Popayan	8227	910	1,042	350	0	281	49	0	0	8,949	83,200	95,692	300
Principe De Paz	8201	50	75	31	No Report Received			0	0	0	0	0	130
Renacer	8225	447	602	452	0	9	0	0	0	28,300	184,000	210,000	350
Samaria	8217	53	86	35	0	20	0	0	0	2,110	10,500	12,500	150
San Lucas	8215	38	56	45	No Report Received			0	0	0	0	0	200
San Marcos	8218	90	129	60	No Report Received			0	0	0	0	0	150
San Pablo	8212	140	160	42	0	32	20	0	0	9,300	19,500	37,700	200
Tulua Mission	8226	85	180	40	No Report Received			0	0	0	0	0	150
Presbytery	8200								11,300				
TOTALS	19	2,902	3,562	1,659	32	492	85	0	11,300	83,567	482,110	595,992	3,300

*Math error corrected. **Purged roll.

CHURCHES, PASTORS, AND CLERKS:

Betania Mission   (4WF)MSCA8204
    Av 5 No 20-12
    (Aereo 851)
    Cali
    Colombia, South America
    ( )894-0624   <S America>
SS: Samuel Guanaquillo   <M3>
    Aereo 10701
    Cali
    Colombia, South America
    FAX: (408)255-5938
    samijg@hotmail.com
CL: Ana Bechara de Montoya
    Aereo 851
    Cali
    Colombia, South America

Bethel   (4MWC)MSCA8205
    Calle 14 Oeste No 48-17
    Cali
    Colombia, South America
    ( )554-7514   <S America>
SS:Rodrigo Torres   <M3>
    Aereo 6365
    Cali
    Colombia, South America
    (011)882-8372
CL: Ana Leyda Meneses
    Aereo 10701
    Cali
    Colombia, South America

Caleb Mission   (4F)MSCA8223
    Av 47 Oeste No 9 A-24
    Montebello
    Colombia, South America
    ( )323-8070   <S America>
PA: Gildardo Agudelo   <M1>
    Cra 73C # 1A-54
    Cali
    Colombia, South America
CL: Carmen Rosa
    Ave 47 Oe 9-51
    Montebello
    Colombia, South America

Central   (4MWC)MSCA8208
    Av Las Americas 19N 18
    Cali
    Colombia, South America
    ( )668-7109   <S America>
PA: Sergio Betancur   <M1>
    Iglesia El Rebano
    Calle 128 sur #48-13
    Caldas,Antioquia
    Colombia, South America
    ( )334-2904
    sergiobetancurposada@hotmail.com
CL: Rocio Triana
    Aereo 6365
    Cali
    Colombia, South America

Divino Redentor   (4MWC)MSCA8206
    Cra 3 No 36-29
    Juan XXIII
    Buenaventur Valle
    Colombia, South America
    ( )242-8399   <S America>
PA: Wilfrido Quinonez   <M1>
    Cra 3 No 36-29
    Juan XXIII
    Buenaventur Valle
    Colombia, South America
    (310)412-1711
    ipc.divinoredentor@gmail.com
CL: Marlen Palacios
    Cra 3 No 36-29
    Juan XXIII
    Buenaventur Valle
    Colombia, South America

Emaus   (4WC)MSCA8219
    Diag 1 sur Cra 49-1
    Buenaventura
    Colombia, South America
    ( )244-2624   <S America>
PA: Manuel Medina   <M1>
    Diag 1 sur Cra 49-1
    Buenaventura
    Colombia, South America
    ( )244-2624
CL: Omairo Valasco Cosme

CAUCA VALLEY PRESBYTERY CONTINUED

Aereo 969
Buenaventura
Colombia, South America

Filipos (4WF)MSCA8211
  Calle 34 #24A-36
  (Aereo 6365)
  Cali
  Colombia, South America
  ( )438-2563 <S America>
PA: Joel Cuartas <M0>
  Calle 34 #24A-36
  Cali
  Colombia, South America
  (000)438-2512
CL: Adriana Gonzalez
  Calle 34 #24A-36
  Cali
  Colombia, South America

Getsemani (ARC)MSCA8210
  Cra 15 No 8-43
  El Cerrito Valle
  Colombia, South America
  ( )256-4261 <S America>
SS: Gilberto Arteaga <M3>
  Aereo 794
  Buenaventura
  Colombia, South America
  (000)256-4261
  pastorgilbertoa@hotmail.com
CL: Amparo Rengifo
  Cra 15 No 8-43
  El Cerrito
  Colombia, South America

Maranatha (4WF)MSCA8220
  Calle 12 No 4-69
  Guapi
  Colombia, South America
  (092)840-0940
  FAX (092)840-0120 <S America>
PA: Alejandro Madrid <M1>
  Calle 12 No 4-69
  Guapi
  Colombia, South America
CL: Magali Angulo
  Calle 12 No 4-69
  Guapi
  Colombia, South America

Nueva Esperanza (F)MSCA8221
  Cra 89 4C-35
  Cali
  Colombia, South America
  ( )332-5849 <South America>
  nuevaesperanza1983@hotmail.com
PA: William Diaz <M1>
  Calle 5 Con Cra 89
  Cali
  Colombia, South America
  ( )332-5849
  nuevaesperanza1983@hotmail.com
CL: Fabiola Ariza
  Avenida de las Americas
  #19N-18 Presbiterio del Valle
  Cali
  Colombia, South America
  (316)419-8414
  fatvioleta@hotmail.com

Nueva Jerusalen (4F)MSCA8222
  Cra 73 CN No 1 A 54 Lourdes
  Cali
  Colombia, South America
  ( )323-3009 <S America>
SS: Fabian Florez <M3>
  Cra 73 CN No 1 A 54 Lour des
  Cali Valle
  Colombia, South America
  ( )323-4447
  fabianflorezpastor@yahoo.es
CL: Adriana Montenegro
  Aereo 6365
  Cali Valle
  Colombia, South America

Popayan (ARC)MSCA8227
  Cra 9 No 6 6N 87 Bello Horizonte
  Popayan
  Colombia, South America
  (092)823-8988 <S America>
PA: Jhony Montano <M1>
  Cra 9 No 6 6N 87 Bello Horizonte
  Popayan
  Colombia, South America
  (092)823-8988
CL: Irma Cecilia Medina
  Cra 5 #19N-56
  Popayan
  Colombia, South America

Principe De Paz (4WC)MSCA8201
  Cra 27 #7-48
  Cali
  Colombia, South America
  ( )556-6527 <S America>
PA: Mario Gaviria <M1>
  Cra 27 No 7-48
  Cali
  Colombia, South America
  ( )372-3869
  pastormariogaviria@hotmail.com
CL: Holber Molina
  Carrera 27 #7-48
  Cali
  Colombia, South America

Renacer (4WF)MSCA8225
  Diag 26M Trv 73A-69
  Cali
  Colombia, South America
  ( )422-3940 <S America>
SS: Wilson Lopez <M3>
  Diag 26 M Trv 73 A 69
  Cali
  Colombia, South America
  ( )327-2543
CL: Maria Onix Lopez
  Diag 26K #73 A-66
  Cali
  Colombia, South America

Samaria (4MWC)MSCA8217
  Tranv 30 No 17F-122
  (Aereo 4290)
  Cali
  Colombia, South America
  ( )448-5880 <S America>
PA: Juan Bautista <M1>
  Tranv 30 No 17F-122
  Cali

Colombia, South America
  ( )442-4562
CL: Maria Josefa Martinez
  Aereo 4290
  Cali
  Colombia, South America

San Lucas (4WC)MSCA8215
  Cll 26 No 29 53
  Palmira
  Colombia, South America
  ( )272-7584 <S America>
SS: Fernando Osorio <M3>
  Cll 26 No 29 53
  Palmira
  Colombia, South America
  ( )272-7584
  sanlucaspalmira@hotmail.com
CL: Janneth Naranto
  Aereo 329
  Palmira
  Colombia, South America

San Marcos (4MWC)MSCA8218
  Cll 46 A No 4N-25
  (Aereo 6453)
  Cali
  Colombia, South America
  ( )446-3311 <S America>
PA: Roberto Fonseca <M1>
  Cll 46 A No 4N 25
  Colombia, South America
  ( )446-7370
CL: Luz Dazy Ceballos
  Cll 46 A No 4N-25
  Aereo 6453
  Cali
  Colombia, South America

San Pablo (4MWC)MSCA8212
  Cra 8 No 5-27
  Guacari
  Colombia, South America
  ( )253-2751 <S America>
PA: Aldrin Calero <M1>
  Cra 8 No 5-27
  Colombia, South America
  ( )253-0453
SS: Alexander Quintero <M3>
  Carrera 13 #3-81
  Guacari
  Colombia, South America
CL: Luis Mayorga
  Carrera 13 # 3-81
  Guacari
  Colombia, South America

Tulua Mission (4WF)MSCA8226
  Cll 41A No 26-26
  Tulua
  Colombia, South America
  ( )224-5004 <S America>
PA: Fhanor Pejendino <M1>
  Cll 41 A No 26-26
  Tulua
  Colombia, South America
  (317)654-5750
CL: Arnaldo Tajama
  Cra 26 #36-40
  Tulua
  Colombia, South America

CAUCA VALLEY PRESBYTERY CONTINUED

OTHERS ON MINISTERIAL ROLL:

Ariza, Fabiola   \<M1 WC\>
   Ave 3 Norte 19N-18
   Cali
   Colombia, South America
   fatvioleta@hotmail.com
   (316)419-8414

De Jimenez, Luciria Aguirre   \<M1 WC\>
   Ave 3 Norte 19N-18
   Cali
   Colombia, South America
   (300)686-9161
   pastorluciana50@yahoo.com.co

Giraldo, William   \<M1 WC\>
   CLL 62 No 1B 11
   Buenaventura
   Colombia, South America
   ( )439-5436

Pejendino, Socorro   \<M1 WC\>
   Cll 41 A No 26-26
   Tulua
   Colombia, South America
   (317)654-5750

Racines, Jairo   \<M1 WC\>
   CLL 39 No 13-40
   Cali
   Colombia, South America
   (311)385-6546

Rodriguez, Jairo Hernan   \<M1 WC\>
   Cll 42 No 80B 64
   Cali-Valle
   Colombia, South America
   jairo.hrodriguez@hotmail.com
   (572)377-8741

Sanchez, Sol Maria   \<M1 WC\>
   Av Americas 19N - 18
   Cali-Valle
   Colombia, South America
   solmarias@starmedia.com

Solis, Arcadio   \<M1 WC\>
   Crr 42 D1 No 55-69
   Cali
   Colombia, South America
   ( )328-5486

Valencia, Jorge   \<M1 WC\>
   Cra 89 4C-35
   Cali
   Colombia, South America
   ( )332-5840

Wallace, Boyce   \<M1 MY\>
   Cra 101 No 15-93
   Cali
   Colombia, South America
   ( )339-1579
   hbwcali@yahoo.com

OTHER LICENTIATES ON ROLL:

Orozeo Ariza, Juan Carlos   \<M2\>
   Aereo 6365
   Cali Vale
   Colombia, South America

OTHER CANDIDATES ON ROLL:

Caicedo, Efrain   \<M3\>
   Aereo 6365
   Cali
   Colombia, South America

Hoyos, Javier   \<M3\>
   Calle 34 24A-36
   Cali
   Colombia, South America

Lubo, Jaime   \<M3\>
   AA 6365
   Montebello
   Colombia, South America

Paredes, Fabio   \<M3\>
   Carerra 7 # 1-76
   La Cruztala
   Ipiales
   Colombia, South America

Piamba, Juan Carlos   \<M3\>
   Cra 7 #21N-35
   Popayan
   Colombia, South America

Choctaw Presbytery
MISSION SYNOD

GENERAL		MEMBERSHIP			CHANGES				FINANCES			
1.Church Number	2.Active	3.Total	4.Church School	5.Prof. of Faith	6.Gains	7.Losses	8.Children Baptized	9. OUR UNITED OUT-REACH	10. Total Out-Reach Giving	11. All Other Expenses	12. Total Income Received	13. Value Church Prop. 1=1000
1	2	3	4	5	6	7	8	9	10	11	12	13
Coal Creek	6102	4	26	16	0	0	2	0		391	6,851	5,558	11
Lone Star	6105	8	22	16	No Report Received			0		0	0	0	50
McGee Chapel	6106	37	37	20	No Report Received			0		0	0	0	100
Panki Bok	6108	2	4	2	No Report Received			0		0	0	0	6
Pigeon Roost	6109	10	25	6	0	3	0	0		460	3,140	3,600	35
Rock Creek	6111	4	15	4	0	0	1	0		1,690	0	2,146	25
Round Lake	6112	9	9	20	No Report Received			0		0	0	0	3
Presbytery									1,000				
TOTALS	7	74	138	84	0	3	3	0	1,000	2,541	9,991	11,304	230

CHURCHES, PASTORS, AND CLERKS:

Coal Creek   (4WC)MSCH6102
  Route 1 Box 1215
  Coalgate, OK 74538
  ( )   <Atoka>
PA: Nathan Scott   <M1>
  960 S Katy Road
  Atoka, OK 74525
  (580)364-6155
CL: Lola John
  Route 1 Box 1215
  Coalgate, OK 74538
  (580)258-8244

Lone Star   (2WC)MSCH6105
  PO Box 44 (mailing)
  206 S Newell Street (physical)
  Coalgate, OK 74538
  ( )   <Atoka>
SS: Hannah Bryan   <M1>
  32 Trenton Lane
  Mead, OK 73449
  (580)775-4955
  hbryan@choctawnation.com
CL: Evangeline Robinson
  PO Box 44
  Boswell, OK 74727
  (580)513-0170
  erobinson@choctawarchiving.com

McGee Chapel   (2EW C)MSCH6106
  PO Box 158
  Broken Bow, OK 74728
  (580)584-2099   <McCurtain>
  FAX: (580)584-2099
  chocpres@pine-net.com
PA: Randy Jacob   <M1>
  PO Box 158
  Broken Bow, OK 74728
  (580)236-2374
  FAX: (580)584-2099
  chocpres@pine-net.com
CL: Betty Jacob
  PO Box 158
  Broken Bow, OK 74728

(580)584-2099
FAX: (580)584-2099
chocpres@pine-net.com

Panki Bok   (2C)MSCH6108
  PO Box 375
  Eagletown, OK 74734
  ( )   <McCurtain>
PA: Randy Jacob   <M1>
  610 W Adams Street
  Broken Bow, OK 74728
  (580)584-2099
  FAX: (580)584-2099
  chocpres@pine-net.com
CL: Mildred Ashalintubbi
  PO Box 375
  Eagletown, OK 74734
  (580)835-7336

Pigeon Roost   (2C)MSCH6109
  960 S Katy Road
  Atoka, OK 74525
  (580)889-2292   <Choctaw>
PA: Virginia Espinoza   <M1>
  PO Box 132
  Boswell, OK 74727
  (580)775-4138
  vespinoza@choctawnation.com
CL: Linda Scott
  960 S Katy Road
  Atoka, OK 74525
  (580)889-2292

Rock Creek   (2WC)MSCH6111
  c/o Betty Walton (mailing)
  PO Box 126
  Talihina, OK 74571
  Honobia, OK (physical)
  (918)567-2370   <LeFlore>
PA: Nathan Scott   <M1>
  960 S Katy Road
  Atoka, OK 74525
  (580)364-6155
CL: Betty Walton
  PO Box 126
  Talihina, OK 74571
  (918)567-2370

Round Lake   (1WC)MSCH6112
  Box 127
  Tupelo, OK 74572
  (580)317-7427   <Coal>
PA: Hannah Bryan   <M1>
  32 Trenton Lane
  Mead, OK 73449
  (580)775-4955
  hbryan@choctawnation.com
CL: Vickie McClure
  Box 127
  Tupelo, OK 74572
  (580)317-7427

OTHERS ON MINISTERIAL ROLL:

OTHER CANDIDATES ON ROLL:

Crosby, Ronald   <M3>
  407 N "A" Street
  Calera, OK 74730
Scott, Linda   <M3>
  960 S Katy Road
  Atoka, OK 74525
  (580)889-2292

Columbia Presbytery
TENNESSEE SYNOD

	GENERAL		MEMBERSHIP			CHANGES				FINANCES			
	1.Church Number	2.Active	3.Total	4.Church School	5.Prof. of Faith	6.Gains	7.Losses	8.Children Baptized	9. OUR UNITED OUT-REACH	10. Total Out-Reach Giving	11. All Other Expenses	12. Total Income Received	13. Value Church Prop. 1=1000
	1	2	3	4	5	6	7	8	9	10	11	12	13
Ash Hill	7101	38	66	29	0	1	2	0	2,836	6,338	19,568	26,733	275
Belleview	7104	13	24	5	1	1	2	0	0	6,887	15,778	22,666	535
Boonshill	7106	26	63	26	0	1	1	0	800	3,500	24,604	29,761	321
Champ*	7108	11	11	5	0	0	9	0	0	2,100	27,571	21,568	40
Chapel Hill	7109	28	28	30	1	1	3	0	1,000	4,100	47,300	57,000	410
Columbia	7110	104	104	38	6	10	25	4	1,200	11,077	160,038	151,280	1,500
Elora	7111	5	5	6	0	0	0	0	0	0	10,865	10,421	150
Fayetteville	7112	115	275	70	6	16	8	0	14,400	24,821	219,734	203,538	2,300
Fiducia*	7113	29	26	12	1	12	0	0	0	828	9,057	8,986	75
Flintville	7115	7	7	14	0	0	0	0	0	2,297	8,108	11,324	25
Franklin*	7116	28	28	10	0	0	6	0	0	2,713	73,984	52,500	800
Grace	7145	12	12	0	0	2	2	0	483	1,895	48,645	12,165	10
Green Hill*	7118	13	13	17	3	3	4	0	1,923	4,959	26,113	37,999	86
Harpeth Lick*	7119	29	38	14	0	0	2	0	1,300	4,491	27,156	43,424	200
Hohenwald**	7120	15	18	0	0	0	46	0	0	0	26,935	15,157	250
Howell	7121	59	124	65	0	2	2	0	3,000	23,538	47,824	86,811	750
Jenkins	7144	97	214	65	5	5	2	1	18,857	34,060	194,660	251,428	3,387
Kelso	7122	35	94	26	1	1	1	0	0	5,294	56,177	80,196	180
Kingdom	7123	10	10	5	0	0	0	0	390	2,004	11,934	17,495	175
Lawrenceburg**	7124	28	27	14	1	0	26	1	0	0	98,056	43,540	1,230
Lewisburg, 1st	7125	65	172	77	0	2	12	1	0	4,788	106,086	110,227	500
McCains	7126	41	78	22	0	3	3	0	3,000	11,312	49,438	52,777	464
Mt. Carmel	7127	73	113	25	0	1	2	0	1,000	3,150	82,797	83,629	1,000
Mt. Hebron	7128	5	5	0	0	0	1	0	53	674	9,094	7,659	140
Mt. Joy	7129	58	102	18	0	0	4	0	1,164	2,364	41,513	70,151	300
Mt. Lebanon	7130	54	54	25	2	4	0	0	0	7,123	34,174	43,564	125
Mt. Moriah	7131	53	118	30	0	2	1	0	0	16,900	36,656	52,000	250
Mt. Nebo	7132	7	7	7	0	0	0	0	0	739	18,035	21,853	90
Mt. Pleasant	7133	46	97	19	0	1	1	0	2,640	6,807	46,947	51,811	1,000
New Bethel	7134	8	8	8	0	0	0	0	249	158	1,255	5,075	100
Petersburg	7135	42	47	49	0	1	3	0	10,200	23,079	55,902	78,981	232
Pleasant Mount	7136	34	83	32	0	0	3	0	2,200	9,000	56,900	60,000	500
Richland	7137	121	121	10	0	0	4	0	1,500	2,713	73,984	52,500	150
Santa Fe	7138	20	27	17	0	1	2	0	0	2,993	21,020	27,773	0
Swan	7140	12	12	10	1	1	6	0	100	2,239	35,579	34,155	300
Union Grove*	7141	10	10	10	0	2	0	0	0	3,436	11,279	16,521	100
Waynesboro	7142	66	66	21	2	8	0	0	6,823	17,624	44,447	76,508	787
West Point**	7143	61	72	50	0	0	135	0	1,000	10,531	82,858	106,333	1,000
TOTALS	38	1,503	2,510	929	31	81	183	8	76,118	256,001	1,879,214	2,029,176	19,737

*Math error corrected. **Purged roll.

CHURCHES, PASTORS, AND CLERKS:

Ash Hill   (4WC)TNCO7101
   4930 Ash Hill Road
   Spring Hill, TN 37174
   (931)381-3367   \<Williamson>
PA: James R Miller   \<M1>
   1214 Whitney Drive
   Columbia, TN 38401
   (931)215-2108
   rev.james.miller@charter.net
CL: Helen Logue
   1603 Emerald Court
   Franklin, 37064
   (615)599-6764

Belleview   (4WC)TNCO7104
   1752 Burke Hollow Road (mailing)
   Nolensville, TN 37135
   4724 Murfreesboro Road (physical)
   Franklin, TN 37064
   ( )   \<Williamson>
PA: James R Miller   \<M1>
   1214 Whitney Drive
   Columbia, TN 38401
   (931)381-3367
   rev.james.miller@charter.net
CL: David C Hughes
   1752 Burke Hollow Road
   Nolensville, TN 37135
   (615)395-4935

Boonshill   (4C)TNCO7106
   91 Red Oak Road (mailing)
   Petersburg, TN 37144
   Rt 2 (physical)
   Boonshill, TN
   ( )   \<Lincoln>
OD: Thomas Smith   \<M5>
   467 Gunter Hollow Drive
   Fayetteville, TN 37334
   (931)732-5426
CL: Sammy Luna
   91 Red Oak Road
   Petersburg, TN 37144
   (931)703-0536
   srluna@ardmore.net

COLUMBIA PRESBYTERY CONTINUED

Champ   (2C)TNCO7108
290 Sullenger Bend Road (mailing)
Belvidere, TN 37306
61 Tucker Creek Road (physical)
Mulberry, TN
( )   <Lincoln>
CL: Diann Adams
2800 Hillsboro Road
Huntsville, AL 35805
(256)534-6076

Chapel Hill   (4MWC)TNCO7109
4801 Eagleville Pike (mailing)
302 N Horton Parkway (physical)
Chapel Hill, TN 37034
(931)364-7819   <Marshall>
PA: Joe Wiggins   <M1>
2734 US Highway 41A S
Eagleville, TN 37060
(615)274-2011
CL: Spence Walls
4521 Polaris Drive
Chapel Hill, TN 37034
(931)364-2573
walls.family95@yahoo.com

Columbia   (4MWC)TNCO7110
1106 Nashville Highway
Columbia, TN 38401
(931)388-9177   <Maury>
pastor@fcpccolumbia.com
PA: Calvin Lunn   <M1>
859 Cranford Hollow Road
Columbia, TN 38401
(931)381-2397
pastor@fcpccolumbia.com
CL: Brian Keith Tilghman
1036 Theta Pike
Columbia, TN 38401
(931)698-0141
tilghmanphoto@aol.com

Elora   (2C)TNCO7111
69 Bear Wallow Road (mailing)
Flintville, TN 37335
Elora, TN 37328 (physical)
( )   <Lincoln>
SS: John Blair   <M1>
108 Cliff Drive
Lawrenceburg, TN 38464
(931)762-2480
jnbblair@charter.net
CL: Jim Ramsey
69 Bear Wallow Road
Flintville, TN 37335
(931)937-8765
jim.brenda.ramsey710@gmail.com

Fayetteville   (4WC)TNCO7112
1015 Lewisburg Highway
Fayetteville, TN 37334
(931)433-5441   <Lincoln>
FAX: (931)433-0056
cpc@fpunet.com
PA: Timothy Smith   <M1>
712 Morningside Drive
Fayetteville, TN 37334
(931)438-2820
FAX: (931)433-0056
tims38@hotmail.com
CL: Larry Ventress
1003 First Avenue

Fayetteville, TN 37334
(931)433-5053
FAX: (931)433-0056
dooda49@fpunet.com

Fiducia   (2EW C)TNCO7113
1342 Bethel Road (mailing)
Pulaski, TN 38478
1695 Fiducia Road (physical)
Prospect, TN 38477
( )   <Giles>
PA: John Blair   <M1>
108 W Cliff Drive
Lawrenceburg, TN 38464
(931)766-2480
jnbblair@charter.net
CL: Ewing Brooks
1429 Crooked Hill Road
Pulaski, TN 38478
(931)363-5985

Flintville   (2C)TNCO7115
35 Well Lee Road (mailing)
9 Flintville School Road (physical)
Flintville, TN 37335
( )   <Lincoln>
PA: John Blair   <M1>
108 W Cliff Drive
Lawrenceburg, TN 38464
(931)766-2480
CL: Jimmie D Wicks
35 Wells Lee Road
Flintville, TN 37335
(931)937-8562
bfwicks@bellsouth.net

Franklin   (4MC)TNCO7116
PO Box 1134 (mailing)
615 West Main Street (physical)
Franklin, TN 37065
(615)599-0029   <Williamson>
FAX: (615)807-2959
cp1876@hotmail.com
PA: John Hyden   <M1>
6525 Peytonsville Arno Road
College Grove, TN 37046
(615)975-9584
cp1876@hotmail.com
CL: Dorris Douglass
724 Fair Street
Franklin, TN 37064
(615)790-7914
FAX: (615)595-1247
ansercher@aol.com

Grace   (4C)TNCO7145
PO Box 682462 (mailing)
1153 Lewisburg Pike (physical)
Franklin, TN 37068
(615)794-0370   <Williamson>
gracecpchurchpastor@gmail.com
PA: Fonda Blair   <M1>
PO Box 11093
Murfreesboro, TN 37129
(615)491-2432
blairfonda2010@comcast.net
CL: Lee Bagby
311 E Chownings Court
Franklin, TN 37064
(615)794-9532
bagbyl@bellsouth.net

Green Hill   (3WC)TNCO7118

1900 Unionville-Deason Road
Bell Buckle, TN 37020
(931)294-2040   <Bedford>
SS: Lawrence (Larry) Kelly   <M1>
3471 Highway 41 A North Apt 5
Unionville, TN 37180
(615)934-1517
CL: Angelia Burns
328 Dunnaway Road
Shelbyville, TN 37160
(931)294-5105

Harpeth Lick   (4C)TNCO7119
6981 Arno Allisona Road
College Grove, TN 37046
( )   <Williamson>
SS: Larry Guin   <M1>
125 Glider Loop
Eagleville, TN 37060
(615)668-5236
lguin43@hotmail.com
CL: Virginia Lou Rogers
8876 Horton Highway
College Grove, TN 37046
(615)368-2202
mudpuddle42@gmail.com

Hohenwald   (4MWC)TNCO7120
PO Box 456 (mailing)
201 Park Avenue S (physical)
Hohenwald, TN 38462
(931)796-3657   <Lewis>
CL: Byrne Dunn
617 Oakdale Drive
Hohenwald, TN 38462
(931)796-2806
FAX: (931)796-2153
marvinwilkins@msn.com

Howell   (4MWC)TNCO7121
43 Brown Teal Road
Fayetteville, TN 37334
(931)433-0818   <Lincoln>
PA: Todd Gaskill   <M1>
430 Haysland Road
Petersburg, TN 37144
(931)580-2708
tgaskill@pens.com
CL: Tim Porter
85 Icy Bank Road
Fayetteville, TN 37334
(931)433-8306

Jenkins   (4MWC)TNCO7144
PO Box 518 (mailing)
2501 York Road (physical)
Nolensville, TN 37135
(615)776-2339   <Williamson>
FAX: (615)776-3520
jenkinspastor@gmail.com
PA: Jonathan Watson   <M1>
4017 Claude Drive
Smyrna, TN 37167
jenkinspastor@gmail.com
(615)630-9153
CL: Joyce A Allemore
2442 Fly Road
Nolensville, TN 37135
(615)776-2985
jallemore@yahoo.com

Kelso   (4MWC)TNCO7122
PO Box 28 (mailing)

COLUMBIA PRESBYTERY CONTINUED

16 Teal Hollow Road (physical)
Kelso, TN 37348
( )   <Lincoln>
PA: Kirk Smith   <M1>
813 1st Avenue
Fayetteville, TN 37334
(931)438-8649
kirks37334@att.net
CL: Bill Dickey
1501 Swanson Boulevard
Fayetteville, TN 37334
(931)433-2462

Kingdom   (4C)TNCO7123
4532 Barfield Crescent Road (mailing)
Murfreesboro, TN 37128
800 Kingdom Road (physical)
Unionville, TN 37180
( )   <Bedford>
SS: Larry Guin   <M1>
125 Glider Loop
Eagleville, TN 37060
(615)668-5236
lguin43@hotmail.com
CL: Thelma Shockey
4532 Barfield Crescent Road
Murfreesboro, TN 37128
(615)896-1890

Lawrenceburg   (4MWC)TNCO7124
228 S Military Avenue
Lawrenceburg, TN 38464
(931)762-4343   <Lawrence>
cumberlandpresby@bellsouth.net
PA: Dwight Liles   <M1>
8467 Joy Road
Mount Pleasant, TN 38474
(931)379-0326
dwightliles@att.net
CL: Kaye Luffman
5 Powell Circle
Five Points, TN 38457
(931)556-2252
kluffman@hotmail.com

Lewisburg 1st   (4MWC)TNCO7125
210 Haynes Street (mailing)
402 2nd Avenue N (physical)
Lewisburg, TN 37091
(931)359-3857   <Marshall>
FAX: (931)270-8624
fcpclewisburg@bellsouth.net
PA: Roger Reid   <M1>
1505 Experiment Farm Road
Lewisburg, TN 37091
(931)422-5257
drrtr@yahoo.com
CL: Tammy Caneer-Carter
1400 Green Valley Road
Pulaski, TN 38478
(931)637-7374
FAX: (931)270-8624
cantam@bellsouth.net

McCains   (4MWC)TNCO7126
PO Box 29 (mailing)
3532 McCains Lane (physical)
Columbia, TN 38401
(931)540-0160   <Maury>
PA: Tommy Clark   <M1>
124 Roberta Drive
Memphis, TN 38112
(615)430-9158

fattire77@gmail.com
CL: Gary Weatherford
3926 Campbellsville Pike
Columbia, TN 38401
(931)388-0599
gmweatherford@cs.com

Mt Carmel   (4C)TNCO7127
4810 Ash Hill Road (mailing)
Spring Hill, TN 37174
2300 Lewisburg Pike (physical)
Franklin, TN 37064
(615)591-3930   <Williamson>
PA: John Eatherly   <M1>
1377 Moss Road
Chapel Hill, TN 37034
(931)364-2087
jrev@united.net
CL: Peggy S Fisher
4810 Ash Hill Road
Spring Hill, TN 37174
(615)944-9300
fishpest@ymail.com

Mt Hebron   (4C)TNCO7128
59 Giles Hollow Road (mailing)
927 Shelbyville Highway (physical)
Fayetteville, TN 37334
( )   <Lincoln>
PA: Todd Gaskill   <M1>
430 Haysland Road
Petersburg, TN 37144
(931)580-2708
tgaskill@pens.com
CL: Jimmy Buchanan
59 Giles Hollow Road
Fayetteville, TN 37334
(931)433-6446

Mt Joy   (4MWC)TNCO7129
8364 Mt Joy Road
Mount Pleasant, TN 38474
( )   <Maury>
CL: Evelyn Luckett
8432 Mount Joy Road
Mount Pleasant, TN 38474
(931)379-4600

Mt Lebanon   (4EC)TNCO7130
4497 Kedron Road
Spring Hill, TN 37174
( )   <Maury>
mortonco@bellsouth.net
PA: Patric Fife   <M1>
73 Jordan Road
Lawrenceburg, TN 38464
(931)629-8146
pnlfifernak@gmail.com
CL: Judy L Morton
1272 John Sharp Road
Columbia, TN 38401
(931)381-1140
mortonco@bellsouth.net

Mt Moriah   (4C)TNCO7131
485 Agnew Road (mailing)
463 Big Dry Creek Road (physical)
Pulaski, TN 38478
( )   <Giles>
PA: Steve Nave   <M1>
5172 Fall River Road
Leoma, TN 38468
(931)424-0020

thenaves@wildblue.net
CL: Dickson Marks
485 Agnew Road
Pulaski, TN 38478
(931)363-2432

Mt Nebo   (4C)TNCO7132
84 S Old Military Road (mailing)
Saint Joseph, TN 38481
473 Mt Nebo Road (physical)
Iron City, TN 38463
( )   <Lawrence>
LS: Sean Richardson   <M6>
4227 Highway 43 N
Ethridge, TN 38456
(931)829-2094
sean@misterrichardson.com
CL: William B Gabel
104 Spring Street
Saint Joseph, TN 38481
(931)845-4203
stjoemerry@gmail.com

Mt Pleasant   (4EWC)TNCO7133
PO Box 689 (mailing)
504 Florida Avenue (physical)
Mount Pleasant, TN 38474
(931)379-3662   <Maury>
PA: Robert Mullenix   <M1>
1408 Azalee Lane
Chapel Hill, TN 37034
(931)364-4611
glonix@live.com
CL: Rickey Massey
609 Circle Drive
Mount Pleasant, TN 38474
(931)379-3617
rickeymassey@bellsouth.net

New Bethel   (2C)TNCO7134
5060 Reynolds Road
Columbia, TN 38401
(931)364-2378   <Marshall>
SS: John Eatherly   <M1>
1377 Moss Road
Chapel Hill, TN 37034
(931)364-2087
jrev@united.net
CL: James W Hood
1532 Lewisburg Pike
Franklin, TN 37064
(615)591-8689

Petersburg   (4MWC)TNCO7135
PO Box 82 (mailing)
303 Russell Street (physical)
Petersburg, TN 37144
(931)607-1859   <Lincoln>
petersburgpreacher@att.net
PA: Troy Green   <M1>
105 Cobb Hollow Lane
Petersburg, TN 37144
(931)659-6627
thegreens101@att.net
CL: Ann Hemphill
803 Washington Street W Apt B
Fayetteville, TN 37334
(931)433-8380
ahemphill@fpunet.com

Pleasant Mount   (4WC)TNCO7136
609 Woods Drive (mailing)
1620 Fountain Heights Road (physical)

COLUMBIA PRESBYTERY CONTINUED

Columbia, TN 38401
( )   <Maury>
PA: William L Rolman, Jr   <M1>
602 Canyon Drive
Columbia, TN 38401
(931)388-2611
wmrolmanjr@att.net
CL: James H Rochell, Jr
609 Woods Drive
Columbia, TN 38401
(931)388-1947
tnpappy53@yahoo.com

_____
Richland   (4C)TNCO7137
3452 Spring Place Road
Lewisburg, TN 37091
(931)270-6135   <Marshall>
PA: Charles (Buddy) Pope   <M1>
2391 Fairfield Pike
Shelbyville, TN 37160
(931)205-6897
pope6897@yahoo.com
CL: Douglas A Looney
3045 Monte Murrey Road
Lewisburg, TN 37091
(931)359-3781
ld.looney@yahoo.com

_____
Santa Fe   (4WC)TNCO7138
PO Box 58 (mailing)
2630 Santa Fe Pike (physical)
Santa Fe, TN 38482
(931)682-3555   <Maury>
SS: Sherry Ladd   <M1>
4521 Turkey Creek Road
Williamsport, TN 38487
(931)682-2263
revsherryladd@gmail.com
CL: Whitney Seaton
111 W Hardin Drive
Columbia, TN 38401
(931)388-9319

_____
Swan   (4C)TNCO7140
4521 Turkey Creek Road (mailing)
Williamsport, TN 38487
Swan Creek Road (physical)
Centerville, TN 37033
(931)682-2263   <Hickman>
revsherryladd@gmail.com
PA: Sherry Ladd   <M1>
4521 Turkey Creek Road
Williamsport, TN 38487
(931)682-2263
revsherryladd@gmail.com
CL: George C Ladd
4521 Turkey Creek Road
Williamsport, TN 38487
(931)682-2263
gladd@hughes.net

_____
Union Grove   (4C)TNCO7141
2409 Green Mills Road Lot 30 (mailing)
1452 Cliff White Road (physical)
Columbia, TN 38401
(931)486-2799   <Maury>
patricia.cates@att.net
PA: Scott Yates   <M1>
8818 New Town Road
Rockvale, TN 37153
(615)274-3000
scott@scottyates.net
CL: Patricia Cates
2409 Green Mills Road Lot 30
Columbia, TN 38401
(931)486-2799
patricia.cates@att.net

_____
Waynesboro   (4MEWC)TNCO7142
PO Box 234 (mailing)
110 North High Street (physical)
Waynesboro, TN 38485
(931)722-5621   <Wayne>
rainsr@tds.net
CL: Robert (Bob) Raines
105 E Songer Street
Waynesboro, TN 38485
(931)722-5621
rainsr@tds.net

_____
West Point   (4MC)TNCO7143
1431 Spainwood Street (mailing)
1533 Theta Pike (physical)
Columbia, TN 38401
(931)388-7268   <Maury>
PA: Terry Peery   <M1>
1431 Spainwood Street
Columbia, TN 38401
(931)381-6871
coppreacher@gmail.com
CL: Mike McCord
4543 Snow Creek Road
Santa Fe, TN 38482
(931)682-2500

_____
OTHERS ON MINISTERIAL ROLL:

Cole, Dwayne   <M1 RT>
6460 Village Parkway
Anchorage, AK 99504
(907)854-5793
tadpolejr@aol.com
Green, Odis G   <M1 RT>
18 Oakwood Street NW
Rome, GA 30165
Heflin, Robert   <M1 DE>
4144 Meadow Court Drive
Bartlett, TN 38135
(901)382-8198
rdheflin@bellsouth.net

Kinnaman, Richard Terry   <M1 WC>
2018 Spring Meadow Circle
Spring Hill, TN 37174
(615)302-3321
kinnaman91@att.net
Trotter, Wendell   <M1 RT>
1516 Fell Avenue NE
Huntsville, AL 35811
(256)519-6571
wendelltrotter@knology.net

_____
OTHER LICENTIATES ON ROLL:

_____
OTHER CANDIDATES ON ROLL:

King, Mark   <M3>
717 Big Swan Creek Road
Hampshire, TN 38461
(931)626-6915

Covenant Presbytery
MIDWEST SYNOD

GENERAL		MEMBERSHIP			CHANGES				FINANCES				
	1.Church Number	2.Active	3.Total	4.Church School	5.Prof. of Faith	6.Gains	7.Losses	8.Children Baptized	9. OUR UNITED OUT-REACH	10. Total Out-Reach Giving	11. All Other Expenses	12. Total Income Received	13. Value Church Prop. 1=1000
	1	2	3	4	5	6	7	8	9	10	11	12	13
Bayou de Chien	3401	40	77	28	No Report Received			0	0	0	0	0	516
Benton	3403	15	40	15	0	0	0	0	0	1,500	7,000	10,500	215
Bethel	3404	182	363	101	0	3	7	1	11,600	37,931	302,626	340,286	2,500
Calvary	3405	23	52	25	No Report Received			0	0	0	0	0	0332
Camp Ground	5103	22	52	23	0	0	1	0	2,991	6,561	25,106	31,857	695
Chandler	5302	107	387	97	3	5	2	0	9,779	27,507	142,731	184,715	1,502
Ebenezer	5105	20	25	15	No Report Received			0	0	0	0	0	50
Ebenezer Hall	5106	1	11	5	0	0	0	0	943	2,648	8,937	9,417	57
Flat Lick	3606	45	96	30	1	0	4	0	4,334	13,093	97,435	100,313	350
Fredonia	3608	102	240	78	1	4	1	1	17,211	35,051	119,891	170,415	1,015
Gilead	5110	50	155	31	2	5	0	0	1,630	8,946	46,622	63,436	375
Good Spring	3609	25	51	14	0	0	1	0	2,200	19,260	32,169	49,658	140
Highland	3414	91	203	70	0	4	3	1	7,200	39,103	148,944	308,041	1,000
Hopewell	3610	40	103	20	2	4	1	0	720	720	49,615	48,961	120
Hopkinsville	3611	53	70	34	0	0	3	0	3,620	7,008	82,196	37,273	850
Liberty	3406	101	112	59	No Report Received			0	0	0	0	0	700
Lisman	3613	27	45	22	No Report Received			0	1,401	0	0	0	225
Macedonia	3614	22	22	15	1	1	20	0	0	2,175	22,640	24,328	300
Madisonville	3615	40	150	25	No Report Received			0	1,545	0	0	0	356
Margaret Hank	3415	70	107	35	1	9	1	0	4,000	20,000	155,000	71,000	750
Marion First	3616	44	137	20	0	6	0	1	3,185	10,371	80,738	100,581	698
Milburn Chapel	3416	170	408	60	6	15	6	3	0	35,000	167,386	195,000	1,800
Mt. Carmel	3617	80	132	10	0	0	4	0	0	2,266	79,370	34,930	600
Mt. Pleasant	3618	23	27	18	0	0	0	2	0	1,733	16,535	20,538	35
Mt. Sterling	5117	170	252	80	No Report Received			0	0	0	0	0	340
Mt. Zion	5118	10	10	0	0	0	0	0	2,125	6,087	12,349	18,436	35
New Hope	3410	165	236	159	No Report Received			0	14,701	0	0	0	1,550
No. Pleasant Gr	3411	23	53	31	No Report Received			0	0	0	0	0	200
Oak Grove	3412	60	98	40	No Report Received			0	0	0	0	0	400
Oak Grove Union	3619	28	56	20	0	0	2	0	4,978	10,231	42,006	43,490	200
Oakland	3413	45	132	32	No Report Received			0	0	0	0	0	1,250
Piney Fork*	3620	37	77	30	0	0	6	0	1,617	10,587	40,302	52,019	250
Pleasant Valley**	3418	5	7	5	0	0	18	0	0	726	11,237	9,337	150
Providence**	5122	2	28	8	0	0	28	0	0	0	11,689	6,430	70
Providence 1st	3621	8	51	0	No Report Received			0	0	0	0	0	80
Rose Creek	3622	67	67	18	1	1	0	1	2,709	7,935	45,257	53,285	850
Rozzell Chapel	3419	57	97	52	3	3	1	0	3,500	18,647	56,768	87,711	380
Sturgis	3625	215	215	73	3	5	5	0	15,895	22,680	254,892	228,945	2,100
Sugar Grove*	3626	71	145	39	6	0	5	0	3,000	23,000	76,000	84,000	700
Union Chapel	5123	33	54	19	No Report Received			0	0	0	0	0	150
Unity	3422	115	193	65	16	17	4	7	2,400	24,000	162,731	233,865	350
Vaughn's Chapel	3423	48	63	12	No Report Received			0	3,158	0	0	0	400
Village	5125	10	10	11	No Report Received			0	1,000	0	0	0	10
Wheatcroft	3627	32	57	10	No Report Received			0	3,177	0	0	0	110
Woodlawn	3417	72	303	47	1	1	4	0	0	40,058	220,342	266,266	1,744
TOTALS	45	2,666	5,269	1,626	47	83	127	18	130,619	434,824	2,518,514	2,885,033	26,500

*Math error corrected. **Purged roll.

COVENANT PRESBYTERY CONTINUED

CHURCHES, PASTORS, AND CLERKS:

Bayou de Chine　　　(4MWC)MICO3401
2 Kingston Road
Water Valley, KY 42085
(270)355-2089　　　　　　<Graves>
PA: Kenneth Richards　　　　<M1>
2 Kingston Road
Water Valley, KY 42085
(270)355-2089
kenrich111443@hotmail.com
CL: Mark Crass
1990 Kingston Road
Water Valley, KY 42085
(270)355-2381
jimcrassauto10@bellsouth.net

Benton　　　　(4WC)MICO3403
2968 Aurora Highway (mailing)
Hardin, KY 40248
Kentucky Highway 58 (physical)
Benton, KY 42025
(　)　　　　　　　　<Marshall>
PA: Donna Davenport　　　<M1>
3539 State Route 339
Wingo, KY 42088
(270)376-5488
chamberdonna@yahoo.com
CL: Michele Shearer
2969 Aurora Highway
Hardin, KY 42048
(270)354-8656
mshearer92858@hotmail.com

Bethel　　　　(4WC)MICO3404
12304 Wickliffe Road
Kevil, KY 42053
(270)876-7239　　　　<Ballard>
FAX: (270)876-7513
bethelcpchurch@gmail.com
PA: Drew Gray　　　　<M1>
5610 Country Drive Apt 210
Nashville, TN 37211
(615)332-8360
CL: Teresa Higdon
230 Lake Point Drive
Paducah, KY 42003
(270)554-5003
teresa@qservicesco.com

Calvary　　　　(4MC)MICO3405
98 Calvary Church Road
Mayfield, KY 42066
(270)376-5525　　　　<Graves>
CL: Darla Jo Tucker
665 McNutt Road
Wingo, KY 42088
(270)376-2065

Camp Ground　　　(4C)MICO5103
2645 Lick Creek Road (mailing)
70 Tunnel Lane (physical)
Anna, IL 62906
(618)833-9000　　　　<Union>
OD: Dwight Kaylor　　　<M5>
9393 Hamlettsburg Road
Brookport, IL 62910
(270)366-6881
dkaylor70@gmail.com
CL: Sandra Boaz

2645 Lick Creek Road
Anna, IL 62906
(618)833-8216
skboaz@yahoo.com

Chandler　　　　(4MWC)MICO5302
338 S State Street
Chandler, IN 47610
(812)925-6175　　　　<Warrick>
FAX: (812)925-3628
chandlercpc2@hotmail.com
PA: Jesse Thornton　　　<M1>
122 E Cherry Street
Chandler, IN 47610
(812)925-6475
FAX: (812)925-3628
jessthornton@msn.com
CL: Robert Hooper
PO Box 351
Chandler, IN 47610
(812)925-6965
rwhooper@yahoo.com

Ebenezer　　　　(C)MICO5105
Thompsonville, IL 62890
(　)　　　　　　　　<Saline>
CL: Pat Fletcher
24535 Kaskaskia Road
Thompsonville, IL 62890
(618)627-2288

Ebenezer Hall　　　(4WC)MICO5106
9850 Lick Creek Road (mailing)
750 Grand View (physical)
Buncombe, IL 62912
(618)833-8280　　　　<Union>
CL: Carolyn Hammon
9850 Lick Creek Road
Buncombe, IL 62912
(618)833-8280

Flat Lick　　　　(4WC)MICO3606
415 Bennetttown Street (mailing)
Herndon, KY 42236
9355 Lafayette Road (physical))
Herndon, KY 42236
(270)885-1350　　　　<Christian>
pastorsteve88@yahoo.com
PA: Stephen H Guarneros　　<M1>
506 Clifton Court
Hopkinsville, KY 42240
(270)869-7544
pastorsteve88@yahoo.com
CL: Mike Barbee
415 Bennetttown Street
Herndon, KY 42236
(270)498-3664

Fredonia　　　(4MEWC)MICO3608
204 West Pierson Street (mailing)
303 Cassidy Avenue (physical)
Fredonia, KY 42411
(270)545-3481　　　　<Caldwell>
SS: Larry Buchanan　　　<M1>
730 Shelby Road
Salem, KY 42078
(270)988-1880
lbuchanan.tse@gmail.com
CL: Cindy Cruce
46 Penn Drive
Marion, KY 42064

(270)965-4520
ccruce@fredoniavalleybank.com

Gilead　　　　(4EC)MICO5110
3470 Gilead Church Road (mailing)
4385 Gilead Church Road (physical)
Simpson, IL 62985
(618)695-2653　　　　<Johnson>
tim-arm@live.com
PA: William E Martin, Jr　　<M1>
741 Chapel Hill Road
Marion, KY 42064
(870)270-3344
juniormartin@yahoo.com
CL: Tim Armstrong
745 Webb Town Road
Tunnel Hill, IL 62972
(618)559-7021
tim-arm@live.com

Good Spring　　　(2WC)MICO3609
1800 Old Fredonia Road (mailing)
Princeton, KY 42445
4142 Good Spring Road (physical)
Fredonia, KY 42411
(　)　　　　　　　<Caldwell>
SS: N Ray Board　　　<M1>
267 State Route 293 N
Princeton, KY 42445
(270)365-3850
rayboard@att.net
CL: Mike Stephens
1800 Old Fredonia Road
Princeton, KY 42445
(270)559-6032
mwstephens1800@gmail.com

Highland　　　(4MWC)MICO3414
3950 Lovelaceville Road
Paducah, KY 42001
(270)554-3572　　　　<McCracken>
hcpsec@bellsouth.net
PA: Brent Ballow　　　<M1>
715 Highland Church Road
Paducah, KY 42001
(270)564-8891
hcppastor@bellsouth.net
CL: Elaine S Overton
3915 Lovelaceville Road
Paducah, KY 42001
(270)554-1259
jred3915@bellsouth.net

Hopewell　　　　(4C)MICO3610
768 Lola Road (mailing)
1235 Lola Road (physical)
Salem, KY 42078
(270)988-3859　　　　<Livingston>
SS: Troy Newcomb　　　<M3>
PO Box 858
Salem, KY 42078
SS: Larry Buchanan　　　<M1>
730 Shelby Road
Salem, KY 42078
(270)988-1880
lbuchanan.tse@gmail.com
CL: Michael Heneisen
1162 Hampton Road
Salem, KY 42078
(270)988-4856
heneisen@tds.net

COVENANT PRESBYTERY CONTINUED

Hopkinsville   (4MWC)MICO3611
2701 Faircourt
Hopkinsville, KY 42240
(270)886-1464   <Christian>
FAX: (270)885-1531
cumberland1@bellsouth.net
CL: Marcia Ballard
306 Lucky Debonair
Hopkinsville, KY 42240
(270)839-5482

Liberty   (4C)MICO3406
510 Richardson Street (mailing)
150 Liberty Road (physical)
Murray, KY 42071
( )   <Calloway>
PA: Gary Vacca   <M1>
2203 Creekwood Drive
Murray, KY 42071
(270)978-0818
garyvacca@spiritualliving.com
CL: Brenda Lawson
441 Old Shiloh Road
Murray, KY 42071
(270)227-5872
bsnip10@hotmail.com

Lisman   (4EC)MICO3613
2085 State Route 270 W
Clay, KY 42404
( )   <Webster>
PA: John R Shoulta   <M1>
1154 Mt Carmel Road
White Plains, KY 42464
(270)676-3563
johnshoulta@bellsouth.net
CL: Nancy Burnett
451 Jim Villines Road
Dixon, KY 42409
(270)639-6204

Macedonia   (4WC)MICO3614
18030 Beulah Road (mailing)
Princeton, KY 42445
Highway 291 (physical)
Dalton, KY
( )   <Hopkins>
SS: Dennis Weaver   <M2 ST>
2620 Dalton Road
Providence, KY 42450
(731)592-9054
dsweaver@memphisseminary.edu
CL: Narvin Darnall
18030 Beulah Road
Princeton, KY 42445
(279)836-7089
narvin-d@yahoo.com

Madisonville   (4MWC)MICO3615
PO Box 392 (mailing)
1540 Anton Road (physical)
Madisonville, KY 42431
(270)821-5970   <Hopkins>
PA: Jeff French   <M1>
5 Rose Petal Lane
Dawson Springs, KY 42408
(270)993-0855
brojeff7@bellsouth.net
CL: Jean Duncan
330 S Daves Street

Madisonville, KY 42431
(270)821-5138
jduncan42431@att.net

Margaret Hank   (4WC)MICO3415
1526 Park Avenue
Paducah, KY 42001
(270)443-3689   <McCracken>
holyday@vci.net
PA: Christopher Fleming   <M1>
133 Minerva Place
Paducah, KY 42001
(615)424-8561
holyday@vci.net
CL: Amy Fleming
133 Minerva Place
Paducah, KY 42001
(270)443-3689
holyday@vci.net

Marion First   (4MEWC)MICO3616
PO Box 323 (mailing)
224 W Bellville Street (physical)
Marion, KY 42064
(270)965-4746   <Crittenden>
firstcpchurch@mchsi.com
PA: Dee Ann Thompson   <M1>
226 W Bellville Street
Marion, KY 42064
(270)445-0310
deethomp5@hotmail.com
CL: Jo Ann McClure
PO Box 92
Marion, KY 42064
(270)965-3323

Milburn Chapel   (4EC)MICO3416
3760 Metropolis Lake Road
West Paducah, KY 42086
(270)488-2588   <McCracken>
milburnchapel@gmail.com
PA: Douglas Hughes   <M1>
5545 Hocker Road
Paducah, KY 42001
(270)488-2588
milburnchapel@gmail.com
CL: Joe Neal Neftzger
903 E 6th Street
Metropolis, IL 62960
(618)524-5349
milburnchapel@gmail.com

Mt Carmel   (4MW C)MICO3617
11504 Mt Carmel Road (mailing)
11410 Mt Carmel Road (physical)
White Plains, KY 42464
(270)676-3563   <Hopkins>
bshoulta@bellsouth.net
PA: John R Shoulta   <M1>
11504 Mt Carmel Road
White Plains, KY 42464
(270)676-3563
johnshoulta@bellsouth.net
CL: Larry Putman
1319 Mt Carmel Pond River Road
White Plains, KY 42464
(270)676-3628

Mt Pleasant   (4 C)MICO3618
16647 State Route 109
Sullivan, KY 42460

( )   <Union>
PA: Dale Williams   <M1>
3156 State Route 2837
Clay, KY 42404
(270)664-2044
CL: Richard White
2465 State Route 270 E
Sturgis, KY 42459
(270)333-6109
whitefarms1@att.net

Mt Sterling   (4MWC)MICO5117
1780 Mt Sterling Road
Brookport, IL 62910
(618)564-2616   <Massac>
FAX: (618)564-2616
mscpchurch@yahoo.com
PA: David LeNeave   <M1>
8725 Hamletsburg Road
Brookport, IL 62910
(618)564-2437
mscpchurch_bd@yahoo.com
CL: Gary N Angelly
8646 Independence Road
Brookport, IL 62910
(618)564-2874
FAX: (618)564-2874
angelly@djklink.net

Mt Zion   (4WC)MICO5118
PO Box 383 (mailing)
1159 Mt Zion Road (physical)
Dongola, IL 62926
(618)827-4463   <Union>
jsr487@frontier.com
SS: Donna Davenport   <M1>
3539 State Route 339
Wingo, KY 42088
chamberdonna@yahoo.com
(270)376-5488
SS: Philip Brown   <M23 ST>
540 Mt Pisgah Road
Dongola, IL 62926
(618)697-0972
brownlp75@yahoo.com
CL: Sharon R. Resch
PO Box 383
Dongola, IL 62926
(618)827-4463
jsr487@frontier.com

New Hope   (4MWC)MICO3410
7620 Cross Mill Road
Paducah, KY 42001
(270)554-0473   <McCracken>
newhopecpchurch@hotmail.com
PA: Curtis Franklin   <M1>
7620 Cross Mill Road
Paducah, KY 42001
(270)625-1898
brocurtis@fredonia.biz
CL: Leslie Wright
6575 New Hope Church Road
Paducah, KY 42001
(270)534-1699
leslie.wright@mccracken.kyschools.us

North Pleasant Grove   (4WC)MICO3411
Murray, KY 42071
( )   <Calloway>
SS: Charles K Westfall   <M1>

COVENANT PRESBYTERY CONTINUED

94 Honeysuckle Drive
Gilbertsville, KY 42044
(270)362-0816
CL: Fred Kemp
276 Airport Road
Murray, KY 42071

Oak Grove   (4MWC)MICO3412
2465 Magness Road
Benton, KY 42025
(270)437-4606   <Calloway>
PA: Randy Lowe   <M1>
222 McDougal Drive
Murray, KY 42071
(270)753-8255
loweshodle@aol.com
CL: Jeff Gordon
2465 Magness Road
Benton, KY 42025
(270)437-4613
jgordon@wk.net

Oak Grove Union   (4C)MICO3619
Highway 132
Clay, KY 42404
(270)664-0008   <Webster>
jvfulton@wk.net
SS: James V Fulton   <M1>
1520 Oak Grove Road
Benton, KY 42025
(270)437-4320
CL: Daniel M Heady
2564 State Route 132 W
Dixon, KY 42409
(270)748-6848
danielheady@kycourts.net

Oakland   (4MWC)MICO3413
9104 US Highway 68 W
Calvert City, KY 42029
(270)898-2630   <Marshall>
PA: Danny York   <M1>
5420 State Routh 902 W
Fredonia, KY 42411
(270)350-7262
nonnieyork@yahoo.com
CL: John Jenkins
1265 Elva Loop Road
Symsonia, KY 42082
(270)705-3229

Piney Fork   (4WC)MICO3620
4294 Coppers Spring Road
Marion, KY 42064
( )   <Crittenden>
SS: Daniel Hopkins   <M2 ST>
887 Penny Road
Hardin, KY 42048
(270)205-1847
CL: Sarah Ford
220 S Weldon Street
Marion, KY 42064
(270)965-3833

Pleasant Valley   (4C)MICO3418
111 College Drive
Kevil, KY 42053
(270)224-2497   <Ballard>
SS: April Watson   <M1>
529 W Bellville
Marion, KY 42064

(270)965-2850
aprilwatson@hotmail.com
CL: William E Kilby
PO Box 413
La Center, KY 42056
(270)665-5405

Providence   (4WC)MICO5122
335 Providence Road
Carriers Mills, IL 62917
(618)994-2146   <Saline>
CL: Session Clerk
335 Providence Road
Carriers Mills, IL 62917
(618)994-2146

Providence 1st   (4MEWC)MICO3621
305 Locust Street (mailing)
119 Locust Street (physical)
Providence, KY 42450
(270)667-2485   <Webster>
chalit@apex.net
SS: Paul Stone   <M1>
3490 State Route 2837
Clay, Kentucky 42404
(270)664-6244
stonepstc@aol.com
CL: Paul Northern
317 N Broadway
Providence, KY 42450
(270)667-2636

Rose Creek   (4WC)MICO3622
7650 Island Ford Road (mailing)
Hanson, KY 42413
7220 Rose Creek Road (physical)
Nebo, KY 42441
( )   <Hopkins>
PA: Paul Stone   <M1>
3490 State Route 2837
Clay, KY 42404
(270)664-6244
CL: Joseph E Peyton
7650 Island Ford Road
Hanson, KY 42413
(270)619-0636
jepeyton@madisonville.com

Rozzell Chapel   (4C)MICO3419
1258 Rozzell Church Road
Mayfield, KY 42066
(270)623-6866   <Graves>
PA: D Frederick (Fred) Fahl   <M1>
500 3rd Street
Fulton, KY 42041
(270)472-1476
dffahl@gmail.com
CL: Donna Davenport   <M1>
3539 State Route 339
Wingo, KY 42088
(270)804-3526
chamberdonna@yahoo.com

Sturgis   (4MWC)MICO3625
504 N Main Street
Sturgis, KY 42459
(270)333-2851   <Union>
FAX: (270)333-3118
sturgiscpc@att.net
PA: Victor Hassell   <M1>
510 N Main Street

Sturgis, KY 42459
(270)333-9170
FAX: (270)333-3118
hassellvictor@hotmail.com
CL: Barbara B Sutton
849 State Route 950
Morganfield, KY 42437
(270)333-4385

Sugar Grove   (4MWC)MICO3626
585 Sugar Grove Church Road
Marion, KY 42064
(270)965-4435   <Crittenden>
PA: Terra Sisco   <M1>
1299 Mt Sterling Road
Brookport, IL 62910
(618)384-6126
terrasisco@hotmail.com
CL: Gladys Brown
6781 State Route 120
Marion, KY 42064
(270)965-2969
gbrown6781@live.com

Union Chapel   (4C)MICO5123
PO Box 100 (mailing)
2210 Droit Road (physical)
Galatia, IL 62935
( )   <Saline>
PA: Kevin Peyton   <M1>
580 S Timothy Lane
Galatia, IL 62935
(618)841-0076
kevinp21@frontier.net
CL: Jennifer Romonosky
PO Box 100
Galatia, IL 62935
realtorjlr@yahoo.com

Unity   (4MWC)MICO3422
1503 Story Avenue (mailing)
Murray, KY 42071
1929 E Unity Church Road (physical)
Hardin, KY 42048
(270)354-8216   <Marshall>
cprevbhayes@gmail.com
PA: Brian Hayes   <M1>
69 Cactus Drive
Benton, KY 42025
(270)210-8165
cprevbhayes@gmail.com
CL: Jonathan Whisman
5352 Murray Highway
Hardin, KY 42048
(270)437-3949
jwhisman@wk.net

Vaughn's Chapel   (4MWC)MICO3423
4775 Calvert City Road
Calvert City, KY 42029
(270)395-7318   <Marshall>
PA: Wendell Ordway   <M1>
4775 Calvert City Road
Calvert City, KY 42029
(270)395-7318
CL: John P Case
93 W Second Avenue
Calvert City, KY 42029
(270)395-4203

Village   (4C)MICO5125

COVENANT PRESBYTERY CONTINUED

324 County Road 250 N
Norris City, IL 62869
(618)962-3256 <White>
SS: Rudolph Barnett <M1>
RR 5 Box 267
McLeansboro, IL 62859
(618)643-3253
CL: Charles F Edwards
324 County Road 250 N
Norris City, IL 62869
(618)962-3256
(618)962-3256 <White>

_____

Wheatcroft (4WC)MICO3627
PO Box 7 (mailing)
47 Hammock Street E (physical)
Wheatcroft, KY 42463
( ) <Webster>
PA: Dale Williams <M1>
3156 State Route 2837
Clay, KY 42404
(270)664-2802
dalewilliams@roadrunner.com
CL: Jackie Gass
147 Blackford-Sullivan Road
Clay, KY 42404
(270)664-9310

_____

Woodlawn (4MWC)MICO3417
3402 Old Benton Road
Paducah, KY 42002
(270)442-7713 <McCracken>
woodlawnchurch@live.com
PA: David Fackler <M1>
3409 Benton Road
Paducah, KY 42003
(270)442-7713
woodlawnpastor@live.com
CL: Todd Belt
3402 Old Benton Road
Paducah, KY 42002
(270)442-7713
woodlawnyouth@msn.com

_____

OTHERS ON MINISTERIAL ROLL:

Aden, Dare <M1 WC>
1280 Kimber Road
Dongola, IL 62926
(618)827-3625
FAX: (618)827-4612
dare_aden@hotmail.com
Gerard, Eugene S <M1 OM>
615 N 42nd Street
Paducah, KY 42001
(270)443-2889
Heidel, Jason <M1 WC>
218 Morningside Drive
Hopkinsville, KY 42240
(270)498-7380
heidelj@hotmail.com

Lawson, James <M1 OM>
1003 West 3rd Street
Fulton, KY 42041
(270)472-5272
ridgepointefarm@bellsouth.net
Lively, Louella <M1 WC>
196 Vicksburg Estate Road
Benton, KY 42025
(270)527-3776
Mays, Ronald B <M1 PR>
1100 Cindy Lane
Mayfield, KY 42066
(270)247-0070
rbmays@wk.net
Moore, Hillman C <M1 RT>
2500 Marshall Avenue Apt 223
Paducah, KY 42003
(270)876-7163
hillmancm@att.net
Murrie, Willard <M1 RT>
506 11th Street
Vienna, IL 62995
(618)658-2430
Potts, Danny <M1 WC>
418 Eddings Street Apt 2
Fulton, KY 42041
(270)376-2901
Prewitt, Curtis <M1 WC>
3712 Carmel Lane
Paducah, KY 42003
(270)554-9779
prewitt@apex.net
Rudolph, Allie D <M1 WC>
855 Old Rosebower Church Road
Paducah, KY 42003
(270)898-4903
rallie307@aol.com
Russell, Olen (Bud) <M1 WC>
4510 Holly Grove Road
Brighton, TN 38011
(901)476-8379
olen552@aol.com
Shauf, Steve <M1 WC>
3032 Monroe Street
Paducah, KY 42001
(870)346-5021
sshauf@hotmail.com
Shauf, Teresa <M1 WC>
3032 Monroe Street
Paducah, KY 42001
(870)291-2938
theshaufs@hotmail.com
Shirey, John <M1 RT>
10181 State Route 56 W
Sturgis, KY 42459
(270)389-3562
amshirey7@ips.com
Vasseur, Terry <M1 WC>
121 Crossland Road
Murray, KY 42071
(270)554-2468
tvasseur@bellsouth.net

White, Charles <M1 RT>
PO Box 44
Galatia, IL 62935
(618)268-4562
Wilkerson, Patrick <M1 WC>
7719 S Whispering Oak Circle
Powell, TN 37849
(865)617-9126
patrickwilkerson3@gmail.com
Williams, David J <M1 WC>
20 Acorn Drive
Harrisburg, IL 62946
(618)252-1851

_____

OTHER LICENTIATES ON ROLL:

Kerner, Leanne <M2 ST>
156 State Route 348
W Symsonia, KY 42082
(270)851-9709
cooldoll@bellsouth.net
Quinton, Noah <M2 ST>
2912 Waller Omer Road
Sturgis, KY 42459
(270)952-3875
noah.quinton@gmail.com

_____

OTHER CANDIDATES ON ROLL:

Ashley, Jack (Nick) <M3 ST>
2015 E Virginia Street
Evansville, IN 47711
Cain, Greg <M3>
155 Greggstown
Calvert City, KY 42029
(270)816-5259
Hassell, Samantha <M3 ST>
510 N Main Street
Sturgis, KY 42459
(270)333-9170
hassell_samantha@hotmail.com
Hopkins, Wayne <M3>
1413 E Unity Church Road
Hardin, KY 42048
(270)437-4481
Hunt, Shelley <M3>
6035 State Route 506
Marion, KY 42064
sheljean@kynet.biz
(270)704-2189
Impastato, Paulino <M3>
1547 Mt Zion Church Road
Marion, KY 42064
(270)965-9528
Navrkal, Amy <M3>
302 W 3rd Street
Brookport, IL 62910
(618)638-4218
brinkleydanne2@gmail.com

Cumberland Presbytery
MIDWEST SYNOD

GENERAL	1.Church Number	2.Active	3.Total	4.Church School	5.Prof. of Faith	6.Gains	7.Losses	8.Children Baptized	9. OUR UNITED OUTREACH	10. Total Out-Reach Giving	11. All Other Expenses	12. Total Income Received	13. Value Church Prop. 1=1000
	1	2	3	4	5	6	7	8	9	10	11	12	13
Antioch	3101	30	30	16	No Report Received			0	0	0	0	0	300
Auburn	3301	57	100	30	No Report Received			0	0	0	0	0	405
Bald Knob	3302	40	143	32	No Report Received			0	0	0	0	0	250
Bethel	3102	62	62	27	0	1	1	1	2,000	3,956	26,429	31,808	0
Bethel #1	3103	15	69	11	0	0	2	0	1,000	1,754	22,013	19,968	200
Beulah	3501	28	39	35	No Report Received			0	1,249	0	0	0	100
Boiling Springs	3303	16	19	14	No Report Received			0	0	0	0	0	27
Bowling Green	3304	436	433	75	3	3	3	3	17,589	33,776	231,261	265,037	1,100
Bridgeport 1st	3131	108	108	23	No Report Received			0	0	0	0	0	651
Brier Creek	3503	85	160	65	2	2	5	0	7,916	18,799	79,929	98,728	300
Campbellsville	3104	94	186	70	2	2	28	0	0	4,273	125,361	142,130	1,845
Caneyville	3201	3	5	20	0	0	0	0	0	1,325	12,559	13,515	199
Casey's Fork	3105	14	19	14	No Report Received			0	1,304	0	0	0	37
Cedar Flat	3106	26	63	25	No Report Received			0	0	0	0	0	90
Clear Point	3107	27	67	37	No Report Received			0	1,618	0	0	0	100
Clifton Mills	3202	16	38	51	2	0	1	0	0	2,993	22,041	19,860	274
Coyle	3203	41	143	45	2	1	1	0	0	3,279	43,285	46,400	250
Dukes	3204	12	49	7	No Report Received			0	0	0	0	0	300
Ephesus	3205	65	65	12	1	8	2	0	0	1,194	7,255	15,910	150
Fairview	3504	7	28	0	No Report Received			0	1,403	0	0	0	20
Freedom	3207	67	91	54	No Report Received			0	949	0	0	0	450
Garfield	3208	68	109	44	No Report Received			0	0	0	0	0	495
Gasper River	3306	36	49	20	No Report Received			0	0	0	0	0	105
Gill's Chapel	3307	7	24	0	0	0	0	0	0	1,130	19,306	10,762	35
Glasgow	3108	150	206	92	6	10	24	2	0	30,390	111,058	136,253	1,928
Good Hope	3109	25	25	25	1	1	0	0	2,107	2,090	20,678	21,044	50
Green Ridge**	3308	36	58	17	0	0	44	0	5,483	7,703	53,784	55,077	450
Greensburg	3110	135	180	50	0	1	1	0	11,218	19,107	101,572	118,801	1,000
Greenville	3505	17	49	0	No Report Received			0	600	0	0	0	525
Harrodsburg	3111	18	129	15	1	2	7	0	1,530	2,086	13,269	40,552	383
Heartsong	3222	25	25	0	No Report Received			0	1,250	0	0	0	1,650
High Point	3314	23	23	5	0	3	5	0	50	1,000	17,620	15,353	485
Hopewell	3112	14	25	14	0	0	0	0	0	0	24,714	19,324	60
Irvington	3210	15	25	15	No Report Received			0	0	0	0	0	86
Leitchfield	3211	44	74	24	1	2	6	3	3,000	7,026	59,980	70,050	550
Lewisburg	3309	30	73	29	1	1	1	1	500	3,882	69,093	77,273	300
Liberty	3116	30	58	12	0	4	1	0	0	1,872	53,777	57,702	750
Lick Branch	3117	64	191	38	No Report Received			0	250	0	0	0	90
Little Muddy	3310	19	19	15	0	0	0	0	2,670	6,321	21,173	39,727	119
Louisville 1st	3212	64	126	38	No Report Received			0	0	0	0	0	1,000
Magnolia	3214	176	176	50	1	3	3	0	0	6,498	56,155	66,034	500
Monroe Chapel	3119	30	54	25	0	0	1	0	2,435	4,580	23,848	27,340	150
Morgantown	3311	21	21	6	No Report Received			0	0	0	0	0	80
Mt. Moriah	3120	14	30	12	0	0	0	0	0	0	8,680	20,011	62
Mt. Olive	3216	13	13	7	0	0	2	1	0	627	17,585	20,670	70
Mt. Olivet*	3312	30	39	20	0	0	2	0	625	3,159	36,846	40,005	1,121
Mt. Pleasant	3217	50	68	30	2	5	0	2	3,399	5,211	31,183	33,985	175
Mt. Vernon*	3218	24	34	14	0	0	3	0	0	1,489	23,720	30,631	70
Mt. Zion (AC)	3121	5	18	8	No Report Received			0	0	0	0	0	0
Mt. Zion (DC)	3507	30	62	25	1	1	1	0	3,678	8,700	38,198	51,800	255
Neal's Chapel*	3122	19	46	14	0	0	1	0	0	3,046	0	24,753	150
Needham	3219	23	23	10	No Report Received			0	0	0	0	0	6
New Cypress	3508	17	41	10	0	0	0	0	967	1,364	13,710	10,947	122
Oak Forest	3123	98	222	87	4	6	2	0	7,857	15,491	57,683	75,300	115
Owensboro	3509	118	118	63	1	13	44	2	8,716	21,544	151,429	183,814	1,646
Pleasant Hill	3510	4	5	4	No Report Received			0	0	0	0	0	230
Point Pleasant	3313	5	5	0	No Report Received			0	0	0	0	0	0

Cumberland Presbytery　(Continued)
MIDWEST SYNOD

GENERAL		MEMBERSHIP			CHANGES				FINANCES				
	1.Church Number	2.Active	3.Total	4.Church School	5.Prof. of Faith	6.Gains	7.Losses	8.Children Baptized	9. OUR UNITED OUT-REACH	10. Total Out-Reach Giving	11. All Other Expenses	12. Total Income Received	13. Value Church Prop. 1=1000
	1	2	3	4	5	6	7	8	9	10	11	12	13
Poplar Grove	3511	8	41	5	0	0	1	0	1,722	2,334	29,924	17,215	90
Radcliff	3220	28	28	14	No Report Received			0	0	0	0	0	237
Sacramento	3512	104	209	90	3	4	4	3	12,660	24,973	87,121	126,494	134
Salem	3127	9	32	0	No Report Received			0	0	0	0	0	35
Seven Springs	3128	16	35	18	No Report Received			0	0	0	0	0	267
Shiloh*	3129	85	85	32	No Report Received			0	7,126	0	0	0	300
Short Creek	3221	22	55	22	No Report Received			0	2,921	0	0	0	95
Wisdom*	3130	30	27	12	1	0	3	0	0	828	9,056	8,986	75
TOTALS	65	3,041	4,875	1,702	37	77	200	20	115,792	294,741	1,908,881	2,239,740	23,144

*Math error corrected. **Purged roll.

CHURCHES, PASTORS, AND CLERKS:

Antioch　　　　　(4C)MICU3101
　103 Clarksdale Circle (mailing)
　Glasgow, KY 42141
　68 Antioch Church Road (physical)
　Knob Lick, KY 42154
　( )　　　　　　　　<Metcalfe>
SS: Michael E Fancher　　　<M3>
　356 Breeding Road
　Edmonton, KY 42129
　(270)432-3138
　princo1975@live.com
CL: Kathy B Nason
　103 Clarksdale Circle
　Glasgow, KY 42141
　(270)670-4796

Auburn　　　　(4MWC)MICU3301
　Box 6
　Auburn, KY 42206
　(270)542-4304　　　　<Logan>
PA: Grant Minton　　　　<M1>
　PO Box 270
　Auburn, KY 42206
　(270)542-7991
　FAX: (270)271-4603
　gminton@logantele.com
CL: Ashley Engler
　695 Howlett Road
　Auburn, KY 42206
　(270)542-6730

Bald Knob　　　　(4C)MICU3302
　102 Bald Knob Church Road
　Russellville, KY 42276
　( )　　　　　　　　<Logan>
PA: Byron Dumas　　　<M1 OP>
　1775 Theresa Drive
　Clarksville, TN 37043
　(931)358-3348
　lodumas7346@aol.com

CL: Kathleen Tynes
　3175 Caney Fork Road
　Lewisburg, KY 42256
　(270)755-4218

Bethel　　　　(2WC)MICU3102
　454 Iron Mountain Road (mailing)
　Center, KY 42214
　( )　　　　　　　　<Metcalfe>
SS: Keith G Atwell　　　<M1>
　7688 Hardyville Road
　Hardyville, KY 42746
　(270)528-3667
CL: Steven McMullen
　454 Iron Mountain Road
　Center, KY 42214
　(270)565-5440
　mcmfarm@yahoo.com

Bethel #1　　　(4MWC)MICU3103
　1259 Perryville Road (mailing)
　2586 Perryville Road (physical)
　Harrodsburg, KY 40330
　( )　　　　　　　　<Mercer>
PA: John Contini　　　　<M1>
　4344 Poor Ridge Pike
　Lancaster, KY 40444
　(859)339-0747
　john@hillsideheritagefarm.com
CL: James L Wheeler
　1259 Perryville Road
　Harrodsburg, KY 40330
　(859)734-2045
　jlwheeler@roadrunner.com

Beulah　　　　(4WC)MICU3501
　PO Box 233 (mailing)
　320 Beulah Church Road (physical)
　Hartford, KY 42347
　(270)298-3352　　　　<Ohio>
　FAX: (270)298-7007
　cmwsaw2@bellsouth.net
PA: Michael Justice　　　<M1>

　112B Vance Lane
　Russellville, KY 42276
　(270)726-6673
CL: Chuck Westerfield
　PO Box 233
　Hartford, KY 42347
　(270)298-3352
　FAX: (270)298-7007
　smwsaw@connectgradd.net

Boiling Springs　　　(4C)MICU3303
　3360 Highway 259 (mailing)
　2412 Highway 259 (physical)
　Portland, TN 37148
　(615)325-2618　　　　<Sumner>
PA: Chris Darland　　　<M1>
　582 Ada Drive
　Harrodsburg, KY 40330
　(859)734-2254
CL: Pearl Kepley
　3380 Highway 259
　Portland, TN 37148
　(615)325-3645

Bowling Green　　(4MWC)MICU3304
　807 Campbell Lane
　Bowling Green, KY 42104
　(270)781-3295　　　　<Warren>
　FAX: (270)781-2368
　bgcpc@insightbb.com
PA: Steve Delashmit　　　<M1>
　2705 Garrett Drive
　Bowling Green, KY 42104
　(270)796-8822
　FAX: (270)781-2368
CL: Hoy Hodges
　295 Carver Lane
　Alvaton, KY 42122
　(270)843-4008
　hhlaw319@aol.com

Bridgeport 1st　　　(4C)MICU3131
　515 DeKalb Street

CUMBERLAND PRESBYTERY CONTINUED

Bridgeport, PA 19405
(610)275-6942 <Philadelphi>
PA: Donald Grey Barnhouse, Jr <M1>
  51 Harristown Road
  Paradise, PA 17562
  (717)768-0048
  donaldbarnhouse@gmail.com
CL: William McLay
  9 E Brown Street
  Norristown, PA 19401
  (610)277-8295

Brier Creek (4MWC)MICU3503
  3467 State Route 175 N
  Bremen, KY 42325
  (270)525-3611 <Muhlenberg>
PA: Marc Bell <M1>
  3467 State Route 175 N
  Bremen, KY 42325
  (270)846-4203
  marcbell@insightbb.com
CL: Sherry Skimehorn
  59 Whitmer Street
  Central City, KY 42330
  (270)525-3472
  skimehor@bellsouth.net

Campbellsville (4MWC)MICU3104
  500 Cumberland Way
  Campbellsville, KY 42718
  (270)465-4091 <Taylor>
  FAX: (270)469-9651
  firstcpchurch@windstream.net
PA: Wayne E Brooks <M1>
  1505 Parkview Drive
  Campbellsville, KY 42718
  (270)465-9235
  webrooks@windstream.net
CL: Faye Adams
  902 Rosecrest Avenue
  Campbellsville, KY 42718
  (270)789-1791
  newlifeblessed@yahoo.com

Caneyville (4EWC)MICU3201
  PO Box 334 (mailing)
  203 River Park Drive (physical)
  Caneyville, KY 42721
  ( ) <Grayson>
PS: Steven Smith <M3 ST>
  100 Valleyview Drive
  Leitchfield, KY 42754
CL: Mary Alice Woosley-Logsdon
  PO Box 334
  Leitchfield, KY 42721
  (270)230-2818
  FAX: (270)879-9211
  alicewoosley71@yahoo.com

Casey's Fork (1C)MICU3105
  PO Box 186 (mailing)
  Highway 90 (physical)
  Marrowbone, KY 42759
  (502)864-3129 <Cumberland>
CL: Jimmy Mosby
  210 Bombshell Creek Road
  Burkesville, KY 42717

Cedar Flat (C)MICU3106
  1444 Milam Clark Road (mailing)
  Summer Shade, KY 42166

Cedar Flat - Curtis Road (physical)
  Edmonton, KY 42129
  ( ) <Metcalfe>
CL: Janet A Proffitt
  1444 Milam Clark Road
  Summer Shade, KY 42166
  (270)428-4379

Clear Point (4MWEC)MICU3107
  7895 S Jackson Highway
  Horse Cave, KY 42749
  ( ) <Hart>
PA: Darrell Pickett <M1>
  113 Woods Drive
  Glasgow, KY 42141
  (270)834-6102
  dpickett@glasgow-ky.com
CL: Barbara Ogden
  7895 S Jackson Highway
  Horse Cave, KY 42749
  (270)786-2695

Clifton Mills (4WC)MICU3202
  521 Butler Hobbs Road (mailing)
  Hardinsburg, KY 40143
  6406 W Highway 86 (physical)
  Irvington, KY 40146
  (270)547-5717 <Breckinridge>
PA: Don Bruington <M1>
  PO Box 105
  Falls of Rough, KY 40119
  (270)257-2228
CL: Edna M Hobbs
  521 Butler Hobbs Road
  Hardinsburg, KY 40143
  (270)756-2592
  tejthbs@att.net

Coyle (4C)MICU3203
  1285 Centerview Rough River Lane
  Hudson, KY 40145
  (270)257-0851 <Breckinridge>
  tucker_rd@bellsouth.net
PA: Billy Ray Carter <M1>
  33 Mockingbird Drive
  Leitchfield, KY 42754
  (270)259-3897
  cartercbc@windstream.net
CL: Ralph D Tucker
  1285 Centerview Rough River Lane
  Hudson, KY 40145
  (270)257-0851
  tucker_rd@bellsouth.net

Dukes (4C)MICU3204
  4743 Happy Hollow Road (mailing)
  7814 State Route 144 E (physical)
  Hawesville, KY 42348
  (270)927-9577 <Hancock>
  kimwilborn@yahoo.com
SS: Kimberley Wilborn <M3>
  4743 Happy Hollow Road
  Hawesville, KY 42348
  (270)927-9577
  kimwilborn@yahoo.com
CL: Joe Wilborn
  4743 Happy Hollow Road
  Hawesville, KY 42348
  (270)927-9577
  joeandkimwilborn@bellsouth.net

Ephesus (4EC)MICU3205
  2300 Ephesus Church Road (mailing)
  30 Ephesus Church Loop (physical)
  Harned, KY 40144
  ( ) <Breckinridge>
  bridget.keesee@ky.gov
CL: Bridget Keesee
  2300 Ephesus Church Road
  Harned, KY 40144
  (270)756-9278
  bridget.keesee@ky.gov

Fairview (4C)MICU3504
  PO Box 195 (mailing)
  Sacramento, KY 42372
  Fairview Road (physical)
  Bremen, KY
  (270)736-5189 <Muhlenberg>
SS: James E Talley <M1>
  203 Browning Place
  Hopkinsville, KY 42240
  (270)886-4184
CL: Ottis E Markwell
  PO Box 195
  Sacramento, KY 42372
  (270)736-5189

Freedom (4MWC)MICU3207
  224 John Drane Lane (mailing)
  394 John Drane Lane (physical)
  Harned, KY 40144
  (270)617-4016 <Breckinridge>
PA: Jeff McMichael <M1>
  224 John Drane Lane
  Harned, KY 40144
  (270)617-4016
  revmcmichael@outlook.com
CL: Larry Collard
  4634 Highway 261 N
  Hardinsburg, KY 40143
  (270)617-0609

Garfield (4MWC)MICU3208
  PO Box 39 (mailing)
  90 W Highway 86 (physical)
  Garfield, KY 40140
  (270)580-4796 <Breckinridge>
  mccallum@bbtel.com
PA: Frank McCallum <M1>
  PO Box 56
  Garfield, KY 40140
  (270)580-4796
  mccallum@bbtel.com
CL: Stephen J Tabor
  PO Box 39
  Garfield, KY 40140
  (270)536-3297
  btabor@bbtel.com

Gasper River (4C)MICU3306
  3201 Bucksville Road (mailing)
  3005 Bucksville Road (physical)
  Auburn, KY 42206
  (270)542-8998 <Logan>
SS: Byron Dumas <M1 OP>
  1775 Theresa Drive
  Clarksville, TN 37043
  (931)358-3348
CL: Sandy Tinsley
  3201 Bucksville Road
  Auburn, KY 42206

CUMBERLAND PRESBYTERY CONTINUED

(270)542-7900
tinsley@logantele.com

Gill's Chapel (4EC)MICU3307
1733 Stokes Chapel Road (mailing)
Elkton, KY 42220
955 Hermon Road (physical)
Guthrie, KY 42234
(270)755-4282 <Todd>
sam60romines@hotmail.com
PA: Sam Romines <M1>
PO Box 127
Lewisburg, KY 42256
(270)755-4282
sam60romines@hotmail.com
CL: Sam Romines
PO Box 127
Lewisburg, KY 42256
(270)755-4282
sam60romines@hotmail.com

Glasgow (4MWC)MICU3108
101 Cumberland Street
Glasgow, KY 42141
(270)651-3308 <Barren>
gcpc@glasgow-ky.com
SS: Nicholas Smith <M2>
101 Cumberland Street
Glasgow, KY 42141
(270)651-3308
pastornic@gcpchurch.tv
CL: Buelon R (Pete) Moss
101 Cumberland Street
Glasgow, KY 42141
(270)651-3308

Good Hope (2C)MICU3109
700 Dutton Creek Road (mailing)
Lemon Bend Road (physical)
Campbellsville, KY 42718
(270)789-1482 <Taylor>
glwgaw@windstream.net
PA: Earl West <M1>
246 Maple Avenue
Greensburg, KY 42743
(207)932-5010
west5010@windstream.net
CL: Gayle Whitley
700 Dutton Creek Road
Campbellsville, KY 42718
(270)789-1482
glwgaw@windstream.net

Green Ridge (4MWC)MICU3308
7424 Highland Lick Road
Lewisburg, KY 42256
(270)726-8497 <Logan>
brojoe2@logantele.com
PA: Joseph R Vaught <M1>
7424 Highland Lick Road
Lewisburg, KY 42256
(270)726-8497
brojoe2@logantele.com
CL: Shannon Wells
1720 Crawford Road
Lewisburg, KY 42256
(270)277-9977
chps@bellsouth.net

Greensburg (4MEWC)MICU3110
699 Old Hodgenville Road

Greensburg, KY 42743
(270)932-4864 <Green>
greensburgcpc@windstream.net
PA: Kevin T Brantley <M1>
729 Old Hodgenville Road
Greensburg, KY 42743
(270)932-3780
kbrantley1971@windstream.net
CL: Amy Beard
699 Old Hodgenville Road
Greensburg, KY 42743
(270)932-4864
greensburgcpc@windstream.net

Greenville (4WC)MICU3505
234 Sunset Park (mailing)
108 S Cherry Street (physical)
Greenville, KY 42345
(270)338-0882 <Muhlenberg>
PA: Arthur L Burrows, Jr <M1>
PO Box 511
Hopkinsville, KY 42241
(270)886-1301
CL: Joseph Harris
234 Sunset Park
Greenville, KY 42345
(270)338-6555
josephharris234@yahoo.com

Harrodsburg (4MWC)MICU3111
1113 Louisville Road
Harrodsburg, KY 40330
( ) <Mercer>
PA: Geoff Barrett <M1>
155 Maude Lane
Harrodsburg, KY 40330
(859)748-0450
glbarrett@live.com
CL: Nancy R Tatum
4955 Louisville Road
Salvisa, KY 40372
(859)865-4482

Heartsong (4C)MICU3222
6322 Labor Lane (mailing)
6800 S Hurstbourne Parkway (physical)
Louisville, KY 40291
(502)635-8587 <Jefferson>
PA: Jim Butler <M1>
6322 Labor Lane
Louisville, KY 40291
(502)635-8587
jbutler54@insightbb.com
CL: Susan Lawson
6322 Labor Lane
Louisville, KY 40291
(502)968-0006

High Point Community (C)MICU3314
610 Walnut Street (mailing)
Somerset, KY 42501
190 Longview Drive (physical)
West Somerset, KY 42503
(606)271-0842 <Pulaski>
highpointcpc@gmail.com
PA: Fred Michael (Mike) Adams <M1>
42 Julies Way
Somerset, KY 42503
(606)451-9155
fma46@twc.com
CL: Betty Huffman

610 Walnut Street
Somerset, KY 42501
(606)561-3645
betty.huffman@hotmail.com

Hopewell (4C)MICU3112
1012 N Jackson Highway (mailing)
Hardyville, KY 42746
Hopewell Church Road (physical)
Canmer, KY 42722
( ) <Hart>
CL: Kaye Atwell
1012 N Jackson Highway
Hardyville, KY 42746
(270)528-5341
mkatwell@yahoo.com

Irvington (4MWC)MICU3210
4108 Highway 477 (mailing)
Webster, KY 40176
111 W Walnut Street (physical)
Irvington, KY 40146
( ) <Breckinridge>
PA: Charles Meredith <M1>
144 Barbara Circle
Elizabethtown, KY 42701
(270)307-0607
CL: Ruby Bell
4108 Highway 477
Webster, KY 40176
(270)547-7455
rrbells@bbtel.com

Leitchfield (4MC)MICU3211
501 W Chestnut Street
Leitchfield, KY 42754
(270)259-3835 <Grayson>
PA: Brenda Wilson <M1>
35 Collins Drive
Elizabethtown, KY 42701
(270)249-3835
susieq2007@windstream.net
CL: Arita French
245 Embry Road
Leitchfield, KY 42754
(270)259-4457
kenarita@windstream.net

Lewisburg (4MWC)MICU3309
PO Box 127 (mailing)
101 Church Street (physical)
Lewisburg, KY 42256
(270)755-4282 <Logan>
PA: Sam Romines <M1>
PO Box 127
Lewisburg, KY 42256
(270)755-4282
sam60romines@hotmail.com
CL: Ralph Cropper
178 Cardinal Street
Lewisburg, KY 42256
(270)755-2357
ralph.cropper@novelis.com

Liberty (4WC)MICU3116
PO Box 4105 (mailing)
4139 Old Columbia Road (physical)
Campbellsville, KY 42718
(270)849-7377 <Taylor>
PA: Earl West <M1>
246 Maple Avenue

CUMBERLAND PRESBYTERY CONTINUED

Greensburg, KY 42743
(207)932-5010
west5010@windstream.net
CL: Barbara Davenport
216 Happy Hill Drive
Campbellsville, KY 42718
(270)465-3633
teebdee@windstream.net

Lick Branch   (4C)MICU3117
50 B Jones Road (mailing)
7318 Lecta Kino Road (physical)
Glasgow, KY 42141
(270)670-6698   <Barren>
doncynem@gmail.com
OD: Jerry D Martin   <M5>
292 Bristletown Road
Glasgow, KY 42141
(270)678-2476
doncynem@glasgow-ky.com
CL: Nancy Jolly
2979 Kino Road
Glasgow, KY 42141
(270)428-5722
jollyfarms@scrtc.com

Little Muddy   (4MC)MICU3310
1061 Sugar Grove Road (mailing)
170 Little Muddy Church Road (physical)
Morgantown, KY 42261
( )   <Butler>
SS: Carlton Hatcher   <M1>
2111 Robin Road
Bowling Green, KY 42101
(270)842-8488
CL: William Gabe Keen
822 Sugar Grove Road
Morgantown, KY 42261
(270)526-5895

Louisville 1st   (4MWC)MICU3212
4610 Manslick Road
Louisville, KY 40216
(502)368-4709   <Jefferson>
FAX: (502)368-4709
firstcumberland@att.net
PA: Rodney E Harris   <M1>
7420 Conjar Court
Louisville, KY 40214
(502)368-5501
rodneypat@insightbb.com
CL: Carrie Roth
4610 Manslick Road
Louisville, KY 40216
(502)368-4709
firstcumberland@att.net

Magnolia   (4MWC)MICU3214
PO Box 1 (mailing)
235 Old L and N Turkpike (physical)
Magnolia, KY 42757
(270)324-3472   <LaRue>
magnoliacpchurch@gmail.com
SS: Anthony Harris   <M2>
1604 Parkview Drive
Campbellsville, KY 42718
(270)403-1126
aharris044@gmail.com
CL: Charlotte Tucker
1080 Greensburg Road
Hodgenville, KY 42748

(270)358-3090
charlotte.tucker@larue.kyschools.ust

Monroe Chapel   (4C)MICU3119
7688 Hardyville Road (mailing)
Rt 2 Highway 88 (physical)
Hardyville, KY 42746
(270)528-3667   <Hart>
jbuggforbis@hotmail.com
CL: Janie B Forbis
2465 Possum Trot Road
Hardyville, KY 42746
(270)528-3873
jbuggforbis@hotmail.com

Morgantown   (4MWC)MICU3311
308 Helm Lane (mailing)
118 W Ohio Street (physical)
Morgantown, KY 42261
( )   <Butler>
SS: David Hocker   <M3>
309 N Taylor Street
Morgantown, KY 42261
(270)526-6027
dhocker@hocker.com
CL: Carolyn Henderson
308 Helm Lane
Morgantown, KY 42261
(270)526-3439

Mt Moriah   (2C)MICU3120
107 James Street (mailing)
Edmonton, KY 42129
2038 Mt Moriah Road (physical)
Summer Shade, KY 42166
( )   <Metcalfe>
CL: Sandy England
107 James Street
Edmonton, KY 42129
(270)432-3778
englandsim@scrtc.com

Mt Olive   (4WC)MICU3216
1295 Solway Meeting Road (mailing)
Mt Olive Church Road (physical)
Big Clifty, KY 42712
( )   <Hardin>
CL: Gayle Johnson
1295 Solway Meeting Road
Big Clifty, KY 42712
(270)862-4313
vonnie.g0000@yahoo.com

Mt Olivet   (4MEWC)MICU3312
2640 Mt Olivet Road
Bowling Green, KY 42101
(270)843-0223   <Warren>
SS: Robert (Bob) Bunnell   <M1>
329 Lexington Drive
Glasgow, KY 42141
(270)629-6209
bob_bunnell@yahoo.com
CL: Betty Grammer
180 Sir Wilburn Way
Alvaton, KY 42122
(270)781-4435
thememaw02@walmartconnect.com

Mt Pleasant   (4C)MICU3217
364 E Big Reedy Road (mailing)
E Big Reedy Road (physical)

Caneyville, KY 42721
( )   <Edmonson>
PS: Greg Bowen   <M3 ST>
3241 South Fork Road
Glasgow, KY 42141
CL: Gloria Slaughter
364 E Big Reedy Road
Caneyville, KY 42721
(270)286-9372
gslaughter@mtownbank.com

Mt Vernon   (4WC)MICU3218
1870 Brandenburg Road (mailing)
2373 Brandenburg Road (physical)
Leitchfield, KY 42754
( )   <Grayson>
PA: William M Macy   <M1>
1358 Ephesus Church Road
Harned, KY 40144
(270)756-2775
CL: Marcella Lucas
1870 Brandenburg Road
Leitchfield, KY 42754
(270)259-9215

Mt. Zion (AC)   (1C)MICU3121
c/o Lena Bryson
1925 Loren Collins Road
Glens Fork, KY 42741
( )   <Adair>
CL: Lena Bryson
214 Buell Collins Road
Glens Fork, KY 42741
(502)378-6172

Mt Zion (DC)   (4MWC)MICU3507
7447 Knottsville Mt Zion Rd (mailing)
8001 Knottsville Mt Zion Rd (physical)
Philpot, KY 42366
( )   <Daviess>
PA: Dennis J Preston   <M1>
7447 Knottsville Mount Zion Road
Philpot, KY 42366
(270)925-8144
dennis.preston@daviess.kyschools.us
CL: Shirley L Bratcher
3815 Locust Hill Drive
Owensboro, KY 42303
(270)993-4056
slbratcher24@yahoo.com

Neal's Chapel   (4C)MICU3122
62 Oscar Gilpin Road (mailing)
860 Lecta Kino Road (physical)
Glasgow, KY 42141
( )   <Barren>
LS: Bob White   <M6>
313 Cleveland Avenue
Glasgow, KY 42141
(270)651-8529
drbwhite@glasgow-ky.com
CL: Pam H Browning
62 Oscar Gilpin Road
Glasgow, KY 42141
(270)670-1047
pshbrowning@hotmail.com

Needham   (4WC)MICU3219
3179 Meeting Creek Road (mailing)
State Route 84 (physical)
Eastview, KY 42732

CUMBERLAND PRESBYTERY CONTINUED

( )   <Hardin>
PA: Shelby O Haire   <M1>
  3179 Meeting Creek Road
  Eastview, KY 42732
  (270)862-3887
CL: Odelia Dewall
  2548 Meeting Creek Road
  Eastview, KY 42732
  (270)862-4362

_____

New Cypress   (4C)MICU3508
  127 W 23rd Street (mailing)
  Owensboro, KY 42303
  4814 Highway 81 S (physical)
  Rumsey, KY 42371
( )   <McLean>
PA: Terry Fortner   <M1>
  1079 Luzerne Depoy Road
  Greenville, KY 42345
  (270)836-3635
  terryfortner@att.net
CL: Phyllis Davis
  127 W 23rd Street
  Owensboro, KY 42303
  (270)926-6033
  phyllisdavis966@hotmail.com

_____

Oak Forest   (4MWC)MICU3123
  170 Milby Rattliff Road
  Summersville, KY 42782
  (270)932-4685   <Green>
OD: Robert Knight   <M5>
  1360 Free Union Road
  Columbia, KY 42728
  (270)384-0677
CL: Mike Durrett
  170 Milby Rattliff Road
  Summersville, KY 42782
  (270)932-4685
  thedurretts@windstream.net

_____

Owensboro   (4C)MICU3509
  910 Booth Avenue
  Owensboro, KY 42301
  (270)683-4479   <Daviess>
  brotim.cpc@gmail.net
PA: Timothy McGuire   <M1>
  PO Box 42
  Mt Sherman, KY 42764
  (270)766-9027
  brotim.cpc@gmail.com
CL: Becky Pedigo
  2508 Duke Drive Apt 10
  Owensboro, KY 42301
  (270)999-8301
  becky_pdg@yahoo.com

_____

Pleasant Hill   (4MEC)MICU3510
  10851 Highway 593
  Owensboro, KY 42301
  (386)689-9340   <Daviess>
CL: Carole Robertson
  4709 Forrest Drive
  Owensboro, KY 42303
  (270)315-5288

_____

Point Pleasant   (1C)MICU3313
  7030 State Route 269
  Beaver Dam, KY 42320
( )   <Butler>
SS: David Hocker   <M3>

309 N Taylor Street
  Morgantown, KY 42261
  (270)526-6027
CL: Kathy Pharris
  7030 State Route 269
  Beaver Dam, KY 42320
  (270)274-7418
  kathyspharris@yahoo.com

_____

Poplar Grove   (4WC)MICU3511
  2929 Kentucky 254 W (mailing)
  5112 State Highway 1155 (physical)
  Sacramento, KY 42372
( )   <McLean>
PA: James E Talley   <M1>
  203 Browning Place
  Hopkinsville, KY 42240
  (270)886-4184
CL: Gibson H Riggs
  PO Box 224
  Calhoun, KY 42327
  (270)273-3280
  FAX: (270)273-3280
  riggsg@bellsouth.net

_____

Radcliff   (4U)MICU3220
  1751 S Logsdon Parkway
  Radcliff, KY 40159
  (270)351-6199   <Hardin>
  radpres@bbtel.com
OD: John Lentz   <M5>
  1876 Highway 44 E
  Shepherdsville, KY 40165
  (502)543-2659
  lentzhome@aol.com
CL: Patricia T. Crosby
  851 S Archer Street
  Radcliff, KY 40160
  (270)351-8548
  ptcrosby@bbtel.com

_____

Sacramento   (4MWC)MICU3512
  PO Box 257 (mailing)
  40 Lyons Lane (physical)
  Sacramento, KY 42372
  (270)736-5176   <McLean>
  jbutler@iccable.com
PA: John Butler   <M1>
  PO Box 257
  Sacramento, KY 42372
  (270)736-2268
  jbutler@iccable.com
CL: Brenda Lee
  386 Dillahay Dame Loop
  Island, KY 42350
  (270)736-5160

_____

Salem   (2C)MICU3127
  1570 Old Salem Church Road (mailing)
  291 Clay Wright Road (physical)
  Greensburg, KY 42743
( )   <Green>
CL: Joan Cook
  1570 Old Salem Church Road
  Greensburg, KY 42743
  (502)932-5717

_____

Seven Springs   (2C)MICU3128
  1607 Seven Springs Church Road
  Center, KY 42214
  (270)565-4865   <Metcalfe>

PA: Randall Gray   <M1>
  1230 New Liberty Big Meadow Road
  Knob Lick, KY 42154
  (270)432-5322
CL: Louise London
  2466 Highway 1048
  Center, KY 42214
  (270)565-3015

_____

Shiloh   (4MEWC)MICU3129
  252 Tabernacle Road (mailing)
  1186 Shiloh Road (physical)
  Campbellsville, KY 42718
  (270)789-2346   <Taylor>
  ferree047@windstream.net
PA: Ronald L Ferree   <M1>
  2475 Fallen Timber Road
  Campbellsville, KY 42718
  (270)465-1150
  ferree047@windstream.net
CL: Sue Campbell
  333 Campbell Road
  Campbellsville, KY 42718
  (270)465-5492

_____

Short Creek   (4WC)MICU3221
  9312 Owensboro Road (mailing)
  Hollow Church Road (physical)
  Falls of Rough, KY 40119
( )   <Grayson>
PS: Steven Smith   <M3 ST>
  100 Valleyview Drive
  Leitchfield, KY 42754
CL: George Fentress
  11680 Owensboro Road
  Falls of Rough, KY 40119
  (270)879-8883

_____

Wisdom   (2C)MICU3130
  254 Echo Road (mailing)
  State Route 640 (physical)
  Knob Lick, KY 42129
( )   <Metcalfe>
CL: Frances Royse
  491 Cave Ridge Road
  Knob Lick, KY 42154
  (270)432-0112
  froyse@scrtc.com

_____

OTHERS ON MINISTERIAL ROLL:

Akai, Anum   <M1 WC>
  458 Dean Taylor Court
  Simpsonville, KY 40067
  (502)405-3120
Barton, Robert   <M1 RT>
  22460 Klines Resort Road #290
  Three Rivers, MI 49093
  (859)613-2686
  csm2ndinfbde2002@yahoo.com
Blevins, Tom   <M1 WC>
  50 Blevins Road
  Center, KY 42214
  (270)565-1792
Boggs, Robert   <M1 WC>
  89 Maple Leaf Lane
  Leitchfield, KY 42754
  (270)259-5546
Byrd, James F   <M1 WC>
  1158 Cornishville Road
  Harrodsburg, KY 40330

CUMBERLAND PRESBYTERY CONTINUED

(859)734-0534
jfbyrd@bluezoomwifi.com

Clark, Tom   \<M1 WC\>
  62 Oak Trace
  Campbellsville, KY 42718
  (270)469-4377

Cottingim, Tom   \<M1 WC\>
  353 Atwood Drive
  Lexington, KY 40515
  (859)273-3800
  FAX: (859)272-4315
  t.cottingim@insightbb.com

Ferree, Carole   \<M1 WC\>
  2475 Fallen Timber Road
  Campbellsville, KY 42718
  (270)465-1150
  ferree047@wildblue.net

Gary, Brian   \<M1 WC\>
  105 Wilma Avenue
  Radcliff, KY 40160
  (502)351-6938

Jones, Joseph M   \<M1 RT\>
  405 Lakeview Drive
  Campbellsville, KY 42718
  joepegjones@windstream.net

Love, James R   \<M1 WC\>
  14382 Sonora Hardin Springs Road
  Eastview, KY 42732
  (502)862-4119

Milby, Elizabeth L   \<M1 WC\>
  207 Summersville Road
  Greensburg, KY 42743
  (270)932-5659

Neafus, Kenneth R   \<M1 WC\>
  237 Richland Church Road
  Morgantown, KY 42261
  (270)526-6835

Norris, Freddie   \<M1 WC\>
  330 Lexington Drive
  Glasgow, KY 42141
  (270)651-7932

Perkins, William H   \<M1 WC\>
  PO Box 632
  Central City, KY 42330
  (270)754-5333

Ranson, Doris   \<M1 WC\>
  9440 Fenwick Road

Owensboro, KY 42301
(270)229-2875
dorisranson@bellsouth.net

Renner, Wallace   \<M1 WC\>
  1648 Griffith Avenue
  Owensboro, KY 42303
  (270)685-4359
  pwrenner@adelphia.net

Ricketts, Roger   \<M1 WC\>
  205 Contantz Drive
  Canton, MO 63435

Thompson, Eugene   \<M1 WC\>
  2825 Albatross Road
  Del Ray Beach, FL 33444

Thompson, W Fay   \<M1 RT\>
  210 Macbeth Lane
  Glasgow, KY 42141
  (270)646-2218

Tucker, James D   \<M1 WC\>
  PO Box 34
  Mc Daniels, KY 40152
  (270)257-8971

Underwood, Jerrell M   \<M1 RT\>
  PO Box 9
  Garfield, KY 40140
  (270)536-3706

OTHER LICENTIATES ON ROLL:

Watts, Glenn David   \<M2 ST\>
  7400 Willowbend Drive
  Crestwood, KY 40014
  (502)241-0436
  hongkongbrother@hotmail.com

OTHER CANDIDATES ON ROLL:

Craddock, Barry   \<M3\>
  147 Moss Way
  Glasgow, KY 42141

Harrison, Richard   \<M3\>
  93 Earl Jones Road
  Hodgenville, KY 42748

Cumberland East Coast Presbytery
SOUTHEAST SYNOD

GENERAL		MEMBERSHIP			CHANGES				FINANCES			
1.Church Number	2.Active	3.Total	4.Church School	5.Prof. of Faith	6.Gains	7.Losses	8.Children Baptized	9. OUR UNITED OUT-REACH	10. Total Out-Reach Giving	11. All Other Expenses	12. Total Income Received	13. Value Church Prop. 1=1000
1	2	3	4	5	6	7	8	9	10	11	12	13
Hope Korean	2131	15	19	1	No Report Received				500	0	0	0	63
One Way	2137	75	101	48	9	18	21	3	0	4,500	138,000	125,000	255
Sharing*	2141	28	28	6	3	4	0	0	0	100	52,800	60,780	0
Sunnyside			2										
TOTALS	4	118	148	55	12	22	21	3	500	4,600	190,800	185,780	318

*Math error corrected. **Purged roll.

CHURCHES, PASTORS, AND CLERKS:

Hope Korean (C)SECE2131
1189 Hope Road
Tinton Falls, NJ 07724
( ) <Monmouth>
PA: Buhwan Yang <M1>
19 Taylors Run
Tinton Falls, NJ 07712
(732)918-0011
yangmoksa@gmail.com
CL: Session Clerk
1189 Hope Road
Tinton Falls, NJ 07724

One Way (C)SECE2137
9 Carlton Avenue
Port Washington, NY 11050
(516)815-1164 <Queens>
FAX: (516)921-2821
PA: Jin Soo Park <M1>
21155 45th Drive
Bayside, NY 11361
(516)558-7298
jpkorea@daum.net
AP: Si Hoon Park <M1>
511 4th Street #B
Palisades Park, NJ 07650
(201)944-7913
CL: Session Clerk
21155 45th Drive
Bayside, NY 11361
(516)558-7298
jpkorea@daum.net

Outreach (C)SECE2143
800 Silver Lane Room 205
East Hartford, CT 06118
(860)830-6808
lovejcamen@yahoo.com
PA: Sansook Cho <M1>
7 Falmouth Court
Middletown, CT
lovejcamen@yahoo.com
(860)830-6808

CL: Session Clerk
800 Silver Lane Room 205
East Hartford, CT 06118
(860)830-6808
lovejcamen@yahoo.com

Sharing (C)SECE2141
35-24 Union Street 1C
Flushing, NY 11354
(718)460-1118 <Queens>
spcko1188@gmail.com
PA: John Jae Ko <M1 RT>
13955 35th Avenue #5A
Flushing, NY 11354
(718)460-1118
spcko@hanmail.net
CL: Session Clerk
35-24 Union Street 1C
Flushing, NY 11354
spcko1188@gmail.com

Sunnyside (C)SECE0000
27-27 Bayside Lane
Flushing, NY 11354
(718)809-5191
PA: Kio Seob Kim <M1>
14430 35th Avenue Apt A62
Flushing, NY 11354
(718)539-3476
imkioseob@hotmail.com
CL: Session Clerk
14430 35th Avenue Apt A62
Flushing, NY 11354
(718)539-3476
imkioseob@hotmail.com

OTHER LICENTIATES ON ROLL:

Sung, John (M2)
26 Old Orchard Road
Cherry Hill, NJ 08003
(856)751-0227

Presbytery del Cristo
MISSION SYNOD

GENERAL		MEMBERSHIP			CHANGES				FINANCES				
1.Church Number	2.Active	3.Total	4.Church School	5.Prof. of Faith	6.Gains	7.Losses	8.Children Baptized	9. OUR UNITED OUT-REACH	10. Total Out-Reach Giving	11. All Other Expenses	12. Total Income Received	13. Value Church Prop. 1=1000
	1	2	3	4	5	6	7	8	9	10	11	12	13
Chinese	8501	570	570	205	0	23	28	0	30,936	71,952	948,724	975,140	3,500
Desert Gardens	8705	18	24	13	0	0	0	0	0	8,239	37,244	52,156	180
El Paso First	8704	17	30	0	1	3	2	1	1,500	6,572	61,849	54,369	1,000
Grace Fellowship	8510	147	147	91	1	7	3	1	43,333	175,000	360,000	681,000	700
Heights	8701	374	2,487	120	1	7	15	2	0	116,481	722,209	847,432	2604
Lubbock First	8702	108	108	40	0	2	31	1	2,052	3,882	589,993	624,912	2,467
Maranatha	8706	100	100	60	No Report Received			0	0	0	0	0	0
Redeemer	8512	44	44	65	6	6	2	3	5,000	20,815	198,183	218,674	0
St. Andrew	8703	110	210	47	0	12	6	3	6,738	27,518	236,427	292,000	1,200
Trona	8503	4	33	7	0	2	0	0	379	1,432	15,608	14,259	125
Westside	8709	44	58	33	3	5	10	3	600	11,240	81,360	98,702	197
TOTALS	11	1,536	3,811	681	12	65	99	14	90,538	443,131	3,251,597	3,858,644	11,973

*Math error corrected. **Purged roll.

CHURCHES, PASTORS, AND CLERKS:

Chinese (4C)MSDC8501
865 Jackson Street
San Francisco, CA 94133
(415)421-1624   <San Francisco>
FAX: (415)421-1874
church@cumberlandsf.org
PA: Walter Lau   <M1>
865 Jackson Street
San Francisco, CA 94133
(415)421-1624
FAX: (415)421-1874
walter@cumberlandsf.org
AP: Steven Chen   <M1>
865 Jackson Street
San Francisco, CA 94133
(415)421-1624
psalm1305@yahoo.com
AP: Pek Hua Tan   <M1>
7 Belhaven Avenue
Daly City, CA 94015
(415)515-0076
ptan27@yahoo.com
AP: Sonny Wan   <M1>
13 Wexford Place
Aladema, CA 94502
(415)421-1624
sonny@cumberlandsf.org
AP: Alexis Yu   <M1>
1761 Willow Way
San Bruno, CA 94066
(415)421-1624
alexis.yu.k@gmail.com
CL: John Fang
2362 - 39th Avenue
San Francisco, CA 94116
(415)665-3721
johnfang@pacbell.net

Desert Gardens (4C)MSDC8705

10851 E Old Spanish Trail
Tucson, AZ 85748
(520)296-0703   <Pima>
PA: Gerald (Jerry) Hagelin   <M1>
10851 E Old Spanish Trail
Tucson, AZ 85712
(520)275-8110
azcef@cs.com
CL: Bonnie Kopke
10851 E Old Spanish Trail
Tucson, AZ 85748
(520)647-4700
bkopke@cox.net

El Paso First (4WC)MSDC8704
11299 Pebble Hills Boulevard
El Paso, TX 79936
(915)592-6138   <El Paso>
FAX: (915)592-3538
fcpcelp@sbcglobal.net
PA: Alfredo Rincon   <M1>
12008 Fred Carter
El Paso, TX 79936
(915)857-1343
yaanaivitaly@yahoo.com
CL: Norma Frye
3317 Funston Place
El Paso, TX 79936
(915)633-6877
cherokee80@sbcglobal.net

Grace Fellowship (4C)MSDC8510
3265 16th Street
San Francisco, CA 94103
(415)703-6090   <San Francisco>
FAX: (415)864-1543
PA: Sharon Huey   <M1>
3265 16th Street
San Francisco, CA 94103
(415)703-6090
sharon_huey@yahoo.com
AP: Douglas Lee   <M1>

3265 16th Street
San Francisco, CA 94103
(415)703-6090
dlee@gum.org
CL: Matthew Denson
3265 16th Street
San Francisco, CA 94103
(415)247-9421 ext 17
FAX: (415)864-5830
matthew@densons.org

Heights (4WC)MSDC8701
8600 Academy Road NE
Albuquerque, NM 87111
(505)821-1993   <Bernalillo>
FAX: (505)797-8599
AP: Jerry Smyrl   <M1>
3421 Montreal Street NE
Albuquerque, NM 87111
(505)293-0108
jwsmyrl@hotmail.com
AP: Marty Goehring   <M1>
8600 Academy NE
Albuquerque, NM 87111
(505)821-3628
FAX: (505)797-8599
mgoehring@heightscpc.org
AP: Justin Richter   <M1>
8600 Academy Road NE
Albuquerque, NM 87111
(505)363-8738
richteryp@gmail.com
CL: Barbara J Cok
8600 Academy Road NE
Albuquerque, NM 87112
(505)275-0108
FAX: (866)280-0731
barbara@lobo.net

Lubbock First (4WC)MSDC8702
7702 Indiana Avenue
Lubbock, TX 79423

PRESBYTERY DEL CRISTO CONTINUED

(806)792-3553   \<Lubbock\>
joy@cpclubbock.com
PA: Steve Doles   \<M1\>
  7702 Indiana Avenue
  Lubbock, TX 79423
  (806)787-7551
  steve@cpclubbock.com
CL: Diana K Akins
  4712 63rd Street
  Lubbock, TX 79414
  (806)797-5246
  FAX: (806)744-0640
  dkakins48@yahoo.com

Maranatha   (4C)MSDC8706
  PO Box 1040 (mailing)
  San Elizario, TX 79849
  11497 Socorro Road (physical)
  Socorro, TX 79927
  (915)851-8349   \<El Paso\>
  hectoryliz@att.net
PA: Hector Mata   \<M1\>
  PO Box 1040
  San Elizario, TX 79849
  (915)851-5354
  hectoryliz@att.net
AP: Elizabeth Mata   \<M1\>
  PO Box 1040
  San Elizaro, TX 79849
  (915)851-5354
  hectoryliz@att.net
AP: Isaac Mata   \<M1\>
  PO Box 1040
  San Elizario, TX 79849
  (915)851-5354
  isaacmata96@yahoo.com
AP: Lyvia Rincon   \<M1\>
  12008 Fred Carter
  El Paso, TX 79936
  (915)857-1343
  yaanaivitaly@yahoo.com
AP: Manuel (Alex) Saldana   \<M1\>
  536 Telop
  El Paso, TX 79927
  (915)317-9349
  campe13@yahoo.com
CL: Miguel Flores
  PO Box 1040
  San Elizario, TX 79849
  (915)346-2071
  mr_titof@yahoo.com

Redeemer   (4C)MSDC8512
  1224 Fairfax Avenue
  San Francisco, CA 94124
  (415)671-2194   \<San Francisco\>
  info@redeemersf.org
PA: Danny Fong   \<M1\>
  1224 Fairfax Avenue
  San Francisco, CA 94124
  (415)671-2194
  dfong@redeemersf.org
CL: Daniel Kim
  1224 Fairfax Avenue
  San Francisco, CA 94124
  (415)596-6400
  dannydhkim@gmail.com

St Andrew   (4MEWC)MSDC8703
  1415 N Grandview
  Odessa, TX 79761
  (432)367-8603   \<Ector\>

FAX: (432)367-8605
standrewcp@sbcglobal.net
PA: Jimmy Braswell   \<M1\>
  1514 E 10th Street
  Odessa, TX 79761
  (432)335-9346
  jjcgbraz@cableone.net
AP: Sharon Notley   \<M1\>
  16500 S Grey Wolf Apt 5
  Odessa, TX 79766
  (432)210-9059
  sharon_standrewcp@sbcglobal.net
CL: Linda Anglley
  309 E 89th Street
  Odessa, TX 79765
  (432)550-8569
  anglley@yahoo.com

Trona   (4C)MSDC8503
  83456 Argus Avenue
  Trona, CA 93592
  (760)382-8636   \<San Bernardino\>
PA: Dennis Benadom   \<M1\>
  13314 Sage Street
  Trona, CA 93562
  (760)372-4536
  galerose91@msn.com
CL: Cindy Barton
  83426 Argus Avenue
  Trona, CA 93562
  (760)372-4033
  cbarton53@hotmail.com

Westside   (4C)MSDC8709
  PO Box 15209 (mailing)
  4110 Sabana Grande Avenue (physical)
  Rio Rancho, NM 87174
  (505)620-2427   \<Sandoval\>
  nancye320@aol.com
PA: Harry W Chapman   \<M1\>
  4908 El Picador Court
  Rio Rancho, NM 87124
  (505)620-2427
  wrightrev@gmail.com
CL: Sherry Meier
  7113 Hartford Hills Drive NE
  Rio Rancho, NM 87144
  (505)771-0418
  sjmeier53@aol.com

OTHERS ON MINISTERIAL ROLL:

Bondurant, Lee   \<M1 WC\>
  1453 Paseo Del Sur Court
  El Paso, TX 79928
  (915)309-7269
  leebondurant@yahoo.com
Bower, Clay   \<M1 WC\>
  221 Waterlemon Way
  Monroe, NC 28110
  (704)575-9497
  cblower@lzbsoutheast.com
Collins, Paul   \<M1 WC\>
  915 Warm Sands Drive SE
  Albuquerque, NM 87123
  (505)294-3842
  FAX: (505)254-7707
  chapp3@comcast.net
Estes, George R   \<M1 RT\>
  7910 Cloverbrook Lane
  Germantown, TN 38138

(901)755-6673
geoestes@gmail.com
Estes, Sam R, Jr   \<M1 RT\>
  3026 54th Street Apt 311
  Lubbock, TX 79413
  (806)748-6116
Freund, Henry O   \<M1 RT\>
  913 Sam Houston Drive
  Dyersburg, TN 38024
  (731)285-1744
  freundly@att.net
Fung, David   \<M1 WC\>
  1846 Gunston Way
  San Jose, CA 95124
  (408)266-3398
Fung, Lawrence   \<M1 WC\>
  2/F Weeland Plaza
  188 Nam Cheong Street
  Sham Shui Po Kowloon, HONG KONG
  (852)2783-8923
  FAX: (852)2771-2726
  revfung@yahoo.com
Giron, Francisco   \<M1 OM\>
  3451 Los Mochis Way
  Oceanside, CA 92056
  (760)203-0381
  FAX: (760)414-1236
  thegirons@cox.net
Gonzales, Homer   \<M1 WC\>
  8924 Armistice NE
  Albuquerque, NM 87109
  (505)821-4376
  FAX: (505)841-4267
  hgabq1985@gmail.com
Green, Paul   \<M1 RT\>
  5228 Anchorage Avenue
  El Paso, TX 79924
  (915)751-7960
Hess, Jean   \<M1 WC\>
  2200 E Dartmouth Circle
  Englewood, CO 80113
  (303)504-0275
  jeanhess@316denver.com
Hess, Rick   \<M1 WC\>
  2200 E Dartmouth Circle
  Englewood, CO 80113
  (303)504-0275
  rick@densem.edu
Hom, Paul   \<M1 RT\>
  722 24th Avenue
  San Franciso, CA 94121
  (415)751-9766
Kim, Byong Sam   \<M1 RT\>
  6290 Dawnridge Court
  Paradise, CA 95969
  (530)877-4651
Knight, Melissa   \<M1 M9\>
  5730 Haley Road
  Meridian, MS 39305
  (530)632-6472
  revlissa@gmail.com
Lui, Stephen   \<M1 RT\>
  512 16th Avenue
  San Francisco, CA 94118
  (415)386-2302
  FAX: (415)386-2302
Luo, Tian-en   \<M1 WC\>
  87 Berta Circle
  Daly City, CA 94015
  (650)754-9885
  FAX: (650)754-9885
  tianenyang555@gmail.comt

PRESBYTERY DEL CRISTO CONTINUED

Maddux, Cynthia   <M1 WC>
5735 Timber Creek Place Drive Apt 212
Houston, TX 77084
(832)343-8867
cmaddux1962@gmail.com

Mata, Pablo   <M1 WC>
PO Box 1040
San Elizaro, TX 79849
(915)851-8348
pablomata@yahoo.com

McMillan, Lloyd Aaron   <M1 WC>
8600 Academy Road NE
Albuquerque, NM 87111
(505)821-1993
FAX: (505)797-8599
amcmillan@heightscpc.org

McNeese, Michael C   <M1 WC>
16410 Wesley Evans Road
Prairieville, LA 70769
(520)722-1350
mcneesemc@cox.net

O'Mara, Shelia   <M1 M8>
533 Loughton Lane
Arnold, MD 21012
(410)757-5713
chaplainshelia@aol.com

Patterson, Jerry   <M1 WC>
7007 Whitaker Avenue
Van Nuys, CA 91406
(818)994-5828

Shin, Kyung I   <M1 WC>
1805 Gallinas Road NE
Rio Rancho, NM 87144
(505)453-5461
pastorkshin@gmail.com

Sze, Joseph   <M1 WC>
Rau Sao Joaquim, 382
Liberdale, Sao Paulo, SP
CEP 015068-000 Brazil
pastorsze@yahoo.com

Tsujimoto, Mark   <M1 WC>
88 S Broadway Unit 3210
Millbrae, CA 94030

(650)697-6901
mltsujimoto@gmail.com

Wilson, Don   <M1 M9>
7300 Calle Montana NE
Albuquerque, NM 87113
(505)823-2594
don-wilson07@comcast.net

Wong, Bruce   <M1 WC>
716 Duncanville Court
Campbell, CA 95008
(408)628-1723
revbwong@gmail.com

Yu, Pyong San (Sonny)   <M1 WC>
139 Silverado Drive
Santa Teresa, NM 88008
(915)329-3451
pyongsanyu@hotmail.com

OTHER LICENTIATES ON ROLL:

Chamberlin, Edwin (Joey)   <M2 ST>
7385 W Grant Ranch Boulevard Apt 1636
Littleton, CO 80123
ejcham@gmail.com
(817)929-9876

George, Thomas   <M2>
908 N Brown Avenue
Casa Grande, AZ 85222
(640)447-2676
tgeorge@aerogram.net

OTHER CANDIDATES ON ROLL:

Barton, Cindy   <M3>
83426 Argus Avenue
Trona, CA 93562
(760)372-4033
cbarton53@hotmail.com

Bell, Michelle   <M3>
8643 Dry Creek Road Unit 1226
Centennial, CO 80112
(720)344-4040
mabbell@comcast.net

Coati, DeAngelo   <M3 ST>
11280 Pebble Hills Boulevard #165
El Paso, TX 79936
(915)504-9032
spccoatie@yahoo.com

Jimenez, Jacqueline   <M3>
11161 San Ysidro
Socorro, TX 79927
(915)252-8395
jjimenez22282gmail.com

Okala, Achile   <M3>
5887 Newcombe Court
Arvada, CO 80004
(720)880-8511
achileok@me.com

Ralph, Brian   <M3>
6419 S Vinewood Street Apt 205
Littleton, CO 80120
(312)315-6915
ralph1970@gmail.com

Presbytery of East Tennessee
SOUTHEAST SYNOD

GENERAL		MEMBERSHIP			CHANGES				FINANCES				
	1.Church Number	2.Active	3.Total	4.Church School	5.Prof. of Faith	6.Gains	7.Losses	8.Children Baptized	9. OUR UNITED OUT-REACH	10. Total Out-Reach Giving	11. All Other Expenses	12. Total Income Received	13. Value Church Prop. 1=1000
	1	2	3	4	5	6	7	8	9	10	11	12	13
Beaver Creek	2301	500	790	275	2	14	10	3	51,937	81,834	434,482	516,316	3,600
Bethesda*	2201	50	52	40	0	2	0	0	3,524	17,716	34,760	60,162	170
Casa De Fe	2220	45	100	25	No Report Received			0	1,000	0	0	0	0
Cedar Hill	2202	53	178	38	No Report Received			0	8,410	0	0	0	850
Clark's Grove	2302	46	124	30	0	4	0	0	5,887	9,276	50,586	59,863	500
Corntassel	2304	18	38	18	1	0	11	0	2,922	3,847	24,949	29,512	200
Dover**	2203	40	40	15	0	0	31	0	6,676	15,436	62,704	78,140	1,250
Fairview	2204	53	104	48	2	0	1	0	4,622	20,763	79,880	104,763	602
FaithFellowship	2319	86	142	46	0	2	4	0	16,887	26,567	285,800	290,845	1,930
Gass Memorial	2205	3	7	6	0	0	0	0	718	1,903	7,062	9,213	160
Greeneville	2206	399	563	96	6	13	21	0	44,800	89,839	400,231	481,293	4,200
Heartland	2306	60	114	25	0	0	0	0	3,488	8,378	75,770	85,489	550
Knoxville	2305	101	281	71	0	3	4	1	1,100	14,204	226,683	241,530	2,500
Korea 1st	2221	89	132	55	Under Care of Missions Ministry Team				0	0	0	0	0
Lebanon	2207	16	21	10	0	2	0	0	3,340	8,804	43,825	40731	300
Loudon	2307	210	210	174	0	3	4	1	0	15,469	222,820	257,674	3,744
Marietta	2308	70	202	60	4	3	0	1	14,277	41,303	161,255	206,368	600
Maryville 1st	2309	90	233	71	0	4	3	0	2,200	7,696	116,338	125,868	1,561
Mercy	2320	16	26	27	No Report Received			0	770	0	0	0	5
Mohawk	2208	24	62	25	No Report Received			0	1,418	0	0	0	300
Mt. Carmel	2310	56	90	25	0	1	0	0	4,662	17,807	46,676	63,250	300
Mt. Pleasant	2209	26	66	20	0	0	2	2	2,576	6,029	21,582	27,611	100
New Bethel*	2210	16	32	25	No Report Received			0	920	0	0	0	333
New Hope*	2311	36	36	14	No Report Received			0	1,818	0	0	0	575
Oak Ridge**	2313	133	133	48	0	6	14	2	14,771	28,366	219,127	247,493	2,000
Oakland**	2211	10	25	20	No Report Received			0	1,451	0	0	0	100
Oliver Springs	2314	7	9	6	No Report Received			0	716	0	0	0	180
Philadelphia	2212	26	26	26	0	0	1	0	600	1,785	19,450	14,548	300
Pilot Knob	2213	9	9	27	No Report Received			0	880	0	0	0	100
Pleasant Hill	2214	25	31	25	0	0	1	0	2,956	7,331	22,616	29,947	400
Pleasant Vale	2215	11	11	26	No Report Received			0	161	0	0	0	250
Salem	2216	7	37	55	No Report Received			0	0	0	0	0	104
Shiloh	2217	109	216	92	0	1	6	0	11,078	23,879	99,702	119,476	1,021
Sumkim Presby	2222				Under Care of Missions Ministry Team				0	0	0	0	5
Talbott	2218	69	93	35	No Report Received			0	10,361	0	0	0	1,100
Union	2315	199	375	75	9	32	13	3	12,914	54,738	358,811	414,014	2,330
Virtue	2316	69	83	27	1	4	4	1	14,344	17,350	114,947	146,226	1,616
Willoughby*	2219	12	12	12	0	0	3	0	1,582	1,882	13,541	16,609	250
Young's Chapel	2317	102	149	61	2	4	45	0	16,511	34,418	152,856	180,896	1,000
TOTALS	39	2,890	4,851	1,774	29	101	176	17	272,277	541,736	3,241,734	3,782,664	35,086

*Math error corrected. **Purged roll.

PRESBYTERY OF EAST TENNESSEE CONTINUED

CHURCHES, PASTORS, AND CLERKS:

Beaver Creek   (4WC)SEET2301
  7225 Old Clinton Pike
  Knoxville, TN 37921
  (865)938-7245   <Knox>
  FAX: (865)938-1465
  tsweet1@comcast.net
PA: Thomas Sweet   <M1>
  7225 Old Clinton Pike
  Powell, TN 37849
  (865)938-7245
  tsweet1@comcast.net
AP: Fran Vickers   <M1>
  7225 Old Clinton Pike
  Knoxville, TN 37921
  (865)859-0805
  franv3@comcast.net
CL: John Todd
  4912 Montmorency Drive
  Powell, TN 37849
  (865)938-7211
  jtodd4912@comcast.net

Bethesda   (4C)SEET2201
  155 Old Shiloh Road (mailing)
  Greeneville, TN 37745
  16340 Kingsport Highway (physical)
  Fall Branch, TN 37656
  (423)620-7753   <Greene>
  FAX: (423)798-2042
  kcor_98@yahoo.com
PA: Rocky L Johnson   <M1 OP>
  321 Hope Road
  Greeneville, TN 37745
  (423)638-2771
  kcor_98@yahoo.com
CL: Jeff H Hayes
  155 Old Shiloh Road
  Greeneville, TN 37745
  (423)639-8404
  mdlpilot@yahoo.com

Casa De Fe   (PRESC)SEET2220
  493 Main Street, 2nd Floor
  Malden, MA 02148
  (781)322-2685   <Middlesex>
  casadefepastores@verizon.net
PA: Ricardo Franco   <M1>
  7 Hancock Street
  Melrose, MA 02176
  (781)662-0267
  casadefericardo@verizon.net
AP: Josefina Sanchez   <M1>
  7 Hancock Street
  Melrose, MA 02176
  (479)970-8654
  fsfamily64@gmail.com
CL: Myriam Santizo
  125 Pennsylvania Avenue
  Somerville, MA 02145
  (617)666-6763

Cedar Hill   (4EWC)SEET2202
  4170 Newport Highway
  Greeneville, TN 37743
  (423)639-0268   <Greene>
  cedarhill@centurylink.net
CL: Carolyn Harmon
  4435 Newport Highway

Greeneville, TN 37743
  (423)639-3037
  richardharmon09@comcast.net

Clark's Grove   (4WC)SEET2302
  1662 Peppertree Drive (mailing)
  Alcoa, TN 37701
  3137 Old Knoxville Highway (physical)
  Maryville, TN 37802
  (865)982-5280   <Blount>
  FAX: (865)273-8726
  lwaters111@aol.com
OD: Danny Davis   <M5>
  3137 Old Knoxville Highway
  Maryville, TN 37804
  (865)661-6723
  dannydavis617@yahoo.com
CL: Lynn Waters
  1662 Peppertree Drive
  Alcoa, TN 37701
  (865)982-9083
  FAX: (865)379-0654
  lwaters111@aol.com

Corntassel   (4C)SEET2304
  933 Kahite Trail (mailing)
  Vonore, TN 37885
  2100 Povo Road (physical)
  Madisonville, TN 37354
  (423)884-3909   <Monroe>
  miriamf23@tds.net
PA: Gary Hartman   <M1>
  3001 Hines Valley Road
  Lenoir City, TN 37771
  (865)986-4949
  g37771@att.net
CL: Carolyn Swabe
  2203 Povo Road
  Madisonville, TN 37354
  (423)442-4377
  swabec@aol.com

Dover   (4MEWC)SEET2203
  1550 Dover Road
  Morristown, TN 37813
  (423)581-4719   <Hamblen>
  dovercp@comcast.net
CL: John Ayers
  4371 Danbury Drive
  Morristown, TN 37813
  (423)586-6883
  bigorange@charter.net

Fairview   (4MWC)SEET2204
  4720 Snapps Ferry Road
  Afton, TN 37616
  (423)639-9011   <Greene>
PA: Ronnie Duncan   <M1>
  146 Deseree Broyles Road
  Chuckey, TN 37641
  (423)552-0321
  ronkduncan@icloud.com
CL: Rick Taylor
  175 Stone Dam Road
  Chuckey, TN 37641
  (423)470-0216

Faith Fellowship   (4EWC)SEET2319
  PO Box 24162 (mailing)
  Knoxville, TN 37934
  14025 Highway 70 E (physical)

Lenoir City, TN 37772
  (865)988-8522   <Knox>
  info@faithfellowshipcp.org
PA: Jeff Sledge   <M1>
  241 Long Bow Road
  Knoxville, TN 37934
  (865)288-3375
  jeffsledge@charter.net
CL: Larry Byars
  1412 Dempsey Road
  Knoxville, TN 37932
  (865)850-2925
  larry@byars-consulting.com

Gass Memorial   (4C)SEET2205
  PO Box 1767 (mailing)
  815 Gass Memorial Road (physical)
  Greeneville, TN 37744
  (423)278-7610   <Greene>
  FAX: (423)638-3452
  gassch@comcast.net
PA: Rex Brown   <M1>
  134 Everhart Drive
  Greeneville, TN 37745
  (423)639-4298
CL: George C Mays
  PO Box 1767
  Greeneville, TN 37744
  (423)638-8624
  FAX: (423)638-3452
  g.mays@comcast.net

Greeneville   (4MEWC)SEET2206
  201 N Main Street
  Greeneville, TN 37745
  (423)638-4119   <Greene>
  FAX: (423)636-1017
  office@gcpchurch.org
PA: James W Lively   <M1>
  906 Lyle Circle
  Greeneville, TN 37745
  (423)798-1959
  FAX: (423)636-1017
  jlively@gcpchurch.org
AP: Roy E Blakeburn   <M1>
  111 Park Place
  Greeneville, TN 37743
  (423)787-9609
  FAX: (423)636-1017
AP: Abby Cole Keller   <M1>
  4415 Fieldstone Drive
  Kingsport, TN 37664
  (423)863-6565
  colekeller@yahoo.com
AP: Melissa Malinoski   <M1>
  9087 Fenmore Cove
  Cordova, TN 38016
  (420)620-0089
  FAX: (423)636-1017
  mmalinoski@memphisseminary.edu
CL: Dick Parrack
  201 N Main Street
  Greeneville, TN 37745
  (423)638-4119
  FAX: (423)636-1017
  parrackd@embarqmail.com

Heartland   (4MWC)SEET2306
  160 Harrison Road
  Lenoir City, TN 37772
  (865)986-3018   <Loudon>

PRESBYTERY OF EAST TENNESSEE CONTINUED

lccpc@icx.net
PA: Kenneth P Phillips   <M1>
6419 Town Creek Road East
Lenoir City, TN 37772
(865)986-7344
CL: Jennifer L Smith
1085 Crestview Circle
Lenoir City, TN 37772
(865)986-5099
jlleslie@chartertn.net

_____

Knoxville   (4WC)SEET2305
6900 Nubbin Ridge Drive
Knoxville, TN 37919
(865)588-8581   <Knox>
FAX: (865)588-8581
firstcpc@earthlink.net
PA: Michael Wilkinson   <M1>
6900 Nubbin Ridge Drive
Knoxville, TN 37919
(334)517-6568
pastormike@kfcpc.comcastbiz.net
CL: Dianne Pipkin
1725 Covey Rise Trail
Knoxville, TN 37922
(865)675-2872
pndpip@aol.com

_____

Korea First   (PRESC)SEET2221
Seoul
South Korea
( )   <Korea >
CL: Jin Ho Kim
c/o Ernest Gillis
605-3 Anyang 8 Dong
South Korea
sergiobetancur@starmedia.com

_____

Lebanon   (4MEC)SEET2207
2117 Murray Street (mailing)
Morristown, TN 37814
714 Lebanon Road (physical)
Jefferson City, TN 37760
( )   <Jefferson>
PA: Howard E Shipley   <M1>
3800 Dan Drive
Morristown, TN 37814
(423)581-1092
hshipley@charter.net
CL: Frances McCarter
2117 Murray Street
Morristown, TN 37814
(423)586-6292
lofmcar@aol.com

_____

Loudon   (4MWC)SEET2307
PO Box 373 (mailing)
503 College Avenue (physical)
Loudon, TN 37774
(865)458-2270   <Loudon>
FAX: (865)458-5360
loudoncpc@bellsouth.net
PA: Robert N Coker   <M1>
721 Lakeview Drive
Loudon, TN 37774
(865)458-8791
FAX: (865)458-5360
nickcoker@bellsouth.net
CL: Russ Newman
623 Mulberry Street
Loudon, TN 37773

(865)282-1977
mulberry623@yahoo.com

_____

Marietta   (4MC)SEET2308
11402 Hardin Valley Road (mailing)
1922 Marietta Church Road (physical)
Knoxville, TN 37932
(865)693-0080   <Knox>
mariettacpc@comcast.net
PA: Randall Mayfield   <M1>
12470 Daisywood Drive
Knoxville, TN 37932
(865)769-4756
FAX: (865)769-4756
mayfield07@comcast.net
CL: Virgil R Hubbard
2122 Campbell Station Road
Knoxville, TN 37932
(865)740-4863
vrhubbard@comcast.net

_____

Maryville First   (4MWC)SEET2309
1301 E Broadway
Maryville, TN 37804
(865)982-7860   <Blount>
firstcumberland@gmail.com
PA: Ronald L Longmire   <M1>
2041 Eckles Drive
Maryville, TN 37804
(865)984-1647
ronaldlongmire@charter.net
CL: Tom Longmire
630 Garfield Street
Alcoa, TN 37701
(865)983-3604

_____

Mercy   (4C)SEET2320
634 Martel Road
Lenoir City, TN 37772
(865)660-7579   <Knox>
iglesiapcmisericordia@gmail.com
PA: Alfonso Oscar Marquez   <M1>
389 Bethel Drive
Lenoir City, TN 37772
(865)660-7579
amarquez61@bellsouth.net
CL: Miguel Angel Gonzalez
200 Bethel Drive
Lenor City, TN 37772
(865)227-2710
mgonzalez865@bellsouth.net

_____

Mohawk   (4MWC)SEET2208
PO Box 7 (mailing)
50 Soville Loop (physical)
Mohawk, TN 37810
( )   <Greene>
SS: Chris Franklin   <M2>
104 Delta Circle
Greeneville, TN 37743
(423)972-3609
chrisfranklin104@comcast.net
CL: Velta Rhea Riley
2149 Phillipe Road
Mohawk, TN 37810
(423)235-6179

_____

Mt Carmel   (4EC)SEET2310
PO Box 4 (mailing)
Coalfield, TN 37719
5515 Knoxville Highway (physical)

Oliver Springs, TN 37840
(865)435-9247   <Morgan>
PA: Donald W Acton   <M1>
1186 Jenkins Lane
Knoxville, TN 37922
(865)966-5132
CL: Lisa Layne
714 Back Valley Road
Oliver Springs, TN 37840
(865)382-8817
lalayne64@yahoo.com

_____

Mt Pleasant   (4MWC)SEET2209
3945 Babbs Mill Road
Afton, TN 37616
( )   <Greene>
PA: James L Carter   <M1>
6155 Hummingbird Lane
Whitesburg, TN 37891
(423)587-8423
jandjmt@comcast.net
CL: Louise Gass
701 Franklin Street
Greeneville, TN 37745
(423)639-3731

_____

New Bethel   (3WC)SEET2210
2820 Blue Springs Parkway (mailing)
90 Cox Road (physical)
Greeneville, TN 37743
( )   <Greene>
PA: Rex Brown   <M1>
134 Everhart Drive
Greeneville, TN 37745
(423)639-4298
firstcumberland@gmail.com
CL: Coriece Baxter
2820 Blue Springs Parkway
Greeneville, TN 37743
(423)638-4089

_____

New Hope   (4C)SEET2311
904 Acorn Gap Road
Madisonville, TN 37354
( )   <Monroe>
PA: David L Koopman   <M1>
5606 Brandon Park Drive
Maryville, TN 37804
(865)660-2440
racewthrev@aol.com
CL: Yvonne Wolfe
139 Old Loudon Road
Sweetwater, TN 37874
(423)442-3045

_____

Oak Ridge   (4EWC)SEET2313
PO Box 4836 (mailing)
127 Lafayette (physical)
Oak Ridge, TN 37831
(865)483-8433   <Anderson>
FAX: (865)483-8445
1stcpc@comcast.net
PA: Larry A Blakeburn   <M1>
230 Heathridge Drive
Dyersburg, TN 38024
(731)286-2982
FAX: (731)285-5792
larry@cumberlandchurch.com
CL: Sarah Makin
378 New Henderson Road
Clinton, TN 37716

PRESBYTERY OF EAST TENNESSEE CONTINUED

(865)945-3104
makin1too@aol.com

_____

Oakland   (4C)SEET2211
694 Oakland Road
Telford, TN 37690
(423)257-2258   <Washington>
OD: Parker Street   <M5>
353 Old Stagecoach Road
Jonesborough, TN 37659
CL: Freda Graham
959 Bowmantown Road
Limestone, TN 37681
(423)257-5050

_____

Oliver Springs   (4C)SEET2314
PO Box 175 (mailing)
400 Spring Street (physical)
Oliver Springs, TN 37840
firstcumberland@gmail.com
(   )   <Roane>
PA: Ken Johnson   <M1>
122 Ridge Lane
Clinton, TN 37716
(865)463-7090
kenjoxav122@bellsouth.net
CL: Sid Thurmer
PO Box 175
Oliver Springs, TN 37840
(865)435-5438

_____

Philadelphia   (4MWC)SEET2212
509 Snapp Bridge Road (mailing)
757 Snapp Bridge Road (physical)
Limestone, TN 37681
(   )   <Washington>
CL: Greg Stafford
509 Snapp Bridge Road
Limestone, TN 37681
(423)257-3796
gregandlesa509@comcast.net

_____

Pilot Knob   (2C)SEET2213
515 Marvin Mountain Road (mailing)
445 Gap Creek Road (physical)
Bulls Gap, TN 37711
(   )   <Greene>
LS: Richard Snowden   <M6>
PO Box 6004
Morristown, TN 37815
(423)235-5914
FAX: (423)254-3206
richard.snowden@wallacehardware.com
CL: Joyce Lamb
4185 Gap Creek Road
Bulls Gap, TN 37711
(423)235-6858

_____

Pleasant Hill   (4WC)SEET2214
13385 Kingsport Highway
Chuckey, TN 37641
(   )   <Greene>
PA: Rex Brown   <M1>
134 Everhart Drive
Greeneville, TN 37745
(423)639-4298
firstcumberland@gmail.com
CL: Genevieve M Bolton
15440 Kingsport Highway
Chuckey, TN 37641
(423)234-7942

_____

Pleasant Vale   (4C)SEET2215
525 Pleasant Vale Road
Chuckey, TN 37641
(   )   <Greene>
OD: Chris Bains   <M5>
155 Pelican Lane
Greeneville, TN 37743
(423)525-7497
CL: Howard Collins
3750 Rheatown Road
Chuckey, TN 37641
(423)278-6072

_____

Salem   (4C)SEET2216
695 West Pines Road (mailing)
Afton, TN 37616
1927 Lost Mountain Pike (physical)
Greeneville, TN 37745
(   )   <Greene>
OD: Billy Moore   <M5>
880 Black Bear Road
Greeneville, TN 37745
(423)552-1594
CL: Helen Starnes
695 West Pines Road
Afton, TN 37616
(423)234-0281
cehwstarnes@comcast.net

_____

Shiloh   (4WC)SEET2217
1121 Shiloh Road
Greeneville, TN 37745
(423)639-3763   <Greene>
shilohcpc@embarqmail.com
PA: Tammy L Greene   <M1>
109 Armitage Drive
Greeneville, TN 37745
(423)972-5525
tg6386@aol.com
CL: Jimmy Ricker
1304 Kenney Street
Greeneville, TN 37745
(423)525-7962
jimmyricker@hotmail.com

_____

Sumkim Presbyterian (GESC)SEET2222
#876-15 Dokok-1dong
Kangam-Gu
Seoul, Korea
(023)463-3939   <Korea>
PA: Byung-Jae Choe   <M1>
876-15 Dokok-1dong
Kangnam-Gu
Seoul, Korea
(023)463-3939
CL: Session Clerk Sumkim Presbyterian
#876-15 Dokok-1dong
Kangam-Gu
Seoul, Korea
(023)461-8615

_____

Talbott   (4C)SEET2218
PO Box 116 (mailing)
7410 W Andrew Johnson Hwy (physical)
Talbott, TN 37877
(865)475-1221   <Hamblen>
FAX: (865)475-1221
talbottchurch@bellsouth.net
LS: Richard Snowden   <M6>
PO Box 6004

Morristown, TN 37815
(423)235-5914
FAX: (423)254-3206
richard.snowden@wallacehardware.com
CL: Lon Barry Knight
950 Rocktown Road
Jefferson City, TN 37760
(865)548-8449
lonknight1@hughes.net

_____

Union   (4WC)SEET2315
400 Everett Road
Knoxville, TN 37934
(865)966-9040   <Knox>
FAX: (865)675-3787
union@unioncpchurch.com
PA: Leonard E Turner, Jr   <M1>
12651 Wagon Wheel Circle
Knoxville, TN 37934
(865)966-9040
FAX: (865)675-3787
pastor@unioncpchurch.com
CL: Hugh Turpin
101 E Passmore Lane
Oak Ridge, TN 37830
(865)272-5116
FAX: (865)675-3787
turpinhk@cs.com

_____

Virtue   (4MWC)SEET2316
725 Virtue Road
Knoxville, TN 37934
(865)966-1491   <Knox>
FAX: (865)966-0558
virtuecpchurch@tds.net
PA: Steve Graham   <M1>
11108 Thornton Drive
Knoxville, TN 37934
(865)206-0012
AP: Robert T Spurling Jr   <M1>
127 Wellington Circle
Oak Ridge, TN 37830
(865)803-8582
CL: Jack A Watson
12309 Turkey Creek Road
Knoxville, TN 37934
(865)966-5998
jwatson423@aol.com

_____

Willoughby   (4C)SEET2219
240 Wheeler Road (mailing)
220 Willoughby Road (physical)
Bulls Gap, TN 37711
(   )   <Greene>
SS: Chris Franklin   <M2>
104 Delta Circle
Greeneville, TN 37743
(423)638-5600
chrisfranklin104@comcast.net
CL: Charles Clowers
240 Wheeler Road
Bulls Gap, TN 37711
(423)235-5249

_____

Young's Chapel   (4WC)SEET2317
1705 Lawnville Road
Kingston, TN 37763
(865)376-2192   <Roane>
FAX: (865)376-2196
info@youngschapel.net
PA: Dale Watson   <M1>

PRESBYTERY OF EAST TENNESSEE CONTINUED

1705 Lawnville Road
Kingston, TN 37763
(865)376-2192
revdwatson@comcast.net
CL: Paul McCallie
3340 Kingston Highway
Kingston, TN 37763
(865)376-9199
pt57466@bellsouth.net

OTHERS ON MINISTERIAL ROLL:

Ahn, Da-Wit (David)   <M1 OM>
 1304 Kakyeng-Dong
 Sangdang-Gu Cheongju-City
 Choongbook, Korea
 (043)235-0219
Choi, Ezra   <M1 WC>
 605 Arbor Hollow Circle #203
 Cordova, TN 38018
 (901)236-82635
Dobson, H Wallis   <M1 WC>
 150 Liberty Way
 Greeneville, TN 37745
 (423)798-8947
Fly, William   <M1 OM>
 3002 Trowbridge Drive
 Paragould, AR 72450
 (865)938-6273
 billyfly3@gmail.com
Freeman, A Daniel   <M1 WC>
 210 Dogwood Drive
 Greeneville, TN 37743
 (423)638-5925
Gillis, Ernest H   <M1 WC>
 3273 Bruckner Boulevard
 Snellville, GA 30078
 (770)982-6587
 professorgil64@hotmail.com
Gonzales, Miguel   <M1 WC>
 200 Bethel Drive
 Lenoir City, TN 37772
 (865)988-4238
Greenwell, James C   <M1 WC>
 7165 Wind Whisper Boulevard
 Knoxville, TN 37924
 (865)742-1653
 FAX: (865)742-1653
 greenwelljc@comcast.net
Hester, Mark S   <M1 WC>
 763 Finn Long Road
 Friendsville, TN 37737
 (865)995-1541
 markshester@att.net
Hubbard, Donald   <M1 RT>
 2128 N Campbell Station Road
 Knoxville, TN 37932
 (865)693-0264
 djhubbard@mindspring.com
Ivey, Billy F   <M1 RT>
 409 Rodeo Drive
 Knoxville, TN 37922
 (865)966-5946
 iveybe@tds.net
Jang, WonJeon   <M1 OM>
 Lot2-C Teresa Subdivision
 Tabucan Mandurriao
 Iloilo City 5000, Phillipine
Johnson, Beverly B   <M1 RT>
 801 Riverhill Drive Apt 308
 Athens, GA 30606

(865)977-0405
 bevloujohnson@aol.com
Kelly, Patrick L   <M1 M9>
 1449 Rainbow Road
 Mountain City, TN 37681
 (423)727-4067
Keown, Gale J   <M1 RT>
 2130 Cason Lane
 Murfreesboro, TN 37128
 (865)805-5451
Kim, YoungHo (Steve)   <M1 WC>
 B02 Hyundai I-Space 1608-2
 Burim Dong, Dong An Gu
 AnYang City, Kyunggi Do S Korea
 (231)348-8033
 paidion4377@naver.com
Lee, Sang-Do   <M1 OM>
 1342 Seocho-2dong
 Seocho-Gu
 Seoul, Korea
 (023)474-8405
Lim, Keum-Taek   <M1 WC>
 1342 Seocho-2dong
 Seocho-Gu
 Seoul, Korea
 (023)474-8405
 limkt114@hanmail.net
Malinoski, T J   <M1 DE>
 9087 Fenmore Cove
 Cordova, TN 38016
 (423)972-1239
 mlmalinoski@comcast.net
Marquez, Martha   <M1 WC>
 389 Bethel Drive
 Lenoir City, TN 37772
 (865)660-7579
McConnell, Donald R   <M1 RT>
 147 Confederacy Circle
 Knoxville, TN 37934
 (865)288-0230
 donjoyce515@hotmail.com
McGuire, James D   <M1 WC>
 220 Southwind Circle #2
 Greenville, TN 37745
 (423)638-6380
 jmcguire915@comcast.net
Melson, Glenda   <M1 M9>
 331 Tickle Weed Road
 Swansea, SC 29160
 (417)588-2758
 gmelson@fidnet.com
Middleton, Bill S   <M1 RT>
 12826 Union Road
 Knoxville, TN 37922
 (865)966-1706
 revbill@charter.net
Nicholson, Casey   <M1 WC>
 1020 Tusculum Boulevard
 Greeneville, TN 37745
 (423)639-0268
 caseynicholson@mac.com
Ortiz, Milton   <M1 DE>
 8846 N Cortona Circle
 Cordova, TN 38018
 (901)486-6679
 mortiz@cumberland.org
Park, Bo-Seong   <M1 OM>
 304-28 Sinlim-Dong, Kwanak-Gu
 Seoul, Korea
 (002)884-3474
Pickard, Ronald   <M1 WC>

6292 Golden Drive
 Morristown, TN 37814
 (423)587-9735
Prenshaw, Rebecca   <M1 WC>
 1100 Albemarie Lane
 Knoxville, TN 37923
 (865)531-1954
 bprenshaw@yahoo.com
Richardson, W Jean   <M1 RT>
 7533 Lancashire Boulevard
 Powell, TN 37849
 (865)947-3111
 jeanandregena@frontier.com
Scott, Jerry   <M1 M9>
 2310 Sentell Drive
 Maryville, TN 37803
 (865)803-3669
 dmjlscott@yahoo.com
Sweet, Don   <M1 RT>
 3008 Shropshire Boulevard
 Powell, TN 37849
 (865)938-7435
 mariondon77@netscape.com
West, Fred E, Jr   <M1 WC>
 510 Cedaredge Drive
 New Smyrna, FL 32168
 (206)409-8321
 jwest616@earthlink.net
Yu, Wn-yong   <M1 OM>
 325-1 DongHyen-Dong
 Jecheon-city
 Choongbuk, Korea
 (043)652-0540
 lifeyu@hanmail.net

OTHER LICENTIATES ON ROLL:

Choi, Justin   <M2 ST>
 605 Arbor Hollow Circle Apt 203
 Cordova, TN 38018
 (901)605-4542
 flymetothemoon@hotmail.com
Choi, Sean   <M2 ST>
 7565 Macon Road
 Cordova, TN 38016
 (901)826-2993
 esloveh2@hotmail.com
Overton, Twanda   <M2 ST>
 616 S Cox Street
 Memphis, TN 38104
 (865)591-8881
 tdeeov@yahoo.com

OTHER CANDIDATES ON ROLL:

Brown, Whitney   <M3 ST>
 137 Roberta Drive
 Memphis, TN 38112
 (865)387-0002
 whitneymbrown@gmail.com
Craig, Aaron   <M3>
 325 Cherry Avenue
 McKenzie, TN 38201
 (731)352-6718
Frazier, Shawn   <M3 ST>
 459 Forrest Avenue
 McKenzie, TN 38201
 (865)414-8394

PRESBYTERY OF EAST TENNESSEE CONTINUED

Hamby, Gary   <M3>
700 W 6th Avenue
Lenoir City, TN 37771
(731)986-2635

Mejia, Salvador   <M3 ST>
7618 S Highway 72
Loudon, TN 37774
(865)661-8267

Sweet-Brockman, Anna   <M3>
210 E Main Street Apt B
Greenfield, TN 38230
(865)803-8582
amsweet@memphisseminary.edu

Wright, Tim   <M3>
165 Quaker Knob Road
Chuckey, TN 37641
(423)639-0634
tdwright1123@yahoo.com

Grace Presbytery
SOUTHEAST SYNOD

	GENERAL	MEMBERSHIP			CHANGES				FINANCES				
	1.Church Number	2.Active	3.Total	4.Church School	5.Prof. of Faith	6.Gains	7.Losses	8.Children Baptized	9. OUR UNITED OUT-REACH	10. Total Out-Reach Giving	11. All Other Expenses	12. Total Income Received	13. Value Church Prop. 1=1000
	1	2	3	4	5	6	7	8	9	10	11	12	13
Antioch	0701	31	38	24	0	0	2	0	1,377	4,159	15,968	13,771	150
Beersheba	0702	159	197	85	5	13	1	2	18,552	43,298	178,505	221,798	1,200
Branchville	0106	152	166	46	No Report Received			0	0	0	0	0	1,650
Cairo	0704	12	24	7	0	1	0	0	0	3,712	18,136	23,257	140
Christ	0303	70	93	25	2	3	3	2	1,335	3,400	90,680	92,250	1,340
Coker	0705	52	101	25	1	5	6	1	1,657	4,708	91,322	105,944	1,935
Columbus	0706	149	149	70	0	10	4	0	4,000	6,000	144,498	137,405	1,500
Crestline	0102	30	32	19	No Report Received			0	6,000	0	0	0	1,500
El Camino	0310	62	70	20	0	5	2	0	1,000	3,900	57,811	65,132	530
Enon	0707	195	261	123	8	14	3	5	1,200	22,397	257,865	270,029	1,050
Erin	0601	57	99	39	0	0	2	0	0	4,089	52,665	58,646	221
First Hispanic+	0307	78	78	9	0	3	1	0	0	543	97,851	91,226	175
Forrest Avenue	0403	166	115	8	0	0	1	0	2,296	3,216	20,384	23,600	240
Gadsden	0402	91	158	43	1	6	4	1	13,493	27,443	114,172	143,480	800
Glencoe	0404	85	247	70	No Report Received			0	250	0	0	0	2,000
Grace Commun	0407	78	129	24	4	10	6	0	9,779	19,122	80,608	122,826	1,200
Greens Chapel	0208	40	71	25	0	0	0	0	6,992	12,571	58,967	77,461	819
Groverton*	0602	28	42	14	16	48	20	1	0	10,097	23,235	33,332	0
Helena	0108	47	50	37	1	10	5	0	2,000	10,953	74,821	85,774	700
Homewood*	0111	78	115	45	1	2	4	1	11,550	25,465	216,093	235,859	2,025
Hope	0308	104	126	20	6	13	2	0	6,457	14,401	143,687	158,088	1,985
Hopewell	0101	21	23	10	0	2	4	0	3,600	6,900	47,352	49,463	1,227
House of Prayer	0214	180	180	180	No Report Received			0	0	0	0	0	450
Hueytown 1st*	0109	20	102	6	No Report Received			0	0	0	0	0	385
Immanuel	0311	24	20	10	No Report Received			0	2,197	0	0	0	0
McLeod Chapel	0708	15	20	10	No Report Received			0	0	0	0	0	350
Mt. Zion	0709	22	22	20	No Report Received			0	4,336	0	0	0	650
New Hope	0104	189	223	90	9	8	3	0	27,484	91,277	188,696	279,973	2,250
Oldham Chapel	0405	14	14	10	No Report Received			0	0	0	0	0	325
Piedmont	0406	69	80	71	1	7	2	1	2,400	4,500	79,086	86,421	1,101
Pleasant Hill	0710	14	32	5	0	0	1	0	0	727	27,780	22,899	160
Roca DeSalvacion	0115	29	65	9	9	12	3	5	0	1,050	47,268	63,758	41
Rocky Ridge	0105	74	225	40	2	3	5	1	23,240	28,359	181,438	199,386	1,200
Salem	0607	50	58	20	0	0	2	0	1,100	6,854	28,976	31,386	150
Spring Creek	0113	130	164	97	2	2	1	0	3,600	41,254	204,300	269,000	1,000
Steam Mill**	0608	53	68	65	1	3	32	2	0	16,522	88,765	122,017	340
Union*	0114	45	63	35	0	0	18	0	1,517	3,031	40,311	43,345	500
TOTALS	37	2,717	3,737	1,498	91	209	149	27	157,412	431,423	2,769,810	3,242,275	30,814

*Math error corrected. **Purged roll (x)Closed 2013 +Union church

GRACE PRESBYTERY CONTINUED

CHURCHES, PASTORS, AND CLERKS:

Antioch (2C)SEGR0701
2994 Antioch Church Road
Reform, AL 35481
( )   <Pickens>
PA: William L Benson   <M1>
137 W Lowndes Drive
Columbus, MS 39701
(662)386-3433
willardb715@gmail.com
CL: Reba Carpenter
3951 County Road 45
Reform, AL 35481
(205)375-6042
rebareform@aol.com

Beersheba (4MEWC)SEGR0702
1736 Beersheba Road
Columbus, MS 39702
(662)327-9615   <Lowndes>
FAX: (662)324-8320
officebeersheba@att.net
PA: Timothy Daniel Lee   <M1>
186 Blasingame Drive
Columbus, MS 39702
(601)433-3714
eelmit@bellsouth.net
CL: Charles Studdard
95 Studdard Drive
Columbus, MS 39702
(662)328-8844
FAX: (662)327-8773
clstuddard@emssonline.com

Branchville (4MWC)SEGR0106
80 Hurst Road
Odenville, AL 35120
(205)629-3258   <St Clair>
FAX: (205)629-3258
session@branchvillechurch.org
PA: Keith L. Mariott   <M1>
155 Ridgewood Lane
Odenville, AL 35120
(205)903-5251
kjmariott@windstream.net
CL: Steve Smith
80 Hurst Road
Odenville, AL 35120
session@branchvillechurch.org

Cairo (4MC)SEGR0704
3836 Highway 50 W (mailing)
West Point, MS 39773
Cairo Road (physical)
Cedar Bluff, MS 39741
( )   <Clay>
CL: Judy Chrismond
3836 Highway 50 W
West Point, MS 39773
(662)494-7290
tjchrismond@gmail.com

Christ (4EWC)SEGR0303
19501 Holly Lane
Lutz, FL 33548
(813)909-9789   <Hillsborough>
ccpclutz@verizon.net
PA: Michael Laperche   <M1>
3867 Evergreen Oaks Drive

Lutz, FL 33558
(813)948-8016
pastor-mike@earthlink.net
CL: Jeannie Vaughn
16107 Carden Drive
Odessa, FL 33556
(813)926-6631
jvaughn1@tampabay.rr.com

Coker (4MEWC)SEGR0705
PO Box 262 (mailing)
14705 Romulus Road (physical)
Coker, AL 35452
(205)339-1178   <Tuscaloosa>
cokercpgreg@att.net
SS: Greg Tucker   <M2>
PO Box 262
Coker, AL 35452
(205)541-7484
cokercpgreg@att.net
CL: Retha Channell
15535 Lisenba Drive
Coker, AL 35452
(205)339-8125

Columbus (4EWC)SEGR0706
2698 Ridge Road
Columbus, MS 39705
(662)328-2692   <Lowndes>
fcpcsecretary@att.net
PA: Luke Lawson   <M1>
270 N Ridgeland Circle
Columbus, MS 39705
(662)295-9322
luke_lawson03@hotmail.com
CL: Carol Carley
71 Little Tom Road
Columbus, MS 39705
(662)328-4589
carleyr@bellsouth.net

Crestline (4MWC)SEGR0102
605 Hagood Street
Birmingham, AL 35213
(205)879-6001   <Jefferson>
FAX: (205)968-8105
jan@crestlinechurch.org
PA: Janice M Overton   <M1>
3320 Pipeline Road
Birmingham, AL 35243
(205)281-6819
FAX: (205)968-8105
jan@crestlinechurch.org
CL: Birki Cvacho
1214 Regal Avenue
Birmingham, AL 35213
(205)592-3023
blcvacho@bellsouth.net

El Camino (C)SEGR0310
6248 SW 14th Street (mailing)
6790 SW 12th Street (physical)
West Miami, FL 33144
(305)261-6200   <Dade>
lucatha@aol.com
PA: Luciano Jaramillo   <M1>
6249 SW 14th Street
West Miami, FL 33144
(305)264-1074
ljara@aol.com
CL: Hedemarrie Dussan

6248 SW 14th Street
Miami, FL 33144
(054)812-0613

Enon (4MWC)SEGR0707
PO Box 294 (mailing)
9000 Highway 12 (physical)
Ackerman, MS 39735
(662)285-3303   <Choctaw>
enoncpchurch@dtcweb.net
PA: Jerry L Lawson   <M1>
6039 MS Highway 415
Ackerman, MS 39735
(662)285-8295
lawson@dtcweb.net
CL: Raymond D Gillon Jr
PO Box 294
Ackerman, MS 39735
(601)916-3589
rgillon@dtcweb.net

Erin (4WC)SEGR0601
PO Box 574, Carthage, MS (mailing)
590 Pete Freeman Road (physical)
Union, MS 39051
( )   <Newton>
OD: Scott Engle   <M5>
PO Box 1023
Decatur, MS 39327
(601)683-9586
CL: Lynn Federick
PO Box 574
Carthage, MS 39051
(601)267-4954

First Hispanic (4MWU)SEGR0307
2828 W Kirby Street
Tampa, FL 33614
(813)932-9684   <Hillsborough>
FAX: (813)932-9700
fhpctampafla@aol.com
PA: Alexandri Sosa   <M1>
8607 Villa Largo Drive
Tampa, FL 33613
(813)562-4289
FAX: (813)932-9700
sosapcus@gmail.com
CL: Nivaria F Neff
3845 S Lake Drive U-186
Tampa, FL 33614
(813)765-2745
nivys7@yahoo.com

Forrest Avenue (4MWC)SEGR0403
2316 Forrest Avenue
Gadsden, AL 35904
(256)547-2833   <Etowah>
SS: Lem Lockmiller Jr   <M1>
5068 Louise Street
Hokes Bluff, AL 35903
(256)490-3021
CL: Joe Neal
1110 Cabot Avenue
Gadsden, AL 35904
(256)547-2833
jnwr@aol.com

Gadsden (4MWC)SEGR0402
PO Box 2055 (mailing)
1200 Piedmont Cutoff (physical)
Gadsden, AL 35903

GRACE PRESBYTERY CONTINUED

(256)492-2556   <Etowah>
FAX: (256)492-2525
office@gadsdencp.com
PA: Daniel Barkley   <M1>
2732 Rexford Street
Hokes Bluff, AL 35903
daniel@gadsdencp.com
(256)478-0397
CL: Grace Whitfield (deceased)
245 Monterey Circle
Gadsden, AL 35901
(256)442-1860
FAX: (256)492-2525
gracenaomi@aol.com

_____

Glencoe   (4WC)SEGR0404
200 N College Street
Glencoe, AL 35905
(256)492-1584   <Etowah>
FAX: (256)492-1584
glencoecpchurch@yahoo.com
PA: Rodney McInnis   <M1>
280-B Coley Road
Glencoe, AL 35905
(256)454-2399
mcinnisrodneyand@bellsouth.net
CL: Scott Stewart
200 N College Street
Gadsden, AL 35905
(256)492-1584
stewie242@hotmail.com

_____

Grace Community   (4C)SEGR0407
3515 Highway 14
Millbrook, AL 36054
(334)285-4655   < >
millbrookgcc@gmail.com
SS: Albert Russell   <M2>
375 Ashton Park Drive
Millbrook, AL 36054
(334)290-0399
chemistry.russell@gmail.com
CL: Debbie Silva
3515 Highway 14
Millbrook, AL 36054
(334)290-3884
quilter.deb@gmx.com

_____

Greens Chapel   (4WC)SEGR0208
PO Box 729 (mailing)
81 Greens Chapel Road (physical)
Cleveland, AL 35049
(205)559-7671   <Blount>
SS: W Ray Lathem   <M1>
452 County Road 1462
Cullman, AL 35055
(256)708-1247
lathemray@bellsouth.net
CL: Ben Royal
148 Truman Drive
Cleveland, AL 5049
(205)274-7503
broyal@otelco.net

_____

Groverton   (2C)SEGR0602
222 Leon Harrell Road
Morton, MS 39117
( )   <Scott>
OD: Ronnie Spears   <M5>
101 Shirley Drive
Pelahatchie, MS 39145

CL: Judy Thompson
1824 Irby Road
Morton, MS 39117
(601)732-3572

_____

Helena   (4MC)SEGR0108
PO Box 566 (mailing)
3396 Helena Road (physical)
Helena, AL 35080
(205)663-2174   <Shelby>
helenacpchurch@bellsouth.net
SS: Mike Emsinger   <M3>
4910 Cox Cove
Helena, AL 35080-3424
(205)620-4699
me0573@att.com
CL: Betty Barron
1263 Siskin Drive
Alabaster, AL 35007
205-664-9251
barron1263@asi-web.com

_____

Homewood   (4WC)SEGR0111
513 Columbiana Road
Homewood, AL 35209
(205)942-3051   <Jefferson>
FAX: (205)945-0677
hcpc@homewoodcpc.com
PA: Mathew Derek Jacks   <M1>
341 Shadeswood Drive
Hoover, AL 35226
(205)903-8469
pastorderek@homewoodcpc.com
CL: Melissa Dameron-Vines
1517 Astre Circle
Hoover, AL 25226
(205)422-1253
mdvines73@hotmail.com

_____

Hope   (4WC)SEGR0308
826 S Miller Road
Valrico, FL 33594
(813)684-4689   <Hillsborough>
FAX: (813)655-7919
hopecpc@verizon.net
PA: William E (Eddie) Jenkins   <M1>
1836 S Ridge Drive
Valrico, FL 33594
(813)651-3802
hopechurch4@aol.com
CL: Donna Cachia
4122 Helene Place
Valrico, FL 33594
(813)684-8391
djc1948@msn.com

_____

Hopewell   (4MWC)SEGR0101
2139 Cumberland Drive SE
Bessemer, AL 35023
(205)425-2126   <Jefferson>
SS: James Scott Edwards   <M3>
226 Jasmine Drive
Alabaster, AL 35007
(205)837-4069
jedwards53163@bellsouth.net
CL: Beverly Edwards
226 Jasmine Drive
Alabaster, AL 35007
(205)529-4507
jedwards53163@bellsouth.net

_____

House of Prayer   (4C)SEGR0214
405 E Moulton Street (mailing)
Decatur, AL 35601
170 County Road 730 (physical)
Cullman, AL 35055
(256)355-0947   <Cullman>
FAX: (256)355-0947
nlajap@yahoo.com
PA: Neil Aguiar   <M1>
405 E Moulton Street
Decatur, AL 35601
(256)616-1318
nlajap@yahoo.com
AP: Antonio Mena Rojas   <M1>
1421 1st Street NW
Cullman, AL 35055
(256)531-8193
antonio.mena.7@facebook.com
CL: Andres Esteban
405 E Moulton Street
Decatur, AL 35601
(256)355-0947
FAX: (256)355-0947

_____

Hueytown First   (4MWC)SEGR0109
2711 Clyburne Street (mailing)
4846 15th Street Road (physical)
Hueytown, AL 35023
( )   <Jefferson>
CL: Thomas S Neel
2711 Clyburne Street
Hueytown, AL 35023
(205)491-6772
tardistom@hotmail.com

_____

Immanuel   (4MC)SEGR0311
10235 US Highway 301
Dade City, FL 33525
(352)567-7427   <Pasco>
PA: Charles Reed   <M1>
10235 US Highway 301
Dade City, FL 33525
instchuck12@embarqmail.com
(352)567-7427
CL: Chad Reed
36821 Indian Lake Cemetary Road
Dade City, FL 33523
(352)567-8755
chadrreed@embarqmail.com

_____

McLeod Chapel   (4MC)SEGR0708
305 E Minor Street (mailing)
Macon-Lynn Creek Road (physical)
Macon, MS 39341
(662)726-4609   <Noxubee>
CL: James B Moore III
305 E Minor Street
Macon, MS 39341
(662)726-4609

_____

Mt Zion   (4C)SEGR0709
3044 Wolfe Road
Columbus, MS 39705
(662)328-3778   <Lowndes>
mjmims@muw.edu
CL: Martha Jo Mims
3011 Wolfe Road
Columbus, MS 39705
(662)328-3778
mjmims@muw.edu

_____

GRACE PRESBYTERY CONTINUED

New Hope   (4EWC)SEGR0104
5521 Double Oak Lane
Birmingham, AL 35242
(205)991-5252   <Shelby>
FAX: (205)991-5159
jessie@newhopecpc.org
PA: Donny Acton   <M1>
5521 Double Oak Lane
Birmingham, AL 35242
(205)991-5252
FAX: (205)991-5259
donny@newhopecpc.org
AP: Mindy Acton   <M1>
1413 Oak Ridge Drive
Birmingham, AL 35242
(205)991-3204
FAX: (205)991-5259
mindy@newhopecpc.org
AP: Sherrlyn Frost   <M1>
5557 Surrey Lane
Birmingham, AL 35242
(205)408-0729
FAX: (205)991-5259
sherrlyn@newhopecpc.org
CL: Jessie R Dunnaway
120 Virginia Way
Birmingham, AL 35242
(205)991-7434
FAX: (205)991-5259
jessie@newhopecpc.org

Oldham Chapel   (4EC)SEGR0405
PO Box 537 (mailing)
8767 Greensport Road (physical)
Ashville, AL 35953
(205)594-5727   <St Clair>
SS: Rodney McInnis   <M1>
280-B Coley Road
Glencoe, AL 35905
(256)454-2399
CL: Faye Bowling
PO Box 537
Ashville, AL 35953
(205)594-7171

Piedmont   (4MWC)SEGR0406
23746 AL Highway 9 N
Piedmont, AL 36272
(256)447-7275   <Calhoun>
PA: Jacob Sims   <M1>
23716 Alabamaa Highway 9 N
Piedmont, AL 36272
(205)907-8273
jacobdsims@gmail.com
CL: Charles Needham
201 Needham Drive
Piedmont, AL 36272
(256)447-6897
cneedham_99@yahoo.com

Pleasant Hill   (4MC)SEGR0710
115 Westwood Drive SW (mailing)
7782 CR 181, Eutaw, AL (physical)
Bessemer, AL 35022
(205)425-9659   <Greene>
williambetts7177@gmail.com
LS: William H Betts   <M6>
115 Westwood Drive SW
Bessemer, AL 35022
(205)425-9659
CL: Greg Espey

12034 County Road 60
Eutaw, AL 35462
(205)372-2260
gregandmichel@bellsouth.net

Roca De Salvacion   (C)SEGR0115
2404 Altadena Road
Birmingham, AL 35243
(205)705-3145   <Jefferson>
cpcrocadesalvacion@gmail.com
PA: William Alas   <M1>
612 King Valley Circle
Pelham, AL 35124
(205)966-9411
alas3542085@yahoo.es
CL: Carlos Solito
106 Highway 63
Calera, AL 35040
(205)329-8514

Rocky Ridge   (4WC)SEGR0105
2404 Altadena Road
Birmingham, AL 35243
(205)823-2719   <Jefferson>
rockyridgechurch@bellsouth.net
SS: David Ferguson   <M2>
1841 Pebble Lake Drive
Birmingham, AL 35232
(205)200-9205
fergusondavid15@yahoo.com
AP: Don H Thomas   <M1 RT>
4829 Caldwell Mill Road
Birmingham, AL 35242
(256)742-0785
dhtatn4ybc@cs.com
CL: Cheryl Riley
2416 Altadena Road
Birmingham, AL 35243
(205)790-4342

Salem   (4WC)SEGR0607
PO Box 121 (mailing)
Sebastopol, MS 39359
1220 Highway 487 E (physical)
Walnut Grove, MS 39189
(601)253-2678   <Leake>
sondragould@att.net
PA: Linda Howell   <M1 OP>
PO Box 80050
Keller, TX 76244
(601)942-2015
lshowell1000@yahoo.com
CL: Virginia Gould
1220 Highway 487 E
Walnut Grove, MS 39189
(601)253-2678
sondragould@att.net

Spring Creek   (4MWC)SEGR0113
3411 Spring Creek Road (mailing)
3455 Spring Creek Road (physical)
Montevallo, AL 35115
(205)665-4184   <Shelby>
sccpchurch@yahoo.com
PA: Scott Fowler   <M1>
1900 Alex Mill Road
Montevallo, AL 35115
(205)901-8478
springcreekcp@aol.com
CL: Ben Ingram
15 Quincy Lane

Montevallo, AL 35115
(205)665-4145
ben_ingram@msn.com

Steam Mill   (4WC)SEGR0608
593 Pine Grove Road (mailing)
Walnut Grove, MS 39189
11551 Road 101 (physical)
Union, MS 39365
( )   <Neshoba>
nchambers@hughes.net
PA: Nicholas Chambers   <M1>
11300 Road 101
Union, MS 39365
(601)900-3684
nachambrs@hotmail.com
CL: Myra Bankston
593 Pine Grove Road
Walnut Grove, MS 39189
(601)616-0436
mbankston@ecmhci.com

Union   (4MWC)SEGR0114
PO Box 64 (mailing)
11633 Bama Rock Garden Road (physical)
Vance, AL 35490
( )   <Tuscaloosa>
LS: Herbie Gray   <M6>
2554 A Rocky Ridge
Birmingham, AL 35243
CL: Clifford Odell
11491 Bama Rock Garden Road
Vance, AL 35490
wjsrabbit@aol.com

OTHERS ON MINISTERIAL ROLL:

Acton, Wade   <M1 RT>
1615 Estes Drive
Glencoe, AL 35905
(256)492-8542
ginnyacton@juno.com
Black, Gary G   <M1 WC>
503 S Main Street
Piedmont, AL 36272
(205)447-7142
Brasher, Karen   <M1 WC>
2931 Barker Cypress Road, Apt 415
Houston, TX 77084
(205)777-2420
ekb077@gmail.com
Carter, Patricia   <M1 M9>
2509 Decatur Stratton Road
Decatur, MS 39327
(601)604-3813
revtree@yahoo.com
Chuquimia, Walter   <M1 OM>
18240 S US Highway 301
Winauma, FL 33598
(813)399-4050
walter@beth-el.info
Clark, J Don   <M1 RT>
1601 Lake Ridge Circle
Birmingham, AL 35216
(205)942-4054
jdsjcl@charter.net
Crawford, Roger B   <M1 RT>
541 Highway 25 N
Carthage, MS 39051
(601)298-1899
Davis, C Timothy   <M1 WC>

GRACE PRESBYTERY CONTINUED

8880 Childress Road
West Paducah, KY 42086
(850)995-8383
FAX: (904)994-6003
charles0828@earthlink.net
Edmonds, Wayne   <M1 RT>
  112 Dogwood Trail
  Eclectic, AL 36024
  (334)857-2202
  sweetpea@comlinkinc.net
English, Don W   <M1 WC>
  4311 Guys Court
  Bessemer, AL 35022
  (205)428-4790
Foreman, Samuel L   <M1 WC>
  2811 Laredo Drive
  Hattiesburg, MS 39402
  (601)562-1415
  slfcpc@yahoo.com
Gaither, Randy   <M1 WC>
  No 3 Pacific Street
  Belmopan City
  Belize, Central America
  rgaither@valuelinx.net
Garcia, Ramon   <M1 OM>
  2714 Callista Court Apt 104
  Naples, FL 34114
  (239)200-5714
  revga@hotmail.com
Hartung, J Thomas   <M1 M9 ST>
  2291 Americus Boulevard W Apt 1
  Clearwater, FL 33763
  (727)797-2882
  revtom6@aol.com
Headrick, Anthony   <M1 M8>
  3327 N Eagle Road Ste 110-132
  Meridian, ID 83646
  (619)524-8821
  chaps2a@yahoo.com
Headrick, Christopher   <M1 WC>
  1913 Vestavia Court Apt B
  Vestavia Hills, AL 35216
  (205)240-0979
  bravespop@gmail.com
Headrick, Jerry   <M1 RT>
  9950 Old Stage Road
  Stockton, AL 36579
  (251)377-9744
  willjheadrick@gmail.com
Hunley, Jearl   <M1 RT>
  2618 Canterbury Road
  Columbus, MS 39705
  (662)329-1516
  jdhunley@cableone.net
Johnson, Thomas (Tommy) C   <M1 RT>
  PO Box 566
  Helena, AL 35080
  (205)936-1350
  revtomjohnson@aol.com
Lefavor, David   <M1 M8>
  414 S Monroe Siding Road
  Xenia, OH 45385
  (813)613-4133
  david.lefavor@med.va.gov
Maynard, Terrell D   <M1 RT>
  3 Nelson Cove
  Milan, TN 38358
  (731)437-0056
  terrellmaynard@bellsouth.net
Moore, James R, Sr   <M1 RT>
  2778 Marguerite Street S

Hokes Bluff, AL 35903
(256)494-9030
jmoore@microxl.com
Mora, Wilfredo   <M1 WC>
  17512 SW 153rd Court
  Miami, FL 33187
  (786)554-1478
  moraw68@gmail.com
Morrow, Charles   <M1 RT>
  5032 Pine Grove Road
  Union, MS 39365
  (601)479-0288
  morrowp7@yahoo.com
Payne, Robert (Bob)   <M1 WC>
  1660 3rd Street NW
  Birmingham, AL 35215
  (205)856-2427
  payne.bob.emmet@gmail.com
Ros, Ramiro   <M1 WC>
  107 Bracken Lane
  Brandon, FL 33511
  (813)633-1548
  bethel@gte.net
Rowlett, Ron   <M1 WC>
  22 Diana Drive
  Savannah, GA 31406
  (912)351-0736
Schultz, Don   <M1 RT>
  708 Gateway Lane
  Tampa, FL 33613
  (813)960-1473
Talley, Ed   <M1 WC>
  404 Serenity Circle
  Walland, TN 37886
  (205)854-1886
Thomas, Lynn   <M1 DE>
  4833 Caldwell Mill Lane
  Birmingham, AL 35242
  (205)601-5770
  lynndont@gmail.com
Tobler, Garth   <M1 WC>
  136 Boat Landing Road
  Oneonta, AL 35121
  (205)683-0298
  gatobler@gmail.com
Travieso, Julio   <M1 WC>
  15910 Countrybrook Street
  Tampa, FL 33624
  (813)963-3727
  jutra98@aol.com
Weldon, Mark   <M1 WC>
  1515 Chambliss Drive
  Birmingham, AL 35226
  (205)330-8580
  weldonm@bellsouth.net
Yarce, Omar   <M1 WC>
  10925 Neptune Drive
  Cooper City, FL 33026
  alphavida@gmail.com
  (205)919-9685

OTHER LICENTIATES ON ROLL:

Linski, David   <M2>
  1060 Alpine Way
  Indian Springs, AL 35124
  (205)677-8163
  david.linski@gmail.com
Sumerlin, Larkin   <M2>
  174 Brookgreen Lane
  Indian Springs, AL 35124

(334)357-00007
larkin_sumerlin72@hotmail.com
Thomas, Micaiah   <M2>
  PO Box 5204 SBN 499
  Princeton, NJ 08543
  (205)478-5985
  micaiah.thomas@gmail.com

OTHER CANDIDATES ON ROLL:

Byford, Ken   <M3>
  58 Quincy Lane
  Montevallo, AL 35115
  (205)665-5753
  kenabyford@gmail.com
Ingram, Matthew   <M3>
  29 Quincy Lane
  Montevallo, AL 35115
  (205)914-0829
  mbingram80@gmail.com
Prevost, Abigail   <M3>
  4731 Lafayette Road
  Hopkinsville, KY 42240
  (731)343-5386
  abbyprevost@gmail.com
Seva, Judith   <M3>
  7685 Tara Circle Apt 204
  Naples, FL 34104
  (239)269-3917
  jclthgirl12@gmail.com
Solito, Carlos   <M3>
  106 Highway 63
  Calera, AL 35040
  (205)329-8514
  fcg9700@gmail.com
Tanck, Brian   <M3>
  64 Mercer Street
  Princeton, NJ 08540
  (630)730-1577
  brian.tanck@gmail.com
Yarce, Virginia   <M3>
  10925 Neptune Drive
  Cooper City, Fl 33026
  (954)850-7111
  ginnyyarce@gmail.com

Hong Kong Presbytery
MISSION SYNOD

	1.Church Number	2.Active	3.Total	4.Church School	5.Prof. of Faith	6.Gains	7.Losses	8.Children Baptized	9. OUR UNITED OUT-REACH	10. Total Out-Reach Giving	11. All Other Expenses	12. Total Income Received	13. Value Church Prop. 1=1000
	1	2	3	4	5	6	7	8	9	10	11	12	13
Cheung Chau	8801	21	38	21	0	0	0	0	64	567	50,595	47,858	128
Kowloon	8803	106	289	73	0	2	3	1	1,833	32,875	202,522	203,000	154
Macau	8804	68	148	25	5	9	3	6	1,178	15,509	98,947	142,748	761
Mu Min*	8810	180	283	50	19	24	12	4	850	15,840	287,936	462,448	0
North Point	8805	48	118	40	2	2	1	0	2,248	23,559	115,254	143,249	100
Po Lam	8808	76	132	20	5	6	3	2	386	2,700	250,000	207,500	385
Shatin*	8807	210	226	45	23	30	2	8	1,858	15,000	350,000	485,000	385
Tao Hsien	8806	400	543	200	0	19	5	5	2,575	135,922	619,846	858,158	2,856
Xi Lin	8809	95	162	75	5	7	1	3	3,862	33,971	229,606	261,090	0
Yao Dao	8811	152	179	35	10	17	4	4	1,944	20,220	209,721	211,733	0
TOTALS	10	1,356	2,118	584	69	116	34	33	16,798	289,593	2,179,357	2,685,564	4,384

CHURCHES, PASTORS, AND CLERKS:

Cheung Chau   (4C)MSHK8801
  11 On Wing Centre 2/F
  Pak She Back Street
  Cheung Chau, HONG KONG
  (852)2981-4933   <Hong Kong>
  cccpcmail@yahoo.com.hk
SS: Kelvin Ho   <M2>
  11 On Wing Centre 2/F
  Pak She Back Street
  Cheung Chau, HONG KONG
  (852)2981-4933
  kelvinskho@gmail.com
CL: Wing Hin Cheung
  11 On Wing Centre 2/F
  Pak She Back Street
  Cheung Chau, HONG KONG
  (852)2981-4933
  cccpcmail@yahoo.com.hk

Kowloon   (4WC)MSHK8803
  338-340 Castle Peak Road
  Flat D 2/FL
  Kowloon, HONG KONG
  (852)2386-6563   <Hong Kong>
  FAX: (852)3020-0365
  kcumber@biznetvigator.com
SS: Ting Bong Ha   <M2>
  338-340 Castle Peak Road
  Flat D 2/FL
  Kowloon, HONG KONG
  (852)2386-6563
  FAX: (852)3020-0365
  kcumber@biznetvigator.com
CL: Lai Seung AU
  338-340 Castle Peak Road
  Flat D 2/FL
  Kowloon, HONG KONG
  (852)2386-6563
  FAX: (852)3020-0365
  kcumber@biznetvigator.com

Macau   (4WC)MSHK8804
  258 Carlos D'Assumpcao
  Ed Kin Heng Long 4 Andar LMN
  MACAU
  (853)2892-1702   <Macau>
  cpc_macau@yahoo.com.hk
SS: Eva Watt   <M3>
  258 Carlos D'Assumpcao
  Ed Kin Heng Long 4 Andar LMN
  MACAU
  (853)2892-1702
  eva6e@hotmail.com
CL: Sok Yi Leong
  258 Carlos D'Assumpcao
  Ed Kin Heng Long 4 Andar LMN
  MACAU
  (853)2892-1702
  cpc_macau@yahoo.com.hk

Mu Min   (C)MSHK8810
  2/F Fu Tung Shopping Center
  Tung Chung
  Lantau Island, HONG KONG
  (852)2109-1738   <Hong Kong>
  FAX: (852)2109-1737
  mmcpc@cumberland.org.hk
PA: Patrick Tat Wing So   <M1>
  2/F Fu Tung Shopping Center
  Tung Chung
  Lantau Island, HONG KONG
  (852)2109-1738
  FAX: (852)2109-1737
  pattwso1@gmail.com
AP: So Li Wong   <M1>
  2/F Fu Tung Shopping Center
  Tung Chung
  Lantau Island, HONG KONG
  (852)2109-1738
  FAX: (852)2109-1737
  soliwong@gmail.com
CL: Lai Yuet Liu   <M2>
  2/F Fu Tung Shopping Center
  Tung Chung
  Lantau Island, HONG KONG

  (852)2109-1738
  FAX: (852)2109-1737
  lyliu0914@gmail.com

North Point   (4WC)MSHK8805
  14-16 Tsat Tsz Mui Road
  1/Fl Block B
  North Point, HONG KONG
  (852)2562-2148   <Hong Kong>
  FAX: (852)2564-2898
  northpointcpc@yahoo.com.hk
SS: Eliza Yuk Lan Yau   <M2>
  14-16 TsatTsz Mui Road
  1/Fl Block B
  North Point, HONG KONG
  (852)2562-2148
  FAX: (852)2564-2898
  elizaylyau@yahoo.com.hk
CL: Cindy Chan
  14-16 Tsat Tsz Mui Road
  1/Fl Block B
  North Point, HONG KONG
  (852)2562-2148
  FAX: (852)2564-2898
  northpointcpc@yahoo.com.hk

Po Lam   (ARC)MSHK8808
  Wing B&C, G/F, Ming Wik House
  Kin Ming Estate
  Tseung Kwan O NT, HONG KONG
  (852)2706-0111   <Hong Kong>
  FAX: (852)2706-0114
  polamcpc@yahoo.com.hk
SS: Yim Ngar Wong   <M2>
  Wing B&C G/F Ming Wik House
  Kin Ming Estate
  Tseung Kwan O NT, HONG KONG
  (852)2706-0111
  FAX: (852)2706-0114
  yimngar@yahoo.com.hk
CL: Yim Ngar Wong
  Wing B&C G/F Ming Wik House
  Kin Ming Estate
  Tseung Kwan O NT, HONG KONG

HONG KONG PRESBYTERY CONTINUED

(852)2706-0111
FAX: (852)2706-0114
yimngar@yahoo.com.hk

Shatin   (ARC)MSHK8807
   G/1F 251 Tin Sam Village
   Shatin NT, HONG KONG
   (852)2693-3444   <Hong Kong>
   FAX: (852)2607-2245
   cpcshatin@yahoo.com.hk
PA: Jonathan Chor K Siu   <M1>
   G/1F 251 Tin Sam Village
   Shatin NT, HONG KONG
   (852)2693-3444
   FAX: (852)2607-2245
   cpccksiu@yahoo.com.hk
CL: Angelo Chui
   G/1F 251 Tin Sam Village
   Shatin NT, HONG KONG
   (852)2693-3444
   FAX: (852)2607-2245
   cpcshatin@yahoo.com.hk

Tao Hsien   (4F)MSHK8806
   2/F Welland Plaza
   188 Nam Cheong Street
   Sham Shui Po, Kowloon, HONG KONG
   (852)2783-8923   <Hong Kong>
   FAX: (852)2771-2726
   thchurch@taohsien.org.hk
PA: Amos Pui Chung Yuen   <M1>
   2/F Welland Plaza
   188 Nam Cheong Street
   Sham Shui Po, Kowloon, HONG KONG
   (852)2783-8923
   FAX: (852)277-1272
   revyuen@taohsien.org.hk
CL: Adays Lee
   2/F Welland Plaza
   188 Nam Cheong Street
   Sham Shui Po, Kowloon, HONG KONG
   (852)2783-8923
   FAX: (852)2771-2726
   thchurch@taohsien.org.hk

Xi Lin   (4C)MSHK8809
   28 Hong Yip Street
   Yuen Long, HONG KONG
   (852)2639-9176   <Hong Kong>
   FAX: (853)2639-5620
   info@yuenlongchurch.org
PA: William Kin Keung Yeung   <M1>
   28 Hong Yip Street
   Yuen Long, HONG KONG
   (852)2639-9176
   FAX: (852)2639-5620
   william@xilincpc.org.hk
CL: Loarinne Tang
   28 Hong Yip Street
   Yuen Long, HONG KONG
   (852)2639-9176
   FAX: (852)2639-5620
   loarinne@yuenlongchurch.org

Yao Dao   (4C)MSHK8811
   CPC Yao Dao Primary School
   Tin Yuet Estate
   Tin Shui Wai, NT, HONG KONG
   (852)2617-7872   <Hong Kong>
   FAX: (852)2617-0287
   ydgrowth@yaodaocpc.org

OD: Antony Cheng   <M5>
   CPC Yao Dao Primary School
   Tin Yuet Estate
   Tin Shui Wai, NT, HONG KONG
   (852)2617-7872
   FAX: (852)2617-0287
   antonycycheng@yahoo.com.hk
CL: Kwong Lung Leung
   CPC Yao Dao Primary School
   Tin Yuet Estate
   Tin Shui Wai, NT, HONG KONG
   (852)2617-7872
   FAX: (852)2617-0287
   ydgrowth@yaodaocpc.org

OTHERS ON MINISTERIAL ROLL:

Cheung, Luke   <M1 WC>
   2/F Welland Plaza
   188 Nam Cheong Street
   Sham Shui Po Kowloon, HONG KONG
   (852)2783-8923
   FAX: (852)2771-2726
   luke.cheung@cgst.edu
Hung, Ella Siu Kei   <M1 WC>
   2/F Welland Plaza
   188 Nam Cheong Street
   Sham Shui Po, Kowloon, HONG KONG
   (852)2783-8923
   FAX: (852)2771-2726
   siukee@taohsien.org.hk
Lee, Ted Shu Tak   <M1 WC>
   2/F Welland Plaza
   188 Nam Cheong Street
   Sham Shui Po, Kowloon, HONG KONG
   (852)2783-8923
   FAX: (852)2771-2726
   tedlee@taohsien.org.hk
Leung, Grace Siu Tim Yu   <M1 WC>
   2/F Welland Plaza
   188 Nam Cheong Street
   Sham Shui Po, Kowloon, HONG KONG
   (852)2783-8923
   FAX: (852)2771-2726
   yuleungsiutim@netvigator.com
Yu, Carver Tat Sum   <M1 WC>
   2/F Welland Plaza
   188 Nam Cheong Street
   Sham Shui Po, Kowloon, HONG KONG
   (852)2783-8923
   FAX: (852)2771-2726
   carver.yu@cgst.edu

OTHER LICENTIATES ON ROLL:

Cheung, Percy   <M2>
   G/F & 1/F 251 TinSam Village
   Tai Wai, Shatin, NT, HONG KONG
   (852)2693-3444
   FAX: (852)2607-2245
   percycheung@hotmail.com
Ho, Carmen   <M2>
   Tin Yuet Estate
   Tin Shui Wai NT, HONG KONG
   (852)2617-7872
   FAX: (852)2617-0287
   ho_carcar@yahoo.com.hk
Lam, Janice   <M2>
   G/F & 1/F 251 Tin Sum Village
   Tai Wai, Shatin NT, HONG KONG
   (852)2693-3444

FAX: (852)2607-2245
janiceyeung929@gmail.com
Lee, Priscilla   <M2>
   Tin Yuet Estate
   Tin Shui Wai NT, HONG KONG
   (852)2617-7872
   FAX: (852)2617-0287
   wai_yung_lee@yahoo.com.hk
Li, Chun Wai   <M2>
   1/Fl Block B
   14 TsatTsz Mui Road
   North Point, HONG KONG
   (852)2562-2148
   FAX: (852)2564-2898
   cwli2000hk@yahoo.com.hk
Liu, Lai Yuet   <M2>
   2/F Fu Tung Shopping Centre
   Tung Chung
   Lantau Island NT, HONG KONG
   (852)2109-1738
   FAX: (852)2109-1737
   laiyuet0914@gmail.com
Mak, Daphne Suet Chung   <M2>
   2/F Welland Plaza
   188 Nam Cheong Street
   Sham Shui Po, Kowloon, HONG KONG
   (852)2783-8923
   FAX: (852)2771-2726
   daphne@taohsien.org.hk
Tsui, Jackson   <M2>
   258 Carlos D'Assumpcao
   Ed Kin Heng Long 4 Andar LMN
   MACAU
   (853)2892-1702
   tsuih@yahoo.com
Wong, Samson Chi   <M2>
   2/F Fu Tung Shopping Centre
   Tung Chung
   Lantau Island NT, HONG KONG
   (852)2109-1738
   FAX: (852)2109-1737
   wongchishui@yahoo.com.hk
Yau, Chat Ming   <M2>
   G/F 251 Tin Sum Village
   Shatin NT, HONG KONG
   (852)2693-3444
   FAX: (852)2607-2245
   summerycm@yahoo.com.hk
Yuen, Susanna   <M2>
   28 Hong Yip Street
   Yuen Long, NT, HONG KONG
   (522)639-9176
   FAX: (522)639-5620
   susanna@yuenlongchurch.org
Yung, Karen Wing Man   <M2>
   Flat D 2/F
   338-340 Castle Peak Road
   Kowloon, HONG KONG
   (852)2386-6563
   FAX: (852)3020-0365
   yungyungmiss@yahoo.com.hk

OTHER CANDIDATES ON ROLL:

Hope Presbytery
SOUTHEAST SYNOD

GENERAL		MEMBERSHIP		CHANGES				FINANCES				
	1.Church Number	2.Active 3.Total 4.Church School		5.Prof. of Faith 6.Gains 7.Losses 8.Children Baptized				9. OUR UNITED OUT-REACH	10. Total Out-Reach Giving	11. All Other Expenses	12. Total Income Received	13. Value Church Prop. 1=1000
	1	2	3	4	5	6	7	8	9	10	11	12	13
Allsboro	0501	48	78	27	No Report Received			0	0	0	0	0	300
Baldwin Chapel	0202	45	65	20	6	11	0	0	0	3,838	29,709	33,546	200
Faith	0213	49	107	31	No Report Received			0	10,083	0	0	0	600
Florence 1st	0506	79	124	69	0	3	9	0	1,200	30,430	128,150	157,973	768
Hickory Grove	0507	26	37	16	No Report Received			0	0	0	0	0	150
Hurricane	0508	60	92	30	No Report Received			0	0	0	0	0	300
Maud	0509	10	4	0	No Report Received			0	0	0	0	0	90
Mt. Hester	0510	10	10	7	No Report Received			0	0	0	0	0	200
Mt. Pleasant	0511	7	7	7	0	0	2	0	0	3,200	17,100	30,000	270
Nebo	0512	34	34	24	1	2	2	1	0	1,000	69,220	68,978	1,200
Old Mt Bethel	0513	30	38	25	No Report Received			0	0	0	0	0	65
Park Terrace	0514	30	33	20	No Report Received			0	0	0	0	0	671
Rogersville 1st	0517	122	274	87	4	10	4	5	17,775	19,635	224,120	193,355	1,025
Springfield	0515	89	172	52	4	4	0	0	0	12,397	103,630	124,656	1,000
Union Hill	0516	77	112	51	9	9	2	0	0	14,240	73,343	84,257	1,500
Welti	0212	140	217	78	4	5	8	2	16,010	43,345	122,371	170,022	925
TOTALS	16	856	1,304	544	28	44	27	8	45,068	128,085	767,643	862,787	9,264

*Math error corrected. **Purged roll.

CHURCHES, PASTORS, AND CLERKS:

Allsboro   (4MEWC)SEHO0501
  515 Iuka Road (mailing)
  1925 Allsboro Road (physical)
  Cherokee, AL 35616
  (256)360-2919   <Colbert>
SS: Don F Thomas   <M1 OP>
  400 Park Hill Road
  Collierville, TN 38017
  (901)861-6398
  thomas63981@comcast.net
CL: Dale Johnson
  515 Iuka Road
  Cherokee, AL 35616
  (256)360-2973
  djohnson@bibank.com

Baldwin Chapel   (4MEWC)SEHO0202
  381 County Road 404 (mailing)
  126 County Road 1153 (physical)
  Cullman, AL 35057
  (256)737-1850   <Cullman>
PA: Howard Rodgers   <M1>
  336 County Road 1216
  Vinemont, AL 35179
  (256)739-6296
  djbr421@yahoo.com
AP: Gary Carter   <M1>
  8311 County Road 1082
  Vinemont, AL 35179
  (256)443-8389
  garycarter51@gmail.com
CL: Bonnie Marty
  381 County Road 404

Cullman, AL 35057
(256)734-6399
brmarty45@yahoo.com

Faith   (4WC)SEHO0213
  5821 County Road 1114 (mailing)
  Vinemont, AL 35179
  6880 AL Highway 157 (physical)
  Cullman, AL 35057
  (256)734-0893   <Cullman>
SS: Philip Nickles   <M1>
  5821 County Road 1114
  Vinemont, AL 35179
  (256)620-1977
  nickles.phil@yahoo.com
CL: Philip Nickles
  5821 County Road 1114
  Vinemont, AL 35179
  (256)620-1977
  nickles.phil@yahoo.com

Florence First   (4WC)SEHO0506
  2422 Darby Drive
  Florence, AL 35630
  (256)766-0471   <Lauderdale>
  FAX: (256)766-0736
  fcpoffice@comcast.net
PA: Dwayne McDuff   <M1>
  9770 County Road 5
  Florence, AL 35633
  (256)764-6354
  FAX: (256)766-0736
  fcpdmcduff@comcast.net
CL: Philip Gambrell
  1045 Piedmont Street
  Florence, AL 35630

(256)443-8924
pgambrell@ffcuonline.com

Hickory Grove   (4MC)SECU0507
  75 County Road 59
  Moulton, AL 35650
  (256)306-0025   <Lawrence>
  dhtatn4ybc@cs.com
PA: Tony Gaskin   <M1>
  1414 Saint Joseph Street NW
  Cullman, AL 35055
  (256)338-7893
  tgaskin46@hotmail.com
CL: Noah Williamson
  655 County Road 38
  Mount Hope, AL 35651
  (256)974-9413
  mwilliamson@lawrenceal.org

Hurricane   (4EWC)SEHO0508
  1331 County Road 86 (mailing)
  1000 County Road 156 (physical)
  Rogersville, AL 35652
  (256)247-7483   <Lauderdale>
PA: Jimmy R Cox   <M1>
  2250 County Road 156
  Anderson, AL 35610
  (256)710-1702
  dcox01@msn.com
CL: Bryan Belue
  1331 County Road 86
  Rogersville, AL 35652
  (256)247-7175
  rbeluebigboy@aol.com

Maud   (4MWC)SEHO0509

HOPE PRESBYTERY CONTINUED

2280 Maud Road (mailing)
Gypsy Loop (physical)
Cherokee, AL 35616
(256)360-2811   <Colbert>
CL: Paula Pardue
2280 Maud Road
Cherokee, AL 35616
(256)360-2811

Mt Hester   (4MEWC)SEHO0510
PO Box 174 (mailing)
14720 Mount Hester Road (physical)
Cherokee, AL 35616
( )   <Colbert>
CL: Leigh Ann Malone
2625 Sutton Hill Road
Cherokee, AL 35616
(256)359-6134
leighmalone05@yahoo.com

Mt Pleasant   (4MC)SEHO0511
30 Carolyn Road (mailing)
13575 County Line Road (physical)
Muscle Shoals, AL 35661
(256)446-5397   <Colbert>
SS: Tony Gaskin   <M1>
1414 Saint Joseph Street NW
Cullman, AL 35055
(256)338-7893
tgaskin46@hotmail.com
CL: James Letsinger
8285 2nd Street
Leighton, AL 35646
(256)446-9367

Nebo   (4MEWC)SEHO0512
9491 Highway 101
Lexington, AL 35648
(256)577-5952   <Lauderdale>
nebo9491@gmail.com
PA: Terry Herston   <M1>
390 County Road 95
Rogersville, AL 35652
(256)247-3004
tpaw51@gmail.com
CL: Gerald A McGee
9491 Highway 101
Lexington, AL 35648
(256)577-5952
nebo9491@gmail.com

Old Mt Bethel   (4C)SEHO0513
County Road 51
Rogersville, AL 35652
( )   <Lauderdale>
PA: Terry Herston   <M1>
390 County Road 95
Rogersville, AL 35652
(256)247-3004
tpaw51@gmail.com
CL: Tommy Word
620 County Road 521
Lexington, AL 35648
(256)247-3182
tword1956@gmail.com

Park Terrace   (4MEWC)SEHO0514
100 E Wheeler Avenue
Sheffield, AL 35660
(256)383-8052   <Colbert>
pastor@parkterracechurch.org

PA: George Lee   <M1>
104 Parc Circle
Florence, AL 35630
(256)740-0809
butchleeautos@yahoo.com
CL: Peggy Vickers
112 Pasadena Avenue
Muscle Shoals, AL 35661
(256)383-1992

Rogersville First   (4WC)SEHO0517
16751 Highway 72
Rogersville, AL 35652
(256)247-3339   <Lauderdale>
fcprogersville@yahoo.com
PA: James P Driskell   <M1>
154 Mountain Way
Anderson, AL 35610
(256)648-6758
FAX: (256)247-3339
patprespax@yahoo.com
CL: Kathy W Ezell
275 McGraw Circle
Anderson, AL 35610
(256)247-3625
kwhiteheadezell@aol.com

Springfield   (4MWC)SEHO0515
5400 Highway 101
Rogersville, AL 35652
(256)247-1424   <Lauderdale>
FAX: (256)247-1424
kennymorgan330@hotmail.com
PA: Kenneth P Morgan   <M1>
5400 Highway 101
Rogersville, AL 35652
(256)247-3890
FAX: (256)247-1424
kennymorgan330@hotmail.com
CL: Charles G Lash
170 Meadow Ridge Lane
Rogersville, AL 35652
(256)247-0040

Union Hill   (4MEWC)SEHO0516
6535 Bailey Road
Anderson, AL 35610
(256)233-1841   <Limestone>
PA: Charles Hood   <M1>
1200 County Road 519
Anderson, AL 35610
(256)229-6251
hooddad11@gmail.com
CL: Curtis Usery
28341 Easter Ferry Road
Lester, AL 35647
(256)232-9237

Welti   (4MWC)SEHO0212
8817 County Road 747
Cullman, AL 35055
(256)737-9138   <Cullman>
weltipastor@welticpchurch.com
PA: James L Peyton   <M1>
1455 County Road 643
Cullman, AL 35055
(256)735-3620
jakjpeyton@att.net
CL: Lee Holder
6589 County Road 747
Cullman, AL 35055

(256)739-5136
lholder@tvpinc.com

OTHERS ON MINISTERIAL ROLL:

Brock, Dudley   <M1 WC>
490 County Road 1184
Cullman, AL 35057
(256)734-0893
preacherbrock@att.net
Craig, Peggy Jean   <M1 WC>
825 S 13th Street Floor 2
Philadelphia, PA 19147
(256)277-1147
pjfpeggy@gmail.com
Deaton, John   <M1 WC>
277 School Lane
Springfield, PA 19064
(215)906-7067
deatonjr11@gmail.com
Malone, John W   <M1 RT>
3693 Highway 67 South
Sommerville, AL 35670
(256)778-8237
Parker, Susan   <M1 WC>
655 York Drive
Rogersville, AL 35652
(256)247-3877
park9301@bellsouth.net
Yaple, George H   <M1 RT>
2051 Lost Creek Road
Carbon Hill, AL 35549
(205)924-9921

OTHER LICENTIATES ON ROLL:

OTHER CANDIDATES ON ROLL:

Japan Presbytery
MISSION SYNOD

GENERAL		MEMBERSHIP			CHANGES				FINANCES				
1.Church Number	2.Active	3.Total	4.Church School	5.Prof. of Faith	6.Gains	7.Losses	8.Children Baptized	9. OUR UNITED OUT-REACH	10. Total Out-Reach Giving	11. All Other Expenses	12. Total Income Received	13. Value Church Prop. 1=1000	
	1	2	3	4	5	6	7	8	9	10	11	12	13
Asahi Mission	8315	27	27	7	0	2	1	0	831	1,275	27,802	29,077	7
Den-en Mission	8310	14	40	15	1	1	2	0	284	1,010	52,025	30,052	70
EbinaShionNoOka	8311	105	164	40	1	1	2	1	3,207	19,668	77,884	93,545	73
Higashi Koganei	8301	30	36	4	1	2	1	0	1,036	4,626	56,778	50,117	130
Ichikawa Grace	8314	16	21	8	2	2	0	0	420	901	51,720	28,957	45
Izumi	8312	25	39	7	1	1	4	0	528	3,741	38,212	41,953	19
Kibougaoka	8302	170	332	110	2	3	5	0	4,972	32,211	108,749	260,633	471
Koza*	8303	522	1,135	412	15	18	41	0	16,833	113,630	564,326	677,303	1,512
KunitachiNozomi	8306	63	104	50	2	2	3	0	2,135	10,012	73,313	83,475	170
Mata De	8313	31	56	22	0	0	4	0	416	885	57,218	29,086	17
Megumi	8309	39	48	7	1	1	2	0	1,416	6,349	59,361	59,308	72
Naruse	8305	55	118	14	1	1	1	0	2,003	9,994	64,810	73,478	96
Sagamino	8304	29	56	11	0	0	0	0	1,280	4,251	36,467	35,716	174
Shibusawa	8307	38	102	20	2	2	1	0	1,754	6,476	58,474	68,189	273
TOTALS	14	1,164	2,278	727	29	36	67	1	37,115	215,029	1,309,159	1,460,889	3,129

*Math error corrected. **Purged roll.

CHURCHES, PASTORS, AND CLERKS:

Asahi Mission   (4F)MSJA8315
 1F Miyabi-Bldg
 1-19-21 Honcho Tsurugamine
 Asahi-ku Yokohama, Kanagawa-Ken
 241-0021 JAPAN
 (045)489-3720   <Japan>
 FAX: (045)953-2588
 asahi_ch@yahoo.co.jp
PA: Atsushi Suzuki   <M1>
 53-17 Higashi Kibogaoka Asahi-ku
 Yokohama, Kanagawa-ken
 241-0826 JAPAN
 (045)362-2603
 FAX: (045)362-2603
 asyuwa98@m10.alpha-net.ne.jp
CL: Session Clerk Asahi Mission Point
 1F Miyabi-Bldg
 1-19-21 Honcho Tsurugamine
 Asahi-ku Yokohama, Kanagawa-Ken
 241-0021 JAPAN
 (045)489-3720
 FAX: (045)953-2588
 asahi_ch@yahoo.co.jp

Den-en Mission   (4MC)MSJA8310
 9-41-2 Kamitsuruma-honcho
 Sagamihara-Shi, Kanagawa-Ken
 228-0818 JAPAN
 (042)744-6804   <Japan>
 FAX: (042)744-6804
 den-en@church.ne.jp
PA: Kazuhiko Furuhata   <M1>
 #310, 9-41-15 Kamitsurumahoncho
 Sagamihara-shi, Kanagawa-ken
 252-0318 JAPAN
 (042)814-7802

FAX: (042)814-7802
cpc.furuhata@gmail.com
CL: Takashi Kanazashi
 3-6-406 Shimoyuzuki
 Hachiouji-shi, Tokyo
 197-0732 JAPAN
 (042)675-6895
 fredericfchopin@gmail.com

Ebina Shion No Oka (4MWC)MSJA8311
 3-17-57 Nakashinden
 Ebina-shi, Kanagawa-ken
 243-0422 JAPAN
 (046)234-3426   <Japan>
 ebinazion@gmail.com
PA: Yukio Tamai   <M1>
 3-17-57 Nakashinden
 Ebina-shi, Kanagawa-ken
 243-0422 JAPAN
 (046)234-3426
 yukiotamai@me.com
CL: Hiroko Fushimi
 2-4-7 Rinkan Yamato-shi
 Kanagawa-ken
 242-0003 JAPAN
 (046)275-3801
 FAX: (046)725-3801
 hrkfsm@hotmail.com

Higashi Koganei   (4MWC)MSJA8301
 2-14-16 Higashi-cho
 Koganei-shi, Tokyo
 184-0011 JAPAN
 (042)231-1279   <Japan>
 FAX: (042)231-1279
PA: Shigeru Katsuki   <M1>
 2-14-16 Higashi-cho
 Koganei-shi, Tokyo
 184-0011 JAPAN

(042)232-3640
shigeru.katsuki@nifty.com
CL: Eiko Imai
 3-4-19 Higashi-cho
 Koganei-shi, Tokyo
 184-0011 JAPAN
 (042)232-1417

Ichikawa Grace Mission (4MF)MSJA8314
 1-11-20 Kokubu
 Ichikawa-shi, Chiba-ken
 272-0834 JAPAN
 (047)369-7540   <Japan>
 FAX: (047)369-7540
 ichikawa-grace@mbi.nifty.com
PA: Yasuo Masuda   <M1>
 1-11-20 Kokubu
 Ichikawa-shi, Chiba-ken
 272-0834 JAPAN
 (047)369-7540
 FAX: (047)369-7540
 fwgc6854@mb.infoweb.ne.jp
CL: Session Clerk Ichikawa Grace Mission
 1-11-20 Kokubu
 Ichikawa-shi, Chiba-ken
 272-0834 JAPAN
 (047)369-7540
 FAX: (047)369-7540

Izumi   (4WC)MSJA8312
 4194-13 Izumi-cho Izumi-ku
 Yokohama, Kanagawa-ken
 245-0016 JAPAN
 (045)803-1749   <Japan>
 FAX: (045)361-4351
 izumi@kyokai.org
PA: Kenji Ushioda   <M1>
 2-47-3 Akuwa-higashi Seya-ku
 Yokohama, Kanagawa-ken

JAPAN PRESBYTERY CONTINUED

243-0023 JAPAN
(046)361-4351
ushioda@jc.ejnet.ne.jp
CL: Kenji Ushioda
2-47-3 Akuwa-higashi Seya-ku
Yokohama, Kanagawa-ken
246-0023 JAPAN
(046)361-4351
FAX: (045)361-4351
ushioda@jc.ejet.ne.jp

_____

Kibougaoka   (4WMC)MSJA8302
72-2 Naka Kibogaoka
Asahi-ku Yokohama, Kanagawa-ken
241-0825 JAPAN
(045)391-6038   <Japan>
FAX: (045)391-6653
PA: Ryuzo Matsuya   <M1>
72-2 Naka Kibogaoka Asahi-ku
Yokohama, Kanagawa-ken
241-0825 JAPAN
(045)364-8297
matsuya.r@woody.ocn.ne.jp
CL: Kazuhiro Ohashi
2-50-16 Akuwa-Higashi
Seya-ku Yokohama, Kanagawa-ken
246-0023 JAPAN
(045)363-4923
k_0084@nifty.com

_____

Koza   (4MWC)MSJA8303
2-14-1 Minami Rinkan
Yamato-shi, Kanagawa-ken
242-0006 JAPAN
(046)724-1370   <Japan>
FAX: (046)276-9685
cpckoza@koza-church.jp
PA: Masahiro Matsumoto   <M1>
2-14-1 Minami Rinkan
Yamato-shi, Kanagawa-ken
242-0006 JAPAN
(046)275-2767
matsumoto@koza-church.jp
AP: Nobuko Seki   <M1>
4-12-42-403 Shimorenjyaku
Mitaka-shi
242-0004 JAPAN
(042)248-5379
seki@koza-church.jp
CL: Yutaka Shibata
1-18-3 Rinkan Yamato-shi
Kanagawa-ken
241-0003 JAPAN
(046)272-0579
shibata@koza-church.jp

_____

Kunitachi Nozomi   (4MWC)MSJA8306
3-15-9 Higashi
Kunitachi-shi, Tokyo
186-0002 JAPAN
(042)572-7616   <Japan>
FAX: (042)572-7616
nozomi-ch@ceres.ocn.ne.jp
PA: Kenta Karasawa   <M1>
3-15-10 Higashi
Kunitachi-shi, Tokyo
186-0002 JAPAN
(042)575-5549
FAX: (042)575-5549
k-kenta@roy.hi-ho.ne.jp
CL: Keita Komine

3-26-16 Higashi
Kunitachi-shi, Tokyo
186-0002 JAPAN
(042)507-9971
bgmgb65@gmail.com

_____

Mata De Sao Joao   (4MC)MSJA8313
Nucleo Colonial JK
Lote 56 Mata De Sao Joao
48280-000, Bahia, BRAZIL
(5571)9641-1307   <JAPAN>
PA: Keishi Ishitsuka   <M1>
Nucleo Colonial JK
Lote 56 Mata De Sao Joao
48280-000, Bahia, BRAZIL
(5571)9641-1307
kishitsuka@hotmail.com
CL: Shinnichi Hizumi
Nucleo Colonial JK
Lote 56 Mata De Sao Joao
48280-000, Bahia, BRAZIL
(5571)3664-1037
hizumi@uol.com.br

_____

Megumi   (4MWC)MSJA8309
3-355-4 Kami Kitadai Higashi
Yamato-shi, Tokyo
207-0023 JAPAN
(042)564-0593   <Japan>
FAX: (042)567-2977
megumikyokai@gmail.com
PA: Makihiko Arase   <M1>
3-355-4 Kamikitadai Higashi
Yamato-shi, Tokyo
207-0023 JAPAN
(042)567-2977
FAX: (042)567-2977
viator@cb3.so-net.ne.jp
CL: Takao Uchida
4-1505-2 Imokubo
Higashiyamato-shi, Tokyo
2074-0033 JAPAN
(042)567-0145
u-tko47@m3.dion.ne.jp

_____

Naruse   (4WC)MSJA8305
7-20-12 Tamagawa Gakuen
Machida-shi, Tokyo
194-0041 JAPAN
(042)725-9909   <Japan>
FAX: (042)725-9909
cpc-naruse@nifty.com
PA: Yoshimasa Niwa   <M1>
15-402 Narakita Danchi
2913 Naramachi Aoba-ku
Kanagawa-ken, Yokohama
227-0036 JAPAN
(045)961-1540
rsb09335@nifty.com
CL:Toru Abe
5-18-14 Nara Aboba-ku
Yokohama-shi, Kanagawa-ken
227-0038 JAPAN
(045)961-8620
FAX: (045)961-8620
abe.tooru@rouge.plala.or.jp

_____

Sagamino   (4MWC)MSJA8304
4-13-24 Higashihara
Zama-shi, Kanagawa-ken
228-0004 JAPAN

(046)255-6441   <Japan>
FAX: (046)255-6441
sagamino@church.jp
PA: Takehiko Miyai   <M1>
A-201 2-2-48 Higashihara Zama-shi
Kanagawa-ken
228-0004 JAPAN
(046)207-6558
FAX: (046)256-3212
CL: Akimasa Nakano
1-105 Sagaminosakura 5-1
Higashihara Zama-shi
Kanagawa-ken
228-0004 JAPAN
(046)254-8564
nakano.a.ipt@gmail.com

_____

Shibusawa   (4MWC)MSJA8307
1-8-50 Magarimatsu
Hadano-shi, Kanagawa-ken
259-1321 JAPAN
(046)387-1203   <Japan>
FAX: (046)387-1203
PA: Keitaro Ohi   <M1>
1-8-50 Magarimatsu
Hadano-shi, Kanagawa-ken
259-1321 JAPAN
(046)387-1203
FAX: (046)387-1203
keitaro_o@hotmail.com
CL: Kiyoshi Kumon
3-26-5 Shibusawa
Hadano-shi, Kanagawa-ken
259-1322 JAPAN
(046)388-3609
kiyokumon@yahoo.co.jp

_____

OTHERS ON MINISTERIAL ROLL:

Asayama, Masaharu   <M1 RT>
6-3-2-308 Toyogaoka
Tama-shi, Tokyo
206-0031 JAPAN
(042)373-2710
asa@ipcc-21.com
Hamazaki, Takashi   <M1 RT>
1551-1-202 Inokuchi
Nakai-cho Ashigarakami-gun
Kanagawa-ken
259-0151 JAPAN
(046)387-1203
FAX: (046)387-1203
gen22-14@qf7.so-net.ne.jp
Ikushima, Michinobu   <M1 RT>
2074 Nakashinden
Ebina-Shi, Kanagawa-Ken
243-0422 JAPAN
(046)232-9888
m.ikushima@tbz.t-com.ne.jp
Satoh, Iwao   <M1 OM>
8710 Hickory Falls Lane
Pewee Valley, KY 40056
iwaosatoh@gmail.com
(502)210-0852
Yano, Fumitsuta   <M1 WC>
424-4 Kamide, Fjinomiya-shi
Shuizuika-ken   JAPAN
(054)454-0313

_____

OTHER LICENTIATES ON ROLL:

Suzuki, Temote   <M2>

JAPAN PRESBYTERY CONTINUED

9-41-15-310 Honcho Kamitsuruma
Sagamihara-shi, Kanagawa-ken
228-0818 JAPAN
timocsuzuki@gmail.com
Miyajima, Atsushi   \<M2\>
  Rua Araja
  58 Paraiso Sao Joa
  48280-000, Bahia, BRAZIL
  (5571)3664-1037
  ariel.atsushi@gmail.com

Taira, Masanori
  Japan Biblical Theological Seminary
  2-14-1 Minami Rinkan
  Yamoto-shi, Kanagawa-ken
  242-0006 JAPAN
Wada, Ichiro   \<M3\>
  Tokyo Christian University
  3-301-5 Uchino Inzai-shi, Chiba
  270-1347 JAPAN
  (047)646-1141
  ichirowada@gmail.com

OTHER CANDIDATES ON ROLL:

Inoh, Yuki   \<M3\>
  Tokyo Christian University
  3-301-5 Uchino Inzai-shi, Chiba
  270-1347 JAPAN
  (047)646-1141
  yuki_inoh0615@yahoo.co.jp
Miyagi, Ken
  Tokyo Christian University
  3-301-5 Uchino Inzai-shi, Chiba
  270-1347 JAPAN

Missouri Presbytery
GREAT RIVERS SYNOD

	GENERAL	MEMBERSHIP			CHANGES			FINANCES				
	1.Church Number	2.Active	3.Total	4.Church School	5.Prof. of Faith	6.Gains	7.Losses	8.Children Baptized	9. OUR UNITED OUT-REACH	10. Total Out-Reach Giving	11. All Other Expenses	12. Total Income Received	13. Value Church Prop. 1=1000
	1	2	3	4	5	6	7	8	9	10	11	12	13
Bethel	4102	7	7	7	0	0	1	0	100	4,158	5,753	12,361	10
Elk Creek	4304	19	20	16	0	0	0	0	0	500	21,599	23,159	75
Greenfield*	4104	14	14	7	14	20	13	5	0	4,129	40,219	11,564	120
Happy Home	4306	14	24	0	0	0	8	0	2,444	5,631	17,490	23,121	200
Harmony	4203	25	42	8	2	7	1	1	2,768	6,226	26,246	35,168	80
Hopewell	4105	34	34	27	0	2	2	1	4,176	13,172	33,283	37,959	310
Lobb	4209	13	13	14	No Report Received			0	0	0	0	0	170
Mansfield	4308	54	73	30	No Report Received			0	0	0	0	0	75
Marshall	4210	105	206	38	0	14	3	0	12,288	40,911	122,951	122,881	1,000
Montrose	4107	2	17	0	Closing 2015			0	0	0	0	0	32
New Hope (DeC)	4309	17	17	9	2	0	9	0	0	3,597	18,695	21,585	60
Orange	4108	39	39	47	1	2	0	0	2,500	2,907	59,759	73,480	780
Phillipsburg	4311	9	13	6	4	0	1	0	2,000	3,854	13,178	20,234	150
Pierson	4312	10	12	6	0	0	1	0	1,758	9,611	5,960	17,180	125
Pleasant Grove	4109	8	59	0	No Report Received			0	0	0	0	0	30
Salem	4216	9	9	9	0	0	0	0	0	221	8,300	9,644	125
Seymour	4313	15	29	6	No Report Received			0	0	0	0	0	50
Shawnee Mound	4111	4	39	6	0	0	5	0	707	1,251	4,759	7,068	60
Spring Creek	4113	28	36	15	0	0	1	0	3,930	14,650	26,277	42,735	182
Springfield 1st	4314	57	115	45	5	7	51	0	4,656	24,402	97,270	90,382	1,500
Warrensburg	4115	71	71	22	0	0	1	0	1,500	5,918	38,634	51,853	300
White Oak Pond	4315	110	202	81	2	4	30	1	15,983	28,450	104,877	159,825	2,150
TOTALS	22	664	1,091	399	30	58	120	8	54,810	173,668	645,230	760,198	7,584

*Math error corrected. **Purged roll.

CHURCHES, PASTORS, AND CLERKS:

_____

Bethel   (2C)GRMI4102
  14621 Lawrence 1032 (mailing)
  Sarcoxie, MO 64862
  Crossroads Lawrence 1030 & Lawrence 2170 (physical)
  Wentworth, MO
  (417)285-6571   <Lawrence>
SS: Tim Steeley   <M3>
  PO Box 281
  Mt Vernon, MO 65712
  (417)466-4345
  tsteeley@swr5.k12.mo.us
CL: Lana Moore
  14621 Lawrence 1032
  Sarcoxie, MO 64862
  (417)285-6571
  lanajeanmoore@hotmail.com

_____

Elk Creek   (4MEC)GRMI4304
  7423 County Road 3730 (mailing)
  Peace Valley, MO 65788
  US Highway 160 E (physical)
  West Plains, MO 65775
  (417)257-0983   <Howell>
  pastorbrown44@yahoo.com
PA: Dale M Brown   <M1 RT>
  HC 61 Box 4740
  West Plains, MO 65775
  (417)257-0983

  pastorbrown44@yahoo.com
CL: Cindy Rasor
  7423 County Road 3730
  Peace Valley, MO 65788
  (417)256-7353
  rrasor@centurytel.net

_____

Greenfield   (4MC)GRMI4104
  423 Water Street (mailing)
  417 W Water Street (physical)
  Greenfield, MO 65661
  ( )   <Dade>
CL: Debra Kay Bartlett
  423 Water Street
  Greenfield, MO 65661
  (417)637-5678
  debrakaybartlett@gmail.com

_____

Happy Home   (4C)GRMI4306
  510 S Newport Avenue (mailing)
  5604 State Highway ZZ (physical)
  Conway, MO 65632
  ( )   <Webster>
CL: Rex Luallin
  510 S Newport Avenue
  Conway, MO 65632
  (417)589-3804

_____

Harmony   (4WC)GRMI4203
  3508 Scott Street (mailing)
  Saint Joseph, MO 64507

SE State Road Z (physical)
San Antonio, MO 64443
(816)279-0733   <Buchanan>
orvalschafer@aol.com
OD: Marion Cannon   <M5>
  4248 SW State Route N
  Stewartsville, MO 64490
  (816)449-2437
  orvalschafer@aol.com
CL: Viola Schafer
  3508 Scott Street
  Saint Joseph, MO 64507
  (816)279-0733
  orvalschafer@aol.com

_____

Hopewell   (4EWC)GRMI4105
  248 NE 50th Road (mailing)
  273 NE 50th Road (physical)
  Lamar, MO 64759
  (417)682-2396   <Barton>
  FAX: (417)682-3514
  parrishron@att.net
OD: George Haag   <M5>
  301 Gulf Street
  Lamar, MO 64759
  (417)682-3876
CL: Reba Simmons
  63 E Highway C
  Lamar, MO 64759
  (417)884-2810

_____

MISSOURI PRESBYTERY CONTINUED

Lobb   (4MC)GRMI4209
 1410 W Walnut Street(mailing)
 Flynn Road & 7-Highway (physical)
 Independence, MO 64050
 ( )   <Jackson>
OD: Paul J Petralie   <M5>
 1409 Granite Creek Drive
 Blue Springs, MO 64015
 (816)229-2804
CL: Pamela Markey
 1419 W Walnut Street
 Independence, MO 64050
 (816)254-1130
 pammarkey@sbcglobal.net

Mansfield   (4MEC)GRMI4308
 PO Box 673 (mailing)
 307 S Phelps Avenue (physical)
 Mansfield, MO 65704
 ( )   <Wright>
OD: S Larry Scott   <M5>
 2211 Airport Road
 Mansfield, MO 65704
 (417)924-4390
 revslscott@gmail.com
CL: Leon Veenstra
 4680 Highway F
 Hartville, MO 65667
 (417)741-7408
 veenstra@getgoin.net

Marshall   (4MWC)GRMI4210
 1000 S Miami
 Marshall, MO 65340
 (660)886-2402   <Saline>
 pastor_randy_shannon@yahoo.com
PA: Randy Shannon   <M1>
 30282 Highway H
 Marshall, MO 65340
 (660)886-9454
 pastor_randy.shannon@yahoo.com
CL: Brenda Guthrie
 28 Cattle Drive
 Slater, MO 65349
 (660)529-2420
 blguthrie1949@hotmail.com

Montrose   (4MWC)GRMI4107
 204 Kansas
 Montrose, MO 64770
 (816)693-4612   <Henry>
 (closing 2015)
OD: Ron Beardon   <M5>
 214 E 3rd Street
 Appleton City, MO 64724
 (660)476-5322
CL: Kathy Collins
 1542 SW H Highway
 Montrose, MO 64770
 (660)693-4689
 collinsmailbox@yahoo.com

New Hope (DeC)   (4WC)GRMI4309
 230 County Road 2630 (mailing)
 Dent County Road 6200 (physical)
 Salem, MO 65560
 ( )   <Dent>
SS: Michael Reno   <M3>
 52 Rolla Gardens
 Rolla, MO 65401
 (573)578-5321

rollarenomike@gmail.com
CL: Fay J Haxton
 230 County Road 2630
 Salem, MO 65560
 (573)729-5524
 rafay@embarkmail.com

Orange   (4WC)GRMI4108
 109 Agnes (mailing)
 Crane, MO 65633
 15743 Highway K (physical)
 Aurora, MO 65605
 (417)678-5220   <Lawrence>
OD: Joe Wolven   <M5>
 1134 Carico Road
 Galena, MO 65656
 (417)357-4004
 lestesx5@centurytel.net
CL: Leah Estes
 109 Agnes
 Crane, MO 65633
 (417)723-8033
 lestesx5@centurytel.net

Phillipsburg   (4WC)GRMI4311
 11187 Cuba Road (mailing)
 Grovespring, MO 65662
 Grover Street (physical)
 Phillipsburg, MO 65722
 ( )   <Laclede>
CL: Cheryl Brown
 11187 Cuba Drive
 Grovespring, MO 65662
 (417)462-0813
 brownc@hartville.k12.mo.us

Pierson   (4C)GRMI4312
 12754 State Highway M (mailing)
 Billings, MO 65610
 45129 State Highway 413 (physical)
 Billings, MO 65610
 (417)369-2104   <Stone>
OD: George Van Hooser   <M5>
 1839 E Lark Street
 Springfield, MO 65804
CL: Kary Crumpley
 1513 Crumpley Drive
 Marionville, MO 65705
 (417)839-3552
 karycrumpley@gmail.com

Pleasant Grove   (4C)GRMI4109
 PO Box 97 (mailing)
 891 SE Y Highway (physical)
 Knob Noster, MO 65336
 ( )   <Johnson>
 gary.moore@reagan.com
LS: Gary M. Moore
 PO Box 97
 Knob Noster, MO 65336
 (816)830-9308
 gary.moore@reagan.com
CL:Gary M. Moore
 PO Box 97
 Knob Noster, MO 65336
 (816)830-9308
 gary.moore@reagan.com

Salem   (4WC)GRMI4216
 211 NW County Road OO (mailing)
 382 NW County Road H (physical)

Warrensburg, MO 64093
 ( )   <Johnson>
CL: Anne Patrick
 211 NW County Road OO
 Warrensburg, MO 64093
 (660)747-8902
 apatrick52@hotmail.com

Seymour   (4C)GRMI4313
 PO Box 40 (mailing)
 222 Main Street (physical)
 Seymour, MO 65746
 (417)935-2235   <Webster>
OD: Sam Burt   <M5>
 102 E Summit Avenue
 Seymour, MO 65746
 (417)735-2759
CL: Denise Burt
 102 E Summit Avenue
 Seymour, MO 65746
 (417)300-6451
 gerrydburt@gmail.com

Shawnee Mound   (4WC)GRMI4111
 72 NW 1150 Road
 Chilhowee, MO 64733
 ( )   <Henry>
LS: Gary Moore   <M6>
 PO Box 97
 Knob Noster, MO 65336
 (660)563-5675
 garymoore@reagan.com
CL: Doris Hunter
 62 NW 1150 Road
 Chilhowee, MO 64733
 (660)885-3709
 dfhunter@embarqmail.com

Spring Creek   (4EWC)GRMI4113
 307 E 365th Road (mailing)
 Hwy 123 & Hwy A Junction (physical)
 Dunnegan, MO 65640
 (417)754-8498   <Polk>
OD: Scott Garner   <M5>
 1403 E Primrose Lane
 Republic, MO 65738
 (417)732-4218
CL: Gary M Roetto
 307 E 365th Road
 Dunnegan, MO 65640
 (417)754-8498

Springfield First   (4MWC)GRMI4314
 4216 S Charleston Avenue
 Springfield, MO 65804
 (417)883-4248   <Greene>
PA: Andrew (Andy) Eppard   <M1>
 1427 W McGee Street
 Springfield, MO 65807
 (417)862-6434
 reformedminister@yahoo.com
AP: Sang Hoon Park   <M1>
 3504 W Shawnee Drive
 Springfield, MO 65810
 (417)888-0442
CL: Carol Fare
 302 N Market Street
 Nixa, MO 65714
 (417)725-2775
 cjfare52@sbcglobal.net

MISSOURI PRESBYTERY CONTINUED

Warrensburg   (4WC)GRMI4115
  201 Grover Street
  Warrensburg, MO 64093
  (660)747-3021   <Johnson>
PA: Randy Crawshaw   <M1>
  136 NE 1271 Road
  Knob Noster, MO 65336
  (660)563-5149
  randy_crawshaw@yahoo.com
CL: Dana Moore
  113 Larkin Street
  Warrensburg, MO 64093
  (660)747-8777
  djmoore@iland.net

White Oak Pond   (4MWC)GRMI4315
  16549 Highway 5 (mailing)
  16551 Highway 5 (physical)
  Lebanon, MO 65536
  (417)532-5049   <Laclede>
  wopcpc@whiteoakpond.org
PA: Terry Hansen   <M1>
  16549 Highway 5
  Lebanon, MO 65536
  (417)533-8106
  thansen@whiteoakpond.org
CL: Janie Lewis
  1931 King James Drive
  Lebanon, MO 65536
  (417)664-6357

OTHERS ON MINISTERIAL ROLL:

Ang, John   <M1 RT>
  5843 S Farm Road 157
  Springfield, MO 65810
  (417)886-3487
  pastorcares@yahoo.com
Appling, John   <M1 WC>
  1722 S Fairway Avenue
  Springfield, MO 65804
  (417)877-4643
  pegblessings@sbcglobal.net

Appling, Peggy   <M1 WC>
  1722 S Fairway
  Springfield, Missouri 65804
  (417)877-4643
  pegblessings@sbcglobal.net
Bone, Leslie   <M1 M9>
  16504 E George Franklin Drive
  Independence, MO 64055
  (816)373-6625
  lesliebone@comcast.net
Campbell, Gordon C   <M1 WC>
  1469 E Wayland Street
  Springfield, MO 65804
  (417)823-9567
  gofor12@gmail.com
Harris, Edward   <M1 RT>
  10000 Wornall Road Apt 2315
  Kansas City, MO 64114
  (816)214-8977
  ed121@kcrr.com
Plachte, Richard   <M1 RT>
  615 Grover Street
  Warrensburg, MO 64093
  (660)441-4427
  rap@aerobiz.org
Rodden, Linda   <M1 WC>
  363 Cornelison Street
  Lebanon, MO 65536
  (417)588-2207
  linda.rodden@mercy.net
Wieland, Jack G, Jr   <M1 WC>
  PO Box 116
  Napoleon, MO 64074
  (217)823-4331
  jgwieland@hotmail.com

OTHER LICENTIATES ON ROLL:

Carr, Jill   <M2>
  PO Box 1547
  Lebanon, MO 65536
  (417)532-6760
  dig.micah.6.8@gmail.com

OTHER CANDIDATES ON ROLL:

Gibbons, Jeannette   <M3>
  6204 S Haynes Avenue
  Ozark, MO 65721
  (417)889-9862
Griffin, Adam   <M3>
  23502 Clinton Road
  Lebanon, MO 65536
  (417)588-2522
  plowboy3500@hotmail.com
Grounds, Clint   <M3>
  918 Stonewall Apt C
  McKenzie, TN 38201
  (731)415-1422
Roedder, Unhui Grace   <M3>
  419 S Jonathan Avenue
  Springfield, MO 65802
  (417)494-6491
Wolf, Matthew   <M3>
  1178 S Salt Pond
  Marshall, MO 65340
  (660)202-3762

Murfreesboro Presbytery
TENNESSEE SYNOD

	GENERAL	MEMBERSHIP			CHANGES				FINANCES				
	1.Church Number	2.Active	3.Total	4.Church School	5.Prof. of Faith	6.Gains	7.Losses	8.Children Baptized	9. OUR UNITED OUT-REACH	10. Total Out-Reach Giving	11. All Other Expenses	12. Total Income Received	13. Value Church Prop. 1=1000
	1	2	3	4	5	6	7	8	9	10	11	12	13
Algood	7201	21	29	6	No Report Received			0	0	0	0	0	180
Banks	7202	14	14	16	0	0	1	0	1,100	4,942	23,720	32,800	344
Bates Hill*	7203	66	103	37	No Report Received			0	6,037	0	0	0	325
Beech Grove	7204	20	20	10	No Report Received			0	250	0	0	0	423
Belvidere	7205	7	47	7	0	0	0	0	0	325	7,416	6,929	60
Blues Hill	7207	21	33	19	1	1	0	0	5,466	9,821	23,697	33,100	80
Cloyd's**	7208	97	97	45	0	18	28	0	5,000	5,020	199,490	182,814	2,500
Commerce	7209	62	62	42	0	0	0	0	3,000	3,600	54,043	66,074	425
Cookeville 1st	7210	555	629	250	10	12	15	4	51,513	110,596	403,936	514,532	4,600
Cowan	7211	59	72	44	5	18	4	2	10,329	18,376	93,711	112,087	1,880
Dibrell	7212	7	9	9	0	0	0	0	0	0	9,908	12,253	35
Dry Valley	7213	8	10	10	0	0	0	0	0	3,856	6,195	10,051	10
Goshen	7214	95	95	45	No Report Received			0	3,500	0	0	0	874
Gum Creek*	7215	23	23	12	1	4	0	1	300	1,055	22,000	25,461	130
Harmony	7216	61	100	54	2	2	1	1	11,348	22,240	84,794	124,796	1,041
Hickory Valley*	7251	9	9	21	No Report Received			0	0	0	0	0	0
Hillsboro	7217	16	18	6	No Report Received			0	0	0	0	0	250
Jerusalem	7218	43	131	26	0	3	3	0	9,092	13,232	108,656	90,916	275
Joywood	7250	25	36	12	No Report Received			0	0	0	0	0	375
LaGuardo	7219	25	25	3	No Report Received			0	0	0	0	0	150
Lebanon	7220	313	491	230	2	17	7	4	23,000	41,528	338,001	387,774	4,000
Liberty	7222	106	147	56	1	3	2	0	12,866	25,993	115,803	128,562	989
Livingston 1st	7223	10	42	3	No Report Received			0	0	0	0	0	250
LuzD.L.Naciones**	7252	9	20	23	No Report Received			0	0	0	0	0	0
Manchester**	7224	98	221	75	2	2	14	0	19,761	30,384	160,989	197,609	1,300
McMinnville*	7225	12	14	9	No Report Received			0	672	0	0	0	225
Monteagle	7227	5	5	0	0	0	0	0	0	0	7,225	7,305	70
Mt. Carmel*	7228	11	23	0	0	0	7	0	0	947	13,195	15,520	350
Mt. Hermon	7229	9	18	10	No Report Received			0	0	0	0	0	200
Mt. Tabor	7230	32	33	0	0	0	1	0	3,946	7,991	26,950	40,450	138
Mt. Vernon	7231	32	37	26	No Report Received			0	0	0	0	0	410
Murfreesboro	7232	153	415	102	4	9	13	0	12,061	35,341	277,899	299,348	3,245
New Hope	7233	60	68	40	3	5	3	0	200	2,156	84,305	83,000	1,022
Old Zion	7234	10	10	9	0	0	1	0	400	1,836	23,055	24,736	300
Owens Chapel	7235	60	74	14	3	11	2	2	0	6,532	101,341	113,429	210
Providence	7238	14	14	38	No Report Received			0	0	0	0	0	150
Rockvale	7239	82	148	55	1	2	4	0	2,000	5,592	78,532	84,124	1,308
Rocky Glade	7240	67	74	57	4	11	13	2	3,500	10,591	39,318	55,665	350
Ruth Chapel	7241	2	5	0	No Report Received			0	0	0	0	0	3
Sewanee*	7242	22	28	12	No Report Received			0	1,634	0	0	0	225
Smithville	7243	153	167	102	7	16	97	6	22,800	61,700	166,200	224,300	1,700
Suggs Creek	7244	8	8	0	2	4	5	0	200	200	17,278	20,660	120
Union Hill	7246	48	70	52	0	1	1	0	1,156	6,429	51,352	57,781	250
Watertown	7247	12	12	9	0	0	2	0	500	1,223	13,873	17,563	458
Winchester 1st	7249	480	915	450	No Report Received			0	58,179	0	0	0	3,500
TOTALS	45	3,042	4,621	2,046	48	139	224	22	269,810	431,866	2,572,882	2,969,639	34,730

*Math error corrected. **Purged roll.

MURFREESBORO PRESBYTERY CONTINUED

CHURCHES, PASTORS, AND CLERKS:

___

Algood (4WC)TNMU7201
3617 Burton Cove Road (mailing)
Cookeville, TN 38506
Corner Harp & Main Street (physical)
Algood, TN 38506
( ) <Putnam>
PA: Richard Bond <M1>
2425 Fisk Road, Lot 0
Cookeville, TN 38506
(931)526-7610
erbond@frontier.net
CL: Elaine Burton
3617 Burton Cove Road
Cookeville, TN 38506
(931)537-6661
e_burton@frontier.com

___

Banks (4MWC)TNMU7202
846 Luttrell Avenue (mailing)
2933 Banks Pisgah Road (physical)
Smithville, TN 37166
( ) <DeKalb>
SS: Greg Whaley <M3>
4970 Comstock Road
Chapel Hill, TN 37034
(931)364-7637
grewha@mail.com
CL: Robert Joins
846 Luttrell Avenue
Smithville, TN 37166
(615)597-6366
b_joins@hotmail.com

___

Bates Hill (4MEWC)TNMU7203
9957 Nashville Highway
Mc Minnville, TN 37110
(931)939-3235 <Warren>
cavecrew1979@gmail.com
SS: Blake Stephens <M1>
9980 Nashville Highway
Mc Minnville, TN 37110
(931)939-2628
blsteph@edge.net
CL: William R Black
205 Ben Lomond Drive
Mc Minnville, TN 37110
(931)743-9809
cavecrew1979@gmail.com

___

Beech Grove (4MC)TNMU7204
PO Box 26 (mailing)
471 Oscar Crowell Road (physical)
Beechgrove, TN 37018
(931)394-2387 <Coffee>
CL: Crystal B Brandon
269 French Brantley Road
Wartrace, TN 37183
(931)394-2387
no_tenn@hotmail.com

___

Belvidere (4WC)TNMU7205
Walnut Hill Road
Belvidere, TN 37306
( ) <Franklin>
PA: Joseph H Butler <M1>
56 Cline Ridge Road
Winchester, TN 37398
(931)224-8423

jhbu737@bellsouth.net
CL: Alton Smith
123 Post Oak Road
Belvidere, TN 37306
starsmith53@hotmail.com

___

Blues Hill (4MWC)TNMU7207
7292 Short Mountain Road
Mc Minnville, TN 37110
( ) <Warren>
SS: Lyon Walkup <M1>
225 Bertha Owen Road
Morrison, TN 37357
(931)607-3233
dirtroad@blomand.net
CL: Maria Mott
38 Winfree Road
Mc Minnville, TN 37110
(931)934-2425

___

Cloyd's (4WC)TNMU7208
PO Box 277 (mailing)
595 West Division (physical)
Mt Juliet, TN 37121
(615)758-7434 <Wilson>
PA: Michael Reese <M1>
404 Five Oaks Boulevard
Lebanon, TN 37087
(615)443-0457
michaelhreese@bellsouth.net
CL: Vickie Hibdon
7141 Lebanon Road
Mount Juliet, TN 37122
(615)444-6498

___

Commerce (4WC)TNMU7209
351 Borum Road (mailing)
4260 S Commerce Road (physical)
Watertown, TN 37184
(615)237-9409 <Wilson>
crutchmckinwater@aol.com
SS: Denny C Shepard <M1>
8514 Newsom Station Road
Nashville, TN 37221
(615)662-1114
CL: Jacki Crutcher
351 Borum Road
Watertown, TN 37184
(615)237-3310
crutchmckinwater@aol.com

___

Cookeville First (4WC)TNMU7210
565 E 10th Street
Cookeville, TN 38501
(931)526-6585 <Putnam>
FAX: (931)528-2270
charles@cookevillecpchurch.org
PA: Charles McCaskey <M1>
679 Canter Lane
Cookeville, TN 38501
(931)526-4885
charles@cookevillecpchurch.org
AP: Christian Smith <M1>
475 State Street
Cookeville, TN 38501
(931)265-8896
csmith2490@gmail.com
CL: Lanny Knight
521 Chad Lane
Cookeville, TN 38501
(931)528-7800

alknight2@msn.com

___

Cowan (4MC)TNMU7211
PO Box 277 (mailing)
206 Cowan Street W (physical)
Cowan, TN 37318
(931)967-7431 <Franklin>
cowancpchurch@bellsouth.net
PA: Richard "Rocky" Whray <M1>
201 8th Avenue SE
Winchester, TN 37398
(931)636-4844
rocklex1017@att.net
CL: Nancy Wood
215 N Cedar Street
Winchester, TN 37398
(931)968-0893
woodnd@bellsouth.net

___

Dibrell (4C)TNMU7212
128 Mitchell Road (mailing)
Mike Muncey Road (physical)
McMinnville, TN 37110
( ) <Warren>
CL: Jacqulyn S Boyd
128 Mitchell Road
McMinnville, TN 37110
(931)934-2088

___

Dry Valley (4C)TNMU7213
5196 Shady Lane (mailing)
4415 Highway 70 N (physical)
Cookeville, TN 38506
( ) <Putnam>
PA: Richard Bond <M1>
2425 Fisk Road Lot 0
Cookeville, TN 38506
(931)854-0979
CL: Janice F Bohannon
5196 Shady Lane
Cookeville, TN 38506
(931)528-7894
jandan80@gmail.com

___

Goshen (4MWC)TNMU7214
PO Box 881 (mailing)
1262 Williams Cove Road (physical)
Winchester, TN 37398
(931)967-0245 <Franklin>
goshenchurch@cafes.net
PA: Richard Morgan <M1>
1468 Williams Cove Road
Winchester, TN 37398
(931)349-4474
icthuse3@gmail.com
CL: Frances Hanger
251 Whipperwill Lane
Winchester, TN 37398
(931)967-7730
FAX: (931)967-7730
bhanger@bellsouth.net

___

Gum Creek (4C)TNMU7215
1063 Franklin Heights Drive
Winchester, TN 37398
(931)967-6539 <Franklin>
PA: Coyle Campbell <M1>
186 Old Limestone Road
New Market, AL 35761
(256)379-4392
CL: Molly Perry

MURFREESBORO PRESBYTERY CONTINUED

1063 Franklin Heights Drive
Winchester, TN 37398
(931)967-6539

Harmony (4MWC)TNMU7216
8891 Lynchburg Road
Winchester, TN 37398
(931)962-0842 <Franklin>
PA: Joseph H Butler, Jr <M1>
261 Ridgefield Drive
Winchester, TN 37398
(931)224-8423
jhbu737@live.com
CL: Clare Wiseman
8555 Lynchburg Road
Winchester, TN 37398
(931)967-3932
wisrc9802@gmail.com

Hickory Valley (4U)TNMU7251
Sparta, TN 38583
(931)738-5812 <White>
PA: Richard Bond <M1>
1528 Eastlake Drive
Cookeville, TN 38506
(931)526-7610
CL: Kathryn Adcock
1450 Oak Grove Road
Sparta, TN 38583
(931)761-5858
kadcock@blomand.net

Hillsboro (4EC)TNMU7217
PO Box 4
Hillsboro, TN 37342
(931)394-2415 <Coffee>
CL: Robert L Jenkins
68 Hillsboro Viola Road
Hillsboro, TN 37342
(931)596-2745

Jerusalem (4MWC)TNMU7218
7192 Mona Road
Murfreesboro, TN 37129
(615)895-8118 <Rutherford>
PA: Brent Wills <M1>
4607 E Richmond Shop Road
Lebanon, TN 37090
(615)449-3258
bwills9185@yahoo.com
CL: Jimmy C Francis
4657 W Jefferson Pike
Murfreesboro, TN 37129
(615)893-8311
jcfjimmy@aol.com

Joywood (4MWC)TNMU7250
7120 Old Nashville Highway
Murfreesboro, TN 37129
(615)459-6518 <Rutherford>
joywoodchurch@yahoo.com
PA: Jeff Clark <M1>
327 Haynes Haven Lane
Murfreesboro, TN 37129
(615)896-7733
jclark7733@aol.com
CL: Mark Tharp
5018 Willowbend Drive
Murfreesboro, TN 37128
(615)895-4772
markat52@comcast.net

LaGuardo (4WC)TNMU7219
7320 Highway 109 N
Lebanon, TN 37087
(615)444-0419 <Wilson>
OD: Gary Mraz <M5>
8630 Highway 109 N
Lebanon, TN 37087
CL: Nancy Voight
500 Woods Ferry Pike
Lebanon, TN 37087

Lebanon (4MWC)TNMU7220
522 Castle Heights Avenue
Lebanon, TN 37087
(615)444-7453 <Wilson>
FAX: (615)444-6671
lcpsecretary@hotmail.com
PA: Kevin Medlin <M1>
316 Dandelion Drive
Lebanon, TN 37087
(615)444-7453
FAX: (615)444-6671
kmedlin12@hotmail.com
AP: Drew Gray <M1>
5610 Country Drive Apt 210
Nashville, TN 37211
(615)332-8360
CL: Kelly Hendricks
464 Locust Grove Road
Watertown, TN 37184
(615)443-0226
FAX: (615)444-6671

Liberty (4MWC)TNMU7222
317 Liberty Lane
McMinnville, TN 37110
(931)473-3813 <Warren>
libertycpc@gmail.com
PA: Marcus Hayes <M1>
102 River Drive
McMinnville, TN 37110
(270)841-7576
marcus.hayes@att.net
CL: Patty Boyd
35 Lonsvale Drive
McMinnville, TN 37110
(931)473-8059
pattyboyd@blomand.net

Livingston First (4WC)TNMU7223
PO Box 393 (mailing)
110 Byrdstown Highway (physical)
Livingston, TN 38570
(931)823-5115 <Overton>
SS: Donald Ray Fossey, II <M3>
328 Waterloo Road
Cookeville, TN 38506
(931)498-2149
dfossey@twlakes.net
CL: Helen Fossey
611 W 4th Street
Livingston, TN 38570
(931)823-9884

Luz D L Naciones (4F)TNMU7252
114 Northwood Lane
Mc Minnville, TN 37110
( ) <Warren>
PA: Jose Perez <M1>
89 Northwood Lane Apt A102

Mc Minnville, TN 37110
(931)743-5585
CL: Session Clerk
114 Northwood Lane
Mc Minnville, TN 37110
(931)815-9502

Manchester (4MWEC)TNMU7224
838 McArthur Street
Manchester, TN 37355
(931)728-2975 <Coffee>
FAX: (931)728-2975
mancp@cafes.net
PA: Mark Barron <M1>
836 McArthur Street
Manchester, TN 37355
(931)728-2975
FAX: (931)728-2975
mbarron@cafes.net
CL: Debbie Shelton
1255 M G England Road
Manchester, TN 37355
(931)728-9422
debbiebl@cafes.net

McMinnville (4MWC)TNMU7225
115 Peers Street
McMinnville, TN 37110
(931)474-4255 <Warren>
dwalhart@aol.com
PA: Daryl Alhart <M1>
2187 Rutledge Ford Road
Decherd, TN 37324
(931)349-7104
dwalhart@aol.com
CL: Leota Watson
804 W Main Street
Mc Minnville, TN 37110
(931)473-7561
leotaw@blomand.net

Monteagle (4C)TNMU7227
PO Bos 243 (mailing)
343 College Street (physical)
Monteagle, TN 37356
( ) <Grundy>
PA: William F James <M1>
2937 Arthur Drive
Murfreesboro, TN 37127
(615)653-1396
wimjim19@gmail.com
CL: Billie Faye Terrill
PO Box 243
Monteagle, TN 37356
(931)924-2787

Mt Carmel (4MEWC)TNMU7228
1484 Elora Road
Huntland, TN 37345
(931)469-7394 <Franklin>
SS: B J Hancock <M1 RT>
103 W Cowan Street
Cowan, TN 37318
(931)967-8491
CL: Tina M Morrow
714 Baxter Hollow Road
Belvidere, TN 37306
(931)967-3853
ramtmm@netzero.net

Mt Hermon (4MEWC)TNMU7229

MURFREESBORO PRESBYTERY CONTINUED

5544 Mt Hermon Road
Cookeville, TN 38506
( )   <Putnam>
SS: Maury A Norman   <M1 OP>
  1750 Shipley Road
  Cookeville, TN 38501
  (931)526-1644
  maurynorman@yahoo.com
CL: Ruth Shubert
  6799 Cherry Creek Road
  Cookeville, TN 38506
  (931)526-5109

_____
Mt Tabor   (4EC)TNMU7230
  3122 Donard Court (mailing)
  6000 Manchester Highway (physical)
  Murfreesboro, TN 37127
  (615)545-4695   <Rutherford>
  sheila.mcclain4695@gmail.com
PA: Brent Wills   <M1>
  4607 E Richmond Shop Road
  Lebanon, TN 37090
  (615)449-3258
  bwills9185@yahoo.com
CL: Sheila McClain
  3122 Donard Court
  Murfreesboro, TN 37128
  (615)545-4695
  sheila.mcclain4695@gmail.com

_____
Mt Vernon   (4C)TNMU7231
  131 Hickory Hills Drive (mailing)
  Murfreesboro, TN 37128
  11915 Mt Vernon Road (physical)
  Rockvale, TN 37153
  (615)890-9125   <Rutherford>
PA: Judy Taylor Sides   <M1>
  534 Bethany Circle
  Murfreesboro, TN 37128
  (615)895-1627
CL: Gregory L Sides
  534 Bethany Circle
  Murfreesboro, TN 37128
  (615)895-1627

_____
Murfreesboro   (4MEWC)TNMU7232
  907 E Main Street
  Murfreesboro, TN 37130
  (615)893-6755   <Rutherford>
  FAX: (615)893-4553
  firstcp@comcast.net
PA: Christopher Warren   <M1>
  906 Prince Lane
  Murfreesboro, TN 37129
  (615)828-8719
  chris@murfreesborocpc.org
CL: Mary Healey
  2015 Red Mile Road
  Murfreesboro, TN 37127
  (615)896-6337
  jomarhealey@comcast.net

_____
New Hope   (4EWC)TNMU7233
  PO Box 1215 (mailing)
  7845 Coles Ferry Pike (physical)
  Lebanon, TN 37087
  (615)449-7020   <Wilson>
SS: Vernon Burrow   <M1 RT>
  707 Saratoga Drive
  Murfreesboro, TN 37130
  (615)406-6385

vernonburrow@comcast.net
CL: Mary Ann Smith
  1600 Smith Road
  Lebanon, TN 37087
  (615)444-0102
  nwhpchrch0@gmail.com

_____
Old Zion   (4C)TNMU7234
  395 Coventry Drive (mailing)
  Nashville, TN 37211
  7489 Old Kentucky Road (physical)
  Sparta, TN 38583
  ( )   <White>
PA: James A McGill   <M1>
  433 S Walnut Avenue
  Cookeville, TN 38501
  (931)526-6936
  jam7235@frontiernet.net
CL: Kay Armstrong
  268 Tulip Drive
  Sparta, TN 38583
  (615)406-3976

_____
Owens Chapel   (4C)TNMU7235
  PO Box 839 (mailing)
  Sewanee, TN 37375
  3058 Liberty Road (physical)
  Winchester, TN 37398
  (931)636-8076   <Franklin>
  ferguea9@gmail.com
PA: Elizabeth Ferguson   <M1>
  PO Box 839
  Sewanee, TN 37375
  (931)636-8076
  ferguea9@gmail.com
CL: Jimmy McKinney
  1310 Liberty Road
  Winchester, TN 37398
  (931)967-3679
  bigmacj37@comcast.net

_____
Providence   (3C)TNMU7238
  c/o Pierce Dodson(mailing)
  106 Bartonwood Drive
  Lebanon, TN 37087
  Providence Road (physical)
  Hartsville, TN 37074
  ( )   <Trousdale>
CL: Session Clerk
  c/o Pierce Dodson(mailing)
  106 Bartonwood Drive
  Lebanon, TN 37087

_____
Rockvale   (4MEWC)TNMU7239
  PO Box 67 (mailing)
  8769 Rockvale Road (physical)
  Rockvale, TN 37153
  (615)274-3143   <Rutherford>
PA: Joyce Merritt   <M1>
  3929 Snail Shell Cave Road
  Rockvale, TN 37153
  (615)574-3047
CL: Martha A Lannom
  903 Sunset Avenue
  Murfreesboro, TN 37129
  (615)896-1348
  malannom@bellsouth.net
_____
Rocky Glade   (4C)TNMU7240
  PO Box 8 (mailing)
  2017 Rocky Glade Road (physical)

Eagleville, TN 37060
  ( )   <Rutherford>
PA: J. Tommy Jobe   <M1>
  PO Box 8
  Eagleville, TN 37060
  (615)776-7755
  cppreacher@united.net
CL: Bill Lamb
  425 River Eagleville Road
  Eagleville, TN 37060
  (615)274-2275
  billlamb1@bellsouth.net

_____
Ruth Chapel   (2C)TNMU7241
  347 Windle Community Road (mailing)
  146 Windle Community Road (physical)
  Livingston, TN 38570
  ( )   <Overton>
SS: Donald Fossey II   <M3>
  328 Waterloo Road
  Cookeville, TN 38506
  (931)498-2149
  dfossey@twlakes.net
CL: Jo K Smith
  347 Windle Community Road
  Livingston, TN 38570
  (931)823-5916

_____
Sewanee   (4WC)TNMU7242
  Box 11
  Sewanee, TN 37375
  (931)598-0766   <Franklin>
  smdiam@hotmail.com
PA: Steven Diamond   <M1>
  106 Ultimate Court
  Madison, AL 35757
  smdiam@hotmail.com
  (931)636-7336
CL: Paul E Mooney
  Box 11
  Sewanee, TN 37375
  (931)598-0766

_____
Smithville   (4MWC)TNMU7243
  201 S College Street
  Smithville, TN 37166
  (615)597-4197   <DeKalb>
  FAX: (615)597-4397
  office@smithvillecpc.com
PA: Isaac Gray   <M1>
  512 Ed Taft Drive
  Smithville, TN 37166
  (870)373-4731
  revgray08@gmail.com
CL: Wesley A Rogers
  305 S College Street
  Smithville, TN 37166
  (615)597-5549
  wesrogers305@gmail.com

_____
Suggs Creek   (4MWC)TNMU7244
  405 Corinth Road
  Mount Juliet, TN 37122
  ( )   <Wilson>
IP: Larry Green   <M1>
  525 Dearman Street
  Smithville, TN 37166
  (615)597-5832
  larrygreen24@aol.com
CL: Dianna Huff
  167 Eakes Thompson Road

MURFREESBORO PRESBYTERY CONTINUED

Mount Juliet, TN 37122
dhuff1983@bellsouth.net

Union Hill　　　(4MWC)TNMU7246
235 Sykes Road
Brush Creek, TN 38547
(615)683-8327　　　　　　<Smith>
brotherperry@msn.com
SS: Dennis Croslin　　　　　<M3>
165 Maple Street
Gordonsville, TN 38563
(615)934-2383
CL: Robin L Nixon
237 Temperance Hall Highway
Hickman, TN 38567
(615)418-5074
robinlpn@hotmail.com

Watertown　　　(4WC)TNMU7247
510 W Main Street
Watertown, TN 37184
(　)　　　　　　　　　　<Wilson>
OD: Rodger McCann　　　　<M5>
352 Winding River Lane
Sparta, TN 38563
(931)738-0352
CL: Emily Nix
305 Cornwell Avenue
Watertown, TN 37184
(615)237-3488
emilymckin_1@juno.com

Winchester First　　(4WC)TNMU7249
PO Box 176 (mailing)
200 2nd Avenue NW (physical)
Winchester, TN 37398
(931)967-2121　　　　　<Franklin>
FAX: (931)967-8444
wintncp@bellsouth.net
PA: Michael Clark　　　　<M1>
80 Bryan Drive
Winchester, TN 37398
(931)967-2121
book_worm35@comcast.net
AP: Amber Clark　　　　　<M1>
80 Bryan Drive
Winchester, TN 37398
(931)967-2121
revamber@comcast.net
AP: Aaron Ferry　　　　　<M1>
PO Box 176
Winchester, TN 37398
(615)946-3078
amferry815@gmail.com
CL: Tom Mahler
PO Box 176
Winchester, TN 37398
twmahler@gmail.com

OTHERS ON MINISTERIAL ROLL:

Benedict, Mary McCaskey　　<M1 WC>
892 Pen Oak Drive
Cookeville, TN 38501
(931)260-1422
marykat_61@hotmail.com
Clark, Jonathan　　　　　<M1 RT>
88 Woodcrest Drive
Winchester, TN 37398
(931)967-9613
FAX: (931)967-8444

clark3568@bellsouth.net
Diamond, James　　　　　<M1 M9>
PO Box 1220
Smyrna, TN 37167
(615)220-2341
FAX: (615)220-1077
james.diamond007@comcast.net
Estep, William　　　　　<M1 RT>
239 Skyline Drive
Harriman, TN 37748
(865)882-5114
Green, Harry　　　　　　<M1 WC>
45 Wood Way
McMinnville, TN 37110
(931)815-9190
Hackman-Truhan, Deborah　　<M1 WC>
7314 N Miramar Drive
Peoria, IL 61614
(931)537-9040
cprevdeb@hotmail.com
Hayes, Jennifer　　　　　<M1 WC>
102 River Drive
McMinnville, TN 37110
(205)533-1018
Jeffrey, Peter　　　　　<M1 WC>
61 Northwood Drive
McKenzie, TN 38201
(731)352-0792
jeffreyp@bethelu.edu
Johnson, Lanny　　　　　<M1 RT>
120 S Mill Street
Morrison, TN 37357
(931)212-1658
ljohnson37357@gmail.com
Labrada, Hector　　　　　<M1 WC>
74 Cumberland Drive
McMinnville, TN 37110
Logan, Jason　　　　　　<M1 M8>
4895 Diggins Drive
Fort Meade, ND 20755
(410)305-8494
jason.b.logan@dix.army.mil
Malone, Michael　　　　　<M1 WC>
330 Holly Street
Johnson City, TN 37604
(865)692-2415
Martin, James W　　　　　<M1 WC>
1922 Battleground Drive
Murfreesboro, TN 37129
(615)896-4442
(615)859-1493
Matlock, Robert　　　　　<M1 RT>
156 Dovenshire Drive
Fairfield Glade, TN 38558
(931)210-0614
revbobm@msn.com
Nye, John　　　　　　　<M1 WC>
210 Crestview Drive
Mount Juliet, TN 37122
Parks, Sam　　　　　　<M1 WC>
10 Lila Way
Cartersville, GA 60120
(615)529-2465
wsamparks@aol.com

Pittenger, Ronnie M　　　<M1 WC>
547 Southcrest Drive
Nashville, TN 37211
(615)832-8832
Salisbury, Rebecca　　　　<M1 WC>
1033 Twin Oaks Drive
Murfreesboro, TN 37130
(615)410-7801
rebsalisbury@yahoo.com
Warren, Joy　　　　　　<M1 WC>
907 W Main Street
Murfreesboro, TN 37129
(615)828-8719
revjoywarren@gmail.com
Wood, Bennie R　　　　　<M1 RT>
3697 S Mount Juliet Road
Hermitage, TN 37076
(615)449-8651

OTHER LICENTIATES ON ROLL:

Mathis, B J　　　　　　<M2>
675 Newt McKnight Road
McMinnville, TN 37110

OTHER CANDIDATES ON ROLL:

Boggs, Barry　　　　　　<M3>
1039 Johnnie Bud Lane
Cookeville, TN 38501
Cleek, Phillip　　　　　<M3>
188 Cleek Lane
Estill Springs, TN 37330
(931)967-2354
Gibson, Rachel　　　　　<M3>
2520 Cairo Bend Road
Lebanon, TN 37087
(615)453-2724
Heard, Robert　　　　　<M3>
527 Jack Thomas Drive
Manchester, TN 37355
(931)273-9687
Norton, Austin　　　　　<M3>
1498 Bradshaw Boulevard
Cookeville, TN 38506
(931)261-3260
Quevedo, Mariano　　　　<M3>
289 Golf Club Lane
McMinnville, TN 37110
Wright, John　　　　　　<M3>

Nashville Presbytery
TENNESSEE SYNOD

GENERAL		MEMBERSHIP			CHANGES				FINANCES				
	1.Church Number	2.Active	3.Total	4.Church School	5.Prof. of Faith	6.Gains	7.Losses	8.Children Baptized	9. OUR UNITED OUT-REACH	10. Total Out-Reach Giving	11. All Other Expenses	12. Total Income Received	13. Value Church Prop. 1=1000
	1	2	3	4	5	6	7	8	9	10	11	12	13
Arlington	7311	20	40	27	0	0	2	0	0	8,525	42,484	90,277	403
Beech	7301	175	175	96	1	4	112	1	11,167	26,065	242,243	408,916	2,998
Bethel	7302	45	95	60	2	11	3	0	1,200	4,375	131,187	117,336	470
Brenthaven	7331	298	486	170	0	17	10	4	37,834	82,000	358,087	416,032	7,000
Brush Hill+	7325	151	218	92	0	3	7	0	11,230	10,750	220,111	224,604	5,600
Calvary	7342	15	15	0	0	6	10	1	125	0	47,924	46,492	500
Camp Ground	7312	20	20	12	0	0	1	0	0	3,072	38,180	42,918	500
Cane Ridge*	7326	20	20	7	No Report Received			0	0	0	0	0	275
Charlotte+	7303	27	57	19	0	0	0	0	3,561	5,284	38,769	39,361	513
Clarksville	7304	264	264	243	3	8	5	2	38,025	49,432	310,153	680,430	2,500
Concord	7306	26	26	26	No Report Received			0	1,000	0	0	0	105
Cristo Vive	7314				No Report Received			0	0	0	0	0	0
Cumberland Valle	7307	26	43	20	0	0	2	0	3,303	6,040	25,092	33,032	250
Dickson	7308	335	400	119	4	4	1	2	12,000	40,158	190,942	233,465	1,500
Donelson	7327	50	115	64	1	1	3	2	1,200	6,459	76,583	73,133	1,650
Dry Fork*	7309	12	24	0	0	5	0	0	1,000	2,700	6,563	15,790	100
Erin	7310	9	16	0	0	0	1	0	469	1,896	18,692	21,701	350
Goodlettsville	7328	354	354	288	8	18	10	1	0	44,931	424,069	469,000	3,500
Halls Creek	7313	53	53	41	0	0	1	0	0	19,314	24,831	39,035	350
Hendersonville*	7340	17	17	18	2	0	0	0	600	2,545	36,370	35,728	500
Liberty	7315	47	47	49	3	3	8	0	3,651	11,588	87,631	95,573	600
Locust Grove	7316	12	43	8	4	4	5	0	0	495	24,984	38,821	313
Madison 1st	7329	28	52	23	0	2	0	0	5,509	7,868	60,164	63,032	340
Mariah	7317	32	32	20	No Report Received			0	0	0	0	0	150
McAdoo	7318	52	52	30	5	5	1	0	3,325	6,300	68,559	74,859	646
Mt. Denson	7319	50	171	28	3	7	1	0	7,960	16,014	71,345	101,304	730
Mt. Liberty	7320	93	160	49	10	10	3	3	3,300	7,058	103,330	116,925	1,035
Mt. Sharon	7321	95	208	95	0	2	4	0	8,750	17,574	197,974	202,449	1,750
Mt. Sinai	7330	10	10	0	1	1	2	0	0	0	17,694	18,032	300
Mt. View	7322	45	85	15	4	12	0	0	0	3,506	91,549	72,730	450
New Hope	7337	7	7	12	No Report Received			0	0	0	0	0	52
New Providence	7305	28	28	10	4	4	9	0	0	0	37,542	28,881	998
Shiloh	7338	35	67	18	3	0	4	2	300	5,830	56,857	47,738	900
St. Luke	7332	120	305	48	0	1	9	1	20,503	27,922	184,582	205,799	3,535
Sudanese	7341	30	34	0	0	0	14	0	0	0	0	0	24
The Connection	7335				CLOSED 10/31/14								1,250
Tusculum	7333	192	685	195	2	8	14	2		37,530	482,482	557,949	3,405
Waverly	7339	54	187	8	1	9	3	1	0	2,983	82,388	61,527	670
West Nashville	7334	121	402	97	0	10	6	1	19,828	39,758	289,019	299,975	3,894
TOTALS	38	2,867	5,012	1,980	65	159	242	47	202,184	498,863	4,111,165	4,696,526	50,106

*Math error corrected. **Purged roll.

NASHVILLE PRESBYTERY CONTINUED

CHURCHES, PASTORS, AND CLERKS:

Arlington (4WC)TNNA7311
PO Box 624 (mailing)
7 Knight Street (physical)
Erin, TN 37061
(931)289-3597 <Houston>
OD: Paul S Moody
600 Hurricane Loop
Tennessee Ridge, TN 37178
(931)721-3953
CL: Andrea Dillard
85 Victor Lane
Erin, TN 37061
(931)289-4004
adillard@workforceessentials.com

Beech (4MWC)TNNA7301
3216 Long Hollow Pike
Hendersonville, TN 37075
(615)824-3990 <Sumner>
FAX: (615)824-6507
office@beechcp.com
PA: Malcolm Patton <M1>
921 Harris Drive
Gallatin, TN 37066
(615)452-5557
FAX: (615)824-6507
bpatton11@comcast.net
CL: Sarah Ezell
787 New Shackle Island Road
Hendersonville, TN 37075
(615)824-6815
sarahezell2@att.net

Bethel (4MC)TNNA7302
3375 Sango Road
Clarksville, TN 37043
(931)358-3295 <Montgomery>
PA: Stewart Salyer <M1>
2211 Foxfire Road
Clarksville, TN 37043
(931)980-2829
stewart.salyer@gmail.com
CL: Chris Davis
632 Eastwood Court
Clarksville, TN 37043
(931)624-9449
cdavis@cemc.org

Brenthaven (4C)TNNA7331
516 Franklin Road
Brentwood, TN 37027
(615)373-4826 <Williamson>
FAX: (615)373-4869
secretary@brenthaven.org
PA: Kip J Rush <M1>
513 Meadowlark Lane
Brentwood, TN 37027
(615)376-4563
pastor@brenthaven.org
AP: Sandra Shepherd <M1>
525 Summit Oaks Court
Nashville, TN 37221
(615)772-5358
woolywagon@gmail.com
CL: Christi Peppers
5008 Woodland Hills Drive
Brentwood, TN 37027
(615)376-9977
christi.peppers@gmail.com

Brush Hill (4MEWC)TNNA7325
3705 Brush Hill Road
Nashville, TN 37216
(615)227-2504 <Davidson>
FAX: (615)227-0039
bhcpc@birch.net
PA: Kenny Butcher <M1>
4608 Cather Court
Nashville, TN 37214
(615)719-1887
bhpastor@birch.net
AP: Paul Tucker <M1>
3801 Brush Hill Pike
Nashville, TN 37216
(615)430-9158
paultucker@gmail.com
CL: Terri Peltier
403 Cunniff Parkway
Goodlettsville, TN 37072
(615)227-2504
tp1260@aol.com

Calvary (4C)TNNA7342
340 Ringgold Road
Clarksville, TN 37042
(931)645-9200 <Montgomery>
2ourchurch@gmail.com
SS: Choil Ma <M1>
300 Ringgold Road Apt 503
Clarksville, TN 37042
(931)824-2443
choilma@yahoo.com
CL: Gary Lloyd
755 Tommy Oliver Road
Clarksville, TN 37042
(931)647-2718

Camp Ground (4MWC)TNNA7312
88 Campground Road
Erin, TN 37061
(931)289-4605 <Houston>
LS: Terry Mathis <M6>
88 Campground Road
Erin, TN 37061
(931)289-3602
ttmathis@peoplestel.net
CL: Patsy Mullins
6210 Highway 13
Erin, TN 37061
(931)289-3195

Cane Ridge (4EC)TNNA7326
6867 Burkitt Road (mailing)
13412 Old Hickory Boulevard (physical)
Cane Ridge, TN 37013
(615)941-8317 <Davidson>
FAX: (615)941-2985
gdunn6867@comcast.net
LS: Gregory (Greg) Dunn <M6>
6867 Burkitt Road
Cane Ridge, TN 37013
(615)941-8317
FAX: (615)941-2985
gdunn6867@comast.net
CL: Eleanor Willett
145 Greenwood Drive
La Vergne, TN 37086
(615)793-5016
tuffyw9@comcast.net

Charlotte (4WC)TNNA7303
515 Mt Hebron Road (mailing)
3 Court Square (physical)
Charlotte, TN 37036
( ) <Dickson>
SS: Dean Guye <M1>
2759 Highway 70 E
Dickson, TN 37055
(615)446-7687
deanjoy@att.net
CL: Eloise Jones
515 Mount Hebron Road
Charlotte, TN 37036
(615)789-5353
joneseloise515@bellsouth.net

Clarksville (4WC)TNNA7304
1410 Golf Club Lane
Clarksville, TN 37040
(931)648-0817 <Montgomery>
office@clarksvillecpc.com
PA: Stephen L Louder <M1>
98 Gallant Court
Clarksville, TN 37043
(931)217-0369
pastorsteve@clarksvillecpc.com
AP: Paula Louder <M1>
98 Gallant Court
Clarksville, TN 37043
(931)804-4809
paula.louder@cmcss.net
CL: Ashley Kettle
205 Bullock Drive
Clarksville, TN 37040
(931)624-8769
ashleykettle@gmail.com

Concord (4MC)TNNA7306
63 Gander Branch Road
Waverly, TN 37185
( ) <Humphreys>
CL: Phyllis Webb
3571 Fire Tower Road
Erin, TN 37061
(931)289-4601

Cristo Vive (4C)TNNA7314
611 Cheron Road
Madison, TN 37115
( ) <Davidson>
PA: Carlos Cinco <M1>
611 Cheron Road
Madison, TN 37115
(615)586-1269
pastorcinco2020@gmail.com
CL: Session Clerk
611 Cheron Road
Madison, TN 37115

Cumberland Valley (4WC)TNNA7307
285 Cumberland Valley Road
Mc Ewen, TN 37101
(931)582-8050 <Houston>
PA: Jesse L Freeman, Jr <M1>
270 Eastside Road
Burns, TN 37029
(615)202-4594
mptc@bellsouth.net
CL: June R Hicks
1339 Highway 13 S

NASHVILLE PRESBYTERY CONTINUED

Waverly, TN 37185
(931)296-4284

Dickson   (4WC)TNNA7308
500 Highway 70 E
Dickson, TN 37055
(615)446-8511   <Dickson>
FAX: (615)446-7827
office@cumberlandpresbyterian.org
PA: Robert D Truitt   <M1>
1238 Old East Side Road
Burns, TN 37029
(615)740-9180
FAX: (615)446-7827
rdtjct@aol.com
AP: Dean Guye   <M1>
2759 Highway 70 E
Dickson, TN 37055
(615)446-7687
deanjoy@att.net
CL: Mark Rolman
102 Charles Court
Dickson, TN 37055
(615)375-7080
mdrolman@gmail.com

Donelson   (4WC)TNNA7327
2914 Lebanon Road
Nashville, TN 37214
(615)516-9427   <Davidson>
email@donelsoncpchurch.com
PA: Michael Bertsch   <M1 RT>
368 Sunset Island Trail
Gallatin, TN 37066
(423)763-8314
mikebertsch14@gmail.com
CL: Keith C Vanstone
3803 Plantation Drive
Hermitage, TN 37076
(615)210-5010
clerk@donelsoncpchurch.com

Dry Fork   (4C)TNNA7309
174 Dry Fork Creek Road (mailing)
1050 Dry Fork Creek Road (physical)
Bethpage, TN 37022
(615)841-3169   <Sumner>
PA: Ted Bane   <M1>
903 W Old Hickory Boulevard
Madison, TN 37115
(615)975-9343
tedjan95@aol.com
CL: Sue Carr
174 Dry Fork Creek Road
Bethpage, TN 37022
(615)841-3169
suekencarr@nctc.com

Erin   (4MWC)TNNA7310
PO Box 307 (mailing)
4793 E Main Street (physical)
Erin, TN 37061
( )   <Houston>
erincpchurch@gmail.com
SS: Timothy W Ferrell   <M1>
1850 Dunbar Road
Woodlawn, TN 37191
(931)920-2662
ferrelltw@aol.com
CL: Carolyn Zurawski
978 Scotts Chapel Road

Cumberland City, TN 37050
(931)827-3111

Goodlettsville   (4MWC)TNNA7328
226 South Main Street
Goodlettsville, TN 37072
(615)859-5888   <Davidson>
FAX: (615)859-8820
gcpc@comcast.net
PA: Tim Stutler   <M1>
1044 Mansker Farm Boulevard
Hendersonville, TN 37075
(615)859-5888
gcpctim@comcast.net
CL: Doug Newman
675 Windsor Green Boulevard
Goodlettsville, TN 37072
(615)400-4589

Halls Creek   (4EC)TNNA7313
3650 Perrywinkle Branch Road (mailing)
2803 Halls Creek Road (physical)
Waverly, TN 37185
(931)296-7758   <Humphreys>
SS: Gary Carlton   <M1>
108 Greenbrier Street
Dickson, TN 37055
(615)441-8963
gwcarlton@yahoo.com
CL: Jerry Binkley
3650 Perrywinkle Branch Road
Waverly, TN 37185
(931)296-3154
binkleys@hughes.net

Hendersonville   (4WC)TNNA7340
453 Walton Ferry Road
Hendersonville, TN 37075
(615)822-6091   <Sumner>
SS: David West   <M1 M9>
2027 Lucille Street
Lebanon, TN 37087
(217)732-7568
CL: Susan Wyatt
115 Elissa Drive
Hendersonville, TN 37075
(615)948-8242
FAX: (615)824-0195
susandwyatt@comcast.net

Liberty   (4MWC)TNNA7315
725 S Liberty Church Road
Clarksville, TN 37042
( )   <Montgomery>
PA: Rocky Johnson   <M1>
1208 Redwood Drive
Clarksville, TN 37042
(423)620-7753
jjjjgriff@gmail.com
CL: Bob Del Giorno
1510 S Freestone Court
Clarksville, TN 37042
(931)647-1086
bodeno@charter.net

Locust Grove   (4WC)TNNA7316
3449 Locust Church Road
Cunningham, TN 37052
( )   <Montgomery>
SS: Timothy W Ferrell   <M1>
1850 Dunbar Road

Woodlawn, TN 37191
(931)920-2662
ferrelltw@aol.com
CL: Lawanda Black
3192 Budds Creek Road
Palmyra, TN 37142
(931)326-5298
jobee39@hughes.net

Madison First   (4MWC)TNNA7329
735 Argyle Avenue
Madison, TN 37115
(615)868-2888   <Davidson>
FAX: (615)868-2888
madisonfirst@yahoo.com
PA: Johnny Parish   <M1>
114 Savo Bay
Hendersonville, TN 37075
(615)824-5842
johnnyparish@bellsouth.net
CL: Edith Marlin
112 Becker Avenue
Old Hickory, TN 37138
(615)847-4148
edithmarlin@live.com

Mariah   (4MWC)TNNA7317
43 Mariah Church Lane
Waverly, TN 37185
(931)296-5546   <Humphreys>
SS: Nathaniel Mathews   <M2>
1006 Woodland Drive
New Johnsonville, TN 37134
(931)209-6645
bro.nate-mathews@hotmail.com
CL: Anita Gehring
65 Warden Road
Waverly, TN 37185
(931)296-8059

McAdoo   (4WC)TNNA7318
3724 Ashland City Road
Clarksville, TN 37043
(931)362-3091   <Montgomery>
PA: Joe Vick   <M1>
6064 Old Hickory Boulevard
Whites Creek, TN 37189
(615)519-5249
joervick@gmail.com
CL: Sherry Jenkins
4253 Ashland City Road
Clarksville, TN 37043
(931)801-4020
tnweaver44@att.net

Mt Denson   (4MWC)TNNA7319
4558 Highway 161
Springfield, TN 37172
(615)384-3613   <Robertson>
PA: Andrew Ward   <M1>
407 Rose Hill Court
Goodlettsville, TN 37072
(615)456-9136
andrewbward@aol.com
AP: Patricia (Pat) Pickett   <M1 M9>
1460 Cheatham Dam Road
Ashland City, TN 37015
(615)792-4973
tovahtoo@aol.com
CL: Karen C Sweatt
4946 Minnis Road

NASHVILLE PRESBYTERY CONTINUED

Springfield, TN 37172
(615)944-5218
kcsweatt@hotmail.com

_____

Mt Liberty   (4MWC)TNNA7320
3655 Highway 49 E
Charlotte, TN 37036
(615)789-5916   <Dickson>
SS: Justin Griffin   <M1>
3655 Highway 49 E
Charlotte, TN 37036
(615)969-2426
jjjjgriff@gmail.com
CL: Cindy Simpson
3378 Highway 49 E
Charlotte, TN 37036
(615)945-0010
cindyrsimpson@hotmail.com

_____

Mt Sharon   (4MWC)TNNA7321
4634 Mount Sharon Road
Greenbrier, TN 37073
(615)384-8569   <Robertson>
pastor@mtsharoncpchurch.org
PA: Jason Mikel   <M1>
4630 Mt Sharon Road
Greenbrier, TN 37073
(615)243-8938
jasonemikel@gmail.com
AP: Fred Schott, Jr   <M1 RT>
606 Taylor Trail
Springfield, TN 37172
(615)384-8572
fws195@aol.com
CL: James D Jordan
2100 W End Avenue Ste 1150
Nashville, TN 37203
(615)329-2100
FAX: (615)329-2187
jdjordan@gjplaw.com

_____

Mt Sinai   (4WC)TNNA7330
3738 Hydes Ferry Road
Nashville, TN 37218
(615)586-7886   <Davidson>
OD: David Lomax   <M5>
1501 Robert Cartwright Drive
Goodlettsville, TN 37072
(615)753-2493
lomaxdavid53@yahoo.com
CL: Katherine B Pleas
507 Glen Echo Place
Nashville, TN 37215
(615)298-2625
pleas5@hotmail.com

_____

Mt View   (4C)TNNA7322
2359 Leatherwood Road (mailing)
Stewart, TN 37175
282 Hickman Creek Road (physical)
Dover, TN 37058
(931)217-0893   <Stewart>
mvcpchurch@gmail.com
PA: Ronald D Burgess   <M1>
116 Harris Ridge Road
Dover, TN 37058
(931)232-5151
revron4@bellsouth.net
CL: Michelle Sills
126 Ralls Road
Dover, TN 37058

(931)305-8893

_____

New Hope   (4C)TNNA7337
c/o Sharon Cook (mailing)
8009 White Oak Road
Stewart, TN 37175
60 New Hope Road (physical)
Stewart, TN 37175
(   )   <Houston>
CL: Sharon E Cook
8009 White Oak Road
Stewart, TN 37175
(931)721-2513
ricsha55@yahoo.com

_____

New Providence   (4MWC)TNNA7305
1307 Fort Campbell Boulevard
Clarksville, TN 37042
(931)647-4455   <Montgomery>
PA: John Adam Smith   <M1 M9>
916 Allen Road
Nashville, TN 37214
(573)453-8455
john.a.smith.81@gmail.com
CL: Christopher Lively
1532B Second Street
Fort Campbell, KY 42223
(931)802-9982

_____

Shiloh   (4C)TNNA7338
4812 Shiloh-Canaan Road
Palmyra, TN 37142
(931)387-4198   <Montgomery>
greg1013@aol.com
PA: Gregory Jones   <M1>
4808 Shiloh Canaan Road
Palmyra, TN 37142
(931)249-9512
greg1013@aol.com
CL: Judi Moore
2010 Old Harmony Church Road
Adams, TN 37010
(615)505-5206

_____

St Luke   (4MWC)TNNA7332
901 W Old Hickory Boulevard
Madison, TN 37115
(615)868-1982   <Davidson>
stlukecpchurch@gmail.com
PA: Dwayne Tyus   <M1>
901 W Old Hickory Boulevard
Madison, TN 37115
(615)720-2564
dwayne.tyus@gmail.com
CL: Angie Pinson
901 W Old Hickory Boulevard
Madison, TN 37115
(615)337-7311
stlukecpchurch@gmail.com

_____

Sudanese   (F)TNNA7341
c/o First UMC (mailing)
149 W Main Street
407 Owen Drive (physical)
Gallatin, TN 37066
(615)585-2842   <Sumner>
PA: Jock Tut Paleak   <M1>
614 N Water Street Apt #623
Gallatin, TN 37066
(615)585-2842
CL: John Tiang Ping

49 Millwood Drive
Nashville, TN 37217
(615)365-3274

_____

The Connection   (4WC)TNNA7335
(previously named West Side)
215 Bellevue Road
Nashville, TN 37221
(615)646-4030   <Davidson>
CLOSED 10/31/14
(membership transferred to West Nashville)

_____

Tusculum   (4MWC)TNNA7333
477 McMurray Drive
Nashville, TN 37211
(615)833-0742   <Davidson>
tusculumchurch@gmail.com
PA: Roger Patton, Jr   <M1>
1534 Eden Rose Place
Nolensville, TN 37135
(615)975-5526
rogerlpatton@att.net
PA: Raymond De Vries   <M1>
2080 Stanford Village Drive
Antioch, TN 37013
(615)332-3587
ray.devries@comcast.net
CL: Dawn Gannon
3417 County Hill Road
Antioch, TN 37013
(615)399-2782
dawngannon0317@yahoo.com

_____

Waverly   (4MWC)TNNA7339
109 N Church Street
Waverly, TN 37185
(931)296-3232   <Humphreys>
FAX: (931)296-3232
waverlycpc@att.net
SS: Glenn Warren   <M1>
116 Cedar Hill Drive
Waverly, TN 37185
(931)209-5431
gwarren224@gmail.com
CL: Larry Cochran
581 Wisteria Lane
Waverly, TN 37185
(931)296-4450

_____

West Nashville   (4MWC)TNNA7334
6849 Charlotte Pike
Nashville, TN 37209
(615)352-2800   <Davidson>
FAX: (615)352-2801
info@wncp.org
PA: Rickey Page   <M1>
736 Rodney Drive
Nashville, TN 37205
(615)353-7850
FAX: (615)352-2801
rickey.page@wncp.org
CL: Nancy Crowell
707 Newberry Road
Nashville, TN 37205
nancydcrowell@gmail.com

NASHVILLE PRESBYTERY CONTINUED

OTHERS ON MINISTERIAL ROLL:

Acuff, David   \<M1 M8\>
    4969 Quail Lane
    Columbia, SC 29206
    (803)727-3910
    david.acuff@us.army.mil

Baranoski, Timothy   \<M1 M8\>
    8040 Starz Loop
    Killeen, TX 76544
    (615)440-3499
    timothy.i.baranoski@us.army.mil

Bennett, Alfred J   \<M1 RT\>
    7286 Nolensville Road
    Nolensville, TN 37135
    (615)776-5181

Cadenbach, Mark   \<M1 OM\>
    PO Box 66
    Westfield, IA 51062

Cook, Lisa   \<M1 M9\>
    4101 Dalemere Court
    Nashville, TN 37207
    (615)830-6217
    tgoose@comcast.net

Corbin, William   \<M1 PR\>
    7300 N Lamar Road
    Mount Juliet, TN 37122
    (615)459-8998
    raven.rest@comcast.net

Duke, Michael E   \<M1 WC\>
    106 Friar Tuck Drive
    Dickson, TN 37055
    (615)446-6515

Dumas, Byron   \<M1 OM\>
    1775 Theresa Drive
    Clarksville, TN 37043
    (931)552-8772
    bdumas7346@aol.com

Earheart-Brown, Daniel   \<M1 PR\>
    866 N McLean
    Memphis, TN 38107
    jebrown@memphisseminary.edu
    (901)278-0367

Ferguson, E Blant   \<M1 RT\>
    704 Bear Run
    Hiawassee, GA 30546
    (706)896-9296
    blantferg@yahoo.com

Goodwill, James L   \<M1 RT\>
    205 S English Hill Lane
    Hillsborough, NC 27278
    (704)526-8729
    jim@jimgoodwill.com

Gough, Ernest E   \<M1 WC\>
    8366 Highway 70
    Nashville, TN 37221
    (615)646-4372
    eegough@bellsouth.net

Hurley, E C   \<M1 WC\>
    221 Fantasia Way
    Clarksville, TN 37043
    (931)551-6173
    hurleyec@gmail.com

Miller, Carol   \<M1 WC\>
    101 Park Avenue
    Dickson, TN 37055
    (615)441-6656
    lcarolmiller@comcast.net

Norton, Kitty   \<M1 WC\>
    251 Westchase Drive
    Nashville, TN 37205
    (615)584-1464
    kitty.a.norton@vanderbilt.edu

Oliver, Lisa   \<M1 M9 OM\>
    110 Allen Drive
    Hendersonville, TN 37075
    (615)319-6466

Parrish, Steven   \<M1 PR\>
    4610 Dunn Avenue
    Memphis, TN 38117
    (901)743-9545
    sparrish@memphisseminary.edu

Polacek, Fred E   \<M1 WC\>
    907 Graham Drive
    Old Hickory, TN 37138
    (615)754-5328
    revfredp@gmail.com

Rippy, James G   \<M1 WC\>
    442 Trina Street
    Gallatin, TN 37066
    (615)681-7086
    lrippy@live.com

Roddy, Lowell G   \<M1 RT\>
    2583 Hedgerow Lane
    Clarksville, TN 37043
    (931)368-1081
    FAX: (931)221-1032
    lgroddy@yahoo.com

Sims, Edward G   \<M1 RT\>
    2161 N Meadow Drive
    Clarksville, TN 37043
    (931)206-5759
    simseg@aol.com

Smith, Billy T   \<M1 HR\>
    49 Abby Lynn Circle
    Clarksville, TN 37043
    (931)368-0424

Stefan, Gregory   \<M1 WC\>
    1917 Birchwood Street
    East Pearl, PA 17519
    (931)296-5291
    pastorstefan@att.net

Stovall, Jeff   \<M1 WC\>
    2829 Trelawny Drive
    Clarksville, TN 37043
    (931)993-6104
    jeffstovall@juno.com

Tabor, Don M   \<M1 RT\>
    9611 Mitchell Place
    Brentwood, TN 37027
    (615)776-7292
    FAX: (615)373-3356
    dontabor@comcast.net

Varner, Susan   \<M1 M9\>
    1502 Green Mountain Drive
    Little Rock, AR 72211
    (901)371-1249
    smvarner76@yahoo.com

Whitworth, Gary W   \<M1 RT\>
    1706 Old Hickory Boulevard
    Brentwood, TN 37027
    (615)915-4180

Winn, Don   \<M1 WC\>
    375 Cumberland Mountain Circle
    Sunbright, TN 37872
    (615)478-9910
    dwinn_ky@yahoo.com

OTHER LICENTIATES ON ROLL:

Jones, Steve   \<M2 ST\>
    PO Box 368
    Burns, TN 37029
    (615)441-6159

Wheelbarger, J J   \<M2\>
    PO Box 504
    Joelton, TN 37080
    (615)876-6948
    jjwheelbarger@aol.com

Young, Taylor   \<M2\>
    255 Willard Drive
    Nashville, TN 37211
    (615)319-8294
    brandontayloryoung@yahoo.com

OTHER CANDIDATES ON ROLL:

Adams, Hunter   \<M3\>
    603 Red Fox Court
    Burns, TN 37029
    (615)943-7862
    hadams60@bethelu.edu

Cassell, C J   \<M3 ST\>
    825 Aimes Court
    Nashville, TN 37221
    (615)594-2693
    n4cjc@comcast.net

Chall-Hutchinson, Deborah   \<M3\>
    190 Ussery Road
    Clarksville, TN 37043
    (931)905-1671
    challhut@gmail.com

Moore, Kimberly   \<M3\>
    1025 Three Island Ford Road
    Charlotte, TN 37036
    (615)545-1595
    kimberly.a.moore@vanderbilt.edu

Norris, Dakota   \<M3\>
    4750 Highway 431 N
    Springfield, TN 37172
    (615)681-6346
    volsfan2011@gmail.com

Stevens, Brittany   \<M3\>
    606 Huntington Parkway
    Nashville, TN 37211
    (615)719-3362
    bstevens5@my.apsu.edu

Wilkinson, Neal
    403 Enclave Circle
    Nashville, TN 37211
    (615)934-7342

Wilson, Melissa   \<M3 ST\>
    107 Hillwood Drive
    Dickson, TN 37055
    (615)446-7523
    milzwilz@comcast.net

North Central Presbytery
MIDWEST SYNOD

GENERAL		MEMBERSHIP			CHANGES				FINANCES				
	1.Church Number	2.Active	3.Total	4.Church School	5.Prof. of Faith	6.Gains	7.Losses	8.Children Baptized	9. OUR UNITED OUT-REACH	10. Total Out-Reach Giving	11. All Other Expenses	12. Total Income Received	13. Value Church Prop. 1=1000
	1	2	3	4	5	6	7	8	9	10	11	12	13
Bethany	5401	99	344	116	8	0	1	0	15,132	50,456	136,562	151,353	560
Burnt Prairie	5102	16	34	6	No Report Received			0	0	0	0	0	63
Campground	5402	13	15	15	No Report Received			0	0	0	0	0	50
Casey	5201	16	36	13	0	0	1	0	201	2,606	25,087	29,786	50
Christ	5305	8	11	7	No Report Received			0	624	0	0	0	150
Comunidad	5212	25	25	19	No Report Received			0	0	0	0	0	0
Cumb. Chapel	5104	7	7	5	0	0	0	0	0	10,377	13,212	20,539	4
Ebenezer	5203	38	38	30	No Report Received			0	3,780	0	0	0	1,000
Elm River	5107	50	50	69	2	2	1	0	6,354	12,200	40,700	70,665	235
Fairfield	5108	182	324	52	14	14	7	0	0	14,447	208,686	208,880	1,000
Faith	5501	5	13	4	0	0	1	0	4,774	6,303	29,518	51,799	500
Fullerton	5404	28	28	20	0	0	0	0	1,921	3,990	19,567	25,623	50
Georgetown**	5204	22	50	17	0	0	28	0	4,759	4,755	40,760	47,549	112
Good Prospect	5205	89	89	97	0	2	4	0	8,091	30,281	64,702	113,029	1,100
Grace	5502	12	29	16	No Report Received			0	112	0	0	0	245
Knights Chapel	5306	29	36	38	No Report Received			0	0	0	0	0	100
Lebanon North**	5113	50	66	69	0	0	0	95	0	5,399	71,499	75,276	200
Lebanon South	5114				No Report Received			0	0	0	0	0	0
Lincoln 1st	5405	39	91	25	No Report Received			0	5,400	0	0	0	575
Monroe City	5307	8	8	0	No Report Received			0	0	0	0	0	200
Morningside	5304	58	80	21	No Report Received			0	800	0	0	0	1,600
Mt. Gilead	5406	29	49	42	0	0	0	0	1,000	3,995	24,854	29,354	145
Mt. Olivet	5308	14	28	8	0	0	0	0	0	3,017	15,759	18,776	75
Mt. Oval	5116	6	6	10	No Report Received			0	0	0	0	0	10
New Hope	5208	45	107	35	1	0	2	0	7,471	16,918	59,388	79,523	400
Pleasant Grove	5210	14	30	22	0	0	3	0	7,116	23,530	16,252	33,681	182
Shiloh	5409	27	100	22	0	0	1	1	1,000	7,436	20,367	34,531	310
Shinar	5410	31	38	0	No Report Received			0	0	0	0	0	237
Spring Hill	5411	5	5	3	No Report Received			0	0	0	0	0	379
Union North	5124	25	25	20	0	1	2	0	2,039	9,568	32,807	36,529	120
United	5119	52	106	30	No Report Received			0	1,000	0	0	0	790
Willow Creek	5211	77	100	91	2	0	0	1	10,333	25,301	88,912	108,215	1,000
TOTALS	32	1,119	1,968	922	27	19	146	2	81,907	230,579	908,632	1,135,108	11,442

*Math error corrected. **Purged roll.

NORTH CENTRAL PRESBYTERY CONTINUED

CHURCHES, PASTORS, AND CLERKS:

Bethany   (4MWC)MINC5401
　PO Box 384 (mailing)
　219 S Lincoln Street (physical)
　Bethany, IL 61914
　(217)665-3034   <Moultrie>
　bethanycpc@yahoo.com
PA: D Kevin Vanderlaan   <M1>
　12 Willow Street
　Bethany, IL 61914
　(217)620-2723
　pastorkevin2@gmail.com
CL: Dean McReynolds
　399 County Road 1600 N
　Bethany, IL 61914
　(217)665-3420
　wdeanmcreynolds@yahoo.com

Burnt Prairie   (4MWC)MINC5102
　RR 3 Box 947 (mailing)
　Fairfield, IL 62837
　Church Street (physical)
　Burnt Prairie, IL 62820
　(618)925-1185   <White>
LS: Scott D Smothers   <M6>
　RR 5 Box 573
　Fairfield, IL 62837
　(618)842-6009
　lsmothers@myfrontiermail.com
CL: Andy Pottorff
　RR 3 Box 947
　Fairfield, IL 62837
　(618)925-1185
　andypottorff@yahoo.com

Campground   (4WEC)MINC5402
　1497 Hookdale Avenue (mailing)
　Route 4 (physical)
　Greenville, IL 62246
　(618)664-1547   <Bond>
CL: Rodney Reavis
　1497 Hookdale Avenue
　Greenville, IL 62246
　(618)664-1547
　rcreavis@yahoo.com

Casey   (4C)MINC5201
　PO Box 21 (mailing)
　16 N Central (physical)
　Casey, IL 62420
　(217)932-5404   <Clark>
CL: Mary Gard
　7810 N 400th Street
　Casey, IL 62420
　(217)932-2971
　thetoymaker@wildblue.net

Christ   (4MC)MINC5305
　6140 S Meridian
　Indianapolis, IN 46217
　(317)787-9585   <Marion>
CL: Paula Price
　892 Geagan Street
　Greenwood, IN 46143
　(317)709-8138

Comunidad Cristina   (4F)MINC5212
　1714 S 4th Avenue (mailing)
　Maywood, IL 60153

　15N562 Vista Lane (physical)
　Dundee, IL 60118
　(708)223-2185   <Cook>
　pastorccc@clear.net
CL: Noel Taveras
　809 Lexington Circle
　Hanover Park, IL 60133
　(630)965-7113
　cololo809@yahoo.com

Cumberland Chapel   (4C)MINC5104
　1075 County Road 2400E (mailing)
　Route 2 CR 1300 N, CR 1200 E (physical)
　Fairfield, IL 62837
　( )   <Wayne>
PA: J B Gates   <M1>
　PO Box 289
　Enfield, IL 62835
　(618)963-2306
　rjjbgate@hamiltoncom.net
CL: Ronald E Huffman
　1075 County Road 2400E
　Fairfield, IL 62837
　(618)842-9518
　huffmanrj@hotmail.com

Ebenezer   (4WF)MINC5203
　1941 W Belmont Avenue
　Chicago, IL 60657
　(773)528-8218   <Cook>
PA: Eduardo Montoya   <M1>
　270 Windsor Drive
　Roselle, IL 60172
　(630)980-1577
　edmontoya@hotmail.com
CL: Samuel Alvarez
　3740 W Leland Avenue
　Chicago, IL 60625
　(773)509-9165

Elm River   (4EC)MINC5107
　2212 County Highway 2 (mailing)
　2250 County Highway 2 (physical)
　Cisne, IL 62823
　( )   <Wayne>
SS: Ralph Blevins   <M1>
　1623 County Road 2375 E
　Geff, IL 62842
　(618)854-2494
　pastorreblevins@gmail.com
CL: Jack Enlow
　2212 County Highway 2
　Cisne, IL 62823
　(618)854-2492
　enlow@wabash.net

Fairfield   (4MEWC)MINC5108
　1700 W Delaware
　Fairfield, IL 62837
　(618)847-5281   <Wayne>
　FAX: (618)842-2608
PA: Jeff Biggs   <M1>
　1504 Cumberland Drive
　Fairfield, IL 62837
　(618)842-2219
　jeffbiggsonline@gmail.com
CL: Kevan Stum
　15 Brock Lane
　Fairfield, IL 62837
　(618)842-2705

Faith   (4C)MINC5501
　20301 E Ten Mile Road
　St Clair Shores, MI 48080
　(586)775-1524   <Macomb>
CL: Christopher D McMacken
　20396 Erben Street
　St Clair Shores, MI 48081
　(586)771-7855
　cmcmacken@itctransco.com

Fullerton   (4WC)MINC5404
　1105 E Allen Street (mailing)
　Route 48 (physical)
　Farmer City, IL 61848
　( )   <DeWitt>
CL: Duane Runyon
　1105 E Allen Street
　Farmer City, IL 61848
　(309)825-3324
　dprunyon@yahoo.com

Georgetown   (4EWC)MINC5204
　201 Frazier Street
　Georgetown, IL 61846
　(217)662-6988   <Vermilion>
CL: Stephen K Hughes
　1011 E 14th Street
　Georgetown, IL 61846
　(217)662-6988
　hughesst@sbcglobal.net

Good Prospect   (4MWC)MINC5205
　PO Box 5 (mailing)
　301 E Trilla Road (physical)
　Trilla, IL 62469
　(217)234-8529   <Coles>
　trillacp@yahoo.com
CL: Jedd Tolen
　PO Box 8
　Trilla, IL 62469
　trillatolens@gmail.com

Grace   (4C)MINC5502
　1122 Harrison Boulevard
　Lincoln Park, MI 48146
　(313)381-3456   <Wayne>
CL: Dorinda Boyer
　21625 Knights Lane
　Brownstown, MI 48183
　(734)675-7322

Knights Chapel   (4WC)MINC5306
　1285 S County Road 375 W
　Petersburg, IN 47567
　( )   <Pike>
CL: Janet Church
　5541 W County Road 100 S
　Petersburg, IN 47567
　(812)749-3242

Lebanon North   (4C)MINC5113
　Route 5
　Fairfield, IL 62837
　(618)842-5205
　FAX: (618)842-5205   <Wayne>
PA: J C McDuffie   <M1>
　RR 3 Box 574
　Fairfield, IL 62837
　(618)842-5624
　mactrapper4@frontier.com
CL: De Young

NORTH CENTRAL PRESBYTERY CONTINUED

107 W King Street
Fairfield, IL 62837
(618)516-1736

_____
Lebanon South   (4C)MINC5114
Route 3
Galatia, IL 62935
( )   <Saline>
OD: Robert D Craig   <M5>
46030 Sunset Drive
Bay Minette, AL 36507
CL: James Patterson
RR 2
Galatia, IL 62935
(618)268-4471

_____
Lincoln First   (4MEWC)MINC5405
PO Box 596 (mailing)
110 Broadway (physical)
Lincoln, IL 62656
(217)732-7568   <Logan>
cumberland@frontier.com
PA: Steven Blaum   <M1>
184 900 Street
Middletown, IL 62666
(217)871-3339
strab2010@yahoo.com
CL: Ronald (Ron) Hubbard
330 3rd Street
Lincoln, IL 62656
(217)871-5453
rehubb1@gmail.com

_____
Monroe City   (4MWC)MINC5307
PO Box 167 (mailing)
8th & Cleveland Streets (physical)
Monroe City, IN 47557
(812)743-5171   <Knox>
FAX: (812)743-5171
PA: David Parman   <M1>
5034 S Monroe School Road
Monroe City, IN 47557
(812)743-2646
FAX: (812)743-5171
CL: Marjorie Vories
PO Box 167
Monroe City, IN 47557
(812)743-5286
FAX: (812)743-5171

_____
Morningside   (4WC)MINC5304
8419 Newburgh Road
Evansville, IN 47715
(812)473-4700   <Vanderburgh>
FAX: (812)473-4765
morningsidechurch@sbcglobal.net
PA: James Messer   <M1 M8>
3653 Old Madisonville Road
Henderson, KY 42420
(270)827-0711
jcmess@hotmail.com
CL: Karen Gossman
5077 Kenosha Drive
Newburgh, IN 47630
(812)490-6522
km56gossman@yahoo.com

_____
Mt Gilead   (4C)MINC5406
PO Box 494 (mailing)
1077 Mt Gilead Road (physical)
Greenville, IL 62246

( )   <Bond>
CL: Elizabeth File
547 IL Route 140
Pocahontas, IL 62275
(618)664-3216

_____
Mt Olivet   (4C)MINC5308
3153 S State Road 257 (mailing)
4299 S State Road 57 (physical)
Washington, IN 47501
(812)254-4077   <Daviess>
g9barnard@yahoo.com
CL: Karen Barnard
3153 S State Road 257
Washington, IN 47501
(812)254-4077
g9barnard@yahoo.com

_____
Mt Oval   (2C)MINC5116
Route 2
Norris City, IL 62869
( )   <White>
CL: Edward Douglas
950 Washington Road
Omaha, IL 62871
(618)962-3362

_____
New Hope   (4EC)MINC5208
3997 N 100th Street (mailing)
Casey, IL 62420
20955 E 2100th Avenue (physical)
Yale, IL 62481
( )   <Jasper>
royndebbie@hotmail.com
LS: Chris Parr   <M6>
9956 E 2100th Avenue
Hidalgo, IL 62438
(618)793-2704
parpar62432@yahoo.com
CL: Roy Shanks
3997 N 100th Street
Casey, IL 62420
(217)932-2995
royndebbie@hotmail.com

_____
Pleasant Grove   (4EC)MINC5210
6360 E 2100th Avenue (mailing)
Martinsville, IL 62442
4125 E 200th Avenue (physical)
Annapolis, IL 62413
(618)569-4588   <Crawford>
donnie.bailey62@yahoo.com
LS: Bill Ulery   <M6>
10725 E 1500th Road
Marshall, IL 62441
(217)382-4593
CL: Donnie B Bailey
7970 E 1625th Avenue
Robinson, IL 62454
(618)569-4588
donnie.bailey62@yahoo.com

_____
Shiloh   (4MWC)MINC5409
7722 Shiloh Road
Virginia, IL 62691
(217)452-3802   <Cass>
CL: Anna Ruth Long
6614 IL Route 78
Virginia, IL 62691
(217)883-2654
hjlong@casscomm.com

_____
Shinar   (4WC)MINC5410
11383 147th Avenue (mailing)
West Burlington, IA 52655
19705 185th Avenue (physical)
New London, IA 52645
(319)457-2652   <Des Moines>
OD: Shane McCampbell   <M5>
109 Indian Terrace
Burlington, IA 52601
(319)457-2652
revshane777@yahoo.com
CL: Carolyn Schenk
11383 147th Avenue
West Burlington, IA 52655
(319)754-8274
carolynschenk@yahoo.com

_____
Spring Hill   (4C)MINC5411
690 E 1800th Avenue (mailing)
9 miles SW of Beecher City (physical)
Beecher City, IL 62414
( )   <Fayette>
OD: Donald Ray Miller   <M5>
Route 2 Box 136C
Beecher City, IL 62414
(618)487-5648
CL: Nelda Kline
690 E 1800th Avenue
Beecher City, IL 62414
(618)487-5363

_____
Union North   (4C)MINC5124
506 Lakeview Drive (mailing)
635 County Road 2400 E (physical)
Fairfield, IL 62837
(618)847-4061   <Wayne>
PA: Ron Fell   <M1>
PO Box 285
Fairfield, IL 62837
(618)638-3744
r.fell@yahoo.com
CL: Sandra Beckel
506 W Lakeview Drive
Fairfield, IL 62837
(618)842-6400
gonqwik@fairfieldwireless.net

_____
United   (4MC)MINC5119
204 S Powell Street
Norris City, IL 62869
(618)378-3341   <White>
FAX: (618)378-3064
tc_5854@yahoo.com
CL: Nellie Shepard
206 E Eubanks Street
Norris City, IL 62869
(618)378-3997

_____
Willow Creek   (4MWC)MINC5211
6492 E 400th Road
Martinsville, IL 62442
(618)569-4955   <Clark>
PA: Kevin Small   <M1>
6492 E 400th Road
Martinsville, IL 62442
(618)569-4955
revkev61@gmail.com
CL: Norma Calvert
6313 E 400th Road
Martinsville, IL 62442

NORTH CENTRAL PRESBYTERY CONTINUED

(618)569-3035
norma.calvert@yahoo.com

OTHERS ON MINISTERIAL ROLL:

Allen, Gail   <M1 WC>
488 County Road 1650 N
Bethany, IL 61914
(217)665-3387
kallen1_61914@yahoo.com

Aros, Jeremias   <M1 RT>
5649 W Roscoe Street
Chicago, IL 60634
(773)685-4395
jeremiasaros@sbcglobal.net

Axton, Durant   <M1 WC>
2441 SE Browning Road
Evansville, IN 47725
(812)459-0089
FAX: (618)842-2608

Barnett, Rudolph   <M1 WC>
RR 5 Box 267
McLeansboro, IL 62859
(618)643-3253

Bender, Richard J   <M1 WC>
5297 Normandy Place
Evansville, IN 47715
(812)983-9597
richardjbenderjr@yahoo.com

Bunting, Geoff   <M1 WC>
9229 Hedgewood Court
Evansville, IN 47725
(812)925-6630
geoff.bunting@yahoo.com

Compton, Marcia   <M1 ST>
218 N Kirk W
Indianapolis, IN 46234
(317)209-9798
mcomptonma@yahoo.com

Craig, Robert A   <M1 RT>
1408 Business Loop W Apt E313
Columbia, MO 65202
(773)477-8249
v-craig@sbcglobal.net

Dallwig, Roger   <M1 WC>
1661 Hickory Lane
Corydon, IN 47112
(812)705-5071
rcd129@hotmail.com

Dill, Diane   <Advisory Mem>
1105 N State Street Apt E7
Lincoln, IL 62656
(217)617-4400
diedremarie@live.com

Furr, Wayne   <M1 WC>
706 E 6th Street
Coal Valley, IL 61240
(309)791-1691
prespreacher@gmail.com

Gross, Ronald   <M1 RT>
2436 N 420th Street
Oblong, IL 62449
(217)932-2788
juneg@eiis.net

Korb, Leon C   <M1 RT>
15360 E 350 North Road
Ridge Farm, IL 61870
(217)662-8398

Lovelace, John G   <M1 RT>
1202 Cedar Street
New Baden, IL 62265
(812)476-5879
jlove1234@aol.com

Nichols, Oscar Lee   <M1 RT>
1035 N County Road 650E
Trilla, IL 62469
(217)234-6551

Oliveira, Jose   <M1 WC>
7310 Jasmine Drive
Hanover Park, IL 60133
(630)855-0870
valdirsoares@yahoo.com

Richards, Carroll R   <M1 RT M9>
210 Allison Drive
Lincoln, IL 62656
(217)732-7894
FAX: (217)732-7894
dr_cr@comcast.net

Scott, Lisa   <M1 WC>
ADDRESS ON FILE
(816)332-0604
lascott1979@att.net

Shirley, Betty L   <M1 RT>
811 Rotherham Drive
Ballwin, MO 63011
(636)386-3174
therevbls@prodigy.net

Smith, Albert J   <M1 RT>
407 W Main Street Apt 131
Wilkesboro, NC 28697
(217)452-3408
ct_alsmith@casscomm.com

Topar, Shirley   <M1 WC>
2233 Cambridge Drive SE
Grand Rapids, MI 49506
(616)245-0625
s_j_topar@yahoo.com

Wallace, Andrew   <M1 WC>
816 Howard Avenue
Burlingame, CA 94010

Watkins, Robert B   <M1 DE>
235 Misty Drive
Somerset, KY 42503
(319)431-0990
watkr@mac.com

Yarce, Janeth   <M1 WC>
3019 W Calavar Road
Phoenix, AZ 85053
(630)518-0295
janethyarce@yahoo.com

OTHER LICENTIATES ON ROLL:

OTHER CANDIDATES ON ROLL:

Alvarez, Samuel   <M3>
3740 W Leland Avenue
Chicago, IL 60625
(773)509-9165

Sandiford, Holton   <M3>
4227 E 300th Road
Casey, IL 62420
(217)259-3773

Stephenson, Joseph   <M3>
PO Box 129
Bethany, IL 61914
(217)853-7819

Red River Presbytery
MISSION SYNOD

GENERAL	1.Church Number	2.Active	3.Total	4.Church School	5.Prof. of Faith	6.Gains	7.Losses	8.Children Baptized	9. OUR UNITED OUT-REACH	10. Total Out-Reach Giving	11. All Other Expenses	12. Total Income Received	13. Value Church Prop. 1=1000
	1	2	3	4	5	6	7	8	9	10	11	12	13
Burns Flat	6301	87	87	60	6	6	19	0	2,600	24,296	83,181	107,504	1,500
Clinton	6302	121	121	58	3	3	1	0	7,739	12,844	113,572	126,416	1,500
Covenant	6304	81	102	87	0	0	5	0	6,000	31,132	164,551	211,730	1,130
Denton	8404	52	204	30	0	0	2	1	1,500	6,124	62,858	79,000	2,500
Eastlake	6205	50	143	20	2	11	1	0	4,189	5,795	86,624	86,050	1,000
Faith	6201	38	38	0	0	0	4	0	5,077	5,667	110,549	98,654	450
Hubbard	8410	13	13	5	No Report Received			0	0	0	0	0	200
Lake Highlands+	8411	149	149	58	6	6	36	4	0	7,379	282,354	256,900	3,390
Locust Grove	6203	7	11	5	0	0	0	0	200	2,300	25,050	9,600	150
Mangum	6306	16	16	11	0	17	0	0	600	3,187	45,537	12,536	752
Marlow	6305	43	77	21	0	0	3	0	7,828	21,391	94,915	113,807	694
Mesquite	8412	36	47	14	0	6	15	0	0	3,000	72,579	79,742	1,200
Mt. Zion	8414	4	4	20	0	0	0	0	1,873	0	12,890	15,258	60
Newberry	8415	22	22	5	0	10	1	0	500	3,100	18,712	21,194	461
Olney	8416	62	92	35	1	1	1	0	8,646	15,994	82,541	86,458	600
Pathway	8418	1,100	1,954	575	49	181	8	38	2,400	256,818	1,935,368	2,561,343	5,480
Sandy Springs	8420	20	35	7	1	1	1	0	0	6,884	10,089	30,758	200
Shiloh	8421	89	205	62	3	5	3	1	17,892	48,374	172,924	212,364	1,030
St. John	8413	31	74	6	0	0	3	0	5,836	10,297	77,940	79,288	916
St. Luke	8407	83	86	60	No Report Received			0	0	0	0	0	4,743
St. Mark (TX)	8408	52	52	5	0	0	1	0	0	7,995	58,506	61,986	1,048
St. Timothy	8419	136	251	114	No Report Received			0	26,805	0	0	0	2,570
Stonegate	6307	47	47	22	13	15	5	1	8,431	10,219	68,982	89,201	823
Trinity	8409	78	97	29	No Report Received			0	13,549	0	0	0	1,300
Whitney	8424	11	11	4	1	1	1	3	180	1,084	16,612	13,507	100
Zion Valley	8425	14	14	3	0	0	0	0	500	8,142	18,536	28,840	180
TOTALS	26	2,433	3,954	1,316	85	263	112	45	122,345	492,022	3,614,870	4,382,136	33,977

*Math error corrected. **Purged roll. +Union church

CHURCHES, PASTORS, AND CLERKS:

Burns Flat   (4WMC)MSRR6301
PO Box 8 (mailing)
205 Highway 44 (physical)
Burns Flat, OK 73624
(580)562-4706   \<Washita\>
burnsflatcpc@windstream.net
PA: Thomas R Spence   \<M1\>
PO Box 802
Burns Flat, OK 73624
(580)562-4531
tomspence0302@gmail.com
CL: Gene Reeves
Route 2 Box 177
Dill City, OK 73641
(580)674-3763
patsyreeves@windstream.net

Clinton   (4WMC)MSRR6302
500 S 30th Street
Clinton, OK 73601
(580)323-3440   \<Custer\>
PA: Dale Nease   \<M1\>
500 S 30th Street
Clinton, OK 73601
(580)323-7557

CL: Dave Felch
500 S 30th Street
Clinton, OK 73601
(580)323-3111

Covenant   (4MEWC)MSRR6304
15791 State Highway 1W
Ada, OK 74820
(580)332-0799   \<Pontotoc\>
lindasnelling@covenantcpc.org
PA: Linda Snelling   \<M1\>
15791 State Highway 1W
Ada, OK 74820
(580)332-0799
FAX: (580)332-9424
lindasnelling@covenantcpc.org
CL: Randy C Davidson
PO Box 880
Ada, OK 74821
(580)421-6969
randy@d-son.com

Denton   (4MWC)MSRR8404
PO Box 236 (mailing)
1424 Stuart Road (physical)
Denton, TX 76202
(940)387-6811   \<Denton\>
gacakee12@verizon.net

CL: Kathy McIntire
304 Surveyors Road
Aubrey, TX 76227
(940)365-2087
kcm1@att.net

Eastlake   (4C)MSRR6205
700 SW 134th Street
Oklahoma City, OK 73170
(405)799-8987   \<Oklahoma\>
eastlakecumberland@att.net
PA: Leslie A Johnson   \<M1\>
11716 Price Drive
Oklahoma City, OK 73170
(405)248-4232
ljohnson275@cox.net
CL: Ray Sears
821 SW 42nd Street
Moore, OK 73160
(405)703-0779
lrsears@cox.net

Faith   (4WC)MSRR6201
PO Box 690715 (mailing)
2801 S 129th East Avenue (physical)
Tulsa, OK 74169
(918)437-2190   \<Tulsa\>
FAX: (918)437-2199

RED RIVER PRESBYTERY CONTINUED

tulsafaith@att.net
PA: Thomas R Sanders   <M1 DE>
    4201 W Kent Street
    Broken Arrow, OK 74012
    (918)269-0043
    FAX: (918)437-2199
    trsncf@msn.com
CL: Georgia Stevens
    29605 S River Ridge Drive
    Catoosa, OK 74015
    FAX: (918)437-2199
    stevenscabinets@yahoo.com

Hubbard   (4MWC)MSRR8410
    404 N Magnolia
    Hubbard, TX 76648
    (   )   <Hill>
CL: Brenard Nunnelley
    475 H County Road 3350 N
    Hubbard, TX 76648
    (254)576-2468
    bfn76648@aol.com

Lake Highlands   (4WU)MSRR8411
    8525 Audelia Road
    Dallas, TX 75238
    (214)348-2133   <Dallas>
    lhpc@lhpres.org
PA: Perryn Rice   <M1>
    10802 Hayfield Drive
    Dallas, TX 75238
    (931)526-6585
    perryn@lhpres.org
CL: Maureen Ramsay
    8935 Larchwood Drive
    Dallas, TX 75238
    (214)542-6173
    FAX: (214)348-2408
    msramsay@hotmail.com

Locust Grove   (4MWC)MSRR6203
    PO Box 577 (mailing)
    203 E Harriett Avenue (physical)
    Locust Grove, OK 74352
    (918)479-5613   <Mayes>
PA: R Brent Turpen   <M1>
    PO Box 577
    Locust Grove, OK 74352
    (918)479-5613
    mlturpen@hotmail.com
CL: Mayme Miley
    7847 S 438 Road
    Locust Grove, OK 74352
    (918)479-2575

Mangum   (4MEWC)MSRR6306
    314 N Oklahoma
    Mangum, OK 73554
    (580)782-2560   <Greer>
    FAX: (580)782-3485
SS: David Rosales   <M3>
    101 N Lowe
    Hobart, OK 73651
    (580)682-0722
    sagradalut@gmail.com
CL: Jack Cossey
    606 W Sproat Street
    Mangum, OK 73554
    (580)782-2560
    jscossey@att.net

Marlow   (4MWC)MSRR6305
    202 N Sixth
    Marlow, OK 73055
    (580)658-2892   <Stephens>
    rgoodman4gvn@hotmail.com
PA: Robert Goodman   <M1>
    604 N 4th Street
    Marlow, OK 73055
    (580)756-4726
    rgoodman4gvn@hotmail.com
CL: Faye Kimbrough
    1202 W Randall Court
    Duncan, OK 73533
    (580)786-4434

Mesquite   (4C)MSRR8412
    819 N Town East Boulevard
    Mesquite, TX 75150
    (972)270-6923   <Dallas>
    FAX: (972)270-6923
    mcpchurch@gmail.com
IP: Wesley H Johnson   <M1>
    6222 Crestmoor Lane
    Sachse, TX 75048
    (972)429-6129
    wjohnson@transitionconsulting.com
CL: Patricia Chatt
    1705 Windmire Drive
    Mesquite, TX 75181
    (214)394-6513
    FAX: (972)270-6923
    pbchatt@sbcglobal.net

Mt Zion   (2C)MSRR8414
    691 County Road 4108 (mailing)
    Greeneville, TX 75401
    15175 Texas Highway 11 W (physical)
    Cumby, TX 75433
    (903)454-3444   <Hopkins>
    bvwood10@yahoo.com
CL: Virginia Woodworth
    691 County Road 4108
    Greeneville, TX 75401
    (903)454-3444
    bvwood10@yahoo.com

Newberry   (2C)MSRR8415
    PO Box 253 (mailing)
    1301 Newberry Road (physical)
    Millsap, TX 76066
    (   )   <Parker>
SS: Tim Dewhirst   <M3>
    3609 Oakbriar Lane
    Colleyville, TX 76034
    (817)605-8147
    timdew@sbcglobal.net
CL: Royce E Jordan
    1751 Newberry Road
    Millsap, TX 76066
    (940)682-4844

Olney   (4MEWC)MSRR8416
    PO Box 756 (mailing)
    210 S Avenue M (physical)
    Olney, TX 76374
    (940)564-2882   <Young>
    olneycpc@brazosnet.comt
PA: David Carpenter   <M1>
    909 W Elm Street
    Olney, TX 76374
    (940)564-2339

olneycpc@brazosnet.com
CL: Clifton W Key
    PO Box 615
    Olney, TX 76374
    (940)564-2979
    barkey8@brazosnet.com

Pathway   (4EC)MSRR8418
    (previously named St Matthew)
    PO Box 182 (mailing)
    380 NW Tarrant (physical)
    Burleson, TX 76097
    (817)295-5832   <Johnson>
    FAX: (817)295-2576
    info@stmattcpc.org
PA: Rick Owen   <M1>
    3305 Wild Oaks Court
    Burleson, TX 76028
    (817)295-5832
    FAX: (817)295-2576
    rowen@stmattcpc.org
AP: Josh Fortney   <M1>
    765 Windridge Lane
    Burleson, TX 76028
    (214)794-9912
    jfortney@stmattcpc.org
AP: Jeffrey A Gehle   <M1>
    PO Box 182
    Burleson, TX 76097
    (817)295-5832
    jeff.gehle@stmattcpc.org
AP: R Allan Mink   <M2>
    1113 Hidden Glen Court
    Burleson, TX 76028
    (817)295-5832
    FAX: (817)295-2576
    alan.mink@stmattcpc.org
CL: Kim Perkey
    2600 Embry Lane
    Burleson, TX 76028
    (817)235-9061
    kimberley.k.perkey@wellsfargo.com

Sandy Springs   (4C)MSRR8420
    1865 Bones Chapel Road (mailing)
    Rease Road (physical)
    Whitesboro, TX 76273
    (   )   <Grayson>
CL: Billy L Morrow
    1865 Bones Chapel Road
    Whitesboro, TX 76273
    (903)564-5148

Shiloh   (4MEWC)MSRR8421
    7810 Shiloh Road
    Midlothian, TX 76065
    (972)723-3758   <Ellis>
    vernon@sansom.us
PA: Vernon Sansom   <M1>
    104 Cockrell Hill Road
    Ovilla, TX 75154
    (972)825-6887
    vernon@sansom.us
CL: Lynette McCarty
    2160 Springer Road
    Midlothian, TX 76065
    (214)629-6963
    lmccarty@link.com

St John   (4WC)MSRR8413
    6007 W Pleasant Ridge Road

RED RIVER PRESBYTERY CONTINUED

Arlington, TX 76016
(817)478-6219   <Tarrant>
FAX: (817)478-8684
stjohncpc@att.net
CL: Barbara Harrell
  6207 W Poly Webb Road
  Arlington, TX 76016
  (817)229-1796
  baharrell@tx.rr.com

St Luke   (4C)MSRR8407
  1404 Sycamore School Road
  Fort Worth, TX 76134
  (817)293-3778   <Tarrant>
  FAX: (817)293-2750
  office@stlukecpc.org
PA: David Kurtz   <M1>
  1404 Sycamore School Road
  Fort Worth, TX 76134
  (817)683-4783
  davidk36@yahoo.com
CL: Beth McLaughlin
  5462 Rutland Avenue
  Fort Worth, TX 76133
  (817)292-5471
  mcbeth1951@att.net

St Mark (TX)   (4MWC)MSRR8408
  4101 Hardeman Street
  Fort Worth, TX 76119
  (817)536-1315   <Tarrant>
PA: Roosevelt Baugh   <M1>
  4101 Hardeman Street
  Fort Worth, TX 76119
  (817)536-1315
  gmf1220@charter.net
CL: Hazel F Wilson
  2801 Sarah Jane Lane
  Fort Worth, TX 76119
  (817)536-4892
  jesseewilson@charter.net

St Timothy   (4WC)MSRR8419
  PO Box 210338 (mailing)
  3001 Forest Ridge Drive (physical)
  Bedford, TX 76095
  (817)571-7474   <Tarrant>
  FAX: (817)571-7714
  cbrown@sttimothy-cpc.org
CL: Danny Washmon
  PO Box 210338
  Bedford, TX 76095
  (817)571-7474
  washmon@rocketmail.com

Stonegate   (ARC)MSRR6307
  17101 North Western Avenue
  Edmond, OK 73083
  (405)340-7281   <Oklahoma>
  stonegatecpc@gmail.com
PA: Marian Sontowski   <M1>
  17101 North Western Avenue
  Edmond, OK 73083
  (405)340-7281
  stonegatecpc@gmail.com
CL: Jeanette Spilman
  17101 North Western Avenue
  Edmond, OK 73083
  (405)340-7281
  stonegate.clerk@gmail.com

Trinity   (4MEWC)MSRR8409
  7120 W Cleburne Road
  Fort Worth, TX 76133
  (817)292-6149   <Tarrant>
  trinitycpc@sbcglobal.net
PA: Randy L Hardisty   <M1>
  4908 Redondo Street
  Fort Worth, TX 76180
  (817)428-3513
  rhardisty@sbcglobal.net
CL: Betty Jean Cooper
  1108 Trinity Trail
  Saginaw, TX 76131
  (817)306-4877
  bjjacoop@sbcglobal.net

Whitney   (4EC)MSRR8424
  PO Box 582 (mailing)
  108 S Colorado (physical)
  Whitney, TX 76692
  (254)694-3852   <Hill>
PA: Charles A Hendershot   <M1>
  122 Tree Shadow
  Whitney, TX 76692
  (254)694-3852
CL: Lou Webb
  101 Bridge Lane
  Whitney, TX 76692
  (254)694-2879
  joelou2@windstream.net

Zion Valley   (4C)MSRR8425
  2684 South FM 1655
  Chico, TX 76431
  ( )   <Wise>
PA: Barney Hudson   <M1>
  10541 Fossil Hill Drive
  Fort Worth, TX 76131
  (817)851-2960
  barneyrev@gmail.com
CL: Priscilla Moreland
  1177 N State Highway 101
  Chico, TX 76431
  (940)644-2462
  hdpjmoreland@hotmail.com

OTHERS ON MINISTERIAL ROLL:

Aden, Marty   <M1 M9>
  202 Bennington Place
  Wilmington, NC 28412
  (910)795-1092
  maden@ec.rr.com
Baltimore, Claud G   <M1 RT>
  PO Box 1358
  1430 Lakehurst Drive
  Ada, OK 74821
  (580)332-2679
  baltimorejb@earthlink.net
Brown, Chuck   <M1 DE>
  137 St Agnes
  Memphis, TN 38112
  (817)915-2907
  cbrown@sttimothy-cpc.org
Brown, Stephanie S   <M1 M9>
  137 St Agnes
  Memphis, TN 38112
  (901)729-3612
  scrudderbrown7@gmail.com
Condon, Jr, Thomas W   <M1 RT>
  6508 Victoria Avenue

N Richland Hills, TX 76180
(817)656-9334
Ferrol, Ruben   <M1 M9 RT>
  1823 Straford Court
  Allentown, PA 18103
  (610)966-7289
  rubeferrol@msn.com
Gardner, Charles   <M1 RT>
  PO Box 1035
  Elephant Butte, NM 87035
  (719)784-7744
Harris, Wendell   <M1 WC>
  329 N Louis Tittle Avenue
  Mangum, OK 73554
  (580)782-2142
  wendellharris@itlnet.net
Henson, Kevin R   <M1 WC>
  1121 Raleigh Path
  Denton, TX 76208
  (817)354-1182
  khenson@cpch.org
Hong, Soon Gab   <M1 WC>
  13600 Doty Avenue Apt 4
  Hawthorne, CA 90250
  (972)446-0350
  lemuelhong@hotmail.com
Howell, Linda   <M1 WC>
  PO Box 80050
  Keller, TX 76244
  (601)942-2015
  lshowell1000@yahoo.com
Kays, Michael   <M1 WC>
  2505 Canterbury Avenue
  Muskogee, OK 74403
  (918)577-6255
  msppk@suddenlink.net
Lain, Judy   <M1 M9>
  1928 Pine Ridge Drive
  Bedford, TX 76021
  (817)660-8020
  judylane5@gmail.com
Lounsbury-Lombard, Kristi   <M1 M9>
  902 Clearview
  Krum, TX 76249
  (940)435-5077
  kristilounsbury@gmail.com
Madden, Judith Ellen   <M1 WC>
  100 SW Brushy Mound
  Burleson, TX 76028
  (817)295-5832
  jmadden@stmattcpc.org
Martinez, Soledad   <M1 WC>
  2801 Biway Street
  Fort Worth, TX 76114
  (817)812-8247
  ismael3233@sbcglobal.net
McGee, Charles Randall   <M1 WC>
  9037 Groveland Drive
  Dallas, TX 75218
  (214)328-2488
  randallmcgee@sbcglobal.net
Nelson, Charles E   <M1 WC>
  209 Classic Court
  Springtown, TX 76082
  (903)641-5466
  dundeal10@aol.com
Parkhurst, L G, Jr   <M1 WC>
  409 Woodhollow Trail
  Edmond, OK 73012
  (405)341-7477
Petty, Linda Lee   <M1 WC>

RED RIVER PRESBYTERY CONTINUED

4401 W Elgin Street
Broken Arrow, OK 74012
(918)252-4741
Rice, Keith   <M1 M9>
PO Box 582
Itasca, TX 76055
(254)087-2418
rsvkeith@yahoo.com
Rivera, Carlos A   <M1 WC>
Calle Dr Jose Maria Vertiz 1410
Departmento 202B, Colonia Portales
Delegacion Benito
Juarez, C.P. 03300 MEXICO
(52)1-55-31058377
caralrifra@une.net.co
Ruggia, Mario (Bud)   <M1 M9 RT>
603 Rumsey Street
Kiowa, KS 67070
(620)825-4509
ruggia@aol.com
Schmoyer, Donna Marie   <M1 WC>
613 Mound Street
Monongahela, PA 15063
(817)266-6572
schmoyerdm@yahoo.com
Scrudder, Norlan   <M1 RT>
29688 S 534 Road
Park Hill, OK 74451
(918)949-1326
ndscrudder@gmail.com
Sharpe, Michael G   <M1 DE>
3423 Summerdale Drive
Bartlett, TN 38133
(901)276-4572
Shelton, Robert E   <M1 RT>
10508 Royalwood Drive
Dallas, TX 75238
(214)349-7162
bshelton67@yahoo.com
Shelton, Robert M   <M1 RT>
7128 Lakehurst Avenue
Dallas, TX 75230
(214)696-3237

Shugert, Richard   <M1 WC>
5208 Bellis Drive
Fort Worth, TX 76244
(817)913-7211
shugertr@yahoo.com
Smith, Robert H   <M1 WC>
5055 S 76th East Avenue Apt D
Tulsa, OK 74145
(918)671-5520
rhsmith@sstelco.com
Thomas, Cassandra   <M1 RT>
1920 Dancy Street
Fayetteville, NC 28301
(910)488-4897
chcothomas@yahoo.com
Wagner, Hugh   <M1 RT>
12556 Timberline Drive
Garfield, AR 72732
(479)359-0021
hughawagner@gmail.com
Webb, William G   <M1 OM>
7926 S 78th East Avenue
Tulsa, OK 74133
(918)294-9117
Youngman, Betty   <M1 RT>
1471 Creekview Court
Fort Worth, TX 76112
(817)492-4100
bettyy@swbell.net
Zumbrunnen, Craig H   <M1 WC>
1210 Country Club Road Apt 3
Santa Teresa, NM 88008
(580)471-0308
craigzum1@yahoo.com

OTHER LICENIATES ON ROLL:

King, Keith   <M2 ST>
3341 S 137th East Avenue
Tulsa, OK 74134
(918)437-5464
cpkking@yahoo.com

OTHER CANDIDATES ON ROLL:

Bohon, Chris Michael   <M3>
109 NE McAlister Road
Burleson, TX 76028
(817)228-9494
cbohon@stmattcpc.org
Brown, Houston
866 N McLean
Memphis, TN 38107
(817)915-9090
hpbrown95@gmail.com

Robert Donnell Presbytery
SOUTHEAST SYNOD

GENERAL		MEMBERSHIP			CHANGES				FINANCES				
1.Church Number	2.Active	3.Total	4.Church School	5.Prof. of Faith	6.Gains	7.Losses	8.Children Baptized	9. OUR UNITED OUT-REACH	10. Total Out-Reach Giving	11. All Other Expenses	12. Total Income Received	13. Value Church Prop. 1=1000
	1	2	3	4	5	6	7	8	9	10	11	12	13
Alabaster	0107	150	363	30	2	2	7	1	5,672	28,473	196,051	203,339	2,300
Big Cove	0801	19	31	12	0	0	0	0	0	60	26,199	22,294	330
Christ Church	0814	83	109	20	0	5	3	0	10,336	16,335	99,871	117,242	650
Concord	0802	23	79	18	No Report Received			0	2,043	0	0	0	286
East Point	0206	22	69	14	0	1	0	0	950	3,072	31,407	28,984	657
Edgefield	0813	2	3	0	No Report Received			0	0	0	0	0	209
Eidson Chapel	0207	20	51	17	No Report Received			0	0	0	0	0	140
Goosepond	0803	28	47	4	2	2	3	0	1,800	7,007	25,146	32,153	250
Gurley	0804	80	80	25	0	4	0	1	5,705	31,889	134,998	186,381	751
Holly Grove	0805				Closed 3/2014								
Hope+	0812	65	65	14	0	2	3	0	0	5,058	72,181	77,242	568
Huntsville, 1st	0806	58	115	25	0	6	3	0	1,200	7,097	102,300	101,300	1,500
Meridianville	0808	35	41	18	0	1	4	0	0	0	66,530	62,972	1,350
Scottsboro	0809	264	462	124	2	3	6	3	25,781	66,100	228,322	344,972	2,780
Stevenson	0810	142	141	28	0	0	7	1	8,616	29,670	58,298	87,968	1,200
Union Grove	0211	20	27	15	No Report Received			0	0	0	0	0	200
Walnut Grove	0811	20	43	10	No Report Received			0	25	0	0	0	20
TOTALS	16	1,031	1,726	374	6	26	36	6	62,128	194,761	1,041,303	1,264,847	13,191

*Math error corrected. **Purged roll. +Union church

CHURCHES, PASTORS, AND CLERKS:

Alabaster   (4WC)SERD0107
   8828 Highway 119
   Alabaster, AL 35007
   (205)663-3152   <Shelby>
   FAX: (205)663-8323
   fpcalabaster@bellsouth.net
IP: Darren Kennemer   <M1>
   8828 Highway 119
   Alabaster, AL 35007
   (205)663-3152
   FAX: (205)663-8323
   darren.kennemer@va.gov
CL: Margaret Russo
   8828 Highway 119
   Alabaster, AL 35007
   (205)663-3152
   russorm@att.net

Big Cove   (4MWC)SERD0801
   5984 Highway 431 S
   Brownsboro, AL 35741
   (256)518-9657   <Madison>
SS: Philip Nickles   <M1 OP>
   5821 County Road 1114
   Vinemont, AL 35179
   (256)734-9847
   nickles.phil@yahoo.com
CL: Beryl Tidwell
   680 Old Big Cove Road
   Owens Cross Roads, AL 35763
   (256)518-9977
   beryl.tidwell@comcast.net

Christ Church   (4WC)SERD0814

   1580 Jeff Road
   Huntsville, AL 35806
   (256)837-6014   <Madison>
   christchurch@knology.net
PA: Cardelia Howell Diamond   <M1>
   1580 Jeff Road
   Huntsville, AL 35806
   (256)837-6014
   clhdzmhd@hotmail.com
CL: Cheryl Caldwell
   1043 Douglass Road
   Huntsville, AL 35806
   (256)837-6014
   sccz4647@att.net

Concord   (4MWC)SERD0802
   1827 Joe Quick Road
   New Market, AL 35761
   (256)828-4503   <Madison>
CL: Gayle Poole
   215 Sealey Hill Road
   New Market, AL 35761
   (256)829-1147

East Point   (4WC)SERD0206
   1441 US Highway 278 E
   Cullman, AL 35055
   (256)734-0900   <Cullman>
OD: Lee Walton   <M5>
   1441 US Highway 278 E
   Cullman, AL 35055
   (256)620-1302
   lee.walton@wallacestate.edu
CL: Karen Munger
   PO Box 1773
   Cullman, AL 35056
   (256)739-0746

karenamunger@bellsouth.net

Edgefield   (4UC)SERD0813
   411 McMahan Cove Road (mailing)
   Stevenson, AL 35772
   311 County Road 158 (physical)
   Stevenson, AL 35772
   ( )   <Jackson>
CL: Merris Powell
   7434 Alabama Highway 40
   Henagar, AL 35978
   (256)558-0715

Eidson Chapel   (4C)SERD0207
   2680 County Road 1725
   Holly Pond, AL 35083
   ( )   <Cullman>
OD: Floyd Bradford   <M5>
   351 Piney Grove Road W
   Falkville, AL 35622
   (256)784-6510
   FAX: (415)864-1543
CL: Linda Harris
   5910 County Road 747
   Cullman, AL 35058
   (256)734-6697

Goosepond   (4MWC)SERD0803
   1155 East Hancock Drive
   Scottsboro, AL 35769
   (256)259-4386   <Jackson>
   betrich76@gmail.com
CL: Bettie M Jordan
   198 County Road 46
   Hollywood, AL 35752
   (256)437-1546
   betrich76@gmail.com

ROBERT DONNELL PRESBYTERY CONTINUED

Gurley   (4MEWC)SERD0804
   223 Section Line Road
   Gurley, AL 35748
   (256)776-2331   <Madison>
PA: Toy E Brindley   <M1>
   PO Box 335
   Gurley, AL 35748
   (256)776-2331
   gurleycpc@gmail.com
CL: Becky Arnold
   423 Sharps Cove Road
   Gurley, AL 35748
   (256)776-6950
   bailey@darnold.net

Holly Grove   (2C)SERD0805
CLOSED 3/2014

Hope   (4WU)SERD0812
   10001 Bailey Cove Road SE
   Huntsville, AL 35803
   (256)881-4673   <Madison>
   hopepresby@comcast.net
PA: Christie Ashton   <M1>
   10001 Bailey Cove Road SE
   Huntsville, AL 35803
   (256)881-4673
   pastorhope@comcast.net
CL: Cheryl D Hoard
   10001 Bailey Cove Road SE
   Huntsville, AL 35803
   (256)881-4673
   cdhoard@bellsouth.net

Huntsville First   (4EWC)SERD0806
   PO Box 777 (mailing)
   1802 Bankhead Parkway (physical)
   Huntsville, AL 35804
   (256)536-9371   <Madison>
   hsvfcpc@att.net
PA: Richard W Hughes   <M1>
   2954 Bob Wade Lane
   Harvest, AL 35749
   (256)859-3178
   hughesrichard23@gmail.com
CL: Carla Rowley
   PO Box 777
   2012 Brandy Court
   Huntsville, AL 35811
   (256)651-5916
   carla.rowley4@gmail.com

Meridianville   (4MWC)SERD0808
   PO Box 188 (mailing)
   11696 Highway 231/431 N (physical)
   Meridianville, AL 35759
   (256)828-0160   <Madison>
   dptalley@hotmail.com
PA: Keith Lorick   <M1>
   127 Chesapeake Boulevard
   Madison, AL 35757
   (256)325-3865
   keithlorick@knology.net
CL: Donna Talley
   360 Monroe Road
   Meridianville, AL 35759
   (256)683-6111
   dptalley@hotmail.com

Scottsboro   (4WC)SERD0809

PO Box 639 (mailing)
315 S Kyle Street (physical)
Scottsboro, AL 35768
FAX: (256)259-2809
cumberland@scottsboro.org
(256)574-2575   <Jackson>
SS: Micaiah Thomas   <M2 OP>
   PO Box 5204 SBN 499
   Princeton, NJ 08543
   (205)478-5985
   micaiah.thomas@gmail.com
CL: Lilly Noble
   237 County Road 350
   Hollywood, AL 35752
   lillynoble3@yahoo.com

Stevenson   (4MEWC)SERD0810
   112 College Street
   Stevenson, AL 35772
   (256)437-8632   <Jackson>
PA: Perry Whitaker
   202 College Street
   Stevenson, AL 35772
   (256)437-8632
   brotherperry@msn.com
CL: Jen Stewart
   112 College Street
   Stevenson, AL 35772
   (256)437-3116
   jstewart306@hotmail.com

Union Grove   (4WC)SERD0211
   91 County Road 1734 (mailing)
   2760 County Road 1742 (physical)
   Holly Pond, AL 35083
   (256)796-1023   <Cullman>
   johnson9983@att.net
PS: David Hooper   <M6>
   115 County Road 682
   Cullman, AL 35055
   (256)775-2419
   davidhoop165@yahoo.com
CL: Glen Johnson
   91 County Road 1734
   Holly Pond, AL 35083
   (256)796-1023
   johnson9983@att.net

Walnut Grove   (4WC)SERD0811
   PO Box 403 (mailing)
   711 New Hope/Cedar Point Road (physical)
   New Hope, AL 35760
   ( )   <Madison>
PA: James Smith   <M1>
   1949 Little Cove Road
   Owens Cross Roads, AL 35763
   dr.james.smith42@gmail.com
CL: Kathy Pegues
   211 Butler Lane
   New Hope, AL 35760
   (256)723-8740
   mcwoodpeg@nehp.net

OTHERS ON MINISTERIAL ROLL:

Alverson, Elmer L   <M1 RT>
   354 Roy Davis Road
   New Market, AL 35761
   (256)828-4503
   bud@alscomputers.com

Babcock, Edward S, Jr   <M1 RT>
   1007 San Ramone Avenue
   Huntsville, AL 35802
   (256)882-9339
   ejsb1@aol.com
Bynum, Ronald H   <M1 WC>
   121 Sycamore Road
   Gurley, AL 35748
   (256)776-9313
   ronaldbynum@bellsouth.net
Gillis, Aubrey Thomas   <M1 WC>
   PO Box 869
   Silverhill, AL 36576
   (251)947-1638
   FAX: (205)664-8323
   tomgillis63@hotmail.com
Goodwin, Earl   <M1 WC>
   1012 Windsor Parkway
   Moody, AL 35004
   (205)222-1741
   FAX: (205)664-8323
   earlgoodwin@yahoo.com
Hall, Brad   <M1 WC>
   1602 Toll Gate Road SE
   Huntsville, AL 35801
   (256)533-4845
Hall, John D   <M1 WC>
   109 Oddo Lane SE
   Huntsville, AL 35802
   (256)880-5129
   johnhall33@comcast.net
Hall, Roy W   <M1 RT>
   87 Lee Hall Street
   Scottsboro, AL 35769
   (256)259-9340
   royhall@scottsboro.org
Herring, C E (Ed) Jr   <M1 RT>
   969 Campground Circle
   Scottsboro, AL 35769
   (256)259-2721
   edherring@scottsboro.org
Howton, Orvie Ray   <M1 RT>
   4928 Montauk Trail SE
   Owens Cross Road, AL 35763
   (256)533-9224
   arhowton@bellsouth.net
Hughes, Charles   <M1 RT>
   114 Gaul Street
   Estill Springs, TN 37330
   (931)649-5189
   cphugs@cafes.net
Lambert, James   <M1 RT>
   224 Peabody Road
   Meridianville, AL 35759
   (256)828-6850
Livingston, Ronald L   <M1 RT>
   5851 Quantrell Avenue #201
   Alexandria, VA 22312
Matthews, James N   <M1 RT>
   241 Morning Star Drive
   Huntsville, AL 35811
   (256)337-2765
   brojim10@mediacombb.net
Murphree, Hughlen   <M1 WC>
   4298 County Road 1719
   Holly Pond, AL 35083
   (256)796-5352
   hmurph@hiwaay.net

ROBERT DONNELL PRESBYTERY CONTINUED

Phillips-Burk, Pam   <M1 DE>
    3325 Bailey Creek Cove N
    Collierville, TN 38017
    (256)684-5247
    pam@cumberland.org
Reeves, Donald   <M1 RT>
    PO Box 528
    Rainsville, AL 35986
    (256)228-4057
    reevesd@nacc.edu

OTHER CANDIDATES ON ROLL:

Boyd, Tammy   <M3>
    118 County Road 24
    Hanceville, AL 35077
    (256)338-4733

Tennessee-Georgia Presbytery
SOUTHEAST SYNOD

GENERAL		MEMBERSHIP			CHANGES				FINANCES				
	1.Church Number	2.Active	3.Total	4.Church School	5.Prof. of Faith	6.Gains	7.Losses	8.Children Baptized	9. OUR UNITED OUT-REACH	10. Total Out-Reach Giving	11. All Other Expenses	12. Total Income Received	13. Value Church Prop. 1=1000
	1	2	3	4	5	6	7	8	9	10	11	12	13
Bartow	2101	86	150	51	2	3	2	2	5,000	24,398	121,192	133,567	913
Cedar Springs	2119	9	19	5	0	2	0	0	800	2,012	13,995	18,944	323
Charleston	2102	43	55	18	2	6	0	0	4,000	10,611	49,281	58,002	900
Chattanooga 1st	2104	554	554	175	0	7	31	1	5,000	23,267	495,164	513,991	1,500
Cleveland	2108	150	179	87	0	4	3	2	15,573	28,830	287,618	304,235	2,400
Cornerstone Com	2107	12	42	9	No Report Received			0	0	0	0	0	675
Ebenezer*	2110	5	4	0	0	7	3	0	0	887	7,558	10,996	75
El Redill	2149	53	53	39	3	10	12	1	0	5,281	65,432	59,532	780
Falling Water	2111	69	81	29	5	8	9	0	1,000	35,181	100,332	117,162	870
Flint Springs	2112	25	25	0	0	0	1	0	0	423	0	16,852	150
Glory Church*	2144	55	55	7	No Report Received			0	0	0	0	0	2,300
Jasper	2113	30	43	14	0	0	2	0	3,546	3,686	59,372	51,368	750
Kelly's Chapel	2120	13	19	17	No Report Received			0	0	0	0	0	110
Korean Living Sto	2130	30	30	8	Provisional Church			0	50	0	0	0	0
New Hope*	2115	55	82	37	3	3	3	0	1,000	11,100	74,800	85,900	600
Oak Grove	2121	14	28	0	0	0	0	0	0	1,905	10,913	9,552	110
Our Good*	2138	22	22	8	No Report Received			0	0	0	0	0	0
Pine Hill	2117	13	13	14	No Report Received			0	0	0	0	0	70
Prospect United	2116	41	98	20	0	2	2	0	1,618	1,864	80,335	88,503	1,400
Red Bank	2105	265	265	80	No Report Received			0	12,250	0	0	0	2,000
Richard City*	2118	25	65	10	0	3	0	0	900	960	33,240	34,227	900
Silverdale	2106	120	139	35	0	0	12	0	6,252	10,922	2,500	125,011	1,200
South Pittsburg	2123	18	63	0	0	0	1	0	100	500	24,116	25,620	825
Sumach	2124	107	217	92	3	6	11	0	5,000	13,482	132,580	146,062	685
Whitwell*	2122	8	9	10	0	0	6	1	0	621	9,243	13,544	25
TOTALS	25	1,822	2,310	765	18	54	98	7	62,089	175,930	1,467,671	1,813,068	19,561

*Math error corrected. **Purged roll.

TENNESSEE-GEORGIA PRESBYTERY CONTINUED

CHURCHES, PASTORS, AND CLERKS:

Bartow   (4MWEC)SETG2101
  1078 Cassville White Road (mailing)
  Cartersville, GA 30121
  2851 Highway 140 NE (physical)
  Rydal, GA 30171
  (770)382-3896   <Bartow>
  pastormarkbcpcga@gmail.com
PA: Mark Rackley   <M1>
  3060 Highway 140 NE
  Rydal, GA 30171
  (770)382-3790
  pastormarkbcpcga@gmail.com
AP: Min Young Lim   <M3 ST>
  3480 Summit Ridge Parkway
  Duluth, GA 30096
  (770)751-1148
  minyounglim63@gmail.com
CL: James Harris Bagwell
  1078 Cassville White Road
  Cartersville, GA 30121
  (770)382-0747
  shadygrovebeef@aol.com

Cedar Springs   (4C)SETG2119
  495 Cedar Springs Loop (mailing)
  6665 Old Dunlap Road (physical)
  Whitwell, TN 37397
  (   )   <Marion>
PA: Kriss McGowan   <M1>
  900 Alvin York Highway
  Whitwell, TN 37397
  (423)463-8609
  krissmcg658@gmail.com
CL: Sarah Way
  4595 Old Dunlap Road
  Whitwell, TN 37397
  (423)580-7685
  sarahway1958@aol.com

Charleston   (4MEWC)SETG2102
  PO Box 476 (mailing)
  Charleston, TN 37310
  8267 N Lee Highway (physical)
  Cleveland, TN 37312
  (423)336-5004   <Bradley>
PA: Bill Bond   <M1>
  205 Windmere Drive
  Chattanooga, TN 37411
  (423)316-0867
  bill@wcbj.net
CL: Vivian McCormack
  5502 Mouse Creek Road NW
  Cleveland, TN 37312
  (423)479-8230
  mcco6868@bellsouth.net

Chattanooga First   (4WC)SETG2104
  1505 N Moore Road
  Chattanooga, TN 37411
  (423)698-2556   <Hamilton>
  FAX: (423)629-6683
  office@firstcumberland.com
PA: Gary Carver   <M1>
  2810 Cabin Road
  Chattanooga, TN 37404
  (423)698-2556
  FAX: (423)629-6683
  sandgattthecabin@epbfi.com

CL: Christy Miller
  7853 Legacy Park Court
  Chattanooga, TN 37421
  (423)894-8220
  christymiller62@epbfi.com

Cleveland   (4WC)SETG2108
  161 2nd Street NE Ste 3 (mailing)
  200 Church Street NE (physical)
  Cleveland, TN 37311
  (423)476-6751   <Bradley>
  FAX: (423)476-6423
  gchudson3@gmail.com
PA: Jennifer Newell   <M1>
  2322 Maraco Circle
  Chattanooga, TN 37421
  (423)892-5834
  FAX: (423)476-6423
  newelljennifer3@gmail.com
CL: Denise Callais
  161 2nd Street NE Suite 3
  Cleveland, TN 37311
  (423)476-6751

Cornerstone Com   (4MWC)SETG2107
  9632 E Brainerd Road
  Chattanooga, TN 37421
  (423)892-3027   <Hamilton>
  cornerstone3cp@gmail.com
SS: Jerry (Butch) Hullander   <M1>
  767 Rifle Range Road
  Ringgold, GA 30736
  (706)935-4878
  jerryihs@catt.com
CL: Session Clerk
  9632 E Brainerd Road
  Chattanooga, TN 37421
  (423)892-3027
  cornerstone3cp@gmail.com

Ebenezer   (4C)SETG2110
  10699 Griffith Highway (mailing)
  2400 Highway 108(physical)
  Whitwell, TN 37397
  (423)942-1939   <Marion>
  cprevinsv@bellsouth.net
PA: Phillip Layne   <M1>
  10699 Griffith Highway
  Whitwell, TN 37397
  (423)658-5849
  cprevinsv@bellsouth.net
CL: Lloyd Shadrick
  3412 Sequatchie Mountain Road
  Sequatchie, TN 37374
  (423)942-1939

El Redill   (C)SETG2149
  875 Scenic Highway
  Lawrenceville, GA 30045
  (678)698-7971   <Monmouth>
  FAX: (678)225-0127
  mabega@juno.com
PA: Maria (Mabe) Garcia   <M1>
  875 Scenic Highway
  Lawrenceville, GA 30045
  (678)698-7971
  mabega@juno.com
CL: Francia Bryon
  3315 Crooked Stick Drive
  Cumming, GA 30041
  (678)977-8606

elenabry1@yahoo.com

Falling Water   (4WC)SETG2111
  PO Box 2027 (mailing)
  6534 Old Dayton Pike (physical)
  Hixson, TN 37343
  (423)843-3050   <Hamilton>
  james_barry@bellsouth.net
PA: James C Barry   <M1>
  1405 Anna Street
  Hixson, TN 37343
  (903)315-7998
  james_barry@bellsouth.net
CL: Diane J Bunch
  8212 Pierpoint Drive
  Harrison, TN 37341
  (423)802-2763
  topdog23@bellsouth.net

Flint Springs   (4WC)SETG2112
  2225 North East Road SE (mailing)
  Flint Springs Road (physical)
  Cleveland, TN 37311
  (   )   <Bradley>
PA: Kevin Wilson   <M1>
  2225 North East Road SE
  Cleveland, TN 37311
  (423)284-6397
  revkev1000@hotmail.com
CL: James F Mitchell, Jr
  517 Mitchell Road SE
  Cleveland, TN 37323
  (423)479-7649

Glory Church of Jesus Christ(C)SETG2144
  3480 Summit Ridge Parkway
  Duluth, GA 30096
  (   )   < >
PA: David Lee   <M1>
  3480 Summit Ridge Parkway
  Duluth, GA 30096
  (404)641-4359
  gcjcatl@gmail.com
CL: Session Clerk Glory Church
  3480 Summit Ridge Parkway
  Duluth, GA 30096

Jasper   (4MWC)SETG2113
  PO Box 877 (mailing)
  148 College Street (physical)
  Jasper, TN 37347
  (423)942-2188   <Marion>
  FAX: (423)942-2188
SS: James H. Patterson   <M1>
  1305 Falmouth Road
  Chattanooga, TN 37405
  (423)267-8568
  FAX: (423)942-2188
CL: Dorris G Ross
  214 Hancock Road
  Jasper, TN 37347
  (423)942-5224
  FAX: (423)942-2188
  ross37347@charter.net

Kelly's Chapel   (4MC)SETG2120
  3748 Alvin York Highway (mailing)
  470 Highway 27 (physical)
  Whitwell, TN 37397
  (   )   <Marion>
  carolb8667@bellsouth.net

TENNESSEE-GEORGIA PRESBYTERY CONTINUED

OD: Anthony Tucker   <M5>
209 Rock City Trail
Lookout Mountain, GA 30750
CL: Stanley Doyle Davis
280 Condra Street
Whitwell, TN 37397
(423)658-5606

_____

Korean Living Stone   (P)SETG2130
4175 Buford Highway
Duluth, GA 30096
(770)912-7710
PA: Yang Rae Park   <M1>
3340 Bentbill Crossing
Cumming, GA 30041
(770)912-7710
barkmoksa@hanmail.net
CL: Session Clerk Korean Living Stone
4175 Buford Highway
Duluth, GA 30096
(770)912-7710

_____

New Hope   (4MWC)SETG2115
176 E Valley Road (mailing)
196 E Valley Road (physical)
Whitwell, TN 37397
(423)949-3951   <Sequatchie>
PA: Jimmy Byrd   <M1>
176 E Valley Road
Whitwell, TN 37397
(615)289-3347
revjimmybyrd@hotmail.com
CL: James Condra
PO Box 1001
Dunlap, TN 37327
(423)447-8126
jwcondra@bledsoe.net

_____

Oak Grove   (4C)SETG2121
872 Alvin York Highway (mailing)
8150 Griffith Highway (physical)
Whitwell, TN 37397
( )   <Marion>
PA: Phillip H Layne   <M1>
10699 Griffith Highway
Whitwell, TN 37397
(423)658-6421
cprevinsv@bellsouth.net
CL: Martha S Layne
872 Alvin York Highway
Whitwell, TN 37397
(423)658-6421

_____

Our Good   (P)SETG2138
32132 Huntly Circle
Salisbury, MD 21804
(443)783-7502   <Wilomico>
PA: Hyoung S. Choi   <M1>
32132 Huntly Circle
Salisbury, MD 21804
(443)880-6776
pastor0101@naver.com
CL: Session Clerk Our Good Church
32132 Huntly Circle
Salisbury, MD 21804

_____

Pine Hill   (4MC)SETG2117
Rt 2 Box 220 (mailing)
146 Pine Hill Road SW (physical)
McDonald, TN 37353
(423)339-2816   <Bradley>

OD: Russell Maroon   <M5>
7103 Snow Hill Road
Ooltewah, TN 37363
(423)472-1094
CL: Session Clerk
Rt 2 Box 220
McDonald, TN 37353

_____

Prospect United   (4MC)SETG2116
310 New Murraytown Road NW
Cleveland, TN 37312
(423)476-6181   <Bradley>
cloverwreathfarm@hotmail.com
SS: Theresa Martin   <M1>
116 Crisman Street
Chattanooga, TN 37415
(423)903-7260 (cell)
choochootm@usa.net
CL: Betty Brakebill
3512 Windsor Circle NE
Cleveland, TN 37312
(423)479-2731

_____

Red Bank   (4WC)SETG2105
115 Morrison Springs Road
Chattanooga, TN 37415
(423)877-1383   <Hamilton>
rbcpchurch@gmail.com
PA: Jim Buttram   <M1>
103 Golfcrest Lane
Oak Ridge, TN 37830
(865)938-7418
FAX: (865)483-8445
littlejimb@gmail.com
CL: Sylvia Hall
930 Sherry Circle
Hixson, TN 37343
(423)875-3668
hallcad1946@epbfi.com

_____

Richard City   (4MWC)SETG2118
1706 Marion Avenue
South Pittsburg , TN 37380
(423)837-6533   <Marion>
SS: Carlton Harper   <M1>
255 Glenview Circle
Lenoir City, TN 37771
(865)317-1296
carltonharperone@gmail.com
CL: Bill Norman
624 19th Street
South Pittsburg , TN 37380
(423)837-6693
FAX: (423)837-8903
billnorman@catcore.com

_____

Silverdale   (4MEWC)SETG2106
7407 Bonny Oaks Drive
Chattanooga, TN 37421
(423)892-8710   <Hamilton>
FAX: (423)892-7751
CL: Dotty Manis
7939 Clara Chase Drive
Ooltewah, TN 37363
(423)238-4021
dottmae@centurylink.net

_____

South Pittsburg   (4MWC)SETG2123
PO Box 327 (mailing)
400 Elm Avenue (physical)
South Pittsburg, TN 37380

(423)837-6488   <Marion>
spcpc1@yahoo.com
PA: Kriss McGowan   <M1>
900 Alvin York Highway
Whitwell, TN 37397
(423)463-8609
krissmcg658@gmail.com
CL: George Holland
214 Dixie Avenue
South Pittsburg, TN 37380
(423)837-7113
georgehollandsp@att.net

_____

Sumach   (4MWC)SETG2124
PO Box 804 (mailing)
9203 Highway 225 N (physical)
Chatsworth, GA 30705
(706)695-4773   <Murray>
FAX: (706)695-4773
sumachcpchurch@windstream.net
CL: Carolyn Luffman
926 Long Avenue
Chatsworth, GA 30705
(706)695-4346
cizzle44@hotmail.com

_____

Whitwell   (4C)SETG2122
7390 Highway 108
Whitwell, TN 37397
(423)658-5849   <Marion>
PA: Phillip Layne   <M1>
10699 Griffith Highway
Whitwell, TN 37397
(423)658-5849
cprevinsv@bellsouth.net
CL: Odus Caldwell
7390 Highway 108
Whitwell, TN 37397
(423)658-6463

_____

OTHERS ON MINISTERIAL ROLL:
Brister, Glenn   <M1 WC>
3004 Delaware Avenue
McComb, MS 39648
(706)934-8629
bearmountainpenworks@gmail.com
Cho, Sangsook   <M1 WC>
7 Falmouth Court
Middletown, CT 06457
(860)830-6808
lovejcamen@yahoo.com
Han, Seung Chon   <M0>
3075 Landington Way
Duluth, GA 30096
kpc0191@gmail.com
(678)469-5015
Hudson, George Cliff   <M1 DE>
4782 Waverly Court
Ooltewah, TN 37363
(423)238-6333
gchudson3@gmail.com
Jackson, Lamar   <M1 RT>
280 Deer Ridge Drive Apt D
Dayton, TN 37321
(423)570-9348
hljaxn@charter.net
Kang, Jin Koo   <M1 OM>
2310 Hisway
Lawrenceville, GA 30044
(678)462-7526
agatopia@hanmail.net

TENNESSEE-GEORGIA PRESBYTERY CONTINUED

Kelso, James H   <M1 RT>
131 Lords Way
Dawsonville, GA 30534
(706)216-7513
elgato@alltel.net

Kim, Kio Seob   <M1 OM>
14430 35th Avenue Apt A62
Flushing, NY 11354
(718)539-3476

Kim, Mi Young   <M1 WC>
IN KOREA

Kim, Min Soo   <M1 OM>
5350 Taylor Road
Johns Creek, GA 30022
samil2110@yahoo.com
(678)622-2717

Lee, Sarah   <M1 WC>
(no address on file)

Ma, Choil   <M1 WC>
40 Conger Street #1404A
Bloomfield, NJ 07003

March, Kevin   <M1 RT>
1701 Ray Jo Circle
Chattanooga, TN 37421
(423)499-4180
kmadm1@aol.com

Martin, Tom   <M1 WC>
116 Crisman Street
Chattanooga, TN 37415
(423)903-7260 (cell)
choochootm@usa.net

McCarty, John   <M1 M9 RT>
305 W Martindale Drive
Marshall, TX 75672
(423)650-8788
mtsjohn@gmail.com

McGowan, Rhonda   <M1 WC>
900 Alvin York Highway
Whitwell, TN 37397
(423)619-5679
pastorrhonda@mcgowanministries.com

Melton, Samuel D   <M1 RT>
2249 Bucks Pocket Road SE
Oldfort, TN 37362
(423)472-8467

Oh, Taeho   <M1 WC>
42-40 2908th Street #1
Bayside, NY 11361

Prosser, Forest   <M1 RT>
1157 Mountain Creek Road
Chattanooga, TN 37405
(423)877-4114
forestprosser@comcast.net

Ryoo, Hwa Chang   <M1 WC>
450 Island Road Unit 146
Ramsey, NJ 07446

Song, Byung Seon   <M1 WC>
(MOVED TO CANADA)
(404)512-9147

Song, Nam Hun   <M1 WC>
(IN KOREA)

Sumrall, Philip (Phil)   <M1 WC>
107 Barnhardt Circle
Fort Oglethorpe, GA 30742
(423)903-1938
phil.sumrall@gmail.com

Tolley, Robert (Butch)   <M1 WC>
1445 New Murraytown Road NW
Cleveland, TN 37312
(423)837-6488
butchtolley@hotmail.com

Turner, Glyn   <M1 WC>
1660 Chattanooga Valley Road
Flintstone, GA 30725
(585)307-7715
glynturner@outlook.com

Wright, B J   <M1 WC>
301 25th Street
Phenix City, AL 36867
(334)298-2896
bojobo3@yahoo.com

Yi, Woo Young   <M1 WC>
538 River Chase Trail
Duluth, GA 30096

Yoo, Paul   <M1 WC>
IN KOREA
sungyy@msn.com

OTHER LICENTIATES ON ROLL:

Chin, Kwang Sik   <M2>
1168 Palisade Avenue
Fort Lee, NJ 07024
(201)220-3390

Jones, Harold   <M2>
4123 Wilkesview Drive Apt A
Chattanooga, TN 37416
(478)320-4222
harold@personalcharacter.com

Kennedy, Jim   <M2>
3818 Peace Court Apt F
Aberdeen Proving Ground, MD 21005
jpkak@comcast.net

OTHER CANDIDATES ON ROLL:

Garcia, Lucas   <M3>
875 Scenic Highway
Lawrenceville, GA 30045
(678)698-7971
lgvplola@hotmail.com

Hollingshed, Lee   <M3 ST>
3612 Harmony Church Grove Road
Dallas, GA 30132
(770)548-0152
leearmstrong@bellsouth.net

Kang, Eun Hee   <M3>
14715 46th Avenue
Flushing, NY 11355
(718)762-0778

Kollie, Moses   <M3>
760 Harbor Point Court
Lawrenceville, GA 30044
(770)990-2215
kolliemoses70@yahoo.com

Lee, In Mi Chang   <M3>
5260 Coacoochee Terrace
Alpharetta, GA 30022
(404)723-3487
inmi1009@gmail.com

Middleton, Frank, Jr   <M3 ST>
1200 Adele Circle
Slidell, LA 70461
(770)655-0406
fmiddle@bellsouth.net

Park, Young   <M3 ST>
3340 Bentbill Crossing
Cummings, GA 30041
(404)661-6117
barkmogun@gmail.com

Porras, Hernan   <M3>
1485 Rivershyre Parkway
Lawrenceville, GA 30043
(404)468-6012
salvosporgraqcia@aol.com

Scott, Joel   <M3>
1848 Sassafrass Lane
Soddy Daisy, TN 37379
(423)240-2724
saejoescott@gmail.com

Varnell, William   <M3 ST>
6729 Old Dunlop Road
Whitwell, TN 37397
(423)658-0506

Trinity Presbytery
MISSION SYNOD

GENERAL		MEMBERSHIP			CHANGES				FINANCES				
1.Church Number	2.Active	3.Total	4.Church School	5.Prof. of Faith	6.Gains	7.Losses	8.Children Baptized	9. OUR UNITED OUT-REACH	10. Total Out-Reach Giving	11. All Other Expenses	12. Total Income Received	13. Value Church Prop. 1=1000
	1	2	3	4	5	6	7	8	9	10	11	12	13
Antioch	8101	18	20	10	No Report Received			0	1,300	0	0	0	325
Austin, First	8601	34	34	8	0	0	2	1	600	20,319	153,735	222,411	2,325
Bertram	8605	80	173	5	0	3	6	0	2,303	28,838	95,234	83,936	324
Concord	8104	55	96	35	No Report Received			0	10,288	0	0	0	805
Daingerfield	8106	9	12	5	0	0	1	0	500	5,899	19,317	28,569	150
Elmira Chapel*	8111	66	126	40	0	2	10	0	1,726	67,177	167,485	225,806	2,500
Freeport	8103	31	31	5	1	2	1	0	5,250	18,650	44,590	66,049	933
Houston, 1st	8606	132	294	52	0	6	0	1	51,938	132,265	369,874	513,205	3,322
Jefferson	8109	48	61	32	10	11	3	1	0	2,616	95,324	76,469	450
Longview, 1st	8112	53	165	29	0	0	0	0	8,979	29,100	84,313	98,162	660
Marshall	8115	172	333	95	1	14	9	2	32,819	107,968	370,617	491,047	3,037
Mt. Hope	8117	3	3	0	No Report Received			0	0	0	0	0	183
Northminster+	8610	275	275	54	0	16	23	8	0	14,839	299,996	337,909	3,628
Nueva Vida	8612	89	134	26	No Report Received			0	0	0	0	0	0
Oak Grove	8607	6	62	0	No Report Received			0	0	0	0	0	200
Pine Hill	8122	22	59	17	0	0	0	0	1,150	7,425	30,352	35,453	85
Pine Tree*	8113	30	72	22	No Report Received			0	3,348	0	0	0	800
Progress*	8123	6	7	6	No Report Received			0	0	0	0	0	0
Round Rock+	8611	112	113	53	0	6	10	3	0	8,309	148,628	177,269	853
Shepherd/Hills+	8604	301	286	149	6	14	7	2	0	44,533	394,546	482,226	1,100
Shiloh	8125	7	42	0	0	0	0	0	0	1,300	20,766	21,138	65
Stone Oak	8608	115	140	42	No Report Received			0	0	0	0	0	2,200
TOTALS	22	1,645	2,474	710	18	88	80	18	120,201	491,183	2,407,595	2,979,570	24,470

*Math error corrected. **Purged roll. +Union Church

CHURCHES, PASTORS, AND CLERKS:

Antioch   (4MWC)MSTR8101
  PO Box 42 (mailing)
  518 N Antioch Road (physical)
  Quitman, LA 71268
  (318)259-7069   <Jackson>
CL: Jerry L Hanes
  5104 Beech Springs Road
  Quitman, LA 71268
  (318)259-4246
  lindaameme@hotmail.com

Austin First   (4WC)MSTR8601
  6800 Woodrow Avenue
  Austin, TX 78757
  (512)453-8434   <Travis>
  cpaustin@prodigy.net
OD: Ron Stevenson   <M5>
  6800 Woodrow Avenue
  Austin, TX 78757
  (512)453-8434
  austinfirstcp@prodigy.net
CL: Session Clerk
  6800 Woodrow Avenue
  Austin, TX 78757
  (512)453-8434
  cpaustin@prodigy.net

Bertram   (4MEWC)MSTR8605
  PO Box 242 (mailing)
  430 Highway 29 (physical)

Bertram, TX 78605
(512)355-2182   <Burnet>
PA: Daryl Johnson   <M1>
  425 W Vaughan Street
  Bertram, TX 78605
  (512)355-2182
  djchurch@earthlink.net
CL: Tommy Griffis
  1701 County Road 254
  Georgetown, TX 78633
  (512)496-8878
  tbgriffis44@gmail.com

Concord   (4MWC)MSTR8104
  212 County Road 4705
  Troup, TX 75789
  (903)842-4745   <Cherokee>
  FAX: (903)842-4745
  revdad.duane@gmail.com
PA: Duane A Dougherty Jr   <M1>
  212 County Road 4705
  Troup, TX 75789
  (903)842-4745
  revdad.duane@gmail.com
CL: Sandy Mager
  356 County Road 4629
  Troup, TX 75789
  (903)842-3844
  stmager@yahoo.com

Daingerfield   (4MC)MSTR8106
  PO Box 645 (mailing)
  307 Broadnak (physical)

Daingerfield, TX 75638
(903)645-2183   <Morris>
sharjohn@windstream.net
SS: John C Lawson   <M2>
  PO Box 645
  Daingerfield, TX 75638
  (903)645-2183
  sharjohn@windstream.net
CL: John C Lawson
  PO Box 645
  Daingerfield, TX 75638
  (903)645-2183
  sharjohn@windstream.net

Elmira Chapel   (4MWC)MSTR8111
  3501 Elmira Drive
  Longview, TX 75605
  (903)759-2069   <Gregg>
  elmirachapel@aol.com
PA: James M Cantey   <M1>
  3505 Elmira Drive
  Longview, TX 75605
  (903)452-6049
CL: Sherry Poteet
  3501 Elmira Drive
  Longview, TX 75605
  (903)759-2069
  spoteet1@aol.com

Freeport   (4C)MSTR8103
  1402 W Broad Street
  Freeport, TX 77541
PA: Lee Attema   <M1>

TRINITY PRESBYTERY CONTINUED

930 W 8th Street
Freeport, TX 77541
(281)728-6263
SC: Cathy Bettoney
1149 Ash Street
Clute, TX 77531
(979)265-7630
cathybettoney@yahoo.com

Houston First   (4EWC)MSTR8606
2119 Avalon Place
Houston, TX 77019
(713)522-7821   <Harris>
FAX: (713)522-8869
firstcp@cphouston.org
PA: J Geoffrey Knight   <M1>
2119 Avalon Place
Houston, TX 77019
(713)522-7821
FAX: (713)522-8869
geoff@family.net
AP: Freddy Diaz   <M1>
2425 Holly Hall Apt B42
Houston, TX 77054
(832)305-2379
fredglobeus@yahoo.com
CL: Diane Dickson
2119 Avalon Place
Houston, TX 77019
(713)522-7821
FAX: (713)522-8869
firstcp@cphouston.org

Jefferson   (4EC)MSTR8109
501 E Jefferson Street
Jefferson, TX 75657
(903)665-9365   <Marion>
jeffersoncpc@juno.com
PA: Robert (Toby) Davis   <M1>
502 S Alley Street
Jefferson, TX 75657
(901)826-5755
pastortobydavis@gmail.com
CL: Eric S Thomas
250 Berea 1
Jefferson, TX 75657
(903)601-1146
ethomas@etbu.edu

Longview First   (4WC)MSTR8112
2401 Alpine Street
Longview, TX 75601
(903)758-5184   <Gregg>
FAX: (903)757-2572
fcpclongview@sbcglobal.net
CL: Mollie Benson
567 Hidden Forest
Longview, TX 75601
(903)663-0443
FAX: (903)757-2572
fcpclongview@sbcglobal.net

Marshall   (4EWC)MSTR8115
PO Box 1303 (mailing)
501 Indian Spring Road (physical)
Marshall, TX 75671
(903)935-3787   <Harrison>
FAX: (903)935-3193
info@cumberlandofmarshall.org
PA: William Rustenhaven III   <M1>
PO Box 1303
Marshall, TX 75671
(903)935-7275
FAX: (903)935-3193
rusty@cumberlandofmarshall.org

AP: Mary Kathryn Kirkpatrick   <M1>
401 1/2 Henley-Perry Drive
Marshall, TX 75670
(903)930-6236
mkkirpartick@gmail.com
CL: Shirley Jones
104 Hillcrest Terrace
Marshall, TX 75672
(903)938-3980
shopfarm75672@yahoo.com

Mt Hope (CLOSING) (4MC)MSTR8117
Box 66
Joinerville, TX 75658
(903)847-3451   <Rusk>
CL: Anna J Holman
PO Box 115
Joinerville, TX 75658
(903)847-3801

Northminster   (4U)MSTR8610
6800 Tezel Road
San Antonio, TX 78250
(210)680-4825   <Bexar>
FAX: (210)680-4826
npcoffice@npcsatx.org
PA: Robert E Weston   <M1>
11 Summer Bluff
San Antonio, TX 78254
(210)347-0232
FAX: (210)680-4826
rjaweston@gmail.com
CL: Marsha Schendel
8730 Prince Heights
San Antonio, TX 78254
(210)681-4231

Nueva Vida   (F)MSTR8612
4505 Highway 6 N
Suite 700
Houston, TX 77084
(832)593-8355   <Harris>
PA: Ruben D Albarracin   <M1>
7411 Magnolia Shadows Lane
Houston, TX 77095
(281)463-8617
FAX: (281)463-8617
confiaendios@hotmail.com
CL: Patricia Nunez
7303 Hollow Field W
Cypress, TX 77433
(281)855-1881
FAX: (713)533-9735

Oak Grove   (4C)MSTR8607
12951 Ranch Road 2338
Georgetown, TX 78633
( )   <Williamson>
SS: Walter Hoke   <M1>
215 Navajo Trail
Georgetown, TX 78633
(512)869-1948
CL: Wanda Shelton
2355 County Road 226
Florence, TX 76527
(512)579-1325

Pine Hill   (4C)MSTR8122
8236 Farm Road 3019 (mailing)
FM 3019 County Road 3281 (physical)
Winnsboro, TX 75494
( )   <Hopkins>
CL: Elizabeth Aden
404 Yates Street
Mount Vernon, TX 75457

(903)537-7288
libbya1@suddenlink.net

Pine Tree   (4MWC)MSTR8113
PO Box 5340 (mailing)
1805 Pine Tree Road (physical)
Longview, TX 75608
(903)759-2685   <Gregg>
ptcpc@sbcglobal.net
CL: Darlynn Jones
1819 Flagstone Drive
Longview, TX 75605
(903)236-7310
darlynnj@att.net

Progress   (4C)MSTR8123
722 Gewin Lane (mailing)
3643 Progress Church Road (physical)
Pleasant Hill, LA 71065
(318)796-3725   <Sabine>
mamacgewin@yahoo.com
CL: Carolyn W Gewin
722 Gewin Lane
Pleasant Hill, LA 71065
(318)796-3703
mamacgewin@yahoo.com

Round Rock   (4U)MSTR8611
4010 Sam Bass Road
Round Rock, TX 78681
(512)544-2152   <Travis>
rrpc_info@roundrockpresbyterian.org
OD: Catherine Craley   <M5>
4010 Sam Bass Road
Round Rock, TX 78681
CL: Elaine B Dodd
1805 Castleguard Way
Cedar Park, TX 78613
(512)260-0310
doddeb@sbcglobal.net

Shepherd of the Hills   (4U)MSTR8604
5226 W William Cannon Drive
Austin, TX 78749
(512)892-3580   <Travis>
FAX: (512)892-6307
church@shpc.org
OD: Laurance W Coulter   <M5>
5226 W William Cannon Drive
Austin, TX 78749
(512)892-3580
FAX: (512)358-0879
larry@shpc.org
AP: Michael Killeen   <M1>
5226 W William Cannon Drive
Austin, TX 78749
(512)560-0423
FAX: (512)358-0879
mike@shpc.org
AP: Britta Dukes   <M1>
5226 W William Cannon Drive
Austin, TX 78749
(512)892-3580
FAX: (512)358-0879
britta@shpc.org
CL: Clift Bowman
5226 W William Cannon Drive
Austin, TX 78749
(512)288-5839
FAX: (512)358-0879
cbowman24@austin.rr.com

Shiloh   (4C)MSTR8125
4928 County Road 3275 (mailing)
2467 County Road 3205 (physical)

TRINITY PRESBYTERY CONTINUED

Clarksville, TX 75426
(903)427-3785   \<Red River>
shiloh.presbyterian@yahoo.com
PA: Billy Jack Holt   \<M1>
5039 Highway 37 N
Clarksville, TX 75426
(903)428-9909
jackdora@windstream.net
CL: Mary Jo McGill
4928 County Road 3275
Clarksville, TX 75426
(903)427-3785
hoopnmj@yahoo.com

Stone Oak   (4C)MSTR8608
20024 Crescent Oaks
San Antonio, TX 78258
(210)497-7974   \<Bexar>
FAX: (210)497-8724
officemanager@satx.rr.com
PA: Kevin Colvard   \<M1>
27027 Harmony Hills
San Antonio, TX 78260
(205)267-9372
FAX: (210)497-8724
rev_kev@satx.rr.com
CL: Barry Elliott
2204 Sunderidge
San Antonio, TX 78260
(210)884-1749
FAX: (210)497-8724
barrydeanelliott@gmail.com

OTHERS ON MINISTERIAL ROLL:

Bone, W Harold   \<M1 WC>
315 Joey Drive
Bourne, TX 78006
(210)859-5560
revdocbone@yahoo.com
Bowers, Sharon G   \<M1 M9>
1011 Barbara Drive
San Marcos, TX 78666
(512)230-7078
sharon.bowers@gmail.com
Bozeman, Robert   \<M1 HR>
582 Bozeman Loop
Belmont, LA 71406
(318)256-5781
bo@bozemanengineering.com
Chancellor, Hilton   \<M1 HR>
11905 Preserve Vista
Austin, TX 78738
(512)382-1972
hiltontex@aol.com
Davenport, Mark A   \<M1 WC>
1578 Cooks Crossing
Tyler, TX 75703
(205)663-3152
FAX: (205)663-8323
fpcapastor@bellsouth.net
Diaz, Gloria Villa   \<M1 OM>
2425 Holly Hall Apt B42
Houston, TX 77054
(832)758-5871
gloria@newdayinchrist.org
Gonzalez, Nora   \<M1 OM>
2515 Blueberry Lane
Pasadena, TX 77502
(832)202-5572
Hamilton, Lynn   \<M1 WC>
4511 Lucksinger Lane Trailer 1
Austin, TX 78745
(512)443-6813
lhamilton@minister.com

Hannah, Hugh   \<M1 HR>
217 Mitchell Road SE
Cleveland, TN 37323
(423)473-7852
pjhannah23@hotmail.com
Harris, Ernest   \<M1 HR>
610 Turtle Creek Drive
Reno, TX 75462
(903)966-2481
ernieandjeri@wmconnect.com
Jarnagin, Mary   \<M1 WC>
1003 Justin Lane Apt 1017
Austin, TX 78757
(512)367-9922
marjar27@yahoo.com
Kessie, John Paul   \<M1 WC>
225 Clear Springs Road
Georgetown, TX 78628
(512)585-1617
jplmkessie@verizon.com
Lindsay, John V   \<M1 WC>
401 Greenwood Avenue
Marshall, TX 75670
(940)391-1213
Magrill Jr, J Richard   \<M1 HR>
500 Miller Drive
Marshall, TX 75672
(901)685-9454
rmmagrill@gmail.com
McNeese, Mark   \<M1 WC>
3306 Greenlawn Parkway
Austin, TX 78757
(512)302-9223
mam53@prodigy.net
Mills, David M   \<M1 WC>
528 County Road 322
Bertram, TX 78605
(512)355-3511
Montoya, David Montoya   \<M1 WC>
20900 FM 1093 #11208
Richmond, TX 77407
adamonva@gmail.com
Nunn, Donald W   \<M1 WC>
203 Bridgers Hill Road
Longview, TX 75604
(903)297-6074
dwnunn@earthlink.net
Park, Sung In   \<M1 WC>
10109 Loxley Lane
Austin, TX 78717
Parsons, Hugh L   \<M1 HR>
1526 Welch
Houston, TX 77006
(713)522-6126
p-h-parsons@comcast.net
Peters, David J   \<M1 IT>
4010 Sam Bass Road
Round Rock, TX 78681
(512)244-2152
Rush, Robert D   \<M1 OM>
12935 Quail Park Drive
Cypress, TX 77429
(832-559-1500)
rushrd74@comcast.net
Rustenhaven, William, Jr   \<M1 HR>
703 W Burleson Street
Marshall, TX 75670
(903)935-7056
rustenhavendolores@yahoo.com
Santillano, Ray Paul   \<M1 M8>
1270 Polo Road Apt 618
Columbia, SC 29223
(808)349-3308
ray.santillano@us.army.mil

Smith, David R   \<M1 HR>
PO Box 892
Rosepine, LA 70659
(903)297-6074
ogreyfox@att.net
Suenram, Timothy   \<M1 WC>
5704 Tyler Street
Pearland, TX 77581
(832)217-6367
tsuenram@aol.com
Turner, Steven W   \<M1 WC>
7622 Snider Road
Gilmer, TX 75645
(903)738-8831
juxtaposition47@yahoo.com
Wayman, Sam   \<M1 OM>
707 High Hill Creek Road
LaGrange, TX 78945
(979)968-3734
samndonnawayman@gmail.com
Winslett, Don   \<M1 M9>
Baptist Hospital/Pastoral Care
1000 W Moreno Street
Pensacola, FL 32521

OTHER LICENTIATES ON ROLL

OTHER CANDIDATES ON ROLL

West Tennessee Presbytery
GREAT RIVERS SYNOD

GENERAL		MEMBERSHIP		CHANGES				FINANCES				
1.Church Number	2.Active	3.Total	4.Church School	5.Prof. of Faith	6.Gains	7.Losses	8.Children Baptized	9. OUR UNITED OUT-REACH	10. Total Out-Reach Giving	11. All Other Expenses	12. Total Income Received	13. Value Church Prop. 1=1000
1	2	3	4	5	6	7	8	9	10	11	12	13
Antioch Union 9401	21	31	30	No Report Received			0	8,183	0	0	0	343
Atwood 9101	4	7	5	0	0	0	0	287	393	9,208	10,033	200
Barren Springs 9102	5	37	4	No Report Received			0	0	0	0	0	25
Beech 9402	60	72	22	1	1	1	1	2,572	5,653	95,341	65,332	400
Bells Chapel 9403	25	65	16	0	2	0	0	860	1,715	23,543	21,365	500
Bethel (TC) 9301	23	34	15	No Report Received			0	0	0	0	0	300
Bethesda 9404	24	24	15	1	5	1	0	1,350	1,750	25,515	32,876	350
Bethlehem 9405	11	25	8	No Report Received			0	0	0	0	0	70
Bolivar 9202	30	47	6	No Report Received			0	2,702	0	0	0	350
Bradford 9104	49	131	31	No Report Received			0	2,374	0	0	0	175
Brunswick 9302	29	62	12	0	0	1	0	2,726	3,093	42,852	46,449	418
Camden 9105	55	117	40	No Report Received			0	0	0	0	0	900
Camp Ground 9204	16	29	30	No Report Received			0	1,000	0	0	0	175
Claybrook 9205	8	8	6	No Report Received			0	150	0	0	0	10
Cloverdale 9407	3	6	5	No Report Received			0	0	0	0	0	5
Colonial 9305	40	134	23	0	0	5	0	5,785	8,967	104,435	96,049	1,500
Concord 9106	50	56	20	1	3	3	0	0	6,407	45,600	50,968	500
Cool Springs CC 9107	57	67	35	No Report Received			0	521	0	0	0	150
Cool Springs GC 9408	50	50	40	4	6	15	0	4,816	19,630	55,161	72,378	300
Davidson Chapel 9108	41	151	41	No Report Received			0	360	0	0	0	450
Double Springs 9109	49	64	43	0	2	2	0	4,405	7,767	118,618	135,067	565
Dresden 9110	30	42	18	0	0	15	0	3,120	5,103	28,689	31,928	315
Dyer 9409	117	218	73	2	4	5	0	10,514	20,203	130,853	105,142	1,085
Dyersburg, 1st* 9410	367	646	100	9	15	7	6	46,924	166,701	512,559	708,482	5,814
Ebenezer (MC) 9206	6	6	7	No Report Received			0	0	0	0	0	50
Ebenezer (TC) 9303	128	128	60	No Report Received			0	3,900	0	0	0	380
Faith 9308	196	339	107	0	6	5	1	25,050	34,200	268,200	302,400	2,575
Fulton 9412	75	181	50	0	1	0	1		13,582	119,314	131,032	850
Germantown** 9310	118	154	97	1	6	188	3	17,798	31,370	211,918	247,748	1,000
Gleason 9111	22	30	15	0	0	1	0	0	0	23,325	23,332	400
Good Springs 9112	19	54	12	No Report Received			0	0	0	0	0	296
Holly Grove 9304	738	738	260	12	7	4	1	0	32,687	284,678	317,754	1,300
Hopewell (BC) 9207	36	36	33	0	0	3	0	1,570	3,245	19,292	17,562	30
Hopewell (WC) 9115	18	14	18	No Report Received			0	3,194	0	0	0	90
Humboldt 9116	70	114	35	2	5	3	0	8,065	22,820	66,857	82,563	1,000
Hurricane Hill 9413	25	52	12	No Report Received			0	0	0	0	0	130
Jackson, 1st 9208	275	455	178	0	3	14	1	10,041	23,049	330,160	319,475	3,000
Kenton 9414	21	46	23	No Report Received			0	4,236	0	0	0	475
Korean 9322	45	45	10	0	2	7	1	100	1,600	44,688	46,288	500
Lexington First 9209	50	114	25	0	0	1	0	3,701	5,248	38,344	41,526	900
Maple Springs 9210	78	144	20	1	2	3	0	0	4,593	85,968	95,365	485
Martin 9117	42	55	42	0	0	0	0	3,323	5,150	60,000	62,182	175
Mason Hall 9415	7	20	4	No Report Received			0	0	0	0	0	100
McKenzie 9118	358	358	182	1	8	5	2	31,336	51,482	277,213	317,742	3,500
Medina 9119	12	37	15	0	3	0	0	1,260	2,681	21,109	19,167	157
Meridian 9120	65	141	35	No Report Received			0	0	0	0	0	175
Milan 9121	224	324	80	4	8	9	4	2,500	42,645	285,152	345,629	2,500
Mill Creek 9122	20	20	9	No Report Received			0	1,400	0	0	0	50
Morella 9416	6	26	6	No Report Received			0	0	0	0	0	125
Morning Sun 9314	60	84	28	2	2	2	0	3,192	10,360	80,334	87,500	750
Mt. Ararat 9417	89	278	56	1	2	19	0	4,800	23,672	70,600	90,382	500
Mt. Carmel 9315	27	44	14	0	0	0	0	2,266	5,268	17,715	22,673	80
Mt. Olive 9418	12	31	10	No Report Received			0	600	0	0	0	205
Mt. Vernon 9213	35	47	18	0	0	5	0	5,285	11,676	39,190	52,510	380
Mt. Zion 9214	91	192	49	1	1	1	0	18,900	35,795	179,100	196,150	2,000
New Beginnings 9306	138	198	39	No Report Received			0	0	0	0	0	170
New Bethel 9215	46	112	19	1	0	0	0	0	450	21,437	21,437	90
New Bethlehem 9420	4	4	0	0	0	1	0	273	2,824	92	2,490	2
New Ebenezer 9422	67	67	39	No Report Received			0	3,516	0	0	0	45
New Salem (MC) 9216	9	9	0	No Report Received			0	0	0	0	0	100

West Tennessee Presbytery (Continued)
GREAT RIVERS SYNOD

GENERAL		MEMBERSHIP		CHANGES				FINANCES				
1.Church Number	2.Active	3.Total	4.Church School	5.Prof. of Faith	6.Gains	7.Losses	8.Children Baptized	9. OUR UNITED OUT-REACH	10. Total Out-Reach Giving	11. All Other Expenses	12. Total Income Received	13. Value Church Prop. 1=1000
1	2	3	4	5	6	7	8	9	10	11	12	13
New Salem (SC) 9316	49	70	19	0	0	0	0	0	1,818	70,710	77,751	98
New Salem (WC) 9124	15	15	28	No Report Received			0	4,621	0	0	0	75
Newbern 9419	37	49	25	8	10	0	0	8,179	16,239	47,745	103,612	709
Nuevo Empezar 9324	20	25	22	No Report Received			0	3,420	0	0	0	0
North Union 9423	68	75	40	No Report Received			0	1,833	0	0	0	360
Oak Grove 9217	32	108	22	No Report Received			0	1,311	0	0	0	300
Oak Hill 9125	14	14	8	0	0	0	0	689	2,115	3,957	7,287	0
Olive Branch 9312	501	501	158	No Report Received			0	2,196	0	0	0	1,950
Oliver's Chapel 9127	30	74	30	0	6	1	0	3,400	5,270	34,822	33,899	314
Olivet 9220	200	337	100	2	2	11	0	7,425	25,341	286,122	311,463	2,108
Palestine (DC) 9424	5	5	7	No Report Received			0	500	0	0	0	50
Palestine (HC) 9221	53	115	30	1	1	2	1	4,611	8,615	52,930	69,932	150
Parsons, First 9222	35	112	10	0	0	1	0	480	1,200	33,823	33,620	500
Pleasant Green 9129	10	20	8	No Report Received			0	0	0	0	0	100
Pleasant Grove 9317	10	22		No Report Received			0	0	0	0	0	32
Pleasant Union 9318	144	144	25	0	0	6	4	0	7,845	91,710	99,832	300
Poplar Grove 9425	42	72	15	0	1	1	0	4,077	9,720	36,800	47,000	340
Protemus 9426	33	39	47	0	3	1	1	6,283	18,790	45,796	62,831	125
Ramer 9223	16	16	12	No Report Received			0	397	0	0	0	100
Roellen 9428	11	7	7	0	0	0	0	300	1,450	5,470	9,600	60
Rutherford 9429	20	28	20	0	0	0	0	4,354	11,820	43,158	54,502	300
Salem 9430	8	17	16	No Report Received			0	0	0	0	0	135
Savannah, 1st 9224	88	132	71	2	10	3	2	0	16,320	141,898	150,666	1,198
Selmer, Ct. Ave.**9225	61	82	16	1	6	1	0	3,108	0	7,150	60,293	550
Sharon 9130	17	31	13	0	0	1	0	1,000	6,703	38,048	30,626	559
Shiloh (AC) 9226	35	35	22	0	2	2	0	3,344	17,062	37,773	33,502	95
Shiloh (CC) 9131	36	52	0	1	3	2	0	4,135	9,660	38,363	41,352	175
Trezevant 9132	17	27	17	No Report Received			0	0	0	0	0	150
Trimble 9431	4	4	4	No Report Received			0	0	0	0	0	125
Troy 9432	17	24	15	No Report Received			0	670	0	0	0	100
Union City 9433	105	203	69	No Report Received			0	0	0	0	0	2,000
Walnut Grove 9320	14	28	18	No Report Received			0	200	0	0	0	300
West Union 9321	104	227	60	No Report Received			0	2,400	0	0	0	1,500
Woodward's Ch 9434	12	12	20	No Report Received			0	0	0	0	0	30
Yorkville 9435	26	59	22	No Report Received			0	0	0	0	0	575
Zion 9133	6	11	5	No Report Received			0	400	0	0	0	95
TOTALS	96	6,302	9,605	3,235	60	131	365	28	324,288	767,115	4,642,072	5,284,530	54,375

*Math Correction*Math error corrected. **Purged roll.

CHURCHES, PASTORS, AND CLERKS:

Antioch Union (4C)GRWT9401
  6765 Mount Olive Road (mailing)
  486 W Newman Glover Road (physical)
  Union City, TN 38261
  (731)885-6435 <Obion>
PA: Mitch Boulton <M1>
  1606 Ebenezer Road
  Troy, TN 38260
  (731)487-2318
  steelermitch@gmail.com
CL: Sharon Barnes
  5765 Mount Olive Road
  Union City, TN 38261
  (731)885-2521
_____
Atwood (4MWC)GRWT9101

PO Box 203 (mailing)
14010 Church Street (physical)
Atwood, TN 38220
(731)662-7692 <Carroll>
rickylong@tennesseetel.net
SS: Richard Reed <M2>
  236 Madison Street
  Dyer, TN 38330
  (731)692-3604
CL: Ricky Long
  230 Brooks Road
  Atwood, TN 38220
  (731)662-7692
  rickylong@tennesseetel.net
_____
Barren Springs (4C)GRWT9102
  Box 14 (mailing)
  1860 Barren Spring Church Road (physical)
  Hollow Rock, TN 38342

( ) <Carroll>
CL: Cassie Cooper
  Box 14
  Hollow Rock, TN 38342
  (731)586-2167
_____
Beech (4MEC)GRWT9402
  PO Box 553 (mailing)
  880 Beech Chapel Road (physical)
  Union City, TN 38261
  (731)885-1710 <Obion>
  beth.williams@nwtdd.org
PA: Bobby D Williams <M1>
  844 W Highway 22
  Union City, TN 38261
  (731)885-1710
CL: Beth Williams
  844 W Highway 22
  Union City, TN 38281

WEST TENNESSEE PRESBYTERY CONTINUED

(731)885-1710
beth.williams@nwtdd.org

Bells Chapel   (2WC)GRWT9403
309 Bells Chapel Road
Dyer, TN 38330
(731)643-6729   <Gibson>
LS: Dennis Emerson   <M6>
137 Midway Road Apt 25
Dyer, TN 38330
(731)643-6539
dennied53@hotmail.com
CL: Dennis Emerson
137 Midway Road Apt 25
Dyer, TN 38330
(731)643-6539
dennied53@hotmail.com

Bethel (TC)   (1WC)GRWT9301
PO Box 114 (mailing)
Tipton, TN 38071
3406 Tracy Road (physical)
Atoka, TN 38004
(901)837-0343   <Tipton>
SS: Kenneth L McCoy   <M1>
1422 Walton Road
Memphis, TN 38117
(901)682-0891
CL: Cindy Rhodes
PO Box 114
Tipton, TN 38071
(901)837-7793

Bethesda   (4MWC)GRWT9404
10755 State Highway 188 (mailing)
9651 State Highway 188 (physical)
Friendship, TN 38034
( )   <Crockett>
jirvin527@yahoo.com
CL: Jim Irvin
10755 State Highway 188
Friendship, TN 38034
(731)414-7180
jirvin527@yahoo.com

Bethlehem   (4C)GRWT9405
711 Whirmantler Street (mailing)
1469 Bethlehem Road (physical)
Union City, TN 38261
( )   <Obion>
CL: Charlotte Thomas
711 Whirmantler Street
Union City, TN 38261
(731)885-1672

Bolivar   (4MWC)GRWT9202
PO Box 413 (mailing)
448 Nuckolls Road (physical)
Bolivar, TN 38008
(731)658-5459   <Hardeman>
CL: Faye Cromwell
2995 Naylor Road
Toone, TN 38381
(731)658-5329
cromwellr@bellsouth.net

Bradford   (4MWC)GRWT9104
PO Box 186 (mailing)
117 Highway 45 S (physical)
Bradford, TN 38316
(731)742-3397   <Gibson>

PA: Keith Harwell   <M1>
13132 Stinson Street
Milan, TN 38358
(731)613-3780
CL: Don Lannom
PO Box 85
Bradford, TN 38316
(731)742-3838

Brunswick   (4MWC)GRWT9302
PO Box 67 (mailing)
4976 Brunswick Road (physical)
Brunswick, TN 38014
(901)386-0105   <Shelby>
PA: Cory Williams   <M1>
3148 Long Bridge Lane
Arlington, TN 38002
(901)486-5981
coromis@hotmail.com
CL: Mary Ellen Starks
PO Box 142
Brunswick, TN 38014
(901)388-9862

Camden   (4MWC)GRWT9105
239 W Main Street
Camden, TN 38320
(731)584-7598   <Benton>
FAX: (731)584-7598
camdencpoffice@bellsouth.net
SS: Carey Womack   <M1>
114 Doris Street
Camden, TN 38320
(731)220-3900
FAX: (731)584-7598
camdencppastor@bellsouth.net
CL: Nancy D Arnold
PO Box 214
Camden, TN 38320
(731)441-2778
FAX: (731)584-7598
arnldnnc@aol.com

Camp Ground   (4C)GRWT9204
2535 Middleburg Road
Decaturville, TN 38329
( )   <Decatur>
SS: David Hawley   <M1>
127 John Holt Road
Beech Bluff, TN 38313
(731)427-7284
dhpreach@aol.com
CL: Fred Brasher
771 Middleburg Road
Decaturville, TN 38329
(731)852-4400

Claybrook   (C)GRWT9205
1300 US Highway 412 E (mailing)
1364 US Highway 412 E (physical)
Jackson, TN 38305
( )   <Madison>
SS: Jerald D Smith   <M1>
2625 Beech Bluff Road
Beech Bluff, TN 38313
(731)427-9316
jergensmith@aol.com
CL: Martha Wolfe
1300 US Highway 412 E
Jackson, TN 38305
(731)424-4979

jergensmith@aol.com

Cloverdale   (2C)GRWT9407
3891 S Sellers Road (mailing)
3541 Cloverdale Road (physical)
Obion, TN 38240
( )   <Obion>
FAX: (731)538-2383
CL: Billy J Sellers
3891 S Sellers Road
Obion, TN 38240
(731)538-2986
FAX: (731)538-2383
bsellers@ken-tennwireless.com

Colonial   (4MWC)GRWT9305
1500 S Perkins Road
Memphis, TN 38117
(901)682-4747   <Shelby>
SS: Lisa Anderson   <M1 M9>
1790 Faxon Avenue
Memphis, TN 38112
(901)246-8052
anderli90@gmail.com
CL: George R Marston
1042 LaRue Place
Memphis, TN 38122
(901)685-1488
put11599@bellsouth.net

Concord   (3MWC)GRWT9106
153 Herd Law Road
Trenton, TN 38382
( )   <Gibson>
PA: Don McCurley   <M1>
4036 McAllister Street
Milan, TN 38358
(731)723-3623
dcmccurley@hotmail.com
CL: Don Gibson
4225 Christmasville Road
Medina, TN 38355
(731)783-0992

Cool Springs CC   (4C)GRWT9107
240 Little Grove Road
Lavinia, TN 38348
( )   <Carroll>
LS: Robert Barger   <M6>
7127 Highway 104 W
Lavinia, TN 38348
(731)987-2477
rbarger104@att.net
CL: Ann Hammett
8725 US Highway 70
Cedar Grove, TN 38321
(731)987-2516

Cool Springs GC   (4MWC)GRWT9408
37 Cool Spring Road
Trimble, TN 38259
(731)643-6153   <Gibson>
SS: Steve Rogers   <M3>
37 Cool Spring Road
Trimble, TN 38259
(731)882-2229
CL: Mike Pruett
119 Heritage Drive
Rutherford, TN 38369
(731)665-6348
mdpruett@tennesseetel.net

WEST TENNESSEE PRESBYTERY CONTINUED

Davidson Chapel   (4MWC)GRWT9108
399 Laneview Concord Road
Trenton, TN 38382
(731)618-1521
FAX: (731)664-3735
dale.cavaness@horne-llp.com <Gibson>
CL: Dale Cavaness
2093 Brentwood Drive
Milan, TN 38358
(731)618-1521
FAX: (731)664-3735
dale.cavaness@horne-llp.com

Double Springs   (4WC)GRWT9109
18 Double Springs Road
Humboldt, TN 38343
(731)787-6422   <Gibson>
PA: Russell Little   <M1>
29 Cotton Row
Medina, TN 38355
(731)783-3565
russelllittle@bellsouth.net
CL: Linda Fisher
65 Spencer Drive
Medina, TN 38355
(731)613-8355
lfisher@eplus.net

Dresden   (4MWC)GRWT9110
PO Box 131 (mailing)
121 S Wilson Street (physical)
Dresden, TN 38225
( )   <Weakley>
PA: H Walter McClanahan   <M1>
215 White Bros Road
Humboldt, TN 38343
(731)784-1176
waltermac2@hughes.net
CL: Martha Killebrew
PO Box 131
Dresden, TN 38225
(731)364-3294
FAX: (731)364-3500
killebrewm@frontiernet.net

Dyer   (4MEWC)GRWT9409
PO Box 181 (mailing)
256 E College Street (physical)
Dyer, TN 38330
(731)692-2594   <Gibson>
dcpchurch@bellsouth.net
PA: Johnny E Watson   <M1>
272 Madison Street
Dyer, TN 38330
(731)692-3555
rev.jwatson@bellsouth.net
CL: Johnny Ward
46 Old Dyer Trenton Road
Dyer, TN 38330
(731)692-2594
ward3363@bellsouth.net

Dyersburg First   (4WC)GRWT9410
2280 Parr Avenue
Dyersburg, TN 38024
(731)285-5703   <Dyer>
FAX: (731)285-5792
cpoffice@cumberlandchurch.com
AP: Annetta Camp   <M1>
2303 Mill Creek Road

Halls, TN 38040
(731)285-5703
FAX: (731)285-5792
annetta@cumberlandchurch.com
CL: William Mallard
198 Walnut Lane Ext
Dyersburg, TN 38024
(731)285-0837
FAX: (731)287-0873
wem1950@bellsouth.net

Ebenezer (MC)   (2EWC)GRWT9206
Main Street
Mercer, TN 38392
(731)935-2391   <Madison>
CL: Pope Mulherin
8 Prestwick Drive
Jackson, TN 38305
(731)427-3113

Ebenezer (TC)   (4WC)GRWT9303
70 Witherington Road
Mason, TN 38049
( )   <Tipton>
CL: Ann Burlison
564 Baskin Road
Burlison, TN 38015
(901)294-3614
aburlison@tipton-county.com

Faith   (4WC)GRWT9308
3427 Appling Road
Bartlett, TN 38133
(901)377-0526   <Shelby>
FAX: (901)382-2600
faithcumberlandp@bellsouth.net
PA: Steven Shelton   <M1>
7886 Farmhill Cove
Bartlett, TN 38135
(901)377-0526
faithcpcpastor@gmail.com
CL: Karen Patten
5728 North Street
Bartlett, TN 38134
(901)237-0535
mkpatten@outlook.com

Fulton   (4MWC)GRWT9412
PO Box 5343 (mailing)
1159 Parker Road (physical)
South Fulton, TN 38257
(731)479-9912   <Obion>
PA: David Bayer   <M1>
3090 Tom Counce Road
South Fulton, TN 38257
(731)479-3060
dbayer9060@gmail.com
CL: Donald R Moore
155 Cox Road
Fulton, KY 42041
(270)436-2723
donaldmoore9@aol.com

Germantown   (4EWC)GRWT9310
2385 Riverdale
Germantown, TN 38138
(901)755-3884   <Shelby>
FAX: (901)759-3653
cpcgww@aol.com
PA: William Warren   <M1>
7139 Toro Cove

Germantown, TN 38138
(901)755-8058
cpcgww@aol.com
CL: Iva McCutchen
1240 Bristol Drive
Memphis, TN 38119
(901)761-0575
ivesmc@att.net

Gleason   (4MC)GRWT9111
190 David Court (mailing)
McKenzie, TN 38201
171 Smyth Lane (physical)
Gleason, TN 38229
(731)648-5343   <Weakley>
PA: James (Jim) Pinnell   <M1>
1525 Parks Well Road
Gleason, TN 38229
(731)648-5078
revpinnell@hotmail.com
CL: Donald Ray Stephens
190 David Court
McKenzie, TN 38201
(731)352-5852
tuvart@charter.net

Good Springs   (4WC)GRWT9112
180 Barham Road (mailing)
Good Springs Road (physical)
Dukedom, TN 38226
( )   <Weakley>
SS: Dennis Weaver   <M2 ST>
2620 Dalton Road
Providence, KY 42450
(731)592-9054
dsweaver@memphisseminary.edu
CL: Loretta Barham
180 Barham Road
Dukedom, TN 38226
(731)469-9555

Holly Grove   (4MWC)GRWT9304
4538 Holly Grove Road
Brighton, TN 38011
(901)476-8379   <Tipton>
FAX: (901)476-3324
hollygrovecpchurch@att.net
PA: L Ronald McMillan   <M1>
675 Kimberly Drive
Atoka, TN 38004
(901)837-1101
mcmillanron@bellsouth.net
AP: Debbie Marshall   <M1>
1494 Bucksnort Road
Covington, TN 38019
(901)494-1251
dsmarshall05@att.net
CL: Donna E Lindley
4538 Holly Grove Road
Brighton, TN 38011
(901)476-8379
FAX: (901)476-3324
hollygrovecpchurch@att.net

Hopewell (BC)   (2EWC)GRWT9207
2309 Saulsbury Road (mailing)
289 Hopewell Road (physical)
Walnut, MS 38683
( )   <Benton>
PA: Byron Forester   <M1>
2376 Eastwood Place

WEST TENNESSEE PRESBYTERY CONTINUED

Memphis, TN 38112
(901)324-1707
bforester@bellsouth.net
CL: Kathy D Wilburn
2309 Saulsbury Road
Walnut, MS 38683
(662)223-6447
kwilburn@fareselaw.com

_____

Hopewell (WC)   (2WC)GRWT9115
1061 Gaylord Road (mailing)
Route 1 Box 91 (physical)
Sharon, TN 38255
(   )   <Weakley>
CL: Lonnie Hazlewood
1061 Gaylord Road
Sharon, TN 38255
(731)973-2426
lonminh@citlink.net

_____

Humboldt   (4MEWC)GRWT9116
2375 E Mitchell Street
Humboldt, TN 38343
(731)784-2703   <Gibson>
pastor@humboldtcpc.org
PA: Robert Harris   <M1>
619 N 24th Avenue
Humboldt, TN 38343
(731)420-6067
pastor@humboldtcpc.org
CL: Carolyn Hunley
6 Clinton Road
Humboldt, TN 38343
(731)784-2031
carolynhunley16@yahoo.com

_____

Hurricane Hill   (4C)GRWT9413
Newbern, TN 38059
(   )   <Dyer>
CL: Holly Powers
684 Hurricane Hill Road
Dyersburg, TN 38024
(731)285-4436

_____

Jackson First   (4WC)GRWT9208
1730 US Highway 45 Bypass
Jackson, TN 38305
(731)664-1632   <Madison>
FAX: (731)664-1633
fcpc1730@bellsouth.net
PA: Terry M Hunley   <M1>
48 Charleston Square
Jackson, TN 38305
(731)660-5685
thunley1@charter.net
CL: Anne Austin
1730 US Highway 45 Bypass
Jackson, TN 38305
(731)660-2411
ama@eplus.net

_____

Kenton   (4MEWC)GRWT9414
301 W College Street
Kenton, TN 38233
(   )   <Obion>
LS: Charles McCall   <M6>
549 Mason Hall Road
Trimble, TN 38259
(731)297-3288
cmccall@ycinet.net
CL: Paul E Williams

206 Hillside Street
Kenton, TN 38233
(731)749-5656

_____

Korean   (P)GRWT9322
7565 Macon Road
Cordova, TN 38018
(901)755-9101   <Shelby>
hjinlab@hotmail.com
SS: Ho-Jin Lee   <M2>
7565 Macon Road
Cordova, TN 38018
(901)754-7070
hjinlab@hotmail.com
CL: Gong Dickens
7565 Macon Road
Cordova, TN 38018
(901)758-1130

_____

Lexington First   (4MWC)GRWT9209
PO Box 11 (mailing)
931 N Broad Street (physical)
Lexington, TN 38351
(731)968-7176   <Henderson>
patfreelandjones@yahoo.com
PA: C William Jones Jr   <M1>
109 Lakewood Drive
Lexington, TN 38351
(731)967-7618
patfreelandjones@yahoo.com
CL: Teresa Ferguson
7747 Middleburg Road
Scotts Hill, TN 38374
(731)968-9079

_____

Maple Springs   (4MWC)GRWT9210
2625 Beech Bluff Road (mailing)
2005 Beech Bluff Road (physical)
Beech Bluff, TN 38313
(731)424-4065   <Henderson>
PA: Jerald D Smith   <M1>
2625 Beech Bluff Road
Beech Bluff, TN 38313
(731)427-9316
jergensmith@aol.com
CL: Tricia Fowler
37 Fowler Cut Off Road
Beech Bluff, TN 38313
(731)423-1255
tfowler@firstbankonline.com

_____

Martin   (4MWC)GRWT9117
312 E Main Street
Martin, TN 38237
(731)587-3222   <Weakley>
FAX: (731)487-6484
cathyjahr@charter.net
PA: Michael T Lavender   (M1)
308 Main Street
Martin, TN 38237
(731)431-9127
mike_lavender@yahoo.com
CL: Cathy Jahr
142 Rolling Meadows
Martin, TN 38237
(731)587-6484
cathyjahr@charter.net

_____

Mason Hall   (2EWC)GRWT9415
549 Mason Hall Road (mailing)
Trimble, TN 38259

1861 CP Church Road (physical)
Kenton, TN 38233
(   )   <Obion>
mccall.cmccall@gmail.com
CL: Charles McCall
549 Mason Hall Road
Trimble, TN 38259
(731)431-8195
mccall.cmccall@gmail.com

_____

McKenzie   (4WC)GRWT9118
PO Box 133 (mailing)
16835 Highland Drive (physical)
McKenzie, TN 38201
(731)352-2440   <Carroll>
FAX: (731)352-3101
church@mckenziecpc.org
PA: Wood, Kevin L   <M1>
339 David Street
McKenzie, TN 38201
(865)588-8581
FAX: (865)588-8581
revkev7285@earthlink.net
AP: Garrett Burns   <M1>
387 Forrest Avenue
McKenzie. TN 38201
(731)535-3126
gburns2888@gmail.com
CL: June Perritt
PO Box 133
McKenzie, TN 38201
(731)352-2440
FAX: (731)352-3101
church@mckenziecpc.org

_____

Medina   (4EC)GRWT9119
104 Cumberland Street
Medina, TN 38355
(731)618-0192   <Gibson>
PA: Linda H Glenn   <M1>
49 Mason Road
Threeway, TN 38343
(731)618-0192
lindahglenn@click1.net
CL: Mark A Kee
67 Jim Jackson Road
Humboldt, TN 38343
(731)487-1088
markkee24@yahoo.com

_____

Meridian   (4C)GRWT9120
1099 Adams Road (mailing)
2590 Meridian Road (physical)
Greenfield, TN 38230
(   )   <Weakley>
CL: David McBride
1099 Adams Road
Greenfield, TN 38230
(731)235-3058

_____

Milan   (4WC)GRWT9121
6083 S First Street
Milan, TN 38358
(731)686-1851   <Gibson>
office@milancp.org
PA: Doy L Daniels Jr   <M1>
1095 Crestview Drive
Milan, TN 38358
(731)686-1851
FAX: (731)723-9324
revdrdoy@gmail.com

WEST TENNESSEE PRESBYTERY CONTINUED

AP: Corey Cummings   <M1>
1023 W Woodrow Street
Milan, TN 38358
(731)686-1851
corey@milancp.org
CL: Ronnie Parks
62 Hughes Loop
Milan, TN 38358
(731)686-3065
ronnieparks@bellsouth.net

Mill Creek   (4C)GRWT9122
239 Smith Street (mailing)
434 Mill Creek Road (physical)
Puryear, TN 38251
( )   <Henry>
CL: Richard E Vincent
239 Smith Street
Puryear, TN 38251
(731)247-5211
richardearlvincent@yahoo.com

Morella   (2EWC)GRWT9416
51 Morella Road
Kenton, TN 38233
( )   <Gibson>
CL: J C Reed
121 Tull Road
Kenton, TN 38233
(731)749-5545

Morning Sun   (4MC)GRWT9314
2682 Morning Sun Road
Cordova, TN 38016
(901)382-3439   <Shelby>
mscpc13@gmail.com
PA: Joey Edwards   <M1>
5279 Ivy Creek Lane
Lakeland, TN 38002
(901)573-7579
edwardsjoey@bellsouth.net
CL: Gwen Hromada
4350 Thorpe Drive
Mason, TN 38049
(901)466-1154
gwen247@aceweb.com

Mt Ararat   (4WC)GRWT9417
1465 Troy-Hickman Road
Union City, TN 38261
(731)536-5406   <Obion>
PA: Robert A Smith   <M1>
PO Box 501
Newbern, TN 38059
(731)627-3332
ras1957@bellsouth.net
CL: Bobby Hall
664 Mill Creek Road
Troy, TN 38260
(731)536-4798

Mt Carmel   (4C)GRWT9315
106 E Marginal Street (mailing)
2355 Union Drive (physical)
Somerville, TN 38068
( )   <Fayette>
PA: Clinton Buck   <M1>
PO Box 770068
Memphis, TN 38117
(901)682-2358
clintonbuck@aol.com

CL: Harry N Wiles
106 E Marginal Street
Somerville, TN 38068
(901)465-9733

Mt Olive   (4MEC)GRWT9418
76 Yorkville Highway (mailing)
42 Mt Olive Road (physical)
Dyer, TN 38330
( )   <Gibson>
PA: Charles Fike   <M1>
2070 N 1st Street
Milan, TN 38358
(731)686-0224
CL: Carolyn Martin
76 Yorkville Highway
Dyer, TN 38330
(731)692-2773

Mt Vernon   (4MC)GRWT9213
3101 Mt Vernon Road
Ramer, TN 38367
(731)645-6420   <McNairy>
SS: Jeff DeWees   <M1>
3101 Mt Vernon Road
Ramer, TN 38367
(731)645-6420
shg_50@bellsouth.net
CL: Larry Gage
130 Shiloh Terrace Drive
Selmer, TN 38375
(731)645-6828
lgage6828@charter.net

Mt Zion   (4MWC)GRWT9214
480 County Road 401
Falkner, MS 38629
(662)837-7013   <Tippah>
FAX: (662)837-7969
info@mtzioncpc.org
PA: Thomas Richie Lockhart   <M1>
700 County Road 343
Falkner, MS 38629
(662)837-4281
nmsdiamonddawgs@yahoo.com
CL: Jane H Childs
921 County Road 338
Falkner, MS 38629
(662)223-4285
jchilds@wgyates.com

New Beginnings   (4C)GRWT9306
2300 Frayser Boulevard
Memphis, TN 38127
(901)353-4011
PA: Craig Wilson   <M1>
2300 Frayser Boulevard
Memphis, TN 38127
(901)277-4066
craigwilson2300@yahoo.com
SC: Elnora McKinzie
1111 Holmes Street
Memphis, TN 38122
(870)377-2174

New Bethel   (4C)GRWT9215
3708 New Bethel Road
Selmer, TN 38375
( )   <McNairy>
CL: Preston King
3708 New Bethel Road

Selmer, TN 38375
(731)645-3150
kingpreston2828@yahoo.com

New Bethlehem   (2EWC)GRWT9420
1585 Bethlehem Road (mailing)
825 Bethlehem Road (physical)
Newbern, TN 38059
( )   <Dyer>
CL: Mary Bell Murray
1585 Bethlehem Road
Newbern, TN 38059
(731)627-2332
murrayc2@juno.com

New Ebenezer   (4MEWC)GRWT9422
PO Box 364 (mailing)
1606 Ebenezer Road (physical)
Troy, TN 38260
(731)536-4936   <Obion>
PA: Mitch Boulton   <M1>
1606 Ebenezer Road
Troy, TN 38260
(731)487-2318
steelermitch@gmail.com
CL: James R Kendall
2494 W State Route 21
Troy, TN 38260
(731)538-9933

New Salem (MC)   (4C)GRWT9216
453 New Salem Road
Bethel Springs, TN 38315
( )   <McNairy>
SS: Earl Phelps   <M1>
172 Michie Pebble Hill Road
Stantonville, TN 38379
(731)632-5107
FAX: (901)632-9126
phelps.e@juno.com
CL: Malcolm Dickson
153 Harris Road
Bethel Springs, TN 38315
(731)934-7282
FAX: (731)934-0736
robert.dickson@aol.com

New Salem (SC)   (4MWC)GRWT9316
6813 Salem Road
Lakeland, TN 38002
(901)829-3241   <Shelby>
FAX: (901)829-3241
ptcriss@hotmail.com
PA: Paul T Criss   <M1>
6831 Salem Road
Lakeland, TN 38002
(901)626-8462
ptcriss@hotmail.com
CL: Patty Butler Little
6909 Salem Road
Lakeland, TN 38002
(901)829-3218

New Salem (WC)   (3C)GRWT9124
3220 Sharon Highway 89 (mailing)
Highway 89 (physical)
Sharon, TN 38255
( )   <Weakley>
SS: Kermit Travis   <M1>
3220 Sharon Highway 89
Dresden, TN 38225

WEST TENNESSEE PRESBYTERY CONTINUED

(731)364-2315
CL: John C Clark
  215 Rambo Road
  Sharon, TN 38255
  (731)364-3921
  jcjclark@frontiernet.net

_____
Newbern   (4MWC)GRWT9419
  310 E Main
  Newbern, TN 38059
  (731)627-3646   <Dyer>
CL: Jamie Kay Berkley
  403 E Main Street
  Newbern, TN 38059
  (731)676-8626
  jamiekayb@hotmail.com

_____
North Union   (4EC)GRWT9423
  15 Cardwell Road (mailing)
  Dyer, TN 38330
  78 Preacher Dowland Road (physical)
  Kenton, TN 38233
  (731)673-4122   <Gibson>
CL: Chad Murray
  2067 Locust Grove Road
  Newbern, TN 38059
  (731)676-6027
  chadgfc@gmail.com

_____
Nuevo Empezar   (4EC)GRWT9324
  3442 Tutwiler
  Memphis, TN 38122
  (901)644-0513
PA: Bertha Davis   <M1>
  2242 Slocum Avenue
  Memphis, TN 38127
  (901)644-0513
CL: Session Clerk
  3442 Tutwiler Avenue
  Memphis, TN 38122
  (901)644-0513

_____
Oak Grove   (4MC)GRWT9217
  3655 Talley Store Road
  Henderson, TN 38340
  (731)989-3825   <Chester>
  marcus.hayes@att.net
SS: Marcus Hayes   <M1 OP>
  3615 Talley School Road
  Henderson, TN 38340
  (270)841-7576
  marcus.hayes@att.net
CL: Don Terry
  1450 Braund Road
  Henderson, TN 38340
  (731)989-7982
  FAX: (731)989-7982

_____
Oak Hill   (1C)GRWT9125
  5820 Highway 69 N (mailing)
  8295 Highway 69 N (physical)
  Paris, TN 38242
  (   )   <Henry>
PA: Francis Howe   <M1>
  129 Manley Street
  McKenzie, TN 38201
  (731)352-5551
CL: Theresa Rushing
  5820 Highway 69 N
  Paris, TN 38242
  (731)642-3499
  trushing@utm.edu

_____
Olive Branch   (4MWC)GRWT9312
  8161 Germantown Road
  Olive Branch, MS 38654
  (662)893-7347   <Desoto>
  FAX: (901)893-7347
  officefcpc@yahoo.com
PA: James L Ratliff   <M1>
  4027 Club View Drive
  Memphis, TN 38125
  (901)758-0125
  pastorjimfcpc@yahoo.com
CL: Charlie Trapp
  4750 Harvest Knoll Cove N
  Memphis, TN 38125
  (901)626-2952
  charliebethtrapp@bellsouth.net

_____
Oliver's Chapel   (4WC)GRWT9127
  85 Olivers Chapel Road (mailing)
  22 Olivers Chapel Road (physical)
  Bradford, TN 38316
  (731)742-3559   <Gibson>
  FAX: (731)742-3994
  mpybas@yahoo.com
PA: Sam Harwell   <M1>
  23 Lake Hayes Estates Road
  Trenton, TN 38382
  (731)414-2153
  sambharl@yahoo.com
CL: Marcy Tahmazian
  85 Olivers Chapel Road
  Bradford, TN 38316
  (731)742-3097
  FAX: (731)742-3994
  mpybas@yahoo.com

_____
Olivet   (4MWC)GRWT9220
  6095 Highway 226
  Savannah, TN 38372
  (731)925-2685   <Hardin>
  olivetcp@bellsouth.net
PA: James D Pounds   <M1>
  40 Nellie Lane
  Savannah, TN 38372
  (731)925-2685
  olivetcp@bellsouth.net
CL: Walton Williams
  10875 Highway 64
  Savannah, TN 38372
  (731)412-7569

_____
Palestine (DC)   (4C)GRWT9424
  Route 2
  Newbern, TN 38059
  (   )   <Dyer>
CL: Session Clerk Palestine CP Church
  Route 2
  Newbern, TN 38059
  (731)627-9227

_____
Palestine (HC)   (4MWC)GRWT9221
  1010 Nobles Road (mailing)
  6835 Highway 22A (physical)
  Lexington, TN 38351
  (   )   <Henderson>
  mcadamsjc@bellsouth.net
PA: Wayne Tompkins   <M1>
  548 E Columbia Road 23
  Emerson, AR 71740
  (870)807-2874
  waynetompkinsministries@yahoo.com

CL: Cheri McAdams
  1010 Nobles Road
  Luray, TN 38352
  (731)614-0433
  mcadamsjc@bellsouth.net

_____
Parsons First   (4MEWC)GRWT9222
  PO Box 141 (mailing)
  114 Virginia Avenue N (physical)
  Parsons, TN 38363
  (731)847-7148   <Decatur>
PA: David Hawley   <M1>
  127 John Holt Road
  Beech Bluff, TN 38313
  (731)427-7284
  haw177@aol.com
CL: Tony Collett
  6636 Rockhouse Road
  Linden, TN 37096
  (931)589-5103
  tacollett@tds.net

_____
Pleasant Green   (4C)GRWT9129
  c/o Helen Watkins (mailing)
  2776 Highway 105
  Trezevant, TN 38258
  712 Idlewild-Holly Leaf (physical)
  Atwood, TN 38220
  (   )   <Gibson>
OD: Keith Pence   <M5>
  PO Box 703
  Gleason, TN 38229
  (731)819-2553
CL: Helen Watkins
  2776 Highway 105
  Trezevant, TN 38258
  (731)669-1601
  hjoy1@charter.net

_____
Pleasant Grove   (2C)GRWT9317
  2320 Pleasant Grove Road
  Moscow, TN 38057
  (901)877-3287   <Fayette>
CL: Jack Joyner
  2320 Pleasant Grove Road
  Moscow, TN 38057
  (901)877-3287

_____
Pleasant Union   (4MWC)GRWT9318
  9251 Brunswick Road
  Millington, TN 38053
  (901)829-3262   <Shelby>
PA: Matthew Dean Cunningham   <M1>
  1646 Brighton-Clopton Road
  Brighton, TN 38011
  (901)475-4252
  mcunningham0528@comcast.net
CL: Patricia Parks
  8995 Mulberry Road
  Atoka, TN 38004
  (901)829-3012
  pittypat28@aol.com

_____
Poplar Grove   (4C)GRWT9425
  492 Church Road
  Halls, TN 38040
  (731)627-2445   <Lauderdale>
  2Orrs.mn@charter.net
PA: Melvin Orr   <M1>
  806 Washington Street
  Newbern, TN 38059
  (731)627-2445

WEST TENNESSEE PRESBYTERY CONTINUED

2Orrs.mn@charter.net
CL: Larry Keen
323 Pennington Road
Halls, TN 38040
(731)836-5546
lkeen@lctn.com

_____

Protemus   (4EWC)GRWT9426
2372 W Shawtown Road (mailing)
2033 W Shawtown Road (physical)
Troy, TN 38260
( )   <Obion>
LS: James R Gunter   <M6>
6997 Bud Barker Road
Obion, TN 38240
(731)538-9252
CL: Betty Rhamy
2372 W Shawtown Road
Troy, TN 38260
(731)538-9458

_____

Ramer   (4MEWC)GRWT9223
4096 Highway 57 W
Ramer, TN 38367
( )   <McNairy>
OD: Albert Brown   <M5>
1772 Buena Vista Road
Bethel Springs, TN 38315
(731)934-7349
CL: George Armstrong
216 Ballpark Road E
Ramer, TN 38367
(731)645-3987

_____

Roellen   (2C)GRWT9428
6040 Highway 104 E (mailing)
Highway 104 E (physical)
Dyersburg, TN 38024
(731)285-0300   <Dyer>
krector@cableone.net
PA: Dennis Vance   <M1>
1320 Valleywood Drive
Paris, TN 38242
(731)644-3627
rvdvance@hotmail.com
CL: Hal Rector
6040 Highway 104 E
Dyersburg, TN 38024
(731)285-0300
krector@cableone.net

_____

Rutherford   (4MEWC)GRWT9429
945 S Trenton Street (mailing)
113 N Trenton Street (physical)
Rutherford, TN 38369
(731)665-6487   <Gibson>
PA: Hobert Walker   <M1>
PO Box 66
Rutherford, TN 38369
(731)665-7236
rutherfordcpchurch@gmail.com
CL: Joe Bone
945 S Trenton Street
Rutherford, TN 38369
(731)665-7253
jobne@msn.com

_____

Salem   (4MC)GRWT9430
174 Franklin Street (mailing)
184 Franklin Street(physical)
Gadsden, TN 38337
( )   <Crockett>

SS: Karl Schwarz   <M1>
83 W Curtis Street
Bells, TN 38006
(731)663-3987
schw8651@bellsouth.net
CL: Ann Davis
174 Franklin Street
Gadsden, TN 38337
(731)784-4713
cloud31@bellsouth.net

_____

Savannah First   (4WC)GRWT9224
300 Tennessee Street
Savannah, TN 38372
(731)925-4493   <Hardin>
savannah1stcp@hotmail.com
SS: Helen Hamilton   <M3>
245 Elm Street
Savannah, TN 38372
(731)925-7338
helmackham@aol.com
CL: Levin Edwards
300 Tennessee Street
Savannah, TN 38372
(731)925-4493
levinedwards@gmail.com

_____

Selmer Court Ave   (4MWC)GRWT9225
PO Box 741 (mailing)
234 Court Avenue (physical)
Selmer, TN 38375
(731)645-5257   <McNairy>
PA: Richard Reid   <M1>
123 S Fifth Street
Selmer, TN 38375
(731)453-5302
rjreid1964@msn.com
CL: Gwelda W Treece
299 Country Club Lane
Selmer, TN 38375
(731)645-5519
gweldat@bellsouth.net

_____

Sharon   (4MEC)GRWT9130
PO Box 588 (mailing)
5414 US Highway 45 (physical)
Sharon, TN 38255
( )   <Weakley>
SS: David Lancaster   <M1 PR>
426 Fugua Road
Martin, TN 38237
(731)588-5895
lancasterd@bethel-college.edu
CL: Patricia Elam
2275 Mount Vernon Road
Sharon, TN 38255
(731)456-2882
jimelam@frontiernet.net

_____

Shiloh (AC)   (4WC)GRWT9226
c/o Scott Coleman (mailing)
5 County Road 617A
164 County Road 634 (physical)
Corinth, MS 38834
( )   <Alcorn>
PA: Brenda Laurence   <M1>
2823 Nine Mile Road
Enville, TN 38332
(731)687-2022
southernmoma@hotmail.com
CL: LaWanda Burns
37 County Road 750

Corinth, MS 38834
(662)415-1038
ljmburns@gmail.com

_____

Shiloh (CC)   (4C)GRWT9131
2880 Highway 423
McKenzie, TN 38201
( )   <Carroll>
church@shilohcp.org
PA: Melissa Reid Goodloe   <M1>
225 Macedonia Road
McKenzie, TN 38201
(731)412-9657
rev.mgoodloe@shilohcp.org
CL: Vickie Summers
2880 Highway 423
McKenzie, TN 38201
(731)225-6714
vsum1956@gmail.com

_____

Trezevant   (3EC)GRWT9132
PO Box 246 (mailing)
98 Church Street (physical)
Trezevant, TN 38258
(731)669-4525   <Carroll>
CL: James O Hinton
PO Box 246
Trezevant, TN 38258
(731)669-5277
johinton@charter.net

_____

Trimble   (2MC)GRWT9431
PO Box 146 (mailing)
403 Pierce Street (physical)
Trimble, TN 38259
( )   <Dyer>
PA: George A Butler   <M1>
306 Flora Circle
Newbern, TN 38059
(731)627-9416
CL: Hamilton Parks
PO Box 146
Trimble, TN 38259
(731)297-3691

_____

Troy   (4WC)GRWT9432
PO Box 454 (mailing)
308 Main Street (physical)
Troy, TN 38260
( )   <Obion>
PA: Johnnie Welch   <M1>
PO Box 1506
Dyersburg, TN 38025
(731)287-9008
johnniewelch@msn.com
CL: Alan Thompson
171 Country Valley Drive
Troy, TN 38260
(731)536-1107
atthompson2@netzero.com

_____

Union City   (4MW C)GRWT9433
631 E Church Street
Union City, TN 38261
(731)885-9773   <Obion>
FAX: (731)885-9766
uccpc@bellsouth.net
PA: Drew Hayes   <M1>
6322 Labor Lane
Louisville, KY 40291
(731)796-7076
dhayes72@gmail.com

WEST TENNESSEE PRESBYTERY CONTINUED

CL: Pat Wood
822 E Main Street
Union City, TN 38261
(731)885-4489
FAX: (731)885-6500
pat@woodcommunications.com

Walnut Grove   (4MWC)GRWT9320
1383 Walnut Grove Road
Burlison, TN 38015
(901)476-5533   <Tipton>
billyshires@bellsouth.net
PA: Lisa Peterson   <M1>
1770 Magnolia Tree Road
Memphis, TN 38138
(901)754-9316
petersonli@aol.com
CL: Denise Shires
681 Highway 179
Covington, TN 38019
(901)476-4590
billyshires@bellsouth.net

West Union   (4MWC)GRWT9321
3099 W Union Road
Millington, TN 38053
(901)876-5757   <Shelby>
westunionoffice@bigriver.net
PA: James R Hamblin   <M1>
60 Rolling Meadow Drive
Drummonds, TN 38023
(901)840-4747
brojim391@gmail.com
CL: W Judd Stafford
9281 Herring Hill Road
Millington, TN 38053
(901)876-3277
emcmwjs@aol.com

Woodward's Chapel   (2C)GRWT9434
1357 Webster Street (mailing)
Union City, TN 38261
3054 Bud O Yates Road (physical)
Obion, TN 38240
(731)431-9127   <Obion>
FAX: (731)623-4226
SS: Mike Lavender   <M3 ST>
308 Main Street
Martin, TN 38237
(731)253-7308
FAX: (731)623-4226
mikelavender@alumni.vanderbilt.edu
CL: Alvin Minnick
1357 Webster Street
Union City, TN 38261
(731)442-1130
alviniraq2004@yahoo.com

Yorkville   (4MEC)GRWT9435
PO Box 156 (mailing)
17 Newbern Highway (physical)
Yorkville, TN 38389
(731)643-6594   <Gibson>
SS: Rian Puckett   <M2 ST>
42 Jesse Patterson Road
Trenton, TN 38382
(731)288-7743
rppuckett@memphisseminary.edu
CL: Mike Roberts
PO Box 213
Yorkville, TN 38389
(731)643-6237
roberts8@ycinet.net

Zion   (4C)GRWT9133
8670 Highway 436 (mailing)
3890 New Zion Road (physical)
McKenzie, TN 38201
( )   <Carroll>
SS: Jon T Carlock   <M1>
248 Cherry Avenue
McKenzie, TN 38201
(731)693-0003
carlockj@bethelu.edu
SS: Richard Reed   <M2>
236 Madison Street
Dyer, TN 38330
(731)692-3604
CL: Stan Welch
3670 New Zion Road
McKenzie, TN 38201
(731)358-2238

OTHERS ON MINISTERIAL ROLL:

Akin, Hershel W   <M1 WC>
388 Mysen Drive
Cordova, TN 38018
(901)744-8980
Alexander, Merlyn A   <M1 HR>
80 N Hampton Lane
Jackson, TN 38305
m_j_alexander@eplus.net
(731)668-8185
Anderson, Barry L   <M1 DE>
1790 Faxon Avenue
Memphis, TN 38112
(901)725-0924
wa4mff@aol.com
Bagby, Larry   <M1 WC>
3189 Northwood Drive
Memphis, TN 38111
(901)452-1952
Barkley, Daniel   <M1 WC>
399 Laneview Concord Road
Trenton, TN 38382
(731)855-4162
dgbarkley@hotmail.com
Boatright, William R   <M1 WC>
513 S 6th Street
Murray, KY 42071
(270)761-5052
catfish.boat@gmail.com
Brown, Elinor   <M1 DE>
752 Hawthorne Street
Memphis, TN 38107
(901)274-1474
esb@cumberland.org
Brown, Mark   <M1 M9>
752 Hawthorne Street
Memphis, TN 38107
(901)274-1474
dmbrown@utmem.edu
Burns, J B, Jr   <M1 WC>
1020 Maud Road
Cherokee, AL 35616
(256)360-2252
Caperton, Donald   <M1 RT>
285 Britton Ford Road
Springville, TN 38256
(731)593-5096
dandjcaperton@vol.com
Coleman, Don L   <M1 WC>
85 Orchard Lane
Savannah, TN 38372
(731)925-9710
Condron, Dudley   <M1 RT>
1360 Harbert Avenue

Memphis, TN 38104
(901)726-1488
dudleywcondron@aol.com
Corbin, Eric   <M1 WC>
1629 Symington Road
Ranotul, IL 61866
(217)282-9702
eric@corbinzone.com
Crisp, Gregory W   <M1 WC>
635 Eden Brook Lane
Cordova, TN 38018
(901)266-0406
Dyer, Stuart   <M1 WC>
3574 Foxfield Trail
Bartlett, TN 38135
(901)388-0612
Eddleman, Keith   <M1 WC>
2787 Stage Park Drive
Memphis, TN 38134
(901)388-9885
Gam, John   <M1 WC>
1235 Sanders Street
Auburn, AL 36830
Gillock, Ed   <M1 WC>
PO Box 157
Savannah, TN 38372
(731)609-6744
Grimsley, Roger   <M1 WC>
215 N Oak Street
Springfield, TN 37172
Hames, Anne   <M1 M9>
118 Paris Street
McKenzie, TN 38201
(731)352-4066
FAX: (731)352-4069
hamesa@bethel-college.edu
Heflin, Donna S   <M1 WC>
4144 Meadow Court Drive
Bartlett, TN 38135
(901)382-8198
rdheflin@bellsouth.net
Hill, Jody   <M1 WC>
4030 St Andrew Circle
Corinth, MS 38834
(662)512-8226
jody.hill34@gmail.com
Holmes, Aaron G   <M1 WC>
PO Box 171
Atwood, TN 38220
(731)662-7595
agholmes@charter.net
Hubbard, Pratt   <M1 WC>
1565 Eli Brown Road
McKenzie, TN 38201
(731)352-9178
Jackson, Terry   <M1 M9>
1461 Mount Pleasant Road
Hernando, MS 38632
(662)429-9741
Janner, Tony   <M1 WC>
104 Northwood Drive
McKenzie, TN 38201
(731)352-8055
drtonyjanner@yahoo.com
Jeong, Woo S   <M1 WC>
1205 Morganshire Drive
Collierville, TN 38017
(901)302-0558
FAX: (901)854-8185
Jett, Mace T Jr   <M1 WC>
109 Park Street
Martin, TN 38237
(731)587-0805
Kim, Yoong S   <M1 WC>
225 Bayswater Drive
Suwanee, GA 30024

WEST TENNESSEE PRESBYTERY CONTINUED

(678)765-7018
yoongkim1934@yahoo.com
Kleinjan, Lori   <M1 WC>
6516 Farnell Avenue
Memphis, TN 38134
(901)372-8413
lkleinj@prodigy.net
Latimer, James M   <M1 WC>
7621 Richmond
Memphis, TN 38125
(901)787-7875
jimmylatimer@redeemerevangelical.com
Luttrell, Ben   <M1 WC>
262 Main Street
Nettleton, MS 38858
(731)645-5257
Maynard, Geoffery   <M1 WC>
1356 Marcia Road
Memphis, TN 38117
(901)409-5269
McClanahan, Jo Ann   <M1 WC>
215 White Brothers Road
Humboldt, TN 38343
(731)784-1176
joannmcclanahan@hughes.net
McClung, Andy   <M1 WC>
919 Dickinson Street
Memphis, TN 38107
(901)606-6615
scubarev@att.net
McClung, Tiffany   <M1 M9>
919 Dickinson Street
Memphis, TN 38107
(901)606-6615
tmcclung@memphisseminary.edu
Meeks, Brittany   <M1 WC>
1340 Tutwiler Avenue
Memphis, TN 38107
(901)336-9024
bpmeeks@memphisseminary.edu
Minor, Mitzi   <M1 PR>
875 S Cox
Memphis, TN 38104
(901)278-6115
Mosley, Karen   <M1 WC>
PO Box 172154
Memphis, TN 38187
Nash, Zachary   <M1 M8>
(on file in General Assembly Office)
zachary.nash@us.af.mil
Ndoro, Wonder   <M1 WC>
111 Roberta Avenue
Memphis, TN 38112
(901)334-5861
gusungo@yahoo.com
Norton, Thomas H   <M1 RT>
220 Evergreen Garden Drive
Elizabethtown, KY 42701
(353)584-4695
tnorton16@comcast.net
Perkins, Ed   <M1 RT>
721 E Paris Avenue
McKenzie, TN 38201
(731)352-2754
Pinion, Phillip   <M1 WC>
PO Box 87
Union City, TN 38281
(731)885-9175
Powell, Jeff   <M1 WC>
547B Fawn Drive
Henderson, TN 38340
(731)608-2040
jfpowell2003@yahoo.com
Prosser, Robert   <M1 DE>
1021 Old State Route 76
Henry, TN 38231
(731)243-4467

Qualls, Michael   <M1 DE>
3639 Tiffany Oaks Lane
Bartlett, TN 38135
(901)377-0526
FAX: (901)382-2600
mqualls1@yahoo.com
Ragsdale, Donnie   <M1 WC>
915 S Olive Street
Union City, TN 38261
(731)885-0014
Ridgely, Michael   <M1 WC>
5195 Broad Street S
Trezevant, TN 38258
(731)669-3767
Rietz, Allen   <M1 WC>
1239 Hopewell Church Road
Finger, TN 38334
(731)989-7872
Rose, Missy   <M1 DE>
5484 Peyton Randolph Street
Bartlett, TN 38134
(901)378-1133
missyrose3@yahoo.com
Scrivener, Carol   <M1 WC>
746 Willowsprings Boulevard
Franklin, TN 37064
(731)660-6469
csscriv@juno.com
Searcy, James M   <M1 WC>
1307 Lucy Way
Knoxville, TN 37912
(817)293-6132
gsearcy@earthlink.net
Smith, James A   <M1 WC>
8301 Poplar Pike
Germantown, TN 38138
(901)309-1992
james1493@att.net
Thomas, Don F   <M1 WC>
400 Park Hill Road
Collierville, TN 38017
(901)861-6398
thomas63981@comcast.net
Thompson, Tommy   <M1 WC>
9160 Tchulahoma Road
Southaven, MS 38671
(662)393-2552
Todd, Laura   <M1 WC>
3303 Decker Street
Bartlett, TN 38134
(901)496-1443
littlelaurarose@yahoo.com
Truax, Robert Lee, Jr   <M1 M9 RT>
2989 Champions Drive Apt 204
Lakeland, TN 38002
(901)266-5927
Turner, O Gene   <M1 WC>
5160 McSpadden Road
Rives, TN 38253
(731)536-0189
Walker, Michael C   <M1 WC>
1404 Wilshire Drive
Odessa, TX 79761
(731)643-6730
mworator@gmail.com
Ward, Frank   <M1 WC>
46 Henderson Cove
Atoka, TN 38004
(901)837-1972
bamaguy68@xipline.com
Westbrook, James   <M1 RT>
1717 Wedgewood Drive
Union City, TN 38261
(731)884-0918
westbrook731@bellsouth.net

Wheeler, Nathan   <M1 WC>
1255 Wedgewood Street
Memphis, TN 38111
(901)606-9535
nathantyac@gmail.com
White, Diann   <M1 WC>
9394 Alex Dickson Cove
Bartlett, TN 38133
(901)377-7776
diannwhite12@yahoo.com
Wilson, Thomas   <M1 WC>
4543 Lake Vista
Memphis, TN 38128
(901)382-6190
tomjw217@gmail.com

OTHER LICENTIATES ON ROLL:

Dalton, Frank   <M2>
1606 Ebenezer Road
Troy, TN 38260
(731)536-4553
Harwell, Jacob   <M2>
319 Joy Drive
McKenzie, TN 38201
(731)415-1457
rjharwell@student.memphisseminary.edu
Jett-Rand, Dana   <M2>
78 Lester Lane
Martin, TN 38237
(731)587-0805
msdanajett@yahoo.com
Magliolo, Sam   <M2 ST>
14352 Fairview
Byhalia, MS 38611
(662)838-7720
samagliolo@fedex.com
Sims, Joyce   <M2>
6935 Highway 54
Paris, TN 38242
(731)364-3537

OTHER CANDIDATES ON ROLL:

Adams, Jamie   <M3 ST>
403 W Washington
Union City, TN 38261
(731)885-1217
adamsj2@k12tn.net
Dimo, Urelia   <M3>
171 Roberta Drive
Memphis, TN 38112
Gray, Brad   <M3>
6378 Highway 59 S
Mason, TN 38049
(901)475-6140
dgray@aol.com
Hernden, Matthew   <M3 ST>
206 Smith Lane
Brighton, TN 38011
(901)484-7661
mherndren023@gmail.com
Lannom, Pamela   <M3 ST>
220 Bradford Acres
Bradford, TN 38316
(731)742-3838
plannom@yahoo.com
Morris, Cary   <M3>
2167 W Shawtown Road
Troy, TN 38260
(731)538-9477
carey@cyberianwolf.net
Todd, Christopher   <M3 ST>
139 Roberta Drive
Memphis, TN 38112
(901)529-1072
ctodd2@msn.com

ALPHABETICAL ROLL OF MINISTERS

Symbols in this roll:

(M0) - Mentored Minister

(M1) - Ordained Minister

(M2) - Licentiate

(M3) - Candidate

(M4) - Minister of another denomination who through reciprocal agreement is enrolled as a member of presbytery and has temporarily the rights and privileges of such membership according to the Constitution, Article 5.3.

--=<< A >>=--

Acton, Donald W (M1)
1186 Jenkins Lane
Knoxville, TN 37922
(865)966-5132 SEET#2310

Acton, Donny (M1)
1413 Oak Ridge Drive
Birmingham, AL 35242
FAX: (205)991-5259
donny@newhopecpc.org
(205)991-3204 SEGR#0104

Acton, Mindy (M1)
1413 Oak Ridge Drive
Birmingham, AL 35242
FAX: (205)991-5259
mindy@newhopecpc.org
(205)991-3204 SEGR#0104

Acton, Wade (M1)
1615 Estes Drive
Glencoe, AL 35905
ginnyacton@juno.com
(256)492-8542 SEGR#0406

Acuff, David (M1)
4969 Quail Lane
Columbia, SC 29206
david.acuff@us.army.mil
(803)727-3910 TNNA#7300

Adams, Fred Michael (M1)
42 Julies Way
Somerset, KY 42503
fma46@twc.com
(606)451-9155 MICU#3314

Adams, Hunter (M3)
603 Red Fox Court
Burns, TN 37029
hadams60@bethelu.edu
(615)943-7862 TNNA#7300

Adams, Jamie (M3)
403 W Washington
Union City, TN 38261
adamsj2@k12tn.net
(731)885-1217 GRWT#9100

Aden, Dare (M1)
1280 Kimber Road
Dongola, IL 62926
FAX: (618)827-4612
dare_aden@hotmail.com
(618)827-3625 MICO#3400

Aden, Marty (M1)
202 Bennington Place
Wilmington, NC 28412
maden@ec.rr.com
(910)795-1092 MSRR#8400

Agudelo, Gildardo (M1)
Cra 73C # 1A-54
Cali, COLOMBIA, SA
( ) MSCA#8223

Aguiar, Neil (M1)
405 E Moulton Street
Decatur, AL 35601

nlajap@yahoo.com
(256)616-1318 SEGR#0214

Ahn, Da-Wit (David) (M1)
1304 Kakyeng-Dong
Sangdang-Gu Cheongju-City
Choongbook, KOREA
(043)235-0219 SEET#2200

Akai, Anum (M1)
458 Dean Taylor Court
Simpsonville, KY 40067
(502)405-3120 MICU#3100

Akin, Hershel W (M1)
388 Mysen Drive
Cordova, TN 38018
(901)744-8980 GRWT#9100

Alas, William (M1)
612 King Valley Circle
Pelham, AL 35124
alas3542085@yahoo.es
(205)966-9411 SEGR#0115

Albarracin, Ruben D (M1)
7411 Magnolia Shadows Lane
Houston, TX 77095
FAX: (281)463-8617
confiaendios@hotmail.com
(281)463-8617 MSTR#8612

Alexander, Merlyn A (M1)
80 N Hampton Lane
Jackson, TN 38305
m_j_alexander@eplus.net
(731)668-8185 GRWT#9100

Alhart, Daryl (M1)
2187 Rutledge Ford Road
Decherd, TN 37324
dwalhart@aol.com
(931)349-7104 TNMU#7225

Allen, Gail (M1)
488 County Road 1650 N
Bethany, IL 61914
kallen1_61914@yahoo.com
(217)665-3387 MINC#5200

Alvarez, Samuel (M3)
3740 W Leland Avenue
Chicago, IL 60625
(773)509-9165 MINC#5200

Alverson, Elmer L (M1)
354 Roy Davis Road
New Market, AL 35761
budalv@bellsouth.net
(256)828-4503 SERD#0800

Anderson, Barry L (M1)
1790 Faxon Avenue
Memphis, TN 38112
wa4mff@aol.com
(901)725-0924 GRWT#9100

Anderson, Christopher (M2)
131 Roberta Drive
Memphis, TN 38112
csanderson@memphisseminary.edu
(870)805-0886 GRAR#1100

Anderson, Kyle (M3)

828 E Main Street
Batesville, AR 72501
kanderson@mempisseminary.edu
(870)834-5799

Anderson, Lisa (M1)
1790 Faxon Avenue
Memphis, TN 38112
anderli60@gmail.com
(901)246-8052 GRWT#9305

Ang, John (M1)
5843 S Farm Road 157
Springfield, MO 65810
pastorcares@yahoo.com
(417)886-3487 GRMI#4100

Appling, John (M1)
1722 S Fairway Avenue
Springfield, MO 65804
pegblessings@sbcglobal.net
(417)877-4643 GRMI#4100

Appling, Peggy (M1)
1722 S Fairway Avenue
Springfield, MO 65804
pegblessings@sbcglobal.net
(417)877-4643 GRMI#4100

Arase, Makihiko (M1)
3-355-4 Kamikitadai Higashi
Yamato-shi, Tokyo
207-0023, JAPAN
FAX: (042)567-2977
viator@cb3.so-net.ne.jp
(042)567-2977 MSJA#8309

Arias, John Jairo (M3)
Calle 144 Sur #496-08 / Apto 202
Caldas, Antioquia
COLOMBIA, SA
(57)317-693-1162 MSAN#8900

Ariza, Fabiola (M1)
COLOMBIA, SA
fatvioleta@hotmail.com
(316)419-8414 MSCA#8200

Aros, Jeremias (M1)
5649 W Roscoe Street
Chicago, IL 60634
jeremiasaros@sbcglobal.net
(773)685-4395 MINC#5200

Arteaga, Gilberto (M3)
Aereo 794
Buenaventura, COLOMBIA, SA
pastorgilbertoa@hotmail.com
( )256-4261 MSCA#8210

Asayama, Masaharu (M1)
6-3-2-308 Toyogaoka
Tama-shi, Tokyo
206-0031, JAPAN
asa@ipcc-21.com
(042)373-2710 MSJA#8300

Ashley, Jack (Nick) (M3)
2015 E Virginia Street
Evansville, IN 47711
( ) MICO#3400

Ashton, Christie (M1)

MINISTERS CONTINUED

10001 Bailey Cove Road SE
Huntsville, AL 35803
FAX: (256)881-0031
pastorhope@bellsouth.net
(256)881-4673   SERD#0800
Attema, Lee   (M1)
930 W 8th Street
Freeport, TX 77541
(281)728-6263   MSTR#8103
Atwell, Keith G   (M1)
7688 Hardyville Road
Hardyville, KY 42746
FAX: (270)524-9100
(270)528-3667   MICU#3102
Axton, Durant   (M1)
2441 SE Browning Road
Evansville, IN 47725
(812)459-0089   MINC#5200

--=<< B >>==--

Babcock, Edward S, Jr   (M1)
1007 San Ramone Avenue
Huntsville, AL 35802
ejsb1@aol.com
(256)882-9339   SERD#0800
Bagby, Larry   (M1)
3189 Northwood Drive
Memphis, TN 38111
(901)452-1952   GRWT#9100
Ballow, Brent   (M1)
715 Highland Church Road
Paducah, KY 42001
hcppastor@bellsouth.net
(270)564-8891   MICO#3414
Baltimore, Claud G   (M1)
PO Box 1358
1430 Lakehurst Drive
Ada, OK 74821
baltimorejb@earthlink.net
(580)332-2679   MSRR#8400
Bane, Ted   (M1)
903 W Old Hickory Boulevard
Madison, TN 37115
tedjan95@aol.com
(615)975-9343   TNNA#7309
Baranoski, Timothy   (M1)
8040 Starz Loop
Killeen, TX 76544
timothy.i.baranoski@us.army.mil
(615)440-3499   TNNA#7300
Barkley, Daniel   (M1)
2732 Rexford Street
Hokes Bluff, AL 35903
daniel@gadsdencp.com
(256)478-0397   SEGR#0402
Barnett, Rudolph   (M1)
RR 5 Box 267
McLeansboro, IL 62859
(618)643-3253   MINC#5200
Barnhouse, Donald Grey, Jr   (M1)
51 Harristown Road
Paradise, PA 17562
donaldbarnhouse@gmail.com
(610)337-4015   MICU#3131
Barrett, Geoff   (M1)
155 Maude Lane
Harrodsburg, KY 40330
FAX: (256)881-0031
glbarrett@live.com
(859)748-8373   MICU#3111
Barron, Mark   (M1)

836 McArthur Street
Manchester, TN 37355
FAX: (931)728-2975
mbarron@cafes.net
(931)728-2975   TNMU#7224
Barry, James   (M1)
1405 Anna Street
Hixson, TN 37343
james_barry@bellsouth.net
(903)315-7998   SETG#2111
Barton, Cindy   (M3)
83426 Argus Avenue
Trona, CA 93562
cbarton53@hotmail.com
(760)372-4033   MSDC#8700
Barton, Robert   (M1)
22460 Klines Resort Road Lot #290
Three Rivers, MI 49093
csm2ndinfbde2002@yahoo.com
(859)613-2686   MICU#3100
Baugh, Roosevelt   (M1)
4101 Hademan Street
Fort Worth, TX 76119
FAX: (817)534-1339
gmf1220@charter.net
(817)536-1315   MSRR#8408
Bautista, Juan   (M1)
Tranv 30 No 17F-122
Cali
Colombia, South America
( )442-4562   MSCA#8217
Bayer, David   (M1)
9060 Tom Counce Road
South Fulton, TN 38257
dbayer9060@gmail.com
(731)479-3060   GRWT#9412
Bell, Marc   (M1)
3467 State Route 175 N
Bremen, KY 42325
marcbell@insightbb.com
(270)846-4203   MICU#3503
Bell, Michelle   (M3)
8643 Dry Creek Road Unit 1226
Centennial, CO 80112
mabbell@comcast.net
(720)344-4040   MSDC#870
Benadom, Dennis   (M1)
13314 Sage Street
Trona, CA 93562
galerose91@msn.com
(760)372-4536   MSDC#8503
Bender, Richard J   (M1)
5297 Normandy Place
Evansville, IN 47715
richardjbenderjr@yahoo.com
(812)983-9597   MINC#5200
Benedict, Mary McCaskey   (M1)
892 Pen Oak Drive
Cookeville, TN 38501
marykat_61@hotmail.com
(931)260-1422   TNMU#7200
Bennett, Alfred J   (M1)
7286 Nolensville Road
Nolensville, TN 37135
(615)776-5181   TNNA#7300
Benson, William L   (M1)
137 W Lowndes Drive
Columbus, MS 39701
willardb715@gmail.com
(662)386-3433   SEGR#0701
Bertsch, Michael   (M1)
368 Sunset Island Trail

Gallatin, TN 37066
mikebertsch14@gmail.com
(423)763-8314   TNNA#7327
Betancur, Sergio   (M1)
Iglesia El Rebano
Calle 128 sur #48-13
Caldas, Antioquia, COLOMBIA, SA
sergiobetancurposada@hotmail.com
(574)278-0787   MSCA#8208
Biggs, Jeff   (M1)
1504 Cumberland Drive
Fairfield, IL 62837
jeffbiggsonline@gmail.com
(618)842-2219   MINC#5108
Black, Gary G   (M1)
503 S Main Street
Piedmont, AL 36272
(205)447-7142   SEGR#0400
Blackburn, Samuel N   (M1)
6706 S 6th Street
Fort Smith, AR 72908
(479)649-9436   GRAR#1100
Blair, Fonda   (M1)
PO Box 11093
Murfreesboro, TN 37129
blairfonda2010@comcast.net
(615)491-2432   TNCO#7145
Blair, John   (M1)
108 Cliff Drive
Lawrenceburg, TN 38464
jnbblair@charter.net
(931)766-2480   TNCO#7111
Blakeburn, Larry A   (M1)
230 Heathridge Drive
Dyersburg, TN 38024
FAX: (731)285-5792
larry@cumberlandchurch.com
(731)286-2982   SEET#2313
Blakeburn, Roy E   (M1)
111 Park Place
Greeneville, TN 37743
FAX: (423)636-1017
(423)787-9609   SEET#2206
Blandon, Juan Esteban   (M1)
Calle 51 #15-32
barrio Los Naranjos
Dosquebradas, Risaralda
COLOMBIA, SA
juanestebanblandon@yahoo.com
57(314)680-2246   MSAN#8907
Blanton, D B   (M1)
ADDRESS UNKNOWN
( )   GRAR#1100
Blaum, Steve R   (M1)
184 900 Street
Middletown, IL 62666
cumberland@frontier.com
(217)871-3339   MINC#5405
Blevins, Ralph   (M1)
1623 County Road 2375 E
Geff, IL 62842
pastorreblevins@gmail.com
(618)854-2494   MINC#5107
Blevins, Tom   (M1)
50 Blevins Road
Center, KY 42214
(270)565-1792   MICU#3100
Board, N Ray   (M1)
267 State Route 293 N
Princeton, KY 42445
rayboard@att.net
(270)365-0006   MICO#3609

MINISTERS CONTINUED

Boatright, William R (M1)
513 S 6th Street
Murray, KY 42071
catfish.boat@gmail.com
(270)761-5052 GRWT#9100

Boggs, Barry (M3)
1039 Johnnie Bud Lane
Cookeville, TN 38501
( ) TNMU#7200

Boggs, Robert (M1)
89 Maple Leaf Lane
Leitchfield, KY 42754
(270)259-5546 MICU#3100

Bohon, Chris Michael (M3)
109 NE McAlister Road
Burleson, TX 76028
cbohon@stmattcpc.org
(817)228-9494 MSRR#8400

Bond, Bill (M1)
205 Windmere Drive
Chattanooga, TN 37411
bill@wcbj.net
(423)316-0867 SETG#2102

Bond, Richard (M1)
2425 Fisk Road Lot 0
Cookeville, TN 38506
erbond@frontier.net
(931)854-0979 TNMU#7213

Bondurant, Lee (M1)
1453 Paseo Del Sur Court
El Paso, TX 79928
leebondurant@yahoo.com
(915)309-7269 MSDC#8700

Bone, Leslie (M1)
16504 George Franklyn Drive
Independence, MO 64055
lesliebone@comcast.net
(816)373-6625 GRMI#4100

Bone, W Harold (M1)
315 Joey Drive
Bourne, TX 78006
ruaha1@sbcglobal.net
(210)859-5560 MSTR#8100

Boulton, Mitch (M1)
1606 Ebenezer Road
Troy, TN 38260
steelermitch@gmail.com
(731)487-2318 GRWT#9422

Bower, Clay (M1)
221 Waterlemon Way
Monroe, NC 28110
cbower@lzbsoutheast.com
(704)575-9497 MSDC#8700

Bowers, Sharon G (M1)
1011 Barbara Drive
San Marcos, TX 78666
sharon.bowers@gmail.com
(512)230-7078 MSTR#8100

Bowling, Andrew (M1)
20945 Highway 16 E
Siloam Springs, AR 72761
(479)524-6576 GRAR#1100

Bowman, Greg (M3)
3241 South Fork Road
Glasgow, KY 42141
( ) MICU#3217

Boyd, Tammy (M3)
118 County Road 24
Hanceville, AL 35077
(256)338-4733 SERD#0800

Bozeman, Robert (M1)
582 Bozeman Loop

Belmont, LA 71406
bo@bozemanengineering.com
(318)256-5781 MSTR#8100

Bradberry, Jim (M3)
120 Hummingbird Lane
Searcy, AR 72143
(501)278-9750 GRAR#1205

Bradshaw, James (Jim) (M1)
415 S Red Street
Sheridan, AR 72150
(870)942-2525 GRAR#1105

Brantley, Kevin T (M1)
729 Old Hodgenville Road
Greensburg, KY 42743
kbrantley1971@windstream.net
(270)932-3780 MICU#3110

Brasher, Karen (M1)
2931 Barker Cypress Road Apt 415
Houston, TX 77084
ekb077@gmail.com
(205)777-2420 SEGR#0100

Braswell, Jimmy (M1)
1514 E 10th
Odessa, TX 79761
jjcgbraz@cableone.net
(432)335-9346 MSDC#8703

Brewer, Barbara Jean (M1)
1360 White Oak Bluff Road
Rison, AR 71665
(870)325-6449 GRAR#1108

Brindley, Toy (M1)
PO Box 225
Gurley, AL 35748
(256)776-2331 SERD#0804

Brister, Glenn (M1)
3004 Delaware Avenue
McComb, MS 39648
bearmountainpenworks@gmail.com
(706)934-8629 SETG#2100

Brock, Dudley (M1)
490 County Road 1184
Cullman, AL 35057
preacherbrock@att.net
(256)734-0893 SEHO#0500

Brooks, Wayne E (M1)
1505 Parkview Drive
Campbellsville, KY 42718
webrooks@windstream.net
(270)465-9235 MICU#3104

Brown, Amy (M2)
679 Freeze Bend Road
Newport, AR 72112
( ) GRAR#1100

Brown, Charles R (M1)
137 St Agnes
Memphis, TN 38112
cbrown@sttimothy-cpc.org
(817)915-2907 MSRR#8400

Brown, Dale M (M1)
HC 61 Box 4740
West Plains, MO 65775
pastorbrown44@yahoo.com
(417)257-0983 GRMI#4304

Brown, Elinor (M1)
752 Hawthorne Street
Memphis, TN 38107
esb@cumberland.org
(901)274-1474 GRWT#9100

Brown, Houston (M3)
866 N McLean
Memphis, TN 38107
hpbrown95@gmail.com

(817)915-9090 MSRR#8400

Brown, Mark (M1)
752 Hawthorne Street
Memphis, TN 38107
dmbrown@utmem.edu
(901)274-1474 GRWT#9100

Brown, Philip (M2)
540 Mt Pisgah Road
Dongola, IL 62926
brownlp75@yahoo.com
(618)827-3516 MICO#5115

Brown, Rex (M1)
134 Everhart Drive
Greeneville, TN 37745
firstcumberland@gmail.com
(423)639-4298 SEET#2205

Brown, Stephanie S (M1)
137 St Agnes
Memphis, TN 38112
scrudderbrown7@gmail.com
(901)729-3612 MSRR#8400

Brown, Whitney (M3)
137 Roberta Drive
Memphis, TN 38112
(865)387-0002 SEET#2200

Bruington, Don (M1)
PO Box 105
Falls of Rough, KY 40119
(270)257-2228 MICU#3202

Bryan, Hannah (M1)
32 Trenton Lane
Mead, OK 73449
hbryan@choctawnation.com
(580)775-4955 MSCH#6105

Buchanan, Larry (M1)
720 Shelby Road
Salem, KY 42078
(270)988-1880 MICO#3610

Buck, Clinton (M1)
PO Box 770068
Memphis, TN 38117
clintobuck@aol.com
(901)682-2358 GRWT#9315

Bunnell, Robert (Bob) (M1)
329 Lexington Drive
Glasgow, KY 42141
bob_bunnell@yahoo.com
(270)629-6209 MICU#3312

Bunting, Geoff (M1)
9229 Hedgewood Court
Evansville, IN 47725
geoff.bunting@yahoo.com
(812)925-6630 MINC#5200

Burgess, Ronald D (M1)
116 Harris Ridge Road
Dover, TN 37058
revron4@bellsouth.net
(931)232-5151 TNNA#7322

Burns, Garrett (M1)
387 Forrest Avenue
McKenzie, TN 38201
gburns2888@gmail.com
(731)535-3126 GRWT#9118

Burns, J B, Jr (M1)
1020 Maud Road
Cherokee, AL 35616
(256)360-2252 GRWT#9100

Burrow, Vernon (M1)
707 Saratoga Drive
Murfreesboro, TN 37130
vernonburrow@comcast.net
(615)406-6385 TNMU#7233

MINISTERS CONTINUED

Burrows, Arthur L, Jr   (M1)
PO Box 511
Hopkinsville, KY 42241
(270)886-1301   MICU#3505
Butcher, Kenny   (M1)
4608 Cather Court
Nashville, TN 37214
bhpastor@birch.net
(615)719-1887   TNNA#7325
Butler, Jim   (M1)
6322 Labor Lane
Louisville, KY 40291
jbutler54@insightbb.com
(502)635-8587   MICU#3222
Butler, John   (M1)
PO Box 257
Sacramento, KY 42372
jbutler@iccable.com
(270)736-2268   MICU#3512
Butler, Joseph H, Jr   (M1)
56 Cline Ridge Road
Winchester, TN 37398
jhbu737@bellsouth.net
(931)224-8423   TNMU#7205
Buttram, Jim   (M1)
103 Golfcrest Lane
Oak Ridge, TN 37830
FAX: (865)483-8445
littlejimb@gmail.com
(865)938-7418   TNGA#2105
Byford, Ken   (M3)
58 Quincy Lane
Montevallo, AL 35115
kenabyford@gmail.com
(205)665-5753   SEGR#0100
Bynum, Ronald H   (M1)
121 Sycamore Road
Gurley, AL 35748
ronaldbynum@bellsouth.net
(256)776-9313   SERD#0800
Byrd, James F   (M1)
1158 Cornishville Road
Harrodsburg, KY 40330
jfbyrd@bluezoomwifi.com
(859)734-0534   MICU#3100
Byrd, Jimmy   (M1)
176 E Valley Road
Whitwell, TN 37397
FAX: (615)444-6671
revjimmybyrd@gmail.com
(615)289-3347   SETG#2115

--==<< C >>==--

Cadenbach, Mark   (M1)
PO Box 66
Westfield, IA 51062
cadenbm@nctc.net
( )   TNNA#7300
Caicedo, Efrain   (M3)
Aereo 6365
Cali, COLOMBIA, SA
( )   MSCA#8224
Cain, Greg   (M3)
155 Greggstown
Calvert City, KY 42029
(270)816-5259   MICO#3400
Calero, Aldrin   (M1)
Cattara 13 3-81
Guacari, COLOMBIA, SA
( )253-0453   MSCA#8212
Camp, Annetta   (M1)

2303 Mill Creek Road
Halls, TN 38040
FAX: (731)285-5792
annetta@cumberlandchurch.com
(731)285-5703   GRWT#9410
Campbell, Coyle   (M1)
186 Old Limestone Road
New Market, AL 35761
(256)379-4392   TNMU#7215
Campbell, Gordon C   (M1)
1469 E Wayland Street
Springfield, MO 65804
gofor12@gmail.com
(417)823-9567   GRMI#4100
Campbell, Thomas D   (M1)
PO Box 343
601 Park Street
Calico Rock, AR 72519
FAX: (870)297-3151
tdcampbellar@gmail.com
(870)297-2319   GRAR#1503
Campos, Eva   (M3)
PO Box 451405
Miami, FL 33245
(786)426-5997   SEGR#0100
Cantey, James M   (M1)
3505 Elmira Drive
Longview, TX 75605
(903)452-6049   MSTR#8111
Caperton, Donald   (M1)
285 Britton Ford Road
Springville, TN 38256
dandjcaperton@vol.com
(731)593-5096   GRWT#9100
Cardona, Nancy   (M3)
Calle 51 #15-32
Dosquebradas, Risaralda
COLOMBIA, SA
nancycardona10@yahoo.com
(576)322-2938   MSAN#8900
Carlock, Jon T   (M1)
248 Cherry Avenue
McKenzie, TN 38201
carlockj@bethel-college.edu
(731)352-0800   GRWT#9133
Carlton, Gary   (M1)
108 Greenbrier Street
Dickson, TN 37055
gwcarlton@yahoo.com
(270)965-4358   TNNA#7313
Carpenter, David   (M1)
909 W Elm Street
Olney, TX 76374
olneycpc@brazosnet.com
(940)564-2339   MSRR#8416
Carr, Jill   (M2)
PO Box 1547
Lebanon, MO 65536
dig.micah.6.8@gmail.com
(417)532-6760   GRMI#4100
Carter, Billy Ray   (M1)
33 Mockingbird Drive
Leitchfield, KY 42754
cartercbc@windstream.net
(270)259-3897   MICU#3203
Carter, Gary   (M1)
8311 County Road 1082
Vinemont, AL 35179
garycarter51@gmail.com
(256)443-8389   SEHO#0202
Carter, James L   (M1)
6155 Hummingbird Lane

Whitesburg, TN 37891
jandjmt@comcast.net
(423)587-8423   SEET#2200
Carter, Patricia   (M1)
2509 Decatur Stratton Road
Decatur, MS 39327
revtree@yahoo.com
(601)604-3813   SEGR#0100
Carver, Gary   (M1)
2810 Cabin Road
Chattanooga, TN 37411
sandgatthecabin@epbfi.com
(423)698-2556   SETG#2104
Cassell, C J   (M3)
825 Aimes Court
Nashville, TN 37221
n4cjc@comcast.net
(615)594-2693   TNNA#7300
Castaneda, Ricardo   (M1)
Calle 65 #98-45 (Interior 174)
Altos de la Macarena-Robledo La Campina
Medellin, Antioquia, COLOMBIA, SA
rijcah@gmail.com
(574)577-0717   MSAN#8915
Castano, Juan Alexander   (M3)
Calle 127 sur #42-38 Apto 301
Caldas, Antioquia, COLOMBIA, SA
FAX: (574)278-0787
juanalexandercastano@hotmail.com
(574)306-4435   MSAN#8905
Chall-Hutchinson   (M3)
190 Ussery Road
Clarksville, TN 37043
challhut@gmail.com
(931)905-1671   TNNA#7300
Chamberlin, Edwin (Joey)   (M2)
7385 W Grant Ranch Boulevard Apt 1636
Littleton, CO 80123
ejcham@gmail.com
(817)929-9876   MSDC#8700
Chambers, Jason   (M1)
131 E Woods Street
Palestine, AR 72372
jmchambers@memphisseminary.edu
(870)807-1930   GRAR#1103
Chambers, Nicholas   (M1)
11300 Road 101
Union, MS 39365
nachambrs@hotmail.com
(870)231-4909   SEGR#0608
Chancellor, Hilton   (M1)
11905 Preserve Vista
Austin, TX 78738
hiltontex@aol.com
(512)382-1972   MSTR#8100
Chang, Leo   (M1)
819 W Division SE
Springfield, MO 65803
(901)287-9901   GRAR#1100
Chapman, Harry W   (M1)
4908 El Picador Court
Rio Rancho, NM 87124
wrightrev@gmail.com
(505)620-2427   MSDC#8709
Chen, Steven   (M1)
865 Jackson Street
San Francisco, CA 94133
psalm1305@yahoo.com
(415)421-1624   MSDC#8501
Cheung, Luke   (M1)
A-D Flat 3/F 338-340 Castle Peak Road
Cheung Sha Wan

MINISTERS CONTINUED

Kowloon HONG KONG
FAX: (852)2706-0114
luke.cheung@cgst.edu
(852)2794-6781   MSHK#8800
Cheung, Percy   (M2)
G/F & 1/F, 251, Tin Sam Village
Tai Wai, Shatin, NT, HONG KONG
FAX: (852)2607-2245
percycheung@hotmail.com
(852)2693-3444   MSHK#8800
Chin, Kwang Sik   (M2)
1168 Palisade Avenue
Fort Lee, NJ 07024
(201)220-3390   SETG#2100
Cho, Sangsook   (M1)
7 Falmouth Court
Middletown, CT
lovejcamen@yahoo.com
(860)830-6808   SETG#2100
Cho, Sung Wan   (M1)
1603 Coolhurst Avenue
Sherwood, AR 72120
swcho100491@gmail.com
(501)247-5953   GRAR#2135
Choe, Byung-Jae   (M1)
876-15 Dokok-1dong
Kangnam-Gu, Seoul, KOREA
(023)463-3939   SEET#2222
Choi, Ezra   (M1)
605 Arbor Hollow Circle #2103
Cordova, TN 38018
(901)236-8235   SEET#2200
Choi, Hyoung S   (M1)
32132 Huntly Circle
Salisbury, MD 21804
pastor0101@naver.com
(443)880-6776   SETG#2138
Choi, Justin   (M2)
605 Arbor Hollow Circle Apt 203
Cordova, TN 38016
flymetothemoon@hotmail.com
(901)605-4542   SEET#2200
Choi, Sean   (M2)
7565 Macon Road
Cordova, TN 38016
esloveh2@hotmail.com
(901)826-2993   SEET#2200
Chuquimia, Walter   (M1)
18240 S US Highway 301
Wimauma, FL 33598
walter@beth-el.info
(813)399-4050   SEGR#0100
Cinco, Carlos   (M1)
611 Cheron Road
Madison, TN 37115
pastorcinco2020@gmail.com
(615)586-1269   TNNA#7314
Clark, Amber LaCroix   (M1)
80 Bryan Drive
Winchester, TN 37398
revamber@comcast.net
(931)967-2121   TNMU#7249
Clark, J Don   (M1)
1601 Lake Ridge Circle
Birmingham, AL 35216
jdsjcl@charter.net
(205)942-4054   SEGR#0100
Clark, Jeff   (M1)
327 Haynes Haven Lane
Murfreesboro, TN 37129
jclark7733@aol.com
(615)896-7733   TNMU#7250
Clark, Jonathan   (M1)
88 Woodcrest Drive
Winchester, TN 37398
FAX: (931)967-8444

clark3568@bellsouth.net
(931)967-9613   TNMU#7200
Clark, Michael   (M1)
80 Bryan Drive
Winchester, TN 37398
michael.clark@winchestercp.org
(931)967-2121   TNMU#7249
Clark, Tom   (M1)
501 Cherokee Drive
Campbellsville, KY 42718
(270)469-5468   MICU#3100
Clark, Tommy   (M1)
124 Roberta Drive
Memphis, TN 37216
fattire77@gmail.com
(615)430-9158   TNCO#7126
Cleek, Phillip   (M3)
188 Cleek Lane
Estill Springs, TN 37330
(931)967-2354   TNMU#7200
Coati, DeAngelo   (M3)
11280 Pebble Hills Boulevard #165
El Paso, TX 79936
spccoatie@yahoo.com
(915)504-9032   MSDC#8700
Coker, Robert N   (M1)
721 Lakeview Drive
Loudon, TN 37774
FAX: (865)458-5360
nickcoker@bellsouth.net
(865)458-8791   SEET#2307
Cole, Dwayne   (M1)
6460 Village Parkway
Anchorage, AK 99504
tadpolejr@aol.com
(907)854-5793   TNCO#7100
Coleman, Bobby D   (M1)
704 E Webb Street
Mountain View, AR 72560
bobbycoleman@gmail.com
(870)213-5410   GRAR#1514
Coleman, Don L   (M1)
85 Orchard Lane
Savannah, TN 38372
(731)925-9710   GRWT#9100
Collins, Paul   (M1)
915 Warm Sands Drive SE
Albuquerque, NM 87123
FAX: (505)254-7707
chapp3@comcast.net
(505)294-3842   MSDC#8700
Colvard, Kevin   (M1)
20024 Crescent Oaks
San Antonio, TX 78258
FAX: (210)497-8724
rev_kev@satx.rr.com
(205)267-9372   MSTR#8608
Compton, Marcia   (M1)
218 N Kirk W
Indianapolis, IN 46234
mcomptonma@yahoo.com
(317)209-9798   MINC#5200
Condon, Thomas W, Jr   (M1)
6508 Victoria Avenue
N Richland Hills, TX 76180
(817)656-9334   MSRR#8400
Condron, Dudley   (M1)
1360 Harbert Avenue
Memphis, TN 38104
dudleywcondron@aol.com
(901)726-1488   GRWT#9100
Contini, John   (M1)
4344 Poor Ridge Pike
Lancaster, KY 40444
john@hillsidehritagefarm.com
(859)339-0747   MICU#3103

Cook, Carl   (M1)
475 Western Hills Loop
Mountain Home, AR 72653
carlc@suddenlink.net
(870)425-2570   GRAR#1100
Cook, Lisa   (M1)
4101 Dalemere Court
Nashville, TN 37207
tgoose@comcast.net
(615)868-4118   TNNA#7300
Corbin, Eric   (M1)
1629 Symington Road
Rantoul, IL 61866
eric@corbinzone.com
(217)282-9702   GRWT#9100
Corbin, William   (M1)
7300 N Lamar Road
Mount Juliet, TN 37122
raven.rest@comcast.net
(615)459-8998   TNNA#7300
Correa, John Jairo   (M1)
Calle 2 Norte #16-39
Armenia, Quindio, COLOMBIA, SA
FAX: (576)745-4860
jjcedp07@hotmail.com
(318)285-1209   MSAN#8903
Cottingim, Tom   (M1)
353 Atwood Drive
Lexington, KY 40515
FAX: (859)272-4315
t.cottingim@insightbb.com
(859)273-3800   MICU#3100
Coulter, Laurance W   (M1)
5226 W William Cannon Drive
Austin, TX 78749
FAX: (512)892-6307
larry@shpc.org
(512)892-3580   MSTR#8604
Cox, Jimmy R   (M1)
2250 County Road 156
Anderson, AL 35610
dcox01@msn.com
(256)710-1702   SEHO#0508
Craddock, Barry   (M3)
147 Moss Way
Glasgow, KY 42141
( )   MICU#3100
Craig, Aaron   (M3)
325 Cherry Avenue
McKenzie, TN 38201
(731)352-6718   SEET#2200
Craig, Peggy Jean   (M1)
825 S 13th Street Floor 2
Philadelphia, PA 19147
pjfpeggy@gmail.com
(256)277-1147   SEHO#0500
Craig, Robert A   (M1)
1408 Business Loop W Apt E313
Columbia, MO 65202
v-craig@sbcglobal.net
(773)477-8249   MINC#5200
Crawford, Roger B   (M1)
541 Highway 25 N
Carthage, MS 39051
(601)298-1899   SEGR#0100
Crawshaw, Randy   (M1)
136 NE 1271 Road
Knob Noster, MO 65336
randy_crawshaw@yahoo.com
(660)563-5149   GRMI#4115
Crisp, Gregory W   (M1)
635 Eden Brook Lane
Cordova, TN 38018
(901)266-0406   GRWT#9100
Criss, Paul T   (M1)
6831 Salem Road

MINISTERS CONTINUED

Lakeland, TN 38002
ptcriss@hotmail.com
(901)626-8462 GRWT#9316
Crosby, Ronald (M3)
407 N "A" Street
Calera, OK 74730
( ) MSCH#6100
Croslin, Dennis (M3)
165 Maple Street
Gordonsville, TN .38563
(615)934-2383 TNMU#7246
Cuartas, Joel (M0)
Calle 34 #24A-36
Cali, COLOMBIA, SA
(000)438-2512 MSCA#8211
Cummings, Corey (M1)
1023 W Woodrow Street
Milan, TN 38358
corey@milancp.org
(731)686-1851 GRWT#9121
Cunningham, Matthew Dean (M1)
1646 Brighton-Clopton Road
Brighton, TN 38011
mcunningham0528@comcast.net
(901)475-4252 GRWT#9318

--==<< D >>==--

Dalwig, Roger (M1)
1661 Hickory Lane
Corydon, IN 47112
rcd129@hotmail.com
(812)705-5071 MINC#5200
Dalton, Frank (M2)
1606 Ebenezer Road
Troy, TN 38260
(731)536-4553 GRWT#9100
Daniels, Doy L, Jr (M1)
1095 Crestview Drive
Milan, TN 38358
revdrdoy@gmail.com
(731)686-1851 GRWT#9121
Darland, Chris (M1)
582 Ada Drive
Harrodsburg, KY 40330
(859)734-2254 MICU#3303
Davenport, Donna (M1)
3539 State Route 339
Wingo, KY 42088
chamberdonna@yahoo.com
(270)376-5488 MICO#3403
Davenport, Mark A (M1)
1578 Cooks Crossing
Tyler, TX 75703
FAX: (205)663-8323
fpcapastor@bellsouth.net
(205)663-3152 MSTR#8100
Davenport, Vondal (M1)
PO Box 823
Lavaca, AR 72941
(479)965-2036 GRAR#1408
Davis, C Timothy (M1)
8880 Childress Road
West Paducah, KY 42086
FAX: (904)994-6003
charles0828@earthlink.net
(850)995-8383 SEGR#0100
Davis, Robert (Toby) (M1)
502 S Alley Street
Jefferson, TX 75657
pastortobydavis@gmail.com
(901)826-5755 MSTR#8109
Daza, Edilberto (M1)
Cra 12 #8-47
Cartago, Valle
Colombia, South America

presbicartago@gmail.com
57(314)794-1905 MSAN#8906
Daza, Johan (M1)
8148 Yellow Stone Drive
Cordova, TN 38016
jdaza@cumberland.org
(281)793-3869 MSAN#8900
De Jimenez, Luciria Aguirre (M1)
AA6365
COLOMBIA, SA
pastorluciana50@yahoo.com.co
(300)686-9161 MSCA#8200
De Vries, Raymond (M1)
2080 Stanford Village Drive
Antioch, TN 37013
ray.devries@comcast.net
(615)332-3587 TNNA#7333
De Wees, Jeff (M1)
3101 Mt Vernon Road
Ramer, TN 38367
shg_50@bellsouth.net
(731)645-6420 TNNA#9213
Deaton, John (M1)
277 School Lanet
Springfield, PA 19064
deatonjr11@gmail.com
(215)906-7067 SEHO#0500
Deere, Thomas (Tom) (M1)
460 Yukon Drive
Russellville, AR 72802
tdeere@suddenlinkmail.com
(479)498-0318 GRAR#1212
Delashmit, Steve (M1)
2705 Garrett Drive
Bowling Green, KY 42104
FAX: (270)781-2368
(270)796-8822 MICU#3304
Dewhirst, Tim (M3)
3609 Oakbriar Lane
Colleyville, TX 76034
timdew@sbcglobal.net
(817)605-8147 MSRR#8415
Diamond, Cardelia Howell (M1)
1580 Jeff Road
Huntsville, AL 35806
clhdzmhd@hotmail.com
(256)837-6014 SERD#0814
Diamond, James (M1)
PO Box 1220
Smyrna, TN 37167
FAX: (615)220-1077
james.diamond007@comcast.net
(615)220-2341 TNMU#7200
Diamond, Steven (M1)
106 Ultimate Court
Madison, AL 35757
smdiam@hotmail.com
(931)636-7336 SERD#7214
Diaz, Esperanza (M1)
Calle 2 Norte #16-19
Armenia, Quindio, COLOMBIA, SA
jjcedp07@hotmail.com
(576)745-0496 MSAN#8903
Diaz, Freddy (M1)
2425 Holly Hall Apt B42
Houston, TX 77054
fredglobeus@yahoo.com
(832)305-2379 MSTR#8606
Diaz, Gloria Villa (M1)
2425 Holly Hall Apt B42
Houston, TX 77054
gloria@newdayinchrist.org
(832)758-5871 MSTR#8100
Diaz, William (M1)
Calle 5 Con Cra 89
Cali, COLOMBIA, SA

nuevaesperanza1983@hotmail.com
( )332-5849 MSCA#8221
Dimo, Urelia (M3)
171 Roberta Drive
Memphis, TN 38112
( ) GRWT#9100
Dobson, H Wallis (M1)
150 Liberty Way
Greeneville, TN 37745
(423)798-8947 SEET#2200
Doles, Steve (M1)
7702 Indiana Avenue
Lubbock, TX 79423
steve@cpclubbock.com
(806)787-7551 MSDC#8702
Dougherty, Duane A, Jr (M1)
212 County Road 4705
Troup, TX 75789
revdad.duane@gmail.com
(903)842-474 MSTR#8104
Driskell, James P (M1)
154 Mountain Way
Anderson, AL 35610
FAX: (256)247-3339
patprespax@yahoo.com
(256)648-6758 SEHO#0517
Duke, Michael E (M1)
106 Friar Tuck Drive
Dickson, TN 37055
(615)446-6515 TNNA#7300
Dukes, Britta (M1)
5226 W William Cannon Drive
Austin, TX 78749
FAX: (512)892-6307
britta@shpc.org
(512)892-3580 MSTR#8604
Dumas, Byron (M1)
1775 Theresa Drive
Clarksville, TN 37043
bdumas7346@aol.com
(931)552-8772 TNNA#3302
Duncan, Ronnie (M1)
146 Deseree Broyles Road
Chuckey, TN 37641
ronkduncan@icloud.com
(423)552-0321 SEET#2204
Dyer, Stuart (M1)
3574 Foxfield Trail
Bartlett, TN 38135
(901)388-0612 GRWT#9100

--==<< E >>==--

Earheart-Brown, Daniel J (Jay) (M1)
866 N McLean
Memphis, TN 38107
jebrown@memphisseminary.edu
(901)278-0367 TNNA#7300
Eatherly, John (M1)
1377 Moss Road
Chapel Hill, TN 37034
jrev@united.net
(931)364-2087 TNCO#7127
Eddleman, Keith (M1)
2787 Stage Park Drive
Memphis, TN 38134
(901)388-9885 GRWT#9100
Edmonds, Wayne (M1)
112 Dogwood Trail
Eclectic, AL 36024
sweetpea@comlinkinc.net
(334)857-2202 SEGR#0100
Edwards, James Scott (M3)
226 Jasmine Drive
Alabaster, AL 35007
jedwards53163@bellsouth.net

MINISTERS CONTINUED

(205)529-4507   SEGR#0101
Edwards, Joey   (M1)
  5279 Ivy Creek Lane
  Lakeland, TN 38002
  edwardsjoey@bellsouth.net
(901)573-7579   GRWT#9314
Emsinger, Mike   (M3)
  4910 Cox Cove
  Helena, AL 35080
  me0573@att.com
(205)620-4699   SEGR#0108
English, Don W   (M1)
  4311 Guys Court
  Bessemer, AL 35022
(205)428-4790   SEGR#0100
Eppard, Andrew   (M1)
  1427 W McGee Street
  Springfield, MO 65807
  reformedminister@yahoo.com
(417)862-6434   GRMI#4314
Espinoza, Virginia   (M1)
  PO Box 132
  Boswell, OK 74727
  vespinoza@choctawnation.com
(580)434-7971   MSCH#6109
Estep, William   (M1)
  239 Skyline Drive
  Harriman, TN 37748
(865)882-5114   TNMU#7200
Estes, George R   (M1)
  7910 Cloverbrook Lane
  Germantown, TN 38138
  geoestes@gmail.com
(901)755-6673   MSDC#8700
Estes, Sam R, Jr   (M1)
  3026 54th Street
  Lubbock, TX 79413
(806)748-6116   MSDC#8700

--==<< F >>==--

Fackler, David   (M1)
  3409 Benton Road
  Paducah, KY 42003
  woodlawnpastor@live.com
(270)442-7713   MICO#3417
Fahl, D Frederick (Fred)   (M1)
  500 3rd Street
  Fulton, KY 42041
  dffahl@gmail.com
(270)432-3138   MICO#3419
Fancher, Michael E   (M3)
  356 Breeding Road
  Edmonton, KY 42129
  princo1975@live.com
(270)579-3139   MICU#3101
Fell, Ron   (M1)
  PO Box 285
  Fairfield, IL 62837
  r.fell@yahoo.com
(618)638-3744   MINC#5124
Ferguson, David   (M2)
  1841 Pebble Lake Drive
  Birmingham, AL 35232
  fergusondavid15@yahoo.com
(205)200-9205   SEGR#0105
Ferguson, E Blant   (M1)
  704 Bear Run
  Hiawassee, GA 30546
  blantferg@yahoo.com
(706)896-9296   TNNA#7300
Ferguson, Elizabeth   (M1)
  PO Box 839
  Sewanee, TN 37375
  ferguea9@gmail.com
(931)636-8076   TNMU#7235

Ferree, Carole   (M1)
  2475 Fallen Timber Road
  Campbellsville, KY 42718
  ferree047@windstream.net
(270)789-4339   MICU#3100
Ferree, Ronald L   (M1)
  2475 Fallen Timber Road
  Campbellsville, KY 42718
  ferree047@windstream.net
(270)465-1150   MICU#3129
Ferrell, Timothy W   (M1)
  1850 Dunbar Road
  Woodlawn, TN 37191
  ferrelltw@aol.com
(931)920-2662   TNNA#7310
Ferrol, Ruben   (M1)
  1823 Straford Court
  Allentown, PA 18103
  rubeferrol@msn.com
(610)966-7289   MSRR#8400
Ferry, Aaron   (M1)
  PO Box 176
  Winchester, TN 37398
  amferry815@gmail.com
(615)946-3078   TNMU#7249
Fife, Patric   (M1)
  73 Jordan Road
  Lawrenceburg, TN 38464
  pnlfifernak@gmail.com
(931)629-8146   TNCO#7130
Fike, Charles   (M1)
  2070 N 1st Street
  Milan, TN 38358
(731)686-0224   GRWT#9418
Fisk, James R   (M1)
  1946 Lake Vernon Road
  Leesville, LA 71446
  jimfisk95@yahoo.com
(870)367-3086   GRAR#1100
Fleming, Christopher   (M1)
  133 Minerva Place
  Paducah, KY 42001
  holyday@vci.net
(615)424-8561   MICO#3415
Fleming, Patrick T   (M1)
  616 N Border Street
  Benton, AR 72015
  ptfleming@live.com
(501)944-4678   GRAR#1100
Flores, Fabian   (M3)
  Aereo 6365, Cali Valle
  COLOMBIA, SA
  ( )   MSCA#8222
Fly, William   (M1)
  3002 Trowbridge Drive
  Paragould, AR 72450
  billyfly3@gmail.com
(865)938-6273   SEET#2200
Fong, Danny   (M1)
  1224 Fairfax Avenue
  San Francisco, CA 94124
  dfong@redeemersf.org
(415)671-2194   MSDC#8512
Fonseca, Roberto   (M1)
  Cll 46 A No 4N 25
  Colombia, South America
  ( )446-3311   MSCA#8218
Foreman, Samuel L   (M1)
  2811 Laredo Drive
  Hattiesburg, MS 39402
  slfcpc@yahoo.com
(601)562-1415   SEGR#0100
Forester, Byron   (M1)
  2376 Eastwood Place
  Memphis, TN 38112
  bforester@bellsouth.net

(901)324-1707   GRWT#9207
Fortner, Terry   (M1)
  1079 Luzerne Depoy Road
  Greenville, KY 42345
  terryfortner@att.net
(270)821-6541   MICU#3508
Fortney, Josh   (M1)
  765 Windridge Lane
  Burleson, TX 76028
  jfortney@stmattcpc.org
(214)794-9912   MSRR#8418
Fossey, Donald, II   (M3)
  328 Waterloo Road
  Cookeville, TN 38506
  dfossey@twlakes.net
(931)498-2149   TNMU#7223
Fowler, Scott   (M1)
  1900 Alex Mill Road
  Montevallo, AL 35115
  springcreekcp@aol.com
(205)901-8478   SEGR#0113
Franco, Ricardo   (M1)
  7 Hancock Street
  Melrose, MA 02176
  casadefericardo@verizon.net
(781)662-0267   SEET#2220
Franklin, Chris   (M1)
  104 Delta Circle
  Greeneville, TN 37743
  chrisfranklin104@comcast.net
(423)972-3609   SEET#2208
Franklin, Curtis   (M1)
  7620 Cross Mill Road
  Paducah, KY 42001
  brocurtis@fredonia.biz
(270)545-3481   MICO#3410
Frazier, Shawn   (M3)
  459 Forrest Avenue
  McKenzie, TN 38201
(865)414-8394   SEET#2200
Freeman, A Daniel   (M1)
  210 Dogwood Drive
  Greeneville, TN 37743
(423)638-5925   SEET#2200
Freeman, Jesse L, Jr   (M1)
  270 Eastside Road
  Burns, TN 37029
  mptc@bellsouth.net
(615)202-4594   TNNA#7307
French, Jeff   (M1)
  5 Rose Petal Lane
  Dawson Springs, KY 42408
  brojeff7@bellsouth.net
(270)993-0855   MICO#3615
Freund, Henry O   (M1)
  913 Sam Houston Drive
  Dyersburg, TN 38024
  freundly@att.net
(731)285-1744   MSDC#8700
Frost, Sherrlyn   (M1)
  5557 Surrey Lane
  Birmingham, AL 35242
  FAX: (205)991-5259
  sherrlyn@newhopecpc.org
(205)408-0729   SEGR#0104
Fulton, James   (M1)
  1520 Oak Grove Road
  Benton, KY 42025
(270)437-4320   MICO#3619
Fung, David   (M1)
  1846 Gunston Way
  San Jose, CA 95124
(408)266-3398   MSDC#8700
Fung, Lawrence   (M1)
  367 El Dorado Drive
  Daly City, CA 94015

MINISTERS CONTINUED

revfung@yahoo.com
(650)756-1702   MSDC#8700
Furr, Wayne   (M1)
  706 E 6th Street
  Coal Valley, IL 61240
  prespreacher@gmail.com
  (309)791-1691   MINC#5200
Furuhata, Kazuhiko   (M1)
  #310, 9-41-15 Kamitsurumahoncho
  Minamiku Sagamihara-shi
  Kanagawa-ken
  cpc.furuhata@gmail.com
  252-0318, JAPAN
  (501)430-8885   MSJA#8310

--==<< G >>==--

Gaither, Randy   (M1)
  No 3 Pacific Street
  Belmopan City
  BELIZE, CENTRAL AMERICA
  rgaither@valuelinx.net
  ( )   SEGR#0100
Galvis, Alexander   (M3)
  Calle 76 #87-14
  Medellin, Antioquia, COLOMBIA, SA
  alexgt7@hotmail.com
  (300)778-4354   MSAN#8900
Gam, John   (M1)
  1235 Sanders Street
  Auburn, AL 36830
  ( )   GRWT#9100
Garcia, Lucas   (M3)
  875 Scenic Highway
  Lawrenceville, GA 30045
  (678)698-7971   SETG#2100
Garcia, Maria (Mabe)   (M1)
  875 Scenic Highway
  Lawrenceville, GA 30045
  FAX: (678)225-0127
  mabega@juno.com
  (678)698-7971   SETG#2149
Garcia, Ramon   (M1)
  2714 Callista Court Apt 104
  Naples, FL 34114
  revga@hotmail.com
  (239)200-5714   SEGR#0100
Gardner, Charles   (M1)
  PO Box 1035
  Elephant Butte, NM 87935
  (719)784-7744   MSRR#8400
Gary, Brian   (M1)
  105 Wilma Avenue
  Radcliff, KY 40160
  (502)351-6938   MICU#3100
Gaskill, Todd   (M1)
  430 Haysland Road
  Petersburg, TN 37144
  tgaskill@pens.com
  (931)580-2708   TNCO#7121
Gaskin, Tony   (M1)
  1414 Saint Joseph Street NW
  Cullman, AL 35055
  tgaskin46@hotmail.com
  (256)338-7893   SEHO#0507
Gates, J B   (M1)
  PO Box 289
  Enfield, IL 62835
  rjjbgate@hamiltoncom.net
  (618)963-2306   MINC#5104
Gaviria, Mario   (M1)
  Cra 27 #7-48
  Cali, COLOMBIA, SA
  pastormariogaviria@hotmail.com
  (314)773-2601   MSCA#8201
Gehle, Jeffrey A   (M1)

PO Box 182
Burleson, TX 76097
FAX: (817)295-2576
jeff.gehle@stmattcpc.org
(817)295-5832   MSRR#8418
Gentry, Michele   (M1)
  Urb San Jorge casa 28
  Km 8 via a La Tebaida
  Armenia, Quindio, COLOMBIA, SA
  gentry.andes@yahoo.com
  (318)285-1161   MSAN#8900
George, Thomas   (M2)
  908 N Brown Avenue
  Casa Grande, AZ 85222
  tgeorge@aerogram.net
  (640)447-2676   MSDC#8700
Gerard, Eugene S   (M1)
  615 N 42nd Street
  Paducah, KY 42001
  (270)443-2889   MICO#3400
Gibbons, Jeannette   (M3)
  6204 S Haynes Avenue
  Ozark, MO 65721
  (417)889-9862   GRMI#4100
Gibson, Rachel   (M3)
  2520 Cairo Bend Road
  Lebanon, TN 37087
  (615)453-2724   TNMU#7200
Gillis, Aubrey Thomas   (M1)
  PO Box 869
  Silverhill, AL 36576
  FAX: (205)664-8323
  tomgillis63@hotmail.com
  (251)947-1638   SERD#0800
Gillis, Ernest H   (M1)
  3273 Bruckner Boulevard
  Snellville, GA 30078
  professorgil64@hotmail.com
  (770)982-6587   SEET#2200
Gillock, Ed   (M1)
  PO Box 157
  Savannah, TN 38372
  (731)609-6744   GRWT#9100
Giraldo, Andres   (M2)
  Calle 76 #87-14 Apto 202
  Medellin, Antioquia, COLOMBIA, SA
  andresgiraldo@une.net.co
  (574)422-6669   MSAN#8911
Giraldo, Marcela   (M3)
  Calle 68 D #40-15
  Manizales, Caldas, COLOMBIA, SA
  (576)878-5412   MSAN#8900
Giraldo, William   (M1)
  CLL 62 No 18 11
  Cali, COLOMBIA, SA
  ( )439-5436   MSCA#8200
Giron, Francisco   (M1)
  3451 Los Mochis Way
  Oceanside, CA 92056
  FAX: (760)414-1236
  thegirons@cox.net
  (760)203-0381   MSDC#8700
Glenn, Linda H   (M1)
  49 Mason Road
  Threeway, TN 38343
  lindahglenn@click1.net
  (731)618-0192   GRWT#9119
Goehring, Marty   (M1)
  8600 Academy NE
  Albuquerque, NM 87111
  FAX: (505)797-8599
  mgoehring@heightscpc.org
  (505)821-3628   MSDC#8701
Gonzales, Homer   (M1)
  8924 Armistice NE
  Albuquerque, NM 87109

FAX: (505)841-4267
hgabq1985@gmail.com
(505)821-4376   MSDC#8700
Gonzales, Miguel   (M1)
  200 Bethel Drive
  Lenoir City, TN 37772
  (865)988-4238   SEET#2200
Gonzalez, Nora   (M1)
  2515 Blueberry Lane
  Pasadena, TX 77052
  (832)202-5572   MSTR#8100
Goodloe, Melissa Reid   (M1)
  225 Macedonia Road
  McKenzie, TN 38201
  rev.mgoodloe@shilohcp.org
  (731)412-9657   GRWT#9131
Goodman, Robert   (M1)
  604 N Fourth Street
  Marlow, OK 73055
  rgoodman4gvn@hotmail.com
  (580)756-4726   MSRR#6305
Goodwill, James L   (M1)
  205 S English Hill Lane
  Hillsborough, NC 27278
  jim@jimgoodwill.com
  (704)526-8729   TNNA#7300
Goodwin, Earl   (M1)
  1012 Windsor Parkway
  Moody, AL 35004
  FAX: (205)664-8323
  earlgoodwin@yahoo.com
  (205)222-1741   SERD#0800
Gough, Ernest E   (M1)
  8366 Highway 70
  Nashville, TN 37221
  eegough@bellsouth.net
  (615)646-4372   TNNA#7300
Graham, Steve   (M1)
  11108 Thornton Drive
  Knoxville, TN 37934
  (865)206-0012   MICO#2316
Gray, Brad   (M3)
  6378 Highway 59 S
  Mason, TN 38049
  dgray@aol.com
  (901)475-6140   GRWT#9100
Gray, Drew   (M1)
  5610 Country Drive #210
  Nashville, TN 37211
  (615)332-8360   TNMU#7220
Gray, Isaac   (M1)
  512 Ed Taft Road
  Smithville, TN 37166
  revgray08@gmail.com
  (870)373-4731   TNMU#7243
Gray, Randall   (M1)
  1230 New Liberty Big Meadow Road
  Knob Lick, KY 42154
  (270)432-5322   MICU#3128
Green, Harry N   (M1)
  45 Wood Way
  McMinnville, TN 37110
  (931)815-9190   TNMU#7200
Green, Larry   (M1)
  525 Dearman Street
  Smithville, TN 37166
  larrylgreen24@aol.com
  (615)597-5832   TNMU#7244
Green, Odis G   (M1)
  18 Oakwood Street NW
  Rome, GA 30165
  ( )   TNCO#7100
Green, Paul   (M1)
  5228 Anchorage Avenue
  El Paso, TX 79924
  (915)751-7960   MSDC#8700

MINISTERS CONTINUED

Green, Troy   (M1)
105 Cobb Hollow Lane
Petersburg, TN 37144
thegreens101@att.net
(931)659-6627   TNCO#7135

Greene, Tammy L   (M1)
109 Armitage Drive
Greeneville, TN 37745
tg6386@aol.com
(423)972-5525   SEET#2217

Greenwell, James C   (M1)
7165 Wind Whisper Boulevard
Knoxville, TN 37924
FAX: (865)742-1653
greenwelljc@comcast.net
(865)742-1653   SEET#2200

Griffin, Adam   (M3)
23502 Clinton Road
Lebanon, MO 65536
plowboy3500@hotmail.com
(417)588-2522   GRMI#4100

Griffin, Justin   (M1)
3655 Highway 49 E
Charlotte, TN 37036
jjjjgriff@gmail.com
(615)969-2426   TNNA#7320

Grimsley, Roger   (M1)
215 N Oak Street
Springfield, TN 37172
(   )   GRWT#9100

Gross, Ronald   (M1)
2436 N 420th Street
Oblong, IL 62449
juneg@eiis.net
(217)932-2788   MINC#5200

Grounds, Clint   (M3)
918 Stonewall Apt C
McKenzie, TN 38201
(731)415-1422   GRMI#4100

Guarneros, Stephen H   (M1)
506 Clifton Court
Hopkinsville, KY 42240
pastorsteve88@yahoo.com
(270)869-7544   MICO#3606

Guasaquillo, Samuel   (M3)
Aereo 10701, Cali
COLOMBIA, SA
FAX: (408)255-5938
(   )   MSCA#8204

Guerrero, Cruzana   (M2)
Calle 83 #74-179
Medellin, Antioguia, COLOMBIA, SA
(574)257-0613   MSAN#8900

Guerrero, Josue   (M2)
Calle 76 #88-65
Medellin, Antioquia, COLOMBIA, SA
josueggutierrez@yahoo.es
(574)412-3504   MSAN#8900

Guerrero, Luz Dary   (M1)
Calle 22 #25-33
Manizales, Caldas, COLOMBIA, SA
clementinajacobo7@hotmail.com
(576)888-4203   MSAN#8900

Guin, Larry   (M1)
125 Glider Loop
Eagleville, TN 37060
lguin43@hotmail.com
(615)668-5236   TNCO#7123

Guthrie, William   (M1)
11130 Frenchmen Loop Apt B
Maumelle, AR 72113
billybarloe@yahoo.com
(501)584-0019   GRAR#1100

Gutierrez, Libardo   (M2)
Calle 83 #74-179
Medellin, Antioquia, COLOMBIA, SA

guzlibar@yahoo.es
57(314)600-2020   MSAN#8900

Guye, Dean   (M1)
2759 Highway 70 E
Dickson, TN 37055
deanjoy@att.net
(615)446-7687   TNNA#7303

--==<< H >>==--

Ha, Ting Bong   (M2)
3/F 338-340 Castle Peak Road
Kowloon, HONG KONG
FAX: (852)3020-0365
tingbongha@yahoo.com.hk
(852)2386-6563   MSHK#8803

Hackman-Truhan, Deborah   (M1)
7314 N Miramar Drive
Peoria, IL 61614
cprevdeb@hotmail.com
(931)537-9040   TNMU#7200

Hagelin, Gerald   (M1)
10851 E Old Spanish Trail
Tucson, AZ 85712
azcef@cs.com
(520)275-8110   MSDC#8705

Haire, Shelby O   (M1)
3179 Meeting Creek Road
Eastview, KY 42732
(270)862-3887   MICU#3219

Halford, Angela   (M1)
PO Box 191466
Little Rock, AR 72219
(501)407-0065   GRAR#1100

Hall, Brad   (M1)
1602 Toll Gate Road SE
Huntsville, AL 35801
(256)533-4845   SERD#0800

Hall, John D   (M1)
109 Oddo Lane SE
Huntsville, AL 35802
johnhall33@comcast.net
(256)880-5129   SERD#0800

Hall, Roy W   (M1)
87 Lee Hall Street
Scottsboro, AL 35769
royhall@scottsboro.org
(256)259-9340   SERD#0809

Hamazaki, Takashi   (M1)
1551-1-202 Inokuchi Nakai-cho
Ashigarakami-gun
Kanagawa-ken
259-0151, JAPAN
gen22-14@qf7.so-net.ne.jp
(046)543-8550   MSJA#8300

Hamblin, James R   (M1)
60 Rolling Meadow Drive
Drummonds, TN 38023
brojim391@gmail.com
(901)840-4747   GRWT#9321

Hamby, Gary   (M3)
700 W 6th Avenue
Lenoir City, TN 37771
(731)986-2635   SEET#2200

Hames, Anne   (M1)
118 Paris Street
McKenzie, TN 38201
hamesa@bethel-college.edu
(731)352-4066   GRWT#9100

Hamilton, Bruce   (M1)
1037 Binns Drive
Monticello, AR 71655
bruce@hamiltonnet.org
(870)224-5007   GRAR#1106

Hamilton, Helen   (M3)

300 Tennessee Street
Savannah, TN 38372
helmackham@aol.com
(731)925-4493   GRWT#9224

Hamilton, Lynn   (M1)
4511 Lucksinger Lane Trailer 1
Austin, TX 78745
lhamilton@minister.com
(512)443-6813   MSTR#8100

Hamlink, Ronald L   (M1)
PO Box 923
Fairacres, NM 88033
hamronelink@yahoo.com
(505)525-9867   GRAR#1100

Han, Seung Chon   (M0)
3075 Landington Way
Duluth, GA 30096
kpc0191@gmail.com
(678)469-5015   SETG#2100

Hancock, B J   (M1)
103 W Cowan Street
Cowan, TN 37318
(931)967-8491   TNMU#7228

Hannah, Hugh   (M1)
217 Mitchell Road SE
Cleveland, TN 37323
pjhannah23@hotmail.com
(423)473-7852   MSTR#8100

Hansen, Terry   (M1)
16549 Highway 5
Lebanon, MO 65536
(417)533-8106   GRMI#4315

Harbour, Ethan   (M2)
77 Burton Road
Booneville, AR 72927
ethanharbour@gmail.com
(479)849-6329   GRAR#1100

Hardisty, Randy   (M1)
4908 Redondo Street
Fort Worth, TX 76180
rhardisty@sbcglobal.net
(817)428-3513   MSRR#8409

Harper, Carlton   (M1)
255 Glenview Cove
Lenoir City, TN 37771
carltonharperone@gmail.com
(865)317-1296   SETG#2118

Harris, Anthony   (M2)
1604 Parkview Drive
Campbellsville, KY 42718
aharris044@gmail.com
(270)403-1126   MICU#3214

Harris, Edward   (M1)
10000 Wornall Road Apt 2315
Kansas City, MO 64114
ed121@kcrr.com
(816)214-8977   GRMI#4100

Harris, Ernest   (M1)
610 Turtle Creek Drive
Reno, TX 75462
ernieandjeri@wmconnect.com
(903)966-2481   MSTR#8100

Harris, Robert   (M1)
619 N 24th Avenue
Humboldt, TN 38343
pastor@humboldtcpc.org
(731)420-6067   GRWT#9116

Harris, Rodney E   (M1)
7420 Conjar Court
Louisville, KY 40214
rodneypat@insightbb.com
(502)368-5501   MICU#3212

Harris, Wendell   (M1)
329 N Louis Tittle Avenue
Mangum, OK 73554
wendellharris@itlnet.net

MINISTERS CONTINUED

(580)782-2142   MSRR#8400

Harrison, Richard   (M3)
93 Earl Jones Road
Hodgenville, KY 42748
( )   MICU#3100

Hartman, Gary   (M1)
3001 Hines Valley Road
Lenoir City, TN 37771
g37771@att.net
(865)986-4949   SEET#2304

Hartung, J Thomas   (M1)
2291 Americus Boulevard W Apt 1
Clearwater, FL 33763
revtom6@aol.com
(727)797-2882   SEGR#0100

Harwell, Jacob   (M2)
319 Joy Drive
McKenzie, TN 38201
rjharwell@student.memphisseminary.edu
(731)415-1457   GRWT#9100

Harwell, Keith   (M1)
13132 Stinson Street
Milan, TN 38358
(731)613-3780   GRWT#9104

Harwell, Sam   (M1)
23 Lake Hayes Estates Road
Trenton, TN 38382
sambharl@yahoo.com
(731)414-2153   GRWT#9127

Hassell, Samantha   (M3)
510 N Main Street
Sturgis, KY 42459
FAX: (270)333-3118
hassell_samantha@hotmail.com
(270)333-9170   MICO#3400

Hassell, Victor   (M1)
510 N Main Street
Sturgis, KY 42459
FAX: (270)333-3118
hassellvictor@hotmail.com
(270)333-9170   MICO#3625

Hatcher, Carlton   (M1)
2111 Robin Road
Bowling Green, KY 42101
(270)842-8488   MICU#3310

Hawley, David R   (M1)
127 John Holt Road
Beech Bluff, TN 38313
haw177@aol.com
(731)427-7284   GRWT#9204

Hayes, Brian   (M1)
69 Cactus Drive
Benton, KY 42025
cprevbhayes@gmail.com
(270)210-8165   MICO#3422

Hayes, Drew   (M1)
6322 Labor Lane
Louisville, KY 40291
dhayes72@gmail.com
(731)796-7076   GRWT#9433

Hayes, Jennifer   (M1)
3615 Talley Store Road
Henderson, TN 38340
(731)989-3825   TNMU#7200

Hayes, Marcus   (M1)
102 River Drive
McMinnville, TN 37110
marcus.hayes@att.net
(270)841-7576   TNMU#7222

Headrick, Anthony   (M1)
3327 N Eagle Road Ste 110-132
Meridian, ID 83646
chaps2a@yahoo.com
(619)524-8821   SEGR#0100

Headrick, Christopher   (M1)
1913 Vestavia Court Apt B

Vestavia Hills, AL 35216
bravespop@gmail.com
(205)240-0979   SEGR#0100

Headrick, Jerry   (M1)
9950 Old Stage Road
Stockton, AL 36579
willjheadrick@gmail.com
(251)377-9744   SEGR#0100

Heard, Robert   (M3)
527 Jack Thomas Drive
Manchester, TN 37355
(931)273-9687   TNMU#7200

Heflin, Donna S   (M1)
4144 Meadow Court Drive
Bartlett, TN 38135
rdheflin@bellsouth.net
(901)382-8198   GRWT#9100

Heflin, Robert   (M1)
4144 Meadow Court Drive
Bartlett, TN 38135
rdheflin@bellsouth.net
(901)382-8198   TNCO#7100

Heidel, Jason   (M1)
218 Morningside Drive
Hopkinsville, KY 42240
heidelj@hotmail.com
(270)498-7380   MICO#3400

Heilbron, Luz Maria   (M1)
Cra 12 bis #11-51
Pereira, Risaralda, COLOMBIA, SA
pastorapresbi@hotmail.com
(576)333-9295   MSAN#8916

Hendershot, Charles A   (M1)
122 Tree Shadow
Whitney, TX 76692
(254)694-3852   MSRR#8424

Henson, Kevin R   (M1)
1121 Raleigh Path
Denton, TX 76208
khenson@cpch.org
(817)354-1182   MSRR#8400

Heo, Mu Sak   (M1)
170 Applewood Drive #210
Lawrenceville, GA 30046
drhou@hanmail.net
(404)644-6514   SETG#2100

Hernden, Matthew   (M3)
206 Smith Lane
Brighton, TN 38011
mhernden023@gmail.com
(901)484-7661   GRWT#9100

Herring, C E (Ed), Jr   (M1)
969 Campground Circle
Scottsboro, AL 35769
edherring@scottsboro.org
(256)259-2721   SERD#0800

Herston, Terry   (M1)
390 County Road 95
Rogersville, AL 35652
tpaw51@gmail.com
(256)247-3004   SEHO#0513

Hess, Jean   (M1)
2200 E Dartmouth Circle
Englewood, CO 80113
jeanhess@316denver.com
(303)504-0275   MSDC#8700

Hess, Rick   (M1)
2200 E Dartmouth Circle
Englewood, CO 80113
rick@densem.edu
(303)504-0275   MSDC#8700

Hester, Mark S   (M1)
763 Finn Long Road
Friendsville, TN 37737
markshester@att.net
(865)995-1541   SEET#2200

Hill, Jody   (M1)
4030 St Andrew Circle
Corinth, MS 38834
jody.hill34@gmail.com
(662)512-8226   GRWT#9100

Ho, Carmen   (M2)
Tin Yuet Estate
Tin Shui Wai NT, HONG KONG
FAX: (852)2617-0287
ho_carcar@yahoo.com.hk
(852)2617-7872   MSHK#8801
ho_carcar@yahoo.com.hk

Ho, Kelvin   (M2)
11 On Wing Centre, 2/F
Pak She Back Street
Cheung Chau, HONG KONG
kelvinskho@gmail.com
(852)2981-4933   MSHK#8801

Hocker, David   (M3)
309 N Taylor Street
Morgantown, KY 42261
davidhocker@hockerins.com
(270)526-6027   MICU#3311

Hoke, Walter   (M1)
215 Navajo Trail
Georgetown, TX 78633
(512)869-1948   MSTR#8607

Holley, Ann   (M1)
PO Box 345
Lockesburg, AR 71846
FAX: (870)289-2914
ladyrev1115@yahoo.com
(870)289-3421   GRAR#1100

Hollingshed, Lee   (M3)
3612 Harmony Church Grove Road
Dallas, GA 30132
leearmstrong@bellsouth.net
(770)548-0152   SETG#2100

Holmes, Aaron G   (M1)
PO Box 171
Atwood, TN 38220
agholmes@charter.net
(731)662-7595   GRWT#9100

Holt, Billy Jack   (M1)
5039 Highway 37 N
Clarksville, TX 75426
jackdora@windstream.net
(903)428-9909   MSTR#8125

Hom, Paul   (M1)
722 24th Avenue
San Franciso, CA 94121
FAX: (415)386-8423
(415)751-9766   MSDC#8700

Hong, Soon Gab   (M1)
13600 Doty Avenue Apt 4
Hawthorne, CA 90250
lemuelhong@hotmail.com
(972)446-0350   MSRR#8400

Hood, Charles   (M1)
6535 Bailey Road
Anderson, AL 35610
hooddad11@gmail.com
(256)229-6251   SEHO#0516

Hopkins, Daniel   (M2)
887 Penny Road
Hardin, KY 42048
(270)205-1847   MICO#3620

Hopkins, Wayne   (M3)
1413 E Unity Church Road
Hardin, KY 42048
(270)437-4481   MICO#3400

Howe, Francis   (M1)
129 Manley Street
McKenzie, TN 38201
(731)352-5551   GRWT#9125

MINISTERS CONTINUED

Howell, Linda (M1)
PO Box 80050
Keller, TX 76244
lshowell1000@yahoo.com
(601)942-2015 MSRR#0607
Howton, Orvie Ray (M1)
4928 Montauk Trail SE
Owens Cross Road, AL 35763
arhowton@bellsouth.net
(256)533-9224 SERD#0800
Hoyos, Amparo (M2)
Cra 43 #20D-26
Zamora, Antioquia, COLOMBIA, SA
chilalu1147@hotmail.com
(574)278-0784 MSAN#8900
Hoyos, Javier (M3)
Calle 34 24A-36
Cali, COLOMBIA, SA
(   )445-5556 MSCA#8200
Hubbard, Donald (M1)
2128 N Campbell Station Road
Knoxville, TN 37932
djhubbard@mindspring.com
(865)693-0264 SEET#2200
Hubbard, Pratt (M1)
1565 Eli Brown Road
McKenzie, TN 38201
(731)352-9178 GRWT#9100
Hudson, Barney (M1)
10541 Fossil Hill Drive
Fort Worth, TX 76131
barneyrev@gmail.com
(817)851-2960 MSRR#8425
Hudson, George Cliff (M1)
4782 Waverly Court
Ooltewah, TN 37363
gchudson3@gmail.com
(423)238-6333 SETG#2100
Huey, Sharon (M1)
3265 16th Street
San Francisco, CA 94103
sharon_huey@yahoo.com
(415)703-6090 MSDC#8510
Hughes, Charles (M1)
114 Gaul Street
Estill Springs, TN 37330
cphugs@cafes.net
(931)649-5189 SERD#0800
Hughes, Douglas (M1)
5545 Hocker Road
Paducah, KY 42001
milburnchapel@gmail.com
(270)488-2588 MICO#3416
Hughes, Richard W (M1)
2954 Bob Wade Lane
Harvest, AL 35749
hughesrichard23@gmail.com
(256)859-3178 SERD#0806
Hullander, Jerry (Butch) (M1)
767 Rifle Range Road
Greeneville, TN 37743
jerryihs@catt.com
(706)935-4878 SETG#2107
Hung, Ella Siu Kei (M1)
2/F Welland Plaza
188 Nam Cheong Street
Sham Shui Po, Kowloon, HONG KONG
FAX: (852)2771-2726
siukee@taohsien.org.hk
(852)2794-2382 MSHK#8800
Hunley, Jearl (M1)
2618 Canterbury Road
Columbus, MS 39705
jdhunley@cableone.net
(662)329-1516 SEGR#0100
Hunley, Terry M (M1)

48 Charleston Square
Jackson, TN 38305
thunley1@charter.net
(731)660-5685 GRWT#9208
Hunt, Shelley (M3)
6035 State Route 506
Marion, KY 42064
sheljean@kynet.biz
(270)704-2189 MICO#3400
Hurley, E C (M1)
221 Fantasia Way
Clarksville, TN 37043
hurleyec@gmail.com
(931)551-6173 TNNA#7300
Hyden, John (M1)
6525 Peytonsville Arno Road
College Grove, TN 37046
cp1876@hotmail.com
(615)975-9584 TNCO#7116

--==<< I >>==--

Ikushima, Michinobu (M1)
2074 Nakashinden
Ebina-Shi Kanagawa-Ken
243-0422 JAPAN
m.ikushima@tbz.t-com.ne.jp
(046)232-9888 MSJA#8300
Impastato, Paulino (M3)
1547 Mt Zion Church Road
Marion, KY 42064
(270)965-9528 MICO#3400
Ingram, Matthew (M3)
29 Quincy Lane
Montevallo, AL 35115
mbingram80@gmail.com
(205)914-0829 SEGR#0100
Inoh, Yuki (M3)
Tokyo Christian University
3-301-5 Uchino Inzai-shi, Chiba
270-1347 JAPAN
yuki_inoh0615@yahoo.co.jp
(047)646-1141 MSJA#8300
Ishitsuka, Keishi (M1)
Nucleo Colonial JK
Lote 56 Mata De Sao Joao
48280-000, Bahia, BRAZIL
FAX: (5571)3664-1019
kishitsuka@hotmail.com
(5571)3664-1019 MSJA#8313
Ivey, Billy F (M1)
409 Rodeo Drive
Knoxville, TN 37922
iveybe@tds.net
(865)966-5946 SEET#2200

--==<< J >>==--

Jacks, Mathew Derek (M1)
341 Shadeswood Drive
Hoover, AL 35226
pastorderek@homewoodcpc.com
(205)903-8469 SEGR#0111
Jackson, Lamar (M1)
280 Deer Ridge Drive Apt D
Dayton, TN 37321
hljaxn@charter.net
(423)570-9348 SETG#2100
Jackson, Terry (M1)
1461 Mount Pleasant Road
Hernando, MS 38632
(662)429-9741 GRWT#9100
Jacob, Randy (M1)
PO Box 158
Broken Bow, OK 74728
FAX: (580)584-2099

chocpres@pine-net.com
(580)584-2099 MSCH#6106
James, William F (M1)
2937 Arthur Drive
Murfreesboro, TN 37127
wimjim19@gmail.com
(615)653-1396 TNMU#7227
Jang, Won Jeon (M1)
Lot2-C Teresa Subdivision
Tabucan Mandurriao
Iloilo City 5000, Phillippine
(   ) SEET#2200
Janner, R Tony (M1)
104 Northwood Drive
McKenzie, TN 38201
FAX: (731)352-3101
drtonyjanner@yahoo.com
(731)352-8055 GRWT#9100
Jaramillo, Luciano (M1)
6248 SW 14th Street
West Miami, FL 33144
ljara@aol.com
(305)264-1074 SEGR#0310
Jarnagin, Mary L (M1)
1003 Justin Lane Apt 1017
Austin, TX 78757
marjar27@yahoo.com
(512)367-9922 MSTR#8100
Jeffrey, Peter (M1)
61 Northwood Drive
McKenzie, TN 38201
jeffreyp@bethelu.edu
(731)352-0792 TNMU#7200
Jeffrey, Sarah Ann (M1)
5271 Highway 202 E
Yellville, AR 72687
FAX: (870)715-9229
annjeffrey2001@yahoo.com
(870)453-7076 GRAR#1100
Jenkins, Henry (M1)
PO Box 148
Magazine, AR 72943
henryj@magtel.com
(479)969-8352 GRAR#1401
Jenkins, William E (M1)
1836 S Ridge Drive
Valrico, FL 33594
hopechurch4@aol.com
(813)651-3802 SEGR#0308
Jeong, Woo S (M1)
1205 Morganshire Drive
Collierville, TN 38017
(901)302-0558 GRWT#9100
Jett, Mace, Jr (M1)
109 Park Street
Martin, TN 38237
(731)587-0805 GRWT#9117
Jett-Rand, Dana (M2)
78 Lester Lane
Martin, TN 38237
msdanajett@yahoo.com
(731)587-0805 GRWT#9100
Jimenez, Jacqueline (M3)
11161 San Ysidro
Socorro, TX 79927
jjimenez2228@gmail.com
(915)252-8395 MSDC#8700
Jimenez, Jorge Enrique (M3)
Urb Manantiales MzC Casa 6
Armenia, Quindio, COLOMBIA, SA
joenjimu@yahoo.es
(576)749-1166 MSAN#8900
Jobe, J Tommy (M1)
PO Box 8
Eagleville, TN 37060
cppreacher@united.net

MINISTERS CONTINUED

(615)776-7755   TNMU#7240
Johnson, Beverly B   (M1)
801 Riverhill Drive Apt 308
Athens, GA 30606
bevloujohnson@aol.com
(865)977-0405   SEET#2200
Johnson, Daryl   (M1)
425 W Vaughan Street
Bertram, TX 78605
djchurch@earthlink.net
(512)355-2182   MSTR#8605
Johnson, Ken   (M1)
122 Ridge Lane
Clinton, TN 37716
kenjoxav122@bellsouth.net
(865)463-7090   SEET#2314
Johnson, Lanny   (M1)
120 S Mill Street
Morrison, TN 37357
ljohnson37357@gmail.com
(931)212-1658   TNMU#7200
Johnson, Leslie A   (M1)
11716 Price Drive
Oklahoma City, OK 73170
ljohnson275@cox.net
(405)759-3189   MSRR#6205
Johnson, Roberta Smith   (M1)
397 Ouachita 54
Camden, AR 71701
(870)231-5827   GRAR#1309
Johnson, Rocky L   (M1)
1208 Redwood Drive
Clarksville, TN 37042
jjjjgriff@gmail.com
(423)620-7753   TNNA#7315
Johnson, Thomas C   (M1)
PO Box 566
Helena, AL 35080
revtomjohnson@aol.com
(205)936-1350   SEGR#0100
Johnson, Wesley H   (M1)
6222 Crestmoor Lane
Sachse, TX 75048
wjohnson@transitionconsulting.com
(972)270-6923   MSRR#8412
Jones, Gregory   (M1)
4808 Shiloh Canaan Road
Palmyra, TN 37142
greg1013@aol.com
(931)249-9512   TNNA#7338
Jones, Harold   (M2)
4123 Wilkesview Drive Apt A
Chattanooga, TN 37416
harold@personalcharacter.com
(478)320-4222   SETG#2100
Jones, Joseph M   (M1)
405 Lakeview Drive
Campbellsville, KY 42718
joepegjones@windstream.net
( )   MICU#3100
Jones, Michael   (M1)
120 Jennifer Lane
Branson, MO 65616
(417)334-2058   GRAR#1100
Jones, Steve   (M2)
PO Box 368
Burns, TN 37029
(615)441-6159   TNNA#7300
Jones, Victor   (M1)
7017 Highway 177 S
Jordan, AR 72519
mommom@centurytel.net
(870)499-5882   GRAR#1508
Jones, C William, Jr   (M1)
109 Lakewood Drive
Lexington, TN 38351

patfreelandjones@yahoo.com
(731)967-7618   GRWT#9209
Justice, Michael   (M1)
112B Vance Lane
Russellville, KY 42276
(270)726-6673   MICU#3501

--==<< K >>==--

Kang, Eun Hee   (M3)
147-15 46th Avenue
Flushing, NY 11355
(718)762-0778   SETG#2100
Kang, Jin Koo   (M1)
2310 Hisway
Lawrenceville, GA 30044
agatopia@hanmail.net
(678)462-7526   SETG#2100
Karasawa, Kenta   (M1)
3-15-10 Higashi
Kunitachi-shi, Tokyo
186-0002 JAPAN
FAX: (042)575-5549
k-kenta@roy.hi-ho.ne.jp
(042)575-5549   MSJA#8306
Katsuki, Shigeru   (M1)
2-14-16 Higashi-cho
Koganei-shi, Tokyo
184-0011 JAPAN
shigeru.katsuki@nifty.com
(042)231-1279   MSJA#8301
Kays, Michael   (M1)
2505 Canterbury Avenue
Muskogee, OK 74403
msppk@suddenlink.net
(918)577-6255   MSRR#8400
Keller, Abby Cole   (M1)
4415 Fieldstone Drive
Kingsport, TN 37664
colekeller@yahoo.com
(423)863-6565   SEET#2206
Kelly, Lawrence   (M1)
3471 Highway 41 A North Apt 5
Unionville, TN 37180
(615)934-1517   TNCO#7118
Kelly, Patrick L   (M1)
1449 Rainbow Road
Limestone, TN 37681
(423)727-4067   SEET#2200
Kelso, James H   (M1)
131 Lords Way
Dawsonville, GA 30534
elgato@alltel.net
(706)216-7513   SETG#2100
Kenedy, Don   (M3)
5335 Dizzy Dean Road
Booneville, AR 72927
donkennedy@centurytel.net
(479)675-4418   GRAR#1414
Kennedy, Jim   (M2)
3818 Peace Court Apt F
Aberdeen Proving Ground, MD 21005
jpkak@comcast.net
( )   SETG#2100
Kennemer, Darren   (M1)
8828 Highway 119
Alabaster, AL 35007
darren.kennemer@va.gov
(205)663-3152   SERD#0107
Keown, Gale J   (M1)
2130 Cason Lane
Murfreesboro, TN 37128
galeesther@aol.com
(865)805-5451   SEET#2200
Kerner, Leanne   (M2)
156 State Route 348 W

Symsonia, KY 42082
cooldoll@bellsouth.net
(270)851-9709   MICO#3400
Kessie, John Paul   (M1)
225 Clear Springs Road
Georgetown, TX 78628
jplmkessie@verizon.com
(512)585-1617   MSTR#8100
Keung Yung, Amos Chung   (M3)
28 Hong Yip Street
Yuen Long, NT, HONG KONG
FAX: (522)639-5620
amos@xilincpc.org.hk
(522)639-9176   MSHK#8809
Killeen, Michael   (M1)
5226 W William Cannon Drive
Austin, TX 78749
FAX: (512)892-6307
mike@shpc.org
(512)892-3580   MSTR#8604
Kim, Byong Sam   (M1)
6290 Dawnridge Court
Paradise, CA 95969
(530)877-4651   MSDC#8700
Kim, Kio Seob   (M1)
14430 35th Avenue Apt A62
Flushing, NY 11354
(718)539-3476   SETG#2100
Kim, Mi Young   (M1)
(IN KOREA)
( )   SETG#2100
Kim, Min Soo   (M1)
5350 Taylor Road
Johns Creek, GA 30022
samil2110@yahoo.com
(678)622-2717   SETG#2100
Kim, Yoong S   (M1)
225 Bayswater Drive
Suwanee, GA 30024
yoongkim1934@yahoo.com
(678)765-7018   GRWT#9100
Kim, YoungHo (Steve)   (M1)
B02 Hyundai I-Space 1608-2
Burim Dong, Dong An Gu
AnYang City, Kyunggi Do, S KOREA
paidion4377@naver.com
(231)348-8033   SEET#2200
King, Keith   (M2)
3341 S 137th E Avenue
Tulsa, OK 74134
(918)437-5464   MSRR#8400
King, Mark   (M3)
717 Big Swan Creek Road
Hampshire, TN 38461
(931)626-6915   TNCO#7100
Kinnaman, Richard T   (M1)
2018 Spring Meadow Circle
Spring Hill, TN 37174
kinnaman91@att.net
(615)302-3321   TNCO#7100
Kirkpatrick, Mary Kathryn   (M1)
401 1/2 Henley-Perry Drive
Marshall, TX 75670
mkkirkpatrick@gmail.com
(903)930-6236   MSTR#8115
Kleinjan, Lori   (M1)
6516 Farnell Avenue
Memphis, TN 38134
lkleinj@prodigy.net
(901)372-8413   GRWT#9100
Knight, J Geoffrey   (M1)
2119 Avalon Place
Houston, TX 77019
geoff@cphouston.org
(713)522-7821   MSTR#8606
Knight, Melissa   (M1)

MINISTERS CONTINUED

5730 Haley Road
Meridian, MS 39305
revlissa@gmail.com
(530)632-6472   MSDC#8700
Ko, John Jae   (M1)
  13955 35th Avenue #5A
  Flushing, NY 11354
  spcko@hanmail.net
  (718)762-4348   SECE#2141
Kollie, Moses   (M3)
  760 Harbor Point Court
  Lawrenceville, GA 30044
  kolliemoses70@yahoo.com
  (770)990-2215   SETG#2100
Koopman, David L   (M1)
  5606 Brandon Park Drive
  Maryville, TN 37804
  racewthrev@aol.com
  (865)660-2440   SEET#2311
Korb, Leon C   (M1)
  15360 E 350 North Road
  Ridge Farm, IL 61870
  (217)662-8398   MINC#5200
Kurtz, David   (M1)
  1404 Sycamore School Road
  Fort Worth, TX 76134
  davidk36@yahoo.com
  (817)683-4783   MSRR#8407

--=<< L >>=--

Labrada, Hector   (M1)
  74 Cumberland Drive
  McMinnville, TN 37110
  ( )   TNMU#7200
Ladd, Sherry   (M1)
  4521 Turkey Creek Road
  Williamsport, TN 38487
  revsherryladd@gmail.com
  (931)682-2263   TNCO#7138
Lain, Judy   (M1)
  1928 Pine Ridge Drive
  Bedford, TX 76021
  judylane5@gmail.com
  (817)660-8020   MSRR#8400
Lam, Janice   (M2)
  G/F & 1/F 251 Tin Sum Village
  Tai Wai, Shatin NT, HONG KONG
  FAX: (852)2607-2245
  janiceyeung929@gmail.com
  (852)2693-3444   MSHK#8800
Lambert, James   (M1)
  224 Peabody Road
  Meridianville, AL 35759
  (256)828-6850   SERD#0800
Lancaster, David   (M1)
  426 Fugua Road
  Martin, TN 38237
  lancasterd@bethel-college.edu
  (731)588-5895   GRWT#9130
Lannom, Pamela   (M3)
  220 Bradford Acres
  Bradford, TN 38316
  plannom@yahoo.com
  (731)742-3838   GRWT#9100
LaPerche, Michael   (M1)
  3867 Evergreen Oaks Drive
  Lutz, FL 33558
  pastor-mike@earthlink.net
  (727)859-3998   SEGR#0303
Lathem, W Ray   (M1)
  452 County Road 1462
  Cullman, AL 35055
  lathemray@bellsouth.net
  (256)734-7146   SEGR#0208
Latimer, James M   (M1)

7621 Richmond
Memphis, TN 38125
jimmylatimer@redeemerevangelical.com
(901)787-7875   GRWT#9100
Lau, Walter   (M1)
  865 Jackson Street
  San Francisco, CA 94133
  FAX: (415)421-1874
  walter@cumberlandsf.org
  (650)583-7878   MSDC#8501
Laurence, Brenda   (M1)
  2823 Nine Mile Road
  Enville, TN 38332
  southernmoma@hotmail.com
  (731)687-2022   GRWT#9226
Lavender, Michael T   (M1)
  308 Main Street
  Martin, TN 38237
  mike_lavender@yahoo.com
  (731)253-7308   GRWT#9117
Lawson, James   (M1)
  1003 W 3rd Street
  Fulton, KY 42041
  (270)472-5272   MICO#3400
Lawson, Jerry L   (M1)
  6039 MS Highway 415
  Ackerman, MS 39735
  lawson@dtcweb.net
  (662)285-8295   SEGR#0707
Lawson, John C   (M2)
  PO Box 645
  Daingerfield, TX 75638
  sharjohn@windstream.net
  (903)645-2183   MSTR#8106
Lawson, Luke   (M1)
  270 N Ridgeland Circle
  Columbus, MS 39705
  luke_lawson03@hotmail.com
  (662)295-9322   SEGR#0706
Layne, Phillip   (M1)
  10699 Griffith Highway
  Whitwell, TN 37397
  cprevinsv@bellsouth.net
  (423)658-6421   SETG#2110
LeNeave, David   (M1)
  8725 Hamletsburg Road
  Brookport, IL 62910
  mscpchurch_bd@yahoo.com
  (618)564-2437   MICO#5117
Lee, David   (M1)
  3480 Summit Ridge Parkway
  Duluth, GA 30096
  gcjcatl@gmail.com
  (404)641-4359   SETG#2100
Lee, Douglas   (M1)
  3265 16th Street
  San Francisco, CA 94103
  dlee@gum.org
  (415)703-6090   MSDC#8510
Lee, George   (M1)
  104 Parc Circle
  Florence, AL 35630
  butchleeautos@yahoo.com
  (256)740-0809   SEHO#0514
Lee, Ho-Jin   (M2)
  7565 Macon Road
  Cordova, TN 38018
  hjinlab@hotmail.com
  (901)754-7070   GRWT#9322
Lee, In Mi Chang   (M3)
  5260 Coacoochee Terrace
  Alpharetta, GA 30022
  inmi1009@gmail.com
  (404)723-3487   SETG#2100
Lee, Priscilla   (M2)
  Tin Yuet Estate

Tin Shui Wai NT, HONG KONG
FAX: (852)2617-0287
wai_yung_lee@yahoo.com.hk
(852)2617-7872   MSHK#8800
Lee, Sang-Do   (M1)
  1342 Seocho-2dong, Seocho-Gu
  Seoul, KOREA
  (023)474-8405   SEET#2200
Lee, Sarah   (M1)
  ( )   SETG#2100
Lee, Ted Shu Tak   (M1)
  2/F Welland Plaza
  188 Nam Cheong Street
  Sham Shui Po, Kowloon, HONG KONG
  FAX: (852)2771-2726
  tedlee@taohsien.org.hk
  (852)2783-8923   MSHK#8800
Lee, Timothy Daniel   (M1)
  186 Blasingame Drive
  Columbus, MS 39702
  eelmit@bellsouth.net
  (601)433-3714   SEGR#0702
Lefavor, David   (M1)
  414 S Monroe Siding Road
  Xenia, OH 45385
  david.lefavor@med.va.gov
  (813)613-4133   SEGR#0100
Li, Chun Wai   (M2)
  1/F Block B
  14 Tsat Tsz Mui Road
  North Point, Hong Kong
  FAX: (852)2564-2898
  cwli2000hk@yahoo.com.hk
  (852)2562-2148   MSHK#8800
Liles, Dwight   (M1)
  8467 Joy Road
  Mount Pleasant, TN 38474
  dwightliles@att.net
  (931)379-0326   TNCO#7124
Lim, Keum-Taek   (M1)
  1342 Seocho-2dong, Seocho-Gu
  Seoul, KOREA
  limkt114@hanmail.net
  (023)474-8405   SEET#2200
Lim, Min Young   (M3)
  3480 Summit Ridge Parkway
  Duluth, GA 30096
  minyounglim63@gmail.com
  (770)751-1148   SETG#2101
Lindsay, John V   (M1)
  401 Greenwood Avenue
  Marshall, TX 75670
  (940)391-1213   MSTR#8100
Linski, David   (M2)
  1060 Alpine Way
  Indian Springs, AL 35124
  david.linski@gmail.com
  (205)677-8163   SEGR#0100
Little, Russell   (M1)
  29 Cotton Row
  Medina, TN 38355
  russelllittle@bellsouth.net
  (731)783-3565   GRWT#9109
Liu, Lai Yuet   (M2)
  2/F Fu Tung Shopping Center
  Tung Chung
  Lantau Island, HONG KONG
  FAX: (852)2109-1737
  (852)2109-1738   MSHK#8800
Lively, James W   (M1)
  906 Lyle Circle
  Greeneville, TN 37745
  FAX: (423)636-1017
  jlively@gcpchurch.org
  (423)798-1959   SEET#2206
Lively, Louella   (M1)

MINISTERS CONTINUED

196 Vicksburg Estate Road
Benton, KY 42025
(270)527-3776   MICO#3400

Livingston, Ronald L   (M1)
5851 Quantrell Ave #201
Alexandria, VA 22312
( )   SERD#0800

Lockhart, Thomas Richie   (M1)
700 County Road 343
Falkner, MS 38629
nmsdiamonddawgs@yahoo.com
(662)837-7281   GRWT#9214

Lockmiller, Lem Jr   (M1)
5068 Louise Street
Hokes Bluff, AL 35903
(256)490-3021   SEGR#0403

Logan, Jason   (M1)
4895 Diggins Drive
Fort Meade, ND 20755
jason.b.logan@dix.army.mil
(410)305-8494   TNMU#7200

Longmire, Ronald L   (M1)
2041 Eckles Drive
Maryville, TN 37804
ronaldlongmire@charter.net
(865)984-1647   SEET#2309

Lopez, Wilson   (M3)
Diag 26M #73A-69
Cali, COLOMBIA, SA
( )422-3940   MSCA#8225

Lorick, Keith   (M1)
127 Chesapeake Boulevard
Madison, AL 35757
keithlorick@knology.net
(256)325-3865   SERD#0808

Louder, Paula   (M1)
98 Gallant Court
Clarksville, TN 37043
paula.louder@cmcss.net
(615)804-4809   TNNA#7304

Louder, Stephen L   (M1)
98 Gallant Court
Clarksville, TN 37043
pastorsteve@clarksvillecpc.com
(931)217-0369   TNNA#7304

Lounsbury-Lombard, Kristi   (M1)
902 Clearview
Krum, TX 76249
kristilounsbury@gmail.com
(940)435-5077   MSRR#8400

Love, James R   (M1)
14382 Sonora Hardin Springs Road
Eastview, KY 42732
(502)862-4119   MICU#3100

Lovelace, John G   (M1)
1202 Cedar Street
New Baden, IL 62265
jlove1234@aol.com
(812)476-5879   MINC#5200

Lowe, Randy   (M1)
222 McDougal Drive
Murray, KY 42071
loweshodle@aol.com
(270)753-8255   MICO#3412

Lubo, Jaime   (M3)
AA 6365
Montebello, COLOMBIA, SA
( )   MSCA#8223

Lui, Stephen   (M1)
512 16th Avenue
San Francisco, CA 94118
FAX: (415)386-2302
(415)386-2302   MSDC#8700

Lunn, Calvin   (M1)
859 Cranford Hollow Road
Columbia, TN 38401

pastor@fcpccolumbia.com
(931)381-2397   TNCO#7110

Luo, Tian-en   (M1)
87 Berta Circle
Daly City, CA 94015
FAX: (650)754-9885
tianenyang555@gmail.com
(650)754-9885   MSDC#8700

Luttrell, Ben   (M1)
262 Main Street
Nettleton, MS 38858
(731)645-5257   GRWT#9225

--==<< M >>==--

Ma, Choil   (M1)
300 Ringgold Road Apt 503
Clarksville, TN 37042
choilma@yahoo.com
(931)824-2443   TNNA#7342

Macy, William M   (M1)
1358 Ephesus Church Road
Harned, KY 40144
(270)756-2775   MICU#3218

Madden, Judith Ellen   (M1)
100 SW Brushy Mound
Burleson, TX 76028
jmadden@stmattcpc.org
FAX: (512)258-7325
(817)295-5832   MSRR#8400

Maddux, Cynthia   (M1)
5735 Timber Creek Place Drive Apt 212
Houston, TX 77084
cmaddux1962@gmail.com
(823)343-8867   MSDC#8700

Magliolo, Sam   (M2)
14352 Fairview
Byhalia, MS 38611
samagliolo@fedex.com
(662)838-7720   GRWT#9100

Magrill, J Richard, Jr   (M1)
500 Miller Drive
Marshall, TX 75672
rmmagrill@gmail.com
(901)685-9454   MSTR#8100

Mak, Daphne Suet Chung   (M2)
2/F Welland Plaza
188 Nam Cheong Street
Sham Shui Po, Kowloon, HONG KONG
FAX: (852)2771-2726
daphne@taohsien.org.hk
(852)2783-8923   MSHK#8800

Malinoski, Melissa   (M1)
9087 Fenmore Cove
Cordova, TN 38016
FAX: (423)636-1017
mmalinoski@memphisseminary.edu
(420)620-0089   SEET#2206

Malinoski, T J   (M1)
9087 Fenmore Cove
Cordova, TN 38016
mlmalinoski@comcast.net
(423)972-1239   SEET#2200

Malone, John W   (M1)
3693 Highway 67 South
Sommerville, AL 35670
(256)778-8237   SEHO#0500

Malone, Michael   (M1)
330 Holly Street
Johnson City, TN 37604
(865)692-2415   TNMU#7200

March, Kevin   (M1)
1701 Ray Jo Circle
Chattanooga, TN 37421
kmadm1@aol.com
(423)499-4180   SETG#2100

Mariott, Keith L   (M1)
155 Ridgewood Lane
Odenville, AL 35120
kjmariott@windstream.net
(205)903-5251   SEGR#0106

Marquez, Alfonso   (M1)
389 Bethel Drive
Lenoir City, TN 37772
amarquez61@bellsouth.net
(865)660-7579   SEET#2320

Marquez, Martha   (M1)
389 Bethel Drive
Lenoir City, TN 37772
(865)660-7579   SEET#2200

Mars, Stan   (M1)
PO Box 274
Mt Pleasant, AR 72561
smars2@liberty.edu
(217)254-5120   GRAR#1517

Marshall, Debbie   (M1)
1494 Bucksnort Road
Covington, TN 38019
dsmarshall05@att.net
(901)494-1251   GRWT#9304

Martin, James W   (M1)
1922 Battleground Drive
Murfreesboro, TN 37129
(615)896-4442   TNMU#7200

Martin, Theresa   (M1)
116 Crisman Street
Chattanooga, TN 37415
choochootm@usa.net
(423)903-7260   SETG#2116

Martin, Tom   (M1)
116 Crisman Street
Chattanooga, TN 37415
choochootm@usa.net
(423)903-7260 (cell)   SETG#2100

Martin, William E, Jr   (M1)
741 Chapel Hill Road
Marion, KY 42064
juniormartin@yahoo.com
(870)270-3344   GRAR#5110

Martinez, Dagoberto   (M1)
Cra 62D #71-113
Bello, Antioquia
COLOMBIA, SA
(574)452-3466   MSAN#8900

Martinez, Rodrigo   (M1)
Mz2 Casa 21 Urb Casas De Milan
Dosquebradas, Risaralda
COLOMBIA, SA
oikoinonia@gmail.com
(576)322-2177   MSAN#8916

Martinez, Soledad   (M1)
2801 Biway Street
Ft Worth, TX 76114
ismael3233@sbcglobal.net
(817)812-8247   MSRR#8400

Masuda, Yasuo   (M1)
1-11-20 Kokubu
Ichikawa-shi, Chiba-ken
272-0834 JAPAN
FAX: (047)369-7540
fwgc6854@mb.infoweb.ne.jp
(047)369-7540   MSJA#8314

Mata, Elizabeth   (M1)
PO Box 1040
San Elizario, TX 79849
hectoryliz@att.net
(915)851-5354   MSDC#8706

Mata, Hector   (M1)
PO Box 1040
San Elizario, TX 79849
hectoryliz@att.net
(915)851-5354   MSDC#8706

MINISTERS CONTINUED

Mata, Isaac (M1)
PO Box 1040
San Elizario, TX 79849
isaacmata96@yahoo.com
(915)851-5354 MSDC#8706

Mata, Pablo (M1)
230 Flor Blanca
El Paso, TX 79927
pablomata@yahoo.com
(915)319-8407 MSDC#8700

Mathews, Nathaniel (M2)
755 Cherokee Road
New Johnsonville, TN 37134
bro.nate-mathews@hotmail.com
(931)209-6645 TNNA#7300

Mathis, B J (M2)
675 Newt McKnight Road
McMinnville, TN 37110
( ) TNMU#7200

Matlock, Robert (M1)
156 Dovenshire Drive
Fairfield Glade, TN 38558
revbobm@msn.com
(931)210-0614 TNMU#7200

Matsumoto, Masahiro (M1)
2-14-1 Minami Rinkan
Yamato-shi, Kanagawa-ken
242-0006 JAPAN
matsumoto@koza-church.jp
(046)275-2767 MSJA#8313

Matsuya, Ryuzo (M1)
72-2 Naka Kibogaoka Asahi-ku
Yokohama, Kanagawa-ken
241-0825 JAPAN
matsuya.r@woody.ocn.ne.jp
(045)364-8297 MSJA#8302

Matthews, James N (M1)
241 Morning Star Drive
Huntsville, AL 35811
brojim10@mediacombb.net
(256)337-2765 SERD#0800

Mayfield, Randall (M1)
12470 Daisywood Drive
Knoxville, TN 37932
FAX: (865)769-4756
mayfield07@comcast.net
(865)769-4756 SEET#2308

Maynard, Geoffery (M1)
1356 Marcia Road
Memphis, TN 38117
(901)409-5269 GRWT#9100

Maynard, Terrell D (M1)
3 Nelson Cove
Milan, TN 38358
terrellmaynard@bellsouth.net
(731)437-0056 SEGR#0100

Mays, Ronald B (M1)
1100 Cindy Lane
Mayfield, KY 42066
rbmays@wk.net
(270)247-0070 MICO#3400

McCallum, Frank (M1)
PO Box 56
Garfield, KY 40140
mccallum@bbtel.com
(270)580-4796 MICU#3208

McCarty, John (M1)
305 W Martindale Drive
Marshall, TX 75672
mtsjohn@gmail.com
(423)650-8788 SETG#2100

McCaskey, Charles (M1)
679 Canter Lane
Cookeville, TN 38501
charles@cookevillecpchurch.org
(931)526-4885 TNMU#7210

McClanahan, H Walter (M1)
215 White Bros Road
Humboldt, TN 38343
waltermac2@hughes.net
(731)784-1176 GRWT#9110

McClanahan, Jo Ann (M1)
215 White Bros Road
Humboldt, TN 38343
joannmcclanahan@hughes.net
(731)784-1176 GRWT#9100

McClung, Andy (M1)
919 Dickinson Street
Memphis, TN 38107
scubarev@att.net
(901)606-6615 GRWT#9100

McClung, Tiffany (M1)
919 Dickinson Street
Memphis, TN 38107
tmcclung@memphisseminary.edu
(901)606-6615 GRWT#9100

McConnell, Donald R (M1)
147 Confederacy Circle
Knoxville, TN 37934
donjoyce515@hotmail.com
(865)288-0230 SEET#2200

McCoy, Kenneth L (M1)
1422 Walton Road
Memphis, TN 38117
(901)682-0891 GRWT#9301

McCurley, Don (M1)
4036 McAllister Street
Milan, TN 38358
dcmccurley@hotmail.com
(731)723-3623 GRWT#9106

McDuff, Dwayne (M1)
9770 County Road 5
Florence, AL 35633
fcpdmcduff@comcast.net
FAX: (256)766-0736
(256)764-6354 SEHO#0506

McDuffie, J C (M1)
RR 3 Box 574
Fairfield, IL 62837
mactrapper4@frontier.com
(618)842-5624 MINC#5113

McGee, Charles Randall (M1)
9037 Groveland Drive
Dallas, TX 75218
randallmcgee@sbcglobal.net
(214)328-2488 MSRR#8400

McGill, James A (M1)
433 S Walnut Avenue
Cookeville, TN 38501
jam7235@frontiernet.net
(931)526-6936 TNMU#7234

McGowan, Kriss (M1)
900 Alvin York Highway
Whitwell, TN 37397
krissmcg658@gmail.com
(423)463-8609 SETG#2119

McGowan, Rhonda (M1)
900 Alvin York Highway
Whitwell, TN 37379
pastorrhonda@mcgowanministries.com
(423)619-5679 SETG#2100

McGuire, James D (M1)
220 Southwind Circle #2
Greenville, TN 37745
jmcguire915@comcast.net
(423)638-6380 SEET#2200

McGuire, Timothy (M1)
PO Box 42
Mt Sherman, KY 42764
brotim.cpc@gmail.com
(270)766-9027 MICU#3509

McInnis, Rodney (M1)

280-B Coley Road
Glencoe, AL 35905
mcinnisrodneyand@bellsouth.net
(256)454-2399 SEGR#0404

McMichael, Jeff (M1)
224 John Drane Lane
Harned, KY 40144
revmcmichael@outlook.com
(270)617-4016 MICU#3207

McMillan, L Ronald (M1)
675 Kimberly Drive
Atoka, TN 38004
mcmillanron@bellsouth.net
(901)837-1101 GRWT#9304

McMillan, Lloyd Aaron (M1)
8600 Academy Road NE
Albuquerque, NM 87111
FAX: (505)797-8599
amcmillan@heightscpc.org
(505)821-1993 MSDC#8700

McNeese, Mark (M1)
3306 Greenlawn Parkway
Austin, TX 78757
mam53@prodigy.net
(512)32-9223 MSTR#8100

McNeese, Michael C (M1)
16410 Wesley Evans Road
Prairieville, LA 70769
mcneesemc@cox.net
(520)722-1350 MSDC#8700

McSpadden, Nancy (M1)
120 Roberta Drive
Memphis, TN 38112
revnancy77@gmail.com
(870)612-0067 GRAR#1100

Mearns, Duawn (M1)
107 Westoak Place
Hot Springs, AR 71913
lakehamiltoncpc@yahoo.com
(501)276-1266 GRAR#1221

Medlin, Kevin (M1)
316 Dandelion Drive
Lebanon, TN 37087
FAX: (615)444-6671
kmedlin12@hotmail.com
(615)444-7453 TNMU#7220

Meeks, Brittany (M1)
1340 Tutwiler Avenue
Memphis, TN 38107
bpmeeks@memphisseminary.edu
(901)336-9024 GRWT#9100

Meinzer, Alan (M1)
25 Rosewood Road
Batesville, AR 72501
natsdad@suddenlink.net
(870)793-8234 GRAR#1515

Mejia, Salvador (M3)
7618 S Highway 72
Loudon, TN 37774
(865)661-8267 SEET#2200

Melson, Glenda (M1)
331 Tickle Weed Road
Swansea, SC 29160
gmelson@fidnet.com
(417)588-2758 GRMI#4100

Melton, Samuel D (M1)
2249 Bucks Pocket Road SE
Oldfort, TN 37362
(423)472-8467 SETG#2100

Meredith, Charles (M1)
144 Barbara Circle
Elizabethtown, KY 42701
(270)307-0607 MICU#3210

Merritt, Joyce (M1)
3929 Snail Shell Cave Road
Rockvale, TN 37153

MINISTERS CONTINUED

(615)574-3047   TNMU#7239
Messer, James   (M1)
   3653 Old Madisonville Road
   Henderson, KY 42420
   jcmess@hotmail.com
(270)827-0711   MINC#5304
Middleton, Bill S   (M1)
   12826 Union Road
   Knoxville, TN 37922
   revbill@charter.net
(865)966-1706   SEET#2200
Middleton, Frank, Jr   (M3)
   1200 Adele Circle
   Slidell, LA 70461
   fmiddle@bellsouth.net
(770)655-0406   SETG#2100
Mikel, Jason   (M1)
   4630 Mt Sharon Road
   Greenbrier, TN 37073
   jasonemikel@gmail.com
(615)243-8938   TNNA#7321
Milby, Elizabeth L   (M1)
   207 Summersville Road
   Greensburg, KY 42743
(270)932-5659   MICU#3100
Miller, Carol   (M1)
   101 Park Avenue
   Dickson, TN 37055
   lcarolmiller@comcast.net
(615)411-6656   TNNA#7300
Miller, James R   (M1)
   1214 Whitney Drive
   Columbia, TN 38401
   rev.james.miller@charter.net
(931)381-3367   TNCO#7101
Mills, David M   (M1)
   528 County Road 322
   Bertram, TX 78605
(512)355-3511   MSTR#8100
Mink, R Allan   (M2)
   1113 Hidden Glen Court
   Burleson, TX 76028
   FAX: (817)295-2576
   alan.mink@stmattcpc.org
(817)295-5832   MSRR#8418
Minor, Mitzi   (M1)
   875 S Cox
   Memphis, TN 38104
(901)278-6115   GRWT#9100
Minton, Grant   (M1)
   PO Box 270
   Auburn, KY 42206
   FAX: (270)271-4603
   gminton@logantele.com
(270)542-7991   MICU#3301
Miyai, Takehiko   (M1)
   A-201 2-2-48 Higashihara Zama-shi
   Kanagawa-ken
   228-0004 JAPAN
   FAX: (046)256-3212
(046)207-6558   MSJA#8304
Miyajima, Atsushi   (M2)
   Rua Araja
   58 Paraiso Sao Joa
   48280-000, Bahia, BRAZIL
   ariel.atsushi@gmail.com
(5571)3664-1037   MSJA#8313
Montano, Jhony   (M1)
   Cra 9 No 6 6N 87 Bello Horizonte
   Popayan
   Colombia, South America
(092)823-8988   MSCA#8227
Montoya, David   (M1)
   Cra 12 bis #11-69
   Pereira, Risaralda, COLOMBIA, SA
   FAX: (576)324-4110

   adamonva@gmail.com
(576)324-4109   MSAN#8916
Montoya, Eduardo   (M1)
   270 Windsor Drive
   Roselle, IL 60172
   edmontoya@hotmail.com
(630)980-1577   MINC#5203
Moore, Angela   (M1)
   3756 Douglass Avenue
   Memphis, TN 38111
(870)581-2509   GRAR#1100
Moore, Hillman C   (M1)
   2500 Marshall Avenue Apt 223
   Paducah, KY 42003
   hillmancm@att.net
(270)876-7163   MICO#3400
Moore, James R, Sr   (M1)
   2778 Marguerite Street S
   Hokes Bluff, AL 35903
   jmoore@microxl.com
(256)494-9030   SEGR#0100
Moore, Kimberly   (M3)
   1025 Three Island Ford Road
   Charlotte, TN 37036
   kimberly.a.moore@vanderbilt.edu
(615)545-1595   TNNA#7300
Mora, Wilfredo   (M2)
   17512 SW 153rd Court
   Miami, FL 33187
   moraw68@gmail.com
(786)554-1478   SEGR#0100
Morgan, Kenneth P   (M1)
   5400 Highway 101
   Rogersville, AL 35652
   FAX: (256)247-1424
   kennymorgan330@hotmail.com
(256)247-3890   SEHO#0515
Morgan, Richard   (M1)
   1468 Williams Cove Road
   Winchester, TN 37398
   icthuse3@gmail.com
(931)349-4474   TNMU#7214
Morris, Carey   (M3)
   2167 W Shawtown Road
   Troy, TN 38260
   carey@cyberianwolf.net
(731)538-9477   GRWT#9100
Morrow, Charles   (M1)
   5032 Pine Grove Road
   Union, MS 39365
   morrowp7@yahoo.com
(601)479-0288   SEGR#0100
Mosley, Karen   (M1)
   PO Box 172154
   Memphis, TN 38187
( )   GRWT#9100
Mosley, Steve   (M1)
   1200 N Arkansas Avenue
   Russellville, AR 72801
   FAX: (479)880-0071
   stevemosley@hotmail.com
(479)968-1061   GRAR#1216
Moss, Larry   (M1)
   167 Bluegrass Drive
   La Center, KY 42056
(270)292-2000   MICO#3400
Mullenix, Robert   (M1)
   1408 Azalee Lane
   Chapel Hill, TN 37034
   glonix@live.comt
(931)379-3617   TNCO#7133
Murphree, Hughlen   (M1)
   4298 County Road 1719
   Holly Pond, AL 35083
   hmurph@hiwaay.net

(256)796-5352   SERD#0800
Murray, Joshua   (M1)
   126 Ray Avenue
   Monticello, AR 71655
   jdm4428@yahoo.com
(318)259-7828   GRAR#1100
Murrie, Willard   (M1)
   506 11th Street
   Vienna, IL 62995
(618)658-2430   MICO#3400

--==<< N >>==--

Nash, Zachary   (M1)
   (on file in General Assembly Office)
( )   GRWT#9100
Nave, Steve   (M1)
   5172 Fall River Road
   Leoma, TN 38468
   thenaves@wildblue.net
(931)424-0020   TNCO#7131
Navrkal, Amy   (M3)
   302 W 3rd Street
   Brookport, IL 62910
   brinkleydanne2@gmail.com
(618)638-4218   MICO#3400
Ndoro, Wonder   (M1)
   111 Roberta Avenue
   Memphis, TN 38112
   gusungo@yahoo.com
(901)334-5861   GRWT#9100
Neafus, Kenneth R   (M1)
   237 Richland Church Road
   Morgantown, KY 42261
(270)526-6835   MICU#3100
Nease, Dale   (M1)
   500 S 30th Street
   Clinton, OK 73601
(580)323-7557   MSRR#6302
Nelson, Charles E   (M1)
   209 Classic Court
   Springtown, TX 76082
   dundeal10@aol.com
(903)641-5466   MSRR#8410
Newcomb, Troy   (M3)
   PO Box 858
   Salem, KY 42078
( )   MICO#3610
Newell, Jennifer   (M1)
   2322 Maraco Circle
   Chattanooga, TN 37421
   newelljennifer3@gmail.com
(423)892-5834   SETG#2108
Nichols, Oscar Lee   (M1)
   1035 N County Road 650E
   Trilla, IL 62469
(217)234-6551   MINC#5200
Nicholson, Casey   (M1)
   1020 Tusculum Boulevard
   Greeneville, TN 37745
   caseynicholson@mac.com
(423)638-4504   SEET#2200
Nickles, Philip   (M1)
   5821 County Road 1114
   Vinemont, AL 35179
   nickles.phil@yahoo.com
(256)734-9847   SEHO#0213
Niswonger, Richard   (M1)
   20941 Highway 16 E
   Siloam Springs, AR 72761
   rniswonger@cox.net
(479)524-4081   GRAR#1100
Niwa, Yoshimasa   (M1)
   15-402 Narakita Danchi
   2913 Naramachi Aoba-ku
   Yokohama, Kanagawa-ken

MINISTERS CONTINUED

227-0036 JAPAN
FAX: (042)725-9909
rsb09335@nifty.com
(045)961-1540   MSJA#8310
Norman, Maury A   (M1)
1750 Shipley Road
Cookeville, TN 38501
marynorman@yahoo.com
(931)526-1644   TNNA#7229
Norris, Dakota   (M3)
4750 Highway 431 N
Springfield, TN 37172
volsfan2011@gmail.com
(615)681-6346   TNNA#7300
Norris, Freddie   (M1)
330 Lexington Drive
Glasgow, KY 42141
(270)651-7932   MICU#3100
Norton, Austin   (M3)
1498 Bradshaw Boulevard
Cookeville, TN 38506
(931)261-3260   TNMU#7200
Norton, Kitty   (M1)
251 Westchase Drive
Nashville, TN 37205
kitty.a.norton@vanderbilt.edu
(615)584-1464   TNNA#7300
Norton, Thomas H   (M1)
220 Evergreen Garden Drive
Elizabethtown, KY 42701
tnorton16@comcast.net
(353)584-4695   GRWT#9100
Notley, Sharon   (M1)
16500 S Grey Wolf Apt 5
Odessa, TX 79766
sharon_standrewcp@sbcglobal.net
(432)210-9059   MSDC#8703
Nunn, Donald W   (M1)
203 Bridgers Hill Road
Longview, TX 75604
dwnunn@earthlink.net
(903)297-6074   MSTR#8113
Nye, John   (M1)
210 Crestview Drive
Mount Juliet, TN 37122
( )   TNMU#7200

--==<< O >>==--

O'Neal Danhof, Claire   (M1)
301 Whispering Hills Street
Hot Springs, AR 71901
acglenn@aol.com
( )   GRAR#1100
Oh, Taeho   (M1)
42-40 2908th Street #1
Bayside, NY 11361   SETG#2100
Ohi, Keitaro   (M1)
2-14-21 Minami Rinkan
Yamato-shi Kanagawa-ken
242-0006 JAPAN
keitaro_o@hotmail.com
(046)275-9616   MSJA#8303
Okala, Achile   (M3)
5887 Newcombe Court
Arvada, CO 80004
archileok@me.com
(720)820-8511   MSDC#8700
Oliveira, Jose   (M1)
7310 Jasmine Drive
Hanover Park, IL 60133
valdirsoares@yahoo.com
(630)855-0870   MSDC#8700
Oliver, Lisa   (M1)
110 Allen Drive
Hendersonville, TN 37075

(615)319-6466   TNNA#7300
O'Mara, Shelia   (M1)
533 Loughton Lane
Arnold, MD 21012
chaplainshelia@aol.com
(410)757-5713   MSDC#8700
Ordway, Wendell   (M1)
4775 Calvert City Road
Calvert City, KY 42029
(270)395-7318   MICO#3423
Orozco, Joaquin   (M2)
Cra 3 #7-14
Aguadas, Caldas, COLOMBIA, SA
jeob40@hotmail.com
(576)851-4773   MSAN#8900
Orozeo Ariza, Juan Carlos   (M2)
Aereo 6365
Cali Vale, COLOMBIA, SA
( )   MSCA#8200
Orr, Melvin   (M1)
806 Washington Street
Newbern, TN 38059
2Orrs.mn@charter.net
(731)627-2445   GRWT#9425
Ortega, Juan   (M3)
COLOMBIA, SA
jortegaus@yahoo.com
(574)323-9305   MSAN#8900
Ortiz, Jaime   (M1)
Cra 50D #62-69
Medellin, Antioquia, COLOMBIA, SA
(574)421-6339   MSAN#8900
Ortiz, Milton   (M1)
8846 N Cortona Circle
Cordova, TN 38018
mortiz@cumberland.org
(901)486-6679   SEET#2200
Osorio, Fernando   (M3)
Aereo 329
Palmira, COLOMBIA, SA
( )272-7584   MSCA#8215
Overton, Janice M   (M1)
3320 Pipeline Road
Birmingham, AL 35243
FAX: (205)968-8105
jan@crestlinechurch.org
(205)281-6819   SEGR#0102
Overton, Twanda   (M2)
616 S Cox Street
Memphis, TN 38104
tdeeov@yahoo.com
(865)591-8881   SEET#2200
Owen, Rick   (M1)
3305 Wild Oaks Court
Burleson, TX 76028
FAX: (817)295-2576
rowen@stmattcpc.org
(817)295-5832   MSRR#8418

--==<< P >>==--

Page, Rickey   (M1)
736 Rodney Drive
Nashville, TN 37205
FAX: (615)352-2801
rickey.page@wncp.org
(615)353-7850   TNNA#7334
Paleak, Jock Tut   (M1)
614 N Water Street Apt #623
Gallatin, TN 37066
(615)585-2842   TNNA#7341
Paredes, Fabio   (M3)
Carerra 7 # 1-76
La Cruztala, Ipiales, COLOMBIA, SA
(092)773-1036   MSCA#8200
Park, Bo-Seong   (M1)

304-28 Sinlim-Dong, Kwanak-Gu
Seoul, KOREA
(002)884-3474   SEET#2200
Park, Jin Soo   (M1)
21155 45th Drive
Bayside, NY 11361
jpkorea@daum.net
(516)558-7298   SECE#2137
Park, Sang Hoon   (M1)
3504 W Shawnee Drive
Springfield, MO 65810
hesed-park@hanmail.net
(417)888-0442   GRMI#4314
Park, Si Hoon   (M1)
511 4th Street #B
Palisades Park, NJ 07650
(201)944-7913   SECE#2137
Park, Sung In   (M1)
12320 Alameda Trace Circle #1309
Austin, TX 78727
( )   MSTR#8100
Park, Yang Rae   (M1)
4175 Buford Highway
Duluth, GA 30096
barkmoksa@hanmail.net
(770)912-7710   SETG#2130
Park, Young   (M3)
3340 Bentbill Crossing
Cummings, GA 30041
barkmogun@gmail.com
(404)661-6117   SETG#2100
Parker, Susan   (M1)
655 York Drive
Rogersville, AL 35652
park9301@bellsouth.net
(256)247-3877   SEHO#0500
Parkhurst, L G, Jr   (M1)
409 Woodhollow Trail
Edmond, OK 73012
(405)341-7477   MSRR#8400
Parks, Sam   (M1)
10 Lila Way
Cartersville, GA 60120
wsamparks@aol.com
(615)529-2465   TNMU#7200
Parman, David   (M1)
5034 S Monroe School Road
Monroe City, IN 47557
FAX: (812)743-5171
(812)743-2646   MINC#5307
Parish, Johnny   (M1)
114 Savo Bay
Hendersonville, TN 37075
johnnyparish@bellsouth.net
(615)824-5842   TNNA#7329
Parrish, Steven   (M1)
4610 Dunn Avenue
Memphis, TN 38117
sparrish@memphisseminary.edu
(901)743-9545   TNNA#7300
Parsons, Hugh L   (M1)
1526 Welch
Houston, TX 77006
p-h-parsons@comcast.net
(713)522-6126   MSTR#8100
Patterson, James H   (M1)
1305 Falmouth Road
Chattanooga, TN 37405
FAX: (423)942-2188
(423)267-8568   SETG#2113
Patterson, Jerry   (M1)
7007 Whitaker Avenue
Van Nuys, CA 91406
(818)994-5828   MSDC#8700
Patton, Malcolm   (M1)
921 Harris Drive

Gallatin, TN 37066
FAX: (615)824-6507
bpatton11@comcast.net
(615)452-5557 TNNA#7301
Patton, Roger, Jr (M1)
1534 Eden Rose Place
Nolensville, TN 37135
rogerlpatton@att.net
(615)975-5526 TNNA#7333
Payne, Robert (Bob) (M1)
1660 3rd Street NW
Birmingham, AL 35215
payne.bob.emmet@gmail.com
(205)856-2427 SEGR#0100
Pedigo, Russell (M1)
1002 Haney Avenue
El Dorado, AR 71730
russell_pedigo@hotmail.com
(870)862-4689 GRAR#1100
Peery, Terry (M1)
1431 Spainwood Street
Columbia, TN 38401
coppreacher@gmail.com
(931)381-6871 TNCO#7143
Pejendino, Fhanor (M1)
Cra 26 #36-40
Tulua, COLOMBIA, SA
(317)654-5750 MSCA#8226
Pejendino, Socorro (M1)
Cra 26 #36-40
Tulua, COLOMBIA, SA
(317)654-5750 MSCA#8200
Perez, Jose (M1)
3512 Chesnut Ridge Lane
Birmingham, AL 35216
(205)663-3110 TNMU#7200
Perkins, Ed (M1)
721 E Paris Avenue
McKenzie, TN 38201
(731)352-2754 GRWT#9100
Perkins, William H (M1)
PO Box 632
Central City, KY 42330
(270)754-5333 MICU#3100
Peters, David J (M1)
4010 Sam Bass Road
Round Rock, TX 78681
(512)244-2152 MSTR#8100
Peterson, Lisa (M1)
1770 Magnolia Tree Road
Memphis, TN 38138
petersonli@aol.com
(901)754-9316 GRWT#9320
Petty, Linda Lee (M3)
4401 W Elgin Street
Broken Arrow, OK 74012
(918)252-4741 MSRR#8400
Peyton, James L (M1)
1455 County Road 643
Cullman, AL 35055
jakjpeyton@att.net
(256)734-6001 SEHO#0212
Peyton, Kevin (M1)
580 S Timothy Lane
Galatia, IL 62935
kevinp21@frontier.net
(618)841-0076 MICO#5123
Phelps, Earl (M1)
172 Michie Pebble Hill Road
Stanntonville, TN 38379
FAX: (901)632-9126
phelps.e@juno.com
(731)632-5107 GRWT#9216
Phillips, Kenneth P (M1)
6419 Town Creek Road East
Lenoir City, TN 37772

(865)986-7344 SEET#2306
Phillips-Burk, Pam (M1)
3325 Bailey Creek Cove N
Collierville, TN 38017
pam@cumberland.org
(256)684-5247 SERD#0800
Piamba, Juan Carlos (M3)
Cra 7 #21N-35
Popayan, COLOMBIA, SA
(092)838-5761 MSCA#8200
Pickard, Ronald (M1)
6292 Golden Drive
Morristown, TN 37814
(423)587-9735 SEET#2200
Pickett, Darrell (M1)
113 Woods Drive
Glasgow, KY 42141
dpickett@glasgow-ky.com
(270)834-6102 MICU#3107
Pickett, Patricia (M1)
1460 Cheatham Dam Road
Ashland City, TN 37015
tovahtoo@aol.com
(615)792-4973 TNNA#7319
Pinion, Phillip (M1)
PO Box 87
Union City, TN 38281
(731)885-9175 GRWT#9432
Pinnell, James (Jim) (M1)
1525 Parks Well Road
Gleason, TN 38229
revpinnell@hotmail.com
(731)648-5078 GRWT#9111
Pittenger, Ronnie M (M1)
547 Southcrest Drive
Nashville, TN 37211
(615)832-8832 TNMU#7200
Plachte, Richard (M1)
615 Grover Street
Warrensburg, MO 64093
rap@aerobiz.org
(660)441-4427 GRMI#4100
Polacek, Fred E (M1)
907 Graham Drive
Old Hickory, TN 37138
revfredp@gmail.com
(615)754-5328 TNNA#7300
Pope, Charles (Buddy) (M1)
2391 Fairfield Pike
Shelbyville, TN 37160
pope6897@yahoo.com
(931)205-6897 TNCO#7137
Porras, Hernan (M3)
1485 Rivershyre Parkway
Lawrenceville, GA 30043
salvosporgracia@aol.com
(404)468-6012 SETG#2100
Porras, Rene Wilgen (M3)
Cra 4 bis #10-51
La Virginia, Risaralda
COLOMBIA, SA
renewilgen@hotmail.com
(576)367-9529 MSAN#8900
Potts, Danny (M1)
418 Eddings Street Apt 2
Fulton , KY 42041
(270)355-2264 MICO#3400
Pounds, James D (M1)
40 Nellie Lane
Savannah, TN 38372
olivetcp@bellsouth.net
(731)925-2685 GRWT#9220
Powell, Jeff (M1)
547B Fawn Drive
Henderson, TN 38340
jfpowell2003@yahoo.com

(731)608-2040 GRWT#9100
Powell, Omer T (M1)
11856 Sonora Hardin Springs Road
Eastview, KY 42732
(270)862-4720 MICU#3100
Prenshaw, Rebecca (M1)
1100 Albermarie Lane
Knoxville, TN 37923
bprenshaw@yahoo.com
(865)531-1954 SEET#2200
Preston, Dennis (M1)
7447 Knottsville Mount Zion Road
Philpot, KY 42366
dennis.preston@daviess.kyschools.us
(270)925-8144 MICU#3507
Prevost, Abigail (M3)
4731 Lafayette Road
Hopkinsville, KY 42240
abbyprevost@gmail.com
(731)343-5386 SEGR#0100
Prewitt, Curtis (M1)
3712 Carmel Lane
Paducah, KY 42003
prewitt@apex.net
(270)554-9779 MICO#3400
Prosser, Forest (M1)
1157 Mountain Creek Road
Chattanooga, TN 37405
forestprosser@comcast.net
(423)877-4114 SETG#2100
Prosser, Robert (M1)
1021 Old State Route 76
Henry, TN 38231
(731)243-4467 GRWT#9100
Puckett, Rian (M3)
3784 Harrison Street
Batesville, AR 72501
rppuckett@memphisseminary.edu
(731)288-7742 GRWT#9435

--==<< Q >>==--

Qualls, Michael (M1)
3639 Tiffany Oaks Lane
Bartlett, TN 38135
mqualls1@yahoo.com
(901)377-0526 GRWT#9100
Quevedo, Mariano (M3)
289 Golf Club Lane
McMinnville, TN 37110
( ) TNMU#7200
Quinonez, Wilfrido (M1)
Cra 3 No 36-29, Juan XXIII
BuenaventurValle, COLOMBIA, SA
ipc.divinoredentor@gmail.com
(310)412-1711 MSCA#8206
Quintero, Alexander (M3)
Carrera 13 #3-81
Guacari, COLOMBIA, SA
( ) MSCA#8212
Quinton, Noah (M2)
2912 Waller Omer Road
Sturgis, KY 42459
noah.quinton@gmail.com
(270)952-3875 MICO#3400

--==<< R >>==--

Racines, Jairo (M1)
CLL 39 No 13-40
Cali, COLOMBIA, SA
(311)385-6546 MSCA#8200
Rackley, Mark (M1)
3060 Highway 140 NE
Rydal, GA 30171
pastormarkbcpcga@gmail.com

MINISTERS CONTINUED

(770)382-3790 SETG#2101
Ragsdale, Donnie (M1)
915 S Olive Street
Union City, TN 38261
(731)885-0014 GRWT#9100

Ralph, Brian (M3)
6419 S Vinewood Street Apt 205
Littleton, CO 80120
ralph1970@gmail.com
(312)315-6915 MSDC#8700

Ranson, Doris (M1)
9440 Fenwick Road
Owensboro, KY 42301
dorisranson@bellsouth.net
(270)229-2875 MICU#3100

Ratliff, James L (M1)
4027 Club View Drive
Memphis, TN 38125
pastorjimfcpc@yahoo.com
(901)758-0125 GRWT#9312

Reed, Charles (M1)
10235 Highway 301
Dade City, FL 33525
instchuck12@embarqmail.com
(352)567-7427 SEGR#0311

Reed, Richard (M2)
236 Madison Street
Dyer, TN 38330
richardcplist@hotmail.com
(731)692-3604 GRWT#9101

Reese, Michael (M1)
404 Five Oaks Boulevard
Lebanon, TN 37087
michaelhreese@bellsouth.net
(615)443-0457 TNMU#7208

Reeves, Donald (M1)
PO Box 528
Rainsville, AL 35986
reevesd@nacc.edu
(256)228-4057 SERD#0800

Reid, Richard (M1)
123 S Fifth Street
Selmer, TN 38375
rjreid1964@msn.com
(731)453-5302 GRWT#9225

Reid, Roger (M1)
1505 Experiment Farm Road
Lewisburg, TN 37091
drrtr@yahoo.com
(931)422-5257 TNCO#7125

Renner, Wallace (M1)
1648 Griffith Avenue
Owensboro, KY 42303
pwrenner@adelphia.net
(270)685-4359 MICU#3100

Reno, Michael (M3)
52 Rolla Gardens
Rolla, MO 65401
rollarenomike@gmail.com
(573)578-5321 GRMI#4309

Rice, Keith (M1)
PO Box 582
Itasca, TX 76055
rsvkeith@yahoo.com
(254)087-2418 MSRR#8400

Rice, Perryn (M1)
10802 Hayfield Drive
Dallas, TX 75238
perryn@lhpres.org
(931)526-6585 MSRR#8411

Richards, Carroll R (M1)
210 Allison Drive
Lincoln, IL 62656
FAX: (217)732-7894
dr_cr@comcast.net
(217)732-7894 MINC#5200

Richards, Kenneth (M1)
2 Kingston Road
Water Valley, KY 42085
kenrich111443@hotmail.com
(270)355-2089 MICO#3401

Richardson, W Jean (M1)
7533 Lancashire Boulevard
Powell, TN 37849
jeanandregena@frontier.com
(865)947-3111 SEET#2200

Richter, Justin (M1)
8600 Academy Road NE
Albuquerque, NM 87111
richteryp@gmail.com
(505)363-8738 MSDC#8701

Ricketts, Roger (M1)
205 Contantz Drive
Canton, MO 63435
( ) MICU#3100

Ridgely, Michael (M1)
5195 Broad Street S
Trezevant, TN 38258
(731)669-3767 GRWT#9100

Rietz, Allen (M1)
1239 Hopewell Church Road
Finger, TN 38334
(731)989-7872 GRWT#9100

Rincon, Alfredo (M1)
12008 Fred Carter
El Paso, TX 79936
yaanaivitaly@yahoo.com
(915)857-1343 MSDC#8704

Rincon, Lyvia (M1)
12008 Fred Carter
El Paso, TX 79936
yaanaivitaly@yahoo.com
(915)857-1343 MSDC#8706

Rippy, James G (M1)
442 Trina Street
Gallatin, TN 37066
lgrippy@live.com
(615)681-7086 TNNA#7300

Rivera, Carlos A (M1)
Calle Dr Jose Maria Vertiz 1410
Departmento 202B, Colonia Portales
Delegacion Benito
Juarez, C.P. 03300 MEXICO
caralrifra@une.net.co
(52)1-55-31058377 MSRR#8400

Rivera, Cenobia (M1)
Cra 12 #8-47
Cartago, Valle, COLOMBIA, SA
zenobiadedaza@yahoo.com.mx
(572)214-5060 MSAN#8906

Rodden, Linda (M1)
363 Cornelison Street
Lebanon, MO 65536
linda.rodden@mercy.net
(417)588-2207 GRMI#4100

Roddy, Lowell G (M1)
2583 Hedgerow Lane
Clarksville, TN 37043
lgroddy@yahoo.com
(931)368-1081 TNNA#7300

Rodgers, Howard (M1)
336 County Road 1216
Vinemont, AL 35179
djbr421@yahoo.com
(256)739-6296 SEHO#0202

Rodriguez, Jairo Hernan (M1)
Cll 42 No 80B 64
Barrio Versalles
Cali-Valle, COLOMBIA, SA
jairo.hrodriguez@hotmail.com
(572)377-8741 MSCA#8200

Roedder, Unhui Grace (M3)

419 S Jonathan Avenue
Springfield, MO 65802
(417)494-6491 GRMI#4100

Rogers, Steve (M3)
37 Cool Spring Road
Trimble, TN 38259
(731)882-2229 GRWT#9408

Rojas, Antonio Mena (M1)
1421 1st Street NW
Cullman, AL 35055
antonio.mena.7@facebook.com
(256)531-8193 SEGR#0100

Rolman, William L, Jr (M1)
602 Canyon Drive
Columbia, TN 38401
wmrolmanjr@att.net
(931)388-2611 TNCO#7136

Romines, Sam (M1)
PO Box 127
Lewisburg, KY 42256
sam60romines@hotmail.com
(270)755-4282 MICU#3307

Ros, Ramiro (M1)
107 Bracken Lane
Brandon, FL 33511
bethel@gte.net
(813)633-1548 SEGR#0100

Rosales, David (M3)
101 N Lowe
Hobart, OK 73651
sagradalut@gmail.com
(580)682-0722 MSRR#6306

Rose, Missy (M1)
5484 Peyton Randolph Street
Bartlett, TN 38134
missyrose3@yahoo.com
(901)378-1133 GRWT#9100

Rowlett, Ron (M1)
22 Diana Drive
Savannah, GA 31406
(912)351-0736 SEGR#0100

Rudolph, Allie D (M1)
855 Old Rosebower Church Road
Paducah, KY 42003
rallie307@aol.com
(270)898-4903 MICO#3400

Ruggia, Mario (Bud) (M1)
603 Rumsey Street
Kiowa, KS 67070
ruggia@aol.com
(620)825-4509 MSRR#8400

Rush, Kip John (M1)
513 Meadowlark Lane
Brentwood, TN 37027
pastor@brenthaven.org
(615)376-4563 TNNA#7331

Rush, Robert D (M1)
12935 Quail Park Drive
Cypress, TX 77429
rushrd74@comcast.net
(832)559-1500 MSTR#8100

Russell, Albert (M2)
375 Ashton Park Drive
Millbrook, AL 36054
chemistry.russell@gmail.com
(334)290-0399 SEGR#0407

Russell, Olen (Bud) (M1)
4510 Holly Grove Road
Brighton, TN 38011
olen552@aol.com
(901)476-8379 MICO#3400

Rustenhaven, William, III (M1)
PO Box 1303
Marshall, TX 75671
FAX: (903)935-3193
rusty@cumberlandofmarshall.org

MINISTERS CONTINUED

(903)935-6609   MSTR#8115
Rustenhaven, William, Jr   (M1)
703 W Burleson Street
Marshall, TX 75670
rustenhavendolores@yahoo.com
(903)935-7056   MSTR#8100
Ryan, Jack   (M1)
8806 Kennesaw Mountain Drive
Mabelvale, AR 72103
(501)749-8572   GRAR#1100
Ryoo, Hwa Chang   (M1)
450 Island Road Unit 146
Ramsey, NJ 07446   SETG#2100

--==<< S >>==--

Saldana, Manuel (Alex)   (M1)
536 Telop
El Paso, TX 79927
campe13@yahoo.com
(915)317-9349   MSDC#8706
Salisbury, Rebecca   (M1)
1033 Twin Oaks Drive
Murfreesboro, TN 37130
rebsalisbury@yahoo.com
(615)410-7801   TNMU#7200
Salyer, Stewart   (M1)
2211 Foxfire Road
Clarksville, TN 37040
stewart.salyer@gmail.com
(931)980-2829   TNNA#7302
Sanchez, Josefina   (M1)
7 Hancock Street
Melrose, MA 02176
fsfamily64@gmail.com
(479)970-8654   SEET#2220
Sanchez, Sol Maria   (M1)
Av Americas 19 N - 18
Cali Valle
Colombia, South America
solmarias@starmedia.com
(   )   MSCA#8200
Sanders, Thomas R   (M1)
4201 W Kent Street
Broken Arrow, OK 74012
FAX: (918)437-2199
trsncf@msn.com
(918)269-0043   MSRR#6201
Sandiford, Holton   (M3)
4227 E 300th Road
Casey, IL 62420
(217)259-3773   MINC#5200
Sansom, Vernon   (M1)
7810 Shiloh Road
Midlothian, TX 76065
vernon@sansom.us
(972)825-6887   MSRR#8421
Santillano, Ray Paul   (M1)
1270 Polo Road
Columbia, SC 29223
ramon.santillano@us.army.mil
(915)500-4928   MSTR#8100
Satoh, Iwao   (M1)
8710 Hickory Falls Lane
Pewee Valley, KY 40056
iwaosatoh@gmail.com
(502)657-9643   MSJA#8300
Schmoyer, Donna Marie   (M1)
613 Mound Street
Monongahela, PA 15063
schmoyerdm@yahoo.com
(817)266-6572   MSRR#8400
Schott, Fred, Jr   (M1)
606 Taylor Trail
Springfield, TN 37172
(615)384-8572   TNNA#7321

Schultz, Don   (M1)
708 Gateway Lane
Tampa, FL 33613
(813)960-1473   SEGR#0100
Schwarz, Karl   (M1)
83 W Curtis Street
Bells, TN 38006
schw8651@bellsouth.net
(731)663-3987   GRWT#9430
Scott, Jerry   (M1)
2310 Sentell Drive
Maryville, TN 37803
dmjlscott@yahoo.com
(865)809-2621   SEET#2200
Scott, Joel   (M3)
1848 Sassafrass Lane
Soddy Daisy, TN 37379
saejoescott@gmail.com
(423)240-2724   SETG#2100
Scott, Linda   (M3)
960 S Katy Road
Atoka, OK 74525
(580)889-2292   MSCH#6100
Scott, Lisa   (M1)
(On File in General Assembly Office)
lascott1979@att.net
(816)332-0604   MINC#5200
Scott, Nathan   (M1)
960 S Katy Road
Atoka, OK 74525
(580)364-6155   MSCH#6102
Scrivener, Carol   (M1)
746 Willowsprings Boulevard
Franklin, TN 37064
csscriv@juno.com
(731)660-6469   GRWT#9100
Scrudder, Norlan   (M1)
29688 S 534 Road
Park Hill, OK 74451
ndscrudder@gmail.com
(918)949-1326   MSRR#8400
Searcy, James M   (M1)
1307 Lucy Way
Knoxville, TN 37912
gsearcy@earthlink.net
(817)293-6132   GRWT#9100
Seki, Nobuko   (M1)
4-12-42-403 Shimorenjyaku
Mitaka-shi
242-0004 JAPAN
seki@koza-church.jp
(042)248-5379   MSJA#8300
Seva, Judith   (M3)
7685 Tara Circle Apt 204
Naples, FL 34104
jclthgirl12@gmail.com
(239)269-3917   SEGR#0100
Shanley, Dwight   (M1)
16904 Old Mill Road
Little Rock, AR 72206
dwightshanley@att.net
(501)888-4190   GRAR#1100
Shannon, Randy   (M1)
30282 Highway H
Marshall, MO 65340
pastor_randy_shannon@yahoo.com
(660)886-9545   GRMI#4210
Sharpe, Michael G   (M1)
3423 Summerdale Drive
Bartlett, TN 38133
(901)276-4572   MSRR#8400
Shauf, Steve   (M1)
3032 Monroe Street
Paducah, KY 42001
sshauf@hotmail.com

(870)291-2046   MICO#3400
Shauf, Teresa   (M1)
3032 Monroe Street
Paducah, KY 42001
theshaufs@hotmail.com
(870)291-2938   MICO#3400
Shelton, Robert E   (M1)
10508 Royalwood Drive
Dallas, TX 75238
bshelton67@yahoo.com
(214)349-7162   MSRR#8400
Shelton, Robert M   (M1)
7128 Lakehurst Avenue
Dallas, TX 75230
(214)696-3237   MSRR#8400
Shelton, Steven   (M1)
7886 Farmhill Cove
Bartlett, TN 38135
faithcpcpastor@gmail.com
(901)377-0526   GRWT#9308
Shepard, Denny C   (M1)
8514 Newsom Station Road
Nashville, TN 37221
(615)662-1114   TNMU#7209
Shepherd, Sandra   (M1)
525 Summitt Oaks Court
Nashville, TN 37221
woolywagon@gmail.com
(615)772-5358   TNNA#7331
Shin, Kyung I   (M1)
1805 Gallinas Road NE
Rio Rancho, NM 87144
pastorkshin@gmail.com
(505)453-5461   MSDC#8700
Shipley, Howard E   (M1)
3800 Dan Drive
Morristown, TN 37814
hshipley@charter.net
(423)581-1092   SEET#2207
Shirey, John   (M1)
10181 State Route 56 W
Sturgis, KY 42459
amshirey7@ips.com
(270)389-3562   MICO#3400
Shirley, Betty L   (M1)
811 Rotherham Drive
Ballwin, MO 63011
therevbls@prodigy.net
(636)386-3174   MINC#5200
Shoulta, John R   (M1)
1154 Mount Carmel Road
White Plains, KY 42464
johnshoulta@bellsouth.net
(270)676-3563   MICO#3613
Shugert, Rich   (M1)
5208 Bellis Drive
Fort Worth, TX 76244
shugertr@yahoo.com
(817)913-7211   MSRR#8400
Sides, Judy Taylor   (M1)
534 Bethany Circle
Murfreesboro, TN 37128
(615)895-1627   TNMU#7231
Sims, Edward G   (M1)
2161 N Meadow Drive
Clarksville, TN 37043
simseg@aol.com
(931)206-5759   TNNA#7300
Sims, Jacob   (M1)
23716 Alabama Highway 9 N
Piedmont, AL 36272
jacobdsims@gmail.com
(205)907-8273   SEGR#0406
Sims, Joyce   (M2)
5935 Paris Highway 54
Paris, TN 38242

MINISTERS CONTINUED

(731)364-3537   GRWT#9100
Sisco, Terra   (M1)
   1299 Mt Sterling Road
   Brookport, IL 62910
   terrasisco@hotmail.com
   (618)384-6126   MICO#5119
Siu, Jonathan Chor K   (M1)
   251 Tin Sam Estate
   Shatin, HONG KONG
   FAX: (852)2607-2245
   cpccksiu@yahoo.com.hk
   (852)2693-3444   MSHK#8807
Skidmore, Garland   (M1)
   2083 US Highway 278 E
   Hampton, AR 71744
   (870)798-4634   GRAR#1101
Sledge, Jeff   (M1)
   241 Long Bow Road
   Knoxville, TN 37934
   jeffsledge@charter.net
   (865)288-3375   SEET#2319
Small, Kevin   (M1)
   6492 E 400th Road
   Martinsville, IL 62442
   revkev61@gmail.com
   (618)569-4955   MINC#5211
Smith, Albert J   (M1)
   407 W Main Street Apt 131
   Wilkesboro, NC 28697
   ct_alsmith@casscomm.com
   (217)452-3408   MINC#5200
Smith, Billy T   (M1)
   49 Abby Lynn Circle
   Clarksville, TN 37043
   (931)368-0424   TNNA#7300
Smith, Christian   (M1)
   475 State Street
   Cookeville, TN 38501
   csmith2490@gmail.com
   (931)265-8896   SETG#7210
Smith, David R   (M1)
   PO Box 892
   Rosepine, LA 70659
   ogreyfox@att.net
   (903)297-6074   MSTR#8100
Smith, James A   (M1)
   8301 Poplar Pike
   Germantown, TN 38138
   james1493@att.net
   (901)309-1992   GRWT#9100
Smith, James   (M3)
   222 Southcrest Drive SW
   Huntsville, AL 35802
   dr.james.smith@netzero.com
   (256)655-6541   SERD#0800
Smith, Jerald D   (M1)
   2625 Beech Bluff Road
   Beech Bluff, TN 38313
   jergensmith@aol.com
   (731)427-9316   GRWT#9205
Smith, John Adam   (M1)
   916 Allen Road
   Nashville, TN 37214
   john.a.smith.81@gmail.com
   (573)453-8455   TNNA#7305
Smith, Kirk   (M1)
   813 1st Avenue
   Fayetteville, TN 37334
   FAX: (931)438-8649
   kirks37334@att.net
   (931)438-8649   TNCO#7122
Smith, Nicholas   (M2)
   101 Cumberland Street
   Glasgow, KY 42141
   pastornic@gcpchurch.tv
   (270)651-3308   MICU#3108

Smith, Robert A   (M1)
   PO Box 501
   Newbern, TN 38059
   ras1957@bellsouth.net
   (731)627-3332   GRWT#9417
Smith, Robert H   (M1)
   5055 S 76th East Avenue Apt D
   Tulsa, OK 74145
   rhsmith@sstelco.com
   (918)671-5520   MSRR#8400
Smith, Steven   (M3)
   100 Valleyview Drive
   Leitchfield, KY 42754
   (   )   MICU#3201
Smith, Timothy   (M1)
   712 Morningside Drive
   Fayetteville, TN 37334
   FAX: (931)433-0056
   tims38@hotmail.com
   (931)438-2820   TNCO#7112
Smyrl, Jerry   (M1)
   3421 Montreal Street NE
   Albuquerque, NM 87111
   jwsmyrl@hotmail.com
   (505)293-0108   MSDC#8701
Snelling, Linda   (M1)
   15791 State Highway 1W
   Ada, OK 74820
   FAX: (580)332-9424
   lindasnelling@covenantcpc.org
   (580)332-0799   MSRR#6304
Snyder, Joel   (M1)
   224 Lord Lane
   Mountain View, AR 72560
   snyder.joel@ymail.com
   (870)269-9743   GRAR#1504
So, Lai Yuet   (M3)
   2/F Fu Tung Shopping Centre
   Tung Chung
   Lantau Island NT, HONG KONG
   FAX: (852)2109-1737
   laiyuet0914@gmail.com
   (852)2109-1738   MSHK#8800
So, Patrick   (M1)
   2/F Fu Tung Shopping Center
   Tung Chung
   Lantau Island, HONG KONG
   FAX: (852)2109-1737
   pattwso@gmail.com
   (852)2109-1738   MSHK#8810
Solis, Arcadio   (M1)
   Crr 42 D1 No 55-69
   Guapi, COLOMBIA, SA
   (   )328-5486   MSCA#8200
Solito, Carlos   (M3)
   106 Highway 63
   Calera, AL 35040
   fcg9700@gmail.com
   (205)329-8514   SEGR#0100
Song, Byung Seon   (M1)
   (MOVED TO CANADA)
   (404)512-9147   SETG#2100
Song, Nam Hun   (M1)
   (IN KOREA)
   (   )   SETG#2100
Sontowski, Marian   (M1)
   17101 N Western Avenue
   Edmond, OK 73012
   stonegatecpc@gmail.com
   (405)340-7281   MSRR#6307
Sosa, Alexandri   (M1)
   8607 Villa Largo Drive
   Tampa, FL 33613
   FAX: (813)932-9700
   sosapcus@gmail.com
   (813)562-4289   SEGR#0307

Spence, Thomas R   (M1)
   PO Box 809
   Burns Flat, OK 73624
   tomspence0302@gmail.com
   (580)562-4531   MSRR#6301
Spurling, Robert T, Jr   (M1)
   127 Wellington Circle
   Oak Ridge, TN 37830
   (865)803-8582   SEET#2316
Steeley, Tim   (M3)
   PO Box 281
   Mt Vernon, MO 65712
   tsteeley@swr5.k12.mo.us
   (417)466-4345   GRMI#4102
Stefan, Gregory   (M1)
   1917 Birchwood Street
   East Pearl, PA 17519
   pastorstefan@att.net
   (931)296-5291   GRWT#7300
Stephens, Blake   (M1)
   9980 Nashville Highway
   Mc Minnville, TN 37110
   blsteph@edge.net
   (931)939-2628   TNMU#7203
Stephenson, Joseph   (M3)
   PO Box 129
   Bethany, IL 61914
   (217)853-7819   MINC#5200
Stevens, Brittany   (M3
   606 Huntington Parkway
   Nashville, TN 37211
   bstevens5@my.apsu.edu
   (615)719-3362   TNNA#7300
Stone, Paul   (M1)
   3490 State Route 2837
   Clay, KY 42404
   stonepstc@aol.com
   (270)664-6244   MICO#3621
Stovall, Jeff   (M1)
   2829 Trelawny Drive
   Clarksville, TN 37043
   jeffstovall@juno.com
   (931)993-6104   TNNA#7300
Stutler, Tim   (M1)
   1044 Mansker Farm Boulevard
   Hendersonville, TN 37075
   gcpctim@bellsouth.net
   (615)859-5888   TNNA#7328
Suenram, Timothy   (M1)
   5704 Tyler Street
   Pearland, TX 77581
   tsuenram@aol.com
   (832)217-6367   MSTR#8100
Sumerlin, Larkin   (M2)
   174 Brookgreen Lane
   Indian Springs, AL 35124
   larkin_sumerlin72@hotmail.com
   (334)357-0007   SEGR#0100
Sumrall, Phil   (M1)
   107 Barnhardt Circle
   Fort Oglethorpe, GA 30742
   phil.sumrall@gmail.com
   (423)903-1938   SETG#2100
Sung, John   (M2)
   26 Old Orchard Road
   Cherry Hill, NJ 08003
   (856)751-0227   SETG#2100
Suttle, Michael   (M1)
   507 Ouachita 18
   Camden, AR 71701
   m_s_suttle@msn.com
   (870)836-0008   GRAR#1100
Suzuki, Atsushi   (M1)
   53-17 Higashi Kibogaoka
   Asahi-ku Yokohama Kanagawa-ken
   241-0826 JAPAN

MINISTERS CONTINUED

asyuwa98@m10.alpha-net.ne.jp
FAX: (045)362-2603
(045)362-2603   MSJA#8315
Suzuki, Temote   (M2)
    9-14-15-310 Honcho Kamitsuruma
    Sagamihara-shi, Kanagawa-ken
    228-0818 JAPAN
    temo_suzuki@hotmail.com
    ( )   MSJA#8300
Sweet-Brockman, Anna   (M3)
    7225 Old Clinton Pike
    Knoxville, TN 37921
    amsweet@memphisseminary.edu
    (865)803-8582   SEET#2200
Sweet, Don   (M1)
    3008 Shropshire Boulevard
    Powell, TN 37849
    mariondon77@netscape.com
    (865)938-7435   SEET#2200
Sweet, Thomas   (M1)
    2711 Windemere Lane
    Powell, TN 37849
    tsweet1@comcast.net
    (865)938-0508   SEET#2301
Sweigart, John M   (M1)
    PO Box 876
    Dover, AL 72837
    (479)229-4041   GRAR#1100
Sze, Joseph   (M1)
    Rau Sao Joaquim, 382
    Liberdale, Sao Paulo, SP
    CEP 015068-000, BRAZIL
    pastorsze@yahoo.com
    ( )   MSDC#8700

--==<< T >>==--

Tabor, Don M   (M1)
    9611 Mitchell Place
    Brentwood, TN 37027
    FAX: (615)373-3356
    dontabor@comcast.net
    (615)776-7292   TNNA#7300
Taborda, Arturo   (M1)
    Cra 43 #20D-46
    Zamora, Medellin
    Antioquia, COLOMBIA, SA
    chilalu1147@hotmail.com
    (574)267-1351   MSAN#8900
Talley, Edward   (M1)
    404 Serenity Circle
    Walland, TN 37886
    (205)854-1886   SEGR#0405
Talley, James E   (M1)
    203 Browning Place
    Hopkinsville, KY 42240
    (270)886-4184   MICU#3504
Tamai, Yukio   (M1)
    3-17-57 Nakashinden
    Ebina-shi Kanagawa-ken
    243-0422 JAPAN
    yukiotamai@me.com
    (046)234-3426   MSJA#8311
Tan, Pek Hua   (M1)
    7 Belhaven Avenue
    Daly City, CA 94015
    ptan27@yahoo.com
    (415)515-0076   MSDC#8501
Tanck, Brian   (M3)
    64 Mercer Street
    Princeton, NJ 08540
    brian.tanck@gmail.com
    (630)730-1577   SEGR#0100
Terrell, Elizabeth   (M1)
    2073 Vinton Avenue
    Memphis, TN 38104

(901)647-2788   GRAR#1220
Thomas, Cassandra   (M1)
    1920 Dancy Street
    Fayetteville, NC 28301
    chcothomas@yahoo.com
    (910)488-4897   MSRR#8400
Thomas, Don F   (M1)
    400 Park Hill Road
    Collierville, TN 38017
    thomas63981@comcast.net
    (901)861-6398   GRWT#0501
Thomas, Don H   (M1)
    4829 Caldwell Mill Road
    Birmingham, AL 35242
    dhtatn4ybc@cs.com
    (205)742-0785   SEGR#0105
Thomas, Lynn   (M1)
    4833 Caldwell Mill Lane
    Birmingham, AL 35242
    lynndont@gmail.com
    (205)601-5770   SEGR#0100
Thomas, Micaiah   (M2)
    PO Box 5204 SBN 499
    Princeton, NJ 08543
    micaiah.thomas@gmail.com
    (205)478-5985   SEGR#0809
Thompson, Dee Ann   (M1)
    226 W Bellville Street
    Marion, KY 42064
    deethomp5@hotmail.com
    (270)445-0310   MICO#3207
Thompson, Eugene   (M1)
    2825 Albatross Road
    Del Ray Beach, FL 33444
    ( )   MICU#3100
Thompson, Tommy   (M1)
    9160 Tchulahoma Road
    Southaven, MS 38671
    (662)393-2552   GRWT#9100
Thompson, W Fay   (M1)
    210 Macbeth Lane
    Glasgow, KY 42141
    (270)646-2218   MICU#3100
Thornton, Jesse   (M1)
    122 E Cherry Street
    Chandler, IN 47610
    jessthornton@msn.com
    (812)925-6475   MINC#5302
Tobler, Garth   (M1)
    136 Boat Landing Road
    Oneonta, AL 35121
    gatobler@gmail.com
    (205)683-0298   SEGR#0100
Todd, Christopher   (M3)
    139 Roberta Drive
    Memphis, TN 38112
    ctodd21@msn.com
    (901)529-1072   GRWT#9100
Todd, Laura   (M1)
    3303 Decker Street
    Bartlett, TN 38134
    littlelaurarose@yahoo.com
    (901)496-1443   GRWT#9100
Tolley, Robert (Butch)   (M1)
    1445 New Murraytown Road NW
    Cleveland, TN 37312
    butchtolley@hotmail.com
    (423)837-6488   SETG#2100
Tompkins, Wayne   (M1)
    548 E Columbia Road 23
    Emerson, AR 71740
    waynetompkinsministries@yahoo.com
    (870)807-2874   GRWT#9221
Topar, Shirley   (M1)
    2233 Cambridge Drive SE
    Grand Rapids, MI 49506

s_j_topar@yahoo.com
(616)245-0625   MINC#5200
Torres, Rodrigo   (M3)
    Aereo 6365
    Cali, COLOMBIA, SA
    (011)882-8372   MSCA#8205
Travieso, Julio   (M1)
    15910 Countrybrook Street
    Tampa, FL 33624
    jutra98@aol.com
    (813)963-3727   SEGR#0100
Travis, Kermit   (M1)
    3220 Sharon Highway 89
    Dresden, TN 38225
    (731)364-2315   GRWT#9124
Treadaway, Kenneth A   (M1)
    172 Miller County 494
    Texarkana, AR 71854
    treadaways@ark.net
    (870)574-1609   GRAR#1100
Trotter, Wendell   (M1)
    1516 Fell Avenue NE
    Huntsville, AL 35811
    wendelltrotter@knology.net
    (256)519-6571   TNCO#7100
Truax, Robert Lee, Jr   (M1)
    2989 Champions Drive Apt 204
    Lakeland, TN 38002
    (901)266-5927   GRWT#9100
Truitt, Robert D   (M1)
    1238 Old East Side Road
    Burns, TN 37029
    FAX: (615)446-7827
    rdtjct@aol.com
    (615)740-9180   TNNA#7308
Tsui, Jackson   (M2)
    258 Carlos D'Assumpcao
    Ed Kin Heng Long 4 Andar LMN
    Macau
    FAX: (852)2771-2726
    (853)2892-1702   MSHK#8800
Tsujimoto, Mark   (M1)
    88 S Broadway Unit 3210
    Millbrae, CA 94030
    mltsuijimoto@gmail.com
    (650)697-6901   MSDC#8700
Tubb, Gary Robert   (M1)
    103 Forest Drive
    Mountain Home, AR 72653
    grtubb@yahoo.com
    (870)424-0603   GRAR#1505
Tucker, Greg   (M2)
    PO Box 262
    Coker, AL 35452
    cokercpgreg@att.net
    (205)541-7484   SEGR#0705
Tucker, James D   (M1)
    PO Box 34
    Mc Daniels, KY 40152
    (270)257-8971   MICU#3100
Tucker, Paul   (M1)
    3801 Brush Hill Pike
    Nashville, TN 37216
    paultucker@gmail.com
    (615)430-9158   TNNA#7325
Turner, Glyn   (M1)
    1660 Chattanooga Valley Road
    Flintstone, GA 30725
    glynturner@outlook.com
    (585)307-7715   SETG#2100
Turner, O Gene   (M1)
    5160 McSpadden Road
    Rives, TN 38253
    (731)536-0189   GRWT#9100
Turner, Leonard E, Jr   (M1)
    12651 Wagon Wheel Circle

MINISTERS CONTINUED

Knoxville, TN 37934
pastor@unioncpchurch.com
FAX: (865)675-3787
(865)966-8262   SEET#2315
Turner, Steven W   (M1)
7622 Snider Road
Gilmer, TX 75645
FAX: (903)757-2572
fcpclongview@sbcglobal.net
(903)758-5184   MSTR#8112
Turpen, R Brent   (M1)
PO Box 577
Locust Grove, OK 74352
mlturpen@hotmail.com
(918)479-5613   MSRR#6203
Tyus, Dwayne   (M1)
901 W Old Hickory Boulevard
Madison, TN 37115
dwayne.tyus@gmail.com
(615)862-0431   TNNA#7332

--==<< U >>==--

Underwood, Jerrell M   (M1)
PO Box 9
Garfield, KY 40140
(270)536-3706   MICU#3100
Ushioda, Kenji   (M1)
2-47-3 Akuwa-higashi Seya-ku
Yokohama, Kanagawa-ken
246-0023 JAPAN
ushioda@jc.ejnet.ne.jp
(046)361-4351   MSJA#8312

--==<< V >>==--

Vacca, Gary   (M1)
2203 Creekwood Drive
Murray, KY 42071
(270)978-0818   MICO#3406
Valdez, Diana   (M1)
Cra 50 D#62-69
Medellin, Antioquia, COLOMBIA, SA
dianamariavaldezduque@gmail.com
(574)263-2154   MSAN#8915
Valencia, Jorge   (M1)
Aereo 4290
Cali, COLOMBIA, SA
( )332-5840   MSCA#8200
Valencia, Nulbel   (M1)
Diag 11D Casa 11 urbGemelas
Dosquebradas
Risaralda, COLOMBIA, SA
(576)330-7704   MSAN#8900
Van Meter, Bill   (M1)
10626 Highway 41
Charleston, AR 72933
revbill46@gmail.com
(479)965-2998   GRAR#1402
Vance, Dennis   (M1)
1320 Valleywood Drive
Paris, TN 38242
rvdvance@hotmail.com
(731)420-4261   GRWT#9428
Vanderlaan, D Kevin   (M1)
12 Willow Street
Bethany, IL 61914
pastorkevin2@gmail.com
(217)620-2723   MINC#5401
Varilla, Adan Manuel   (M3)
Calle 48 D E #96A-30
Medellin, Antioquia
COLOMBIA, SA   MSAN#8900
Varnell, William   (M3)
6729 Old Dunlop Road
Whitwell, TN 37397

billvatagts@hotmail.com
(423)658-0506   SETG#2100
Varner, Susan   (M1)
1502 Green Mountain Drive Apt 187
Little Rock, AR 72211
smvarner76@yahoo.com
(901)371-1249   TNNA#7300
Vasquez, Alejandro   (M1)
Cra 58 #32A-41 Apt 420
Bello, Antioquia, COLOMBIA, SA
almaesda@une.net.co
(574)451-4816   MSAN#8918
Vasseur, Terry   (M1)
121 Crossland Road
Murray, KY 42071
tvasseur@bellsouth.net
(270)876-8083   MICO#3400
Vaught, Joseph R   (M1)
7424 Highland Lick Road
Lewisburg, KY 42256
brojoe2@logantele.com
(270)726-8497   MICU#3308
Velez, Gabriel   (M1)
CL 8A #16A-26
Dosquebradas
Risaralda, COLOMBIA, SA
(576)330-1168   MSAN#8900
Velez, Gloria Patricia   (M3)
Cra 4 bis #10-51
LaVirginia, Risaralda
COLOMBIA, SA
renewilgen@hotmail.com
(576)385-4517   MSAN#8900
Vick, Joe   (M1)
6064 Old Hickory Boulevard
Whites Creek, TN 37189
joervick@gmail.com
(615)519-5249   TNNA#7318
Vickers, Fran   (M1)
7225 Old Clinton Pike
Knoxville, TN 37921
franv3@comcast.net
(865)859-0805   SEET#2301

--==<< W >>==--

Wada, Ichiro   (M3)
Tokyo Christian University
3-301-5 Uchino Inzai-shi, Chiba
270-1347 JAPAN
ichirowada@gmail.com
(047)646-1141   MSJA#8300
Wagner, Hugh   (M1)
12556 Timberline Drive
Garfield, AR 72732
hughawagner@gmail.com
(479)359-0021   MSRR#8400
Walker, Hobert   (M1)
PO Box 66
Rutherford, TN 38369
rutherfordcpchurch@gmail.com
(731)665-7236   GRWT#9429
Walker, Michael C   (M1)
1404 Wilshire Drive
Odessa, TX 79761
mworator@gmail.com
(731)643-6730   GRWT#9100
Walkup, Lyon   (M1)
225 Bertha Owen Road
Morrison, TN 37357
dirtroad@blomand.net
(931)604-3233   TNMU#7207
Wallace, Andrew   (M1)
816 Howard Avenue
Burlingame, CA 94010
( )   MINC#5200

Wallace, Boyce   (M1)
Cra 101 No 15-93
Cali, COLOMBIA, SA
hbwcali@yahoo.com
( )339-1579   MSCA#8200
Walsh, Devin   (M3)
801 East "M" Street
Russellville, AR 72801
(479)890-6716   GRAR#1100
Wan, Sonny   (M1)
13 Wexford Place
Aladema, CA 94502
sonny@cumberlandsf.org
(415)421-1874   MSDC#8501
Ward, Andrew   (M1)
407 Rose Hill Court
Goodlettsville, TN 37072
andrewbward@aol.com
(615)456-9136   TNNA#7319
Ward, Frank   (M1)
46 Henderson Cove
Atoka, TN 38004
bamaguy68@xipline.com
(901)837-1972   GRWT#9100
Warren, Christopher   (M1)
906 Prince Lane
Murfreesboro, TN 37129
chris@murfreesborocpc.org
(615)828-8719   TNMU#7232
Warren, Elizabeth   (M3)
811 W Wall Street
Morrilton, AR 72110
(501)354-4139   GRAR#1100
Warren, Glenn   (M1)
116 Cedar Hill Drive
Waverly, TN 37185
gwarren224@gmail.com
(931)209-5431   TNNA#7339
Warren, Gordon   (M1)
811 Wall Street
Morrilton, AR 72110
jogordonwarren@suddenlink.net
(501)208-1120   GRAR#1219
Warren, Jo   (M1)
811 Wall Street
Morrilton, AR 72110
pastorjo47@ymail.com
(501)354-4139   GRAR#1211
Warren, Joy   (M1)
907 W Main Street
Murfreesboro, TN 37129
revjoywarren@gmail.com
(615)828-8719   TNMU#7200
Warren, William   (M1)
7139 Toro Cove
Germantown, TN 38138
FAX: (901)759-3653
cpcgww@aol.com
(901)755-8058   GRWT#9310
Washburn, Gloria   (M2)
PO Box 2484
Jordan, AR 72519
grwashburn07@gmail.com
(870)321-4596   GRAR#1100
Watkins, Robert B   (M1)
235 Misty Drive
Somerset, KY 42503
watkr@mac.com
(319)431-0990   MINC#5200
Watson, April   (M1)
529 W Bellville
Marion, KY 42064
aprilwatson@hotmail.com
(270)965-2850   MICO#3418
Watson, Dale   (M1)
1705 Lawnville Road

MINISTERS CONTINUED

Kingston, TN 37763
revdwatson@comcast.net
(865)376-2192 SEET#2317
Watson, Johnny E (M1)
272 Madison Street
Dyer, TN 38330
rev.jwatson@bellsouth.net
(731)692-3555 GRWT#9409
Watson, Jonathan (M1)
PO Box 518
Nolensville, TN 37135
watsonjonathan@bellsouth.net
(615)630-9153 TNCO#7144
Watt, Eva (M3)
258 Carlos D'Assumpcao
Ed Kin Heng Long 4 Andar LMN
MACAU
FAX: (852)2892-1702
eva6e@hotmail.com
(853)2892-1702 MSHK#8804
Watts, Glenn David (M2)
7400 Willowbend Drive
Crestwood, KY 40014
hongkongbrother@hotmail.com
(502)241-0436 MICU#3100
Wayman, Sam (M1)
707 High Hill Creek Road
LaGrange, TX 78945
samndonnawayman@gmail.com
(979)968-3734 MSTR#8100
Weaver, Dennis (M2)
2620 Dalton Road
Providence, KY 42450
dsweaver@memphisseminary.edu
(731)592-9054 MICO#3614
Webb, William G (M1)
7926 S 78th E Avenue
Tulsa, OK 74133
(918)294-9117 MSRR#8400
Welch, Johnie (M1)
PO Box 1506
Dyersburg, TN 38025
johnniewelch@msn.com
(731)287-9008 GRWT#9100
Weldon, Mark (M1)
1515 Chambliss Drive
Birmingham, AL 35226
weldonm@bellsouth.net
(205)330-8580 SEGR#0100
West, David (M1)
2027 Lucille Street
Lebanon, TN 37087
(217)732-7568 TNNA#7340
West, Earl (M1)
246 Maple Avenue
Greensburg, KY 42743
west5010@windstream.net
(207)932-5010 MICU#3116
West, Fred E, Jr (M1)
510 Cedaredge Drive
New Smyrna, FL 32168
jwest616@earthlink.net
(206)409-8321 SEET#2200
Westbrook, James (M1)
1717 Wedgewood Drive
Union City, TN 38261
westbrook731@bellsouth.net
(731)884-0918 GRWT#9100
Westfall, Charles K (M1)
94 Honeysuckle Drive
Gilbertsville, KY 42044
(270)362-0816 MICO#3411
Weston, Robert E (M1)
11 Summer Bluff
San Antonio, TX 78254
rjaweston@gmail.com

(210)347-0232 MSTR#8610
Whaley, Greg (M3)
4970 Comstock Road
Chapel Hill, TN 37034
grewha@mail.com
(931)364-7637 TNMU#7202
Wheelbarger, J J (M2)
PO Box 504
Joelton, TN 37080
jjwheelbarger@aol.com
(615)876-6948 TNNA#7300
Wheeler, Nathan (M1)
1255 Wedgewood Street
Nashville, TN 38111
nathantyac@gmail.com
(901)606-9535 GRWT#9100
Whitaker, Perry Eugene (M1)
235 Sykes Road
Brush Creek, TN 38547
brotherperry@msn.com
(615)631-1844 SERD#0810
White, Charles (M1)
PO Box 44
Galatia, IL 62935
(618)268-4562 MICO#3400
White, Diann (M1)
9394 Alex Dickson Cove
Bartlett, TN 38133
diannwhite12@yahoo.com
(901)377-7776 GRWT#9110
Whitworth, Gary W (M1)
1706 Old Hickory Boulevard
Brentwood, TN 37027
(615)915-4180 TNNA#7300
Whray, Richard "Rocky" (M1)
201 8th Avenue SE
Winchester, TN 37398
rocklex1017@att.net
(931)636-4844 TNMU#7211
Wieland, Jack G Jr (M1)
PO Box 116
Napoleon, MO 64074
jgwieland@hotmail.com
(217)823-4331 GRMI#4100
Wiggins, Joe (M1)
2734 US Highway 41A S
Eagleville, TN 37060
(615)274-2011 TNCO#7109
Wilborn, Kimberley (M3)
4743 Happy Hollow Road
Hawesville, KY 42348
(270)927-9577 MICU#3204
Wilkerson, Patrick (M1)
7719 S Whispering Oak Circle
Powell, TN 37849
patrickwilkerson3@gmail.com
(865)617-9126 MICO#3400
Wilkinson, Michael (M1)
6900 Nubbin Ridge Drive
Knoxville, TN 37919
pastormike@kfcpc.comcastbiz.net
(205)533-2001 SEET#2305
Wilkinson, Neal (M3)
403 Enclave Circle
Nashville, TN 37211
(615)934-7382 TNNA#7300
Williams, Bobby D (M1)
844 W Highway 22
Union City, TN 38261
(731)885-1710 GRWT#9402
Williams, Cory (M1)
3148 Long Bridge Lane
Arlington, TN 38002
coromis@hotmail.com
(901)486-5981 GRWT#9302
Williams, Dale (M1)

3156 State Route 2837
Clay, KY 42404
dalewilliams@roadrunner.com
(270)664-2044 MICO#3618
Williams, David J (M1)
20 Acorn Drive
Harrisburg, IL 629463790
(618)252-1851 MICO#3400
Williamson, Dave (M1)
PO Box 67
Dolph, AR 72528
(870)499-7448 GRAR#1513
Wills, Brent (M1)
4607 E Richmond Shop Road
Lebanon, TN 37090
bwills9185@yahoo.com
(615)449-3258 TNMU#7218
Wilson, Brenda (M1)
35 Collins Drive
Elizabethtown, KY 42701
susieq2007@windstream.net
(270)249-3835 MICU#3211
Wilson, Craig (M1)
2300 Frayser Boulevard
Memphis, TN 38127
craigwilson2300@yahoo.com
(901)277-4066 GRWT#9306
Wilson, Don (M1)
7300 Calle Montana NE
Albuquerque, NM 87113
don-wilson07@comcast.net
(505)823-2594 MSDC#8700
Wilson, Kevin (M1)
2225 North East Road SE
Cleveland, TN 37311
revkev1000@hotmail.com
(423)284-6397 SETG#2112
Wilson, Melissa (M3)
107 Hillwood Drive
Dickson, TN 37055
milzwilz@comcast.net
(615)446-7523 TNNA#7300
Wilson, Thomas (M1)
4543 Lake Vista
Memphis, TN 38128
tomjw217@gmail.com
(901)382-6190 GRWT#9100
Wing So, Patrick Tat (M1)
2/F Fu Tung Shopping Centre
Tung Chung
Lantau Island, HONG KONG
FAX: (852)2109-1737
cpctwso@yahoo.com.hk
(522)109-1738 MSHK#8810
Winn, Don (M1)
375 Cumberland Mountain Circle
Sunbright, TN 37872
dwinn_ky@yahoo.com
(615)478-9910 TNNA#7300
Winslett, Don (M1)
Baptist Hosp/Pastoral Care
1000 W Moreno Street
Pensacola, FL 32521
( ) MSTR#8100
Wolf, Matthew (M3)
1178 S Salt Pond
Marshall, MO 65340
(660)202-3762 GRMI#4100
Womack, Carey (M1)
114 Doris Street
Camden, TN 38320
camdencppastor@bellsouth.net
(731)220-3900 GRWT#9105
Wong, Bruce (M1)
716 Duncanville Court
Campbell, CA 95008

MINISTERS CONTINUED

revbwong@gmail.com
(408)628-1723   MSDC#8700
Wong, Samson   (M2)
CPC Yao Dao Primary School
Tin Yuet Estate
Tin Shui Wai, NT, HONG KONG
FAX: (852)2617-0287
wongchishui@yahoo.com.hk
(852)2617-7872   MSHK#8800
Wong, So Li   (M1)
2/F Fu Tung Shopping Centre
Tung Chung, Lantau Island
HONG KONG
FAX: (852)2109-1737
soliwong@gmail.com
(852)2109-1738   MSHK#8810
Wong, Yim Ngar   (M2)
Wing B&C, G/F, Ming Wik House
Kin Ming Estate
Tseung Kwan O,NT, HONG KONG
FAX: (852)2706-0114
yimngar@yahoo.com.hk
(852)2706-0111   MSHK#8808
Wood, Bennie R   (M1)
3697 S Mount Juliet Road
Hermitage, TN 37076
(615)449-8651   TNMU#7200
Wood, Kevin L   (M1)
339 David Street
McKenzie, TN 38201
FAX: (865)588-8581
revkev7285@earthlink.net
(865)588-8581   GRWT#9100
Wood, Wayne   (M1)
HC 61 Box 600
Calico Rock, AR 72519
FAX: (870)297-3151
bexarwood@centurytel.net
(870)297-2205   GRAR#1100
Woodliff, George   (M1)
310 W Cleveland Street Apt A3
Prairie Grove, AR 72956
mwoodliff@kih.net
(479)410-1933   GRAR#1100
Wooten, Wallace   (M1)
1152 Melrose Road
Lockesburg, AR 71846
(870)289-2224   GRAR#1100
Wright, B J   (M1)
301 25th Street
Phenix City, AL 36867
bojobo3@yahoo.com
(334)298-2896   SETG#2100
Wright, John   (M3)
( )   TNMU#7200
Wright, Tim   (M3)
165 Quaker Knob Road
Chuckey, TN 37641
tdwright1123@yahoo.com
(423)639-0634   SEET#2200

--==<< **X** >>==--

--==<< **Y** >>==--

Yang, Buhwan   (M1)
19 Taylors Run
Tinton Falls, NJ 07712
yangmoksa@gmail.com
(732)458-2203   SECE#2131
Yano, Fumitsuta   (M1)
424-4 Kamide, Fjinomiya-shi
Shuizuika-ken   JAPAN
(054)454-0313   MSJA#8300
Yaple, George H   (M1)

2051 Lost Creek Road
Carbon Hill, AL 35549
(205)924-9921   SEHO#0500
Yarce, Janeth   (M1)
3019 W Calavar Road
Phoenix, AZ 85053
janethyarce@yahoo.com
(630)518-0295   MINC#5200
Yarce, Omar   (M1)
10925 Neptune Drive
Cooper City, FL 33026
alphavida@gmail.com
(205)919-9685   SEGR#0100
Yarce, Virginia   (M3)
10925 Neptune Drive
Cooper City, FL 33026
ginnyyarce@gmail.com
(954)850-7111   SEGR#0100
Yates, Scott   (M1)
8818 New Town Road
Rockvale, TN 37153
scott@scottyates.net
(615)274-3000   TNCO#7141
Yau, Chat Ming   (M2)
G/F 251 Tin Sam Village
Shatin, NT, HONG KONG
FAX: (852)2607-2245
summerycm@yahoo.com.hk
(852)2693-3444   MSHK#8800
Yau, Eliza Yuk Lan Chui   (M2)
14-16 TsatTsz Mui Road
1/Fl Block B North Point
HONG KONG
FAX: (852)2564-2898
elizaylyau@yahoo.com.hk
(852)2562-2148   MSHK#8805
Yeung, William Kin Keung   (M1)
28 Hong Yip Street
Yuen Long, HONG KONG
FAX: (852)263-9562
william@xilincpc.org.hk
(852)2639-9176   MSHK#8809
Yi, Woo Young   (M1)
538 River Chase Trail
Duluth, GA 30096
( )   SETG#2100
Yoo, Paul   (M1)
(IN KOREA)
sungyy@msn.com
( )   SETG#2100
York, Danny   (M1)
5420 State Route 902
Fredonia, KY 42411
nonnieyork@yahoo.com
(270)350-7262   MICO#3413
Young, Taylor   (M2)
255 Willard Drive
Nashville, TN 37211
brandontayloryoung@yahoo.com
(615)319-8294   TNNA#7300
Youngman, Betty   (M1)
1471 Creekview Court
Fort Worth, TX 76112
bettyy@swbell.net
(817)492-4100   MSRR#8400
Yu, Alexis   (M1)
1761 Willow Way
San Bruno, CA 94066
alexis.yu.k@gmail.com
(415)421-1624   MSDC#8501
Yu, Carver Tat Sum   (M1)
2/F Welland Plaza
188 Nam Cheong Street
Sham Shui Po, Kowloon, HONG KONG

FAX: (852)2771-2726
carver.yu@cgst.edu
(852)2794-2382   MSHK#8800
Yu, Grace Siu Tim   (M1)
2/F Welland Plaza
188 Nam Cheong Street
Sham Shui Po, Kowloon, HONG KONG
FAX: (852)2771-2726
yuleungsiutim@netvigator.com
(852)2783-8923   MSHK#8800
Yu, Pyong San (Sonny)   (M1)
139 Silverado Drive
Santa Teresa, NM 88008
pyongsanyu@hotmail.com
(915)329-3451   MSDC#8700
Yu, Wn-yong   (M1)
325-1 DongHyen-Dong
Jecheon-city, Choongbuk, KOREA
lifeyu@hanmail.net
(043)652-0540   SEET#2200
Yuen, Amos Pui Chung   (M1)
2/F Welland Plaza
188 Nam Cheong Street
Sham Shui Po, Kowloon, HONG KONG
FAX: (852)2771-2726
revyuen@taohsien.org.hk
(852)2783-8923   MSHK#8806
Yuen, Susanna   (M2)
28 Hong Yip Street
28 Hong Yip Street
Yuen Long, NT, HONG KONG
FAX: (522)639-5620
susanna@yuenlongcpc.org
(522)639-9176   MSHK#8800
Yung, Karen   (M2)
Flat D, 2/F
338-340 Castle Peak Road
Kowloon, HONG KONG
FAX: (852)3020-0365
(852)2386-6563   MSHK#8800

--==<< **Z** >>==--

Zumbrunnen, Craig   (M1)
1210 Country Club Road Apt 3
Santa Teresa, NM 88008
craigzum1@yahoo.com
(580)471-0308   MSRR#8400

ALPHABETICAL INDEX OF CHURCHES

The four letter abbreviation indicates the synod and presbytery of which the congregation
is a member. The four digit number indicates the church number.
(See pages 10-12 for abbreviations of presbyteries.)

--==<<A>>==--

Alabaster
  AL Alabaster .... SERD#0107
Algood
  TN Algood........................TNMU#7201
Allsboro
  AL Cherokee .... SEHO#0501
Antioch
  AL Reform .... .SEGR#0701
  KY Knob Lick................... MICU#3101
  LA Quitman .... MSTR#8101
Antioch Union
  TN Union City .... GRWT#9401
Appleton
  AR Atkins......................... .GRAR#1202
Arkansas Loving
  AR Little Rock .... GRAR#2135
Arlington
  TN Erin ....TNNA#7311
Armenia
  CO Quindio...................... MSAN#8903
Asahi Mission Point
  JA 241-0021 .... MSJA#8315
Ash Hill
  TN Spring Hill ....TNCO#7101
Atwood
  TN Atwood.......................GRWT#9101
Auburn
  KY Auburn...................... .MICU#3301
Austin, First
  TX Austin..........................MSTR#8601

--==<<B>>==--

Bald Knob
  KY Russellville .... MICU#3302
Baldwin Chapel
  AL Cullman...................... SEHO#0202
Banks
  TN Smithville....................TNMU#7202
Barren Fork
  AR Mount Pleasant .... GRAR#1501
Barren Springs
  TN Hollow Rock...............GRWT#9102
Bartow
  GA Rydal............................SETG#2101
Bates Hill
  TN McMinnville ....TNMU#7203
Bayou de Chien
  KY Water Valley ....MICO#3401
Beaver Creek
  TN Knoxville .... SEET#2301
Beech
  TN Hendersonville........... TNNA#7301
  TN Union City .... GRWT#9402
Beech Grove
  TN Beechgrove ....TNMU#7204
Beersheba
  MS Columbus .... SEGR#0702
Belleview
  TN Franklin.......................TNCO#7104
Bells Chapel
  TN Dyer .... .GRWT#9403
Belvidere
  TN Belvidere....................TNMU#7205

Ben Lomond
  AR Ben Lomond .... GRAR#1301
Benton
  KY Benton .... .MICO#3403
Bertram
  TX Bertram ....MSTR#8605
Betania Mission
  CO Cali .... .MSCA#8204
Bethany
  IL Bethany........................ MINC#5401
Bethel
  CO Cali .... .MSCA#8205
  KY Center .... .MICU#3102
  KY Kevil .... MICO#3404
  MO Wentworth .... GRMI#4102
  TN Atoka..........................GRWT#9301
  TN Clarksville .... TNNA#7302
Bethel #1
  KY Harrodsburg................MICU#3103
Bethesda
  AR Camden...................... .GRAR#1302
  TN Fall Branch...................SEET#2201
  TN Friendship ....GRWT#9404
Bethlehem
  TN Union City .... GRWT#9405
Beulah
  KY Hartford .... MICU#3501
Big Cove
  AL Brownsboro................. SERD#0801
Blues Hill
  TN McMinnville ....TNMU#7207
Boiling Springs
  TN Portland...................... MICU#3303
Bolivar
  TN Bolivar ....GRWT#9202
Booneville
  AR Booneville................... GRAR#1401
Boonshill
  TN Boonshill....................TNCO#7106
Bowling Green
  KY Bowling Green .... MICU#3304
Bradford
  TN Bradford......................GRWT#9104
Branchville
  AL Odenville...................... SEGR#0106
Brenthaven
  TN Brentwood................... TNNA#7331
Bridgeport 1st
  PA Bridgeport....................MICU#3131
Brier Creek
  KY Bremen .... .MICU#3503
Brunswick
  TN Brunswick...................GRWT#9302
Brush Hill
  TN Nashville .... TNNA#7325
Burns Flat
  OK Burns Flat .... MSRR#6301
Burnt Prairie
  IL Burnt Prairie .... MINC#5102
Byron
  AR Calico Rock .... GRAR#1508

--==<<C>>==--

Cairo
  MS Cedarbluff.................... SEGR#0704

Caleb Mission
  CO Montebello.................. MSCA#8223
Calico Rock
  AR Calico Rock .... GRAR#1503
Calvary
  KY Mayfield .... MICO#3405
  TN Clarksville .... TNNA#7342
Camden
  AR Camden...................... GRAR#1303
  TN Camden......................GRWT#9105
Camp Ground
  AR Hampton ....GRAR#1101
  IL Anna .... MICO#5103
  TN Decaturville................GRWT#9204
  TN Erin .... TNNA#7312
Campbellsville
  KY Campbellsville............. MICU#3104
Campground
  IL Greenville .... MINC#5402
Cane Ridge
  TN Cane Ridge.................. TNNA#7326
Caneyville
  KY Caneyville................... MICU#3201
Cartago
  CO Valle...........................MSAN#8906
Casa De Fe
  MA Malden .... SEET#2220
Casey
  IL Casey .... MINC#5201
Casey's Fork
  KY Marrowbone .... MICU#3105
Caulksville
  AR Ratcliff....................... GRAR#1402
Cedar Flat
  KY Edmonton .... MICU#3106
Cedar Hill
  TN Greeneville................. SEET#2202
Cedar Springs
  TN Whitwell .... SETG#2119
Central
  CO Cali .... MSCA#8208
Champ
  TN Mulberry ....TNCO#7108
Chandler
  IN Chandler...................... MICO#5302
Chapel Hill
  TN Chapel Hill...................TNCO#7109
Charleston
  TN Cleveland ....SETG#2102
Charlotte
  TN Charlotte .... TNNA#7303
Chattanooga 1st
  TN Chattanooga ....SETG#2104
Cheung Chau
  HO Cheung Chau..............MSHK#8801
Chinese
  CA San Francisco.............MSDC#8501
Christ
  FL Lutz............................. SEGR#0303
  IN Indianapolis.................. MINC#5305
Christ Church
  AL Huntsville .... SERD#0814
Clark's Grove
  TN Maryville...................... SEET#2302
Clarksville
  TN Clarksville .... TNNA#7304

ALPHABETICAL INDEX OF CHURCHES CONTINUED

Claybrook
TN Jackson........................GRWT#9205
Clear Point
KY Horse Cave ....MICU#3107
Cleveland
TN Cleveland.....................SETG#2108
Clifton Mills
KY Irvington ....MICU#3202
Clinton
OK Clinton........................MSRR#6302
Cloverdale
TN Obion............................GRWT#9407
Cloyd's
TN Mt Juliet.......................TNMU#7208
Coal Creek
OK Coalgate......................MSCH#6102
Coker
AL Coker............................SEGR#0705
Colonial
TN Memphis ....GRWT#9305
Columbia 1st
TN Columbia.....................TNCO#7110
Columbus
MS Columbus ....SEGR#0706
Commerce
TN Watertown....................TNMU#7209
Comunidad Cristiana
IL Dundee ....MINC#5212
Concord
AL New Market ....SERD#0802
TN Trenton.........................GRWT#9106
TN Waverly........................TNNA#7306
TX Troup............................MSTR#8104
Cookeville 1st
TN Cookeville....................TNMU#7210
Cool Springs CC
TN Lavinia.........................GRWT#9107
Cool Springs GC
TN Trimble.........................GRWT#9408
Cornerstone Community
TN Chattanooga.................SETG#2107
Corntassel
TN Madisonville ....SEET#2304
Covenant
OK Ada ....MSRR#6304
Cowan
TN Cowan..........................TNMU#7211
Coyle
KY Hudson ....MICU#3203
Crestline
AL Birmingham ....SEGR#0102
Cristo Vive
TN Madison ....TNNA#7314
Cumberland Chapel
IL Fairfield ....MINC#5104
Cumberland Valley
TN McEwen.......................TNNA#7307

--==<<D>>==--

Daingerfield
TX Daingerfield ....MSTR#8106
Davidson Chapel
TN Trenton.........................GRWT#9108
Den-en Mission
JA 228-0818.......................MSJA#8310
Denton
TX Denton..........................MSRR#8404
Desert Gardens
AZ Tucson..........................MSDC#8705
Dibrell
TN McMinnville ....TNMU#7212

Dickson
TN Dickson ....TNNA#7308
Dilworth
AR Horatio ....GRAR#1304
Divino Redentor
CO Buenaventura...............MSCA#8206
Donelson
TN Nashville ....TNNA#7327
Dosquebradas
CO Risaralda......................MSAN#8907
Double Springs
TN Humboldt ....GRWT#9109
Dover
AR Dover ....GRAR#1203
TN Morristown ....SEET#2203
Dresden
TN Dresden ....GRWT#9110
Dry Fork
TN Bethpage ....TNNA#7309
Dry Valley
TN Cookeville....................TNMU#7213
Dukes
KY Hawesville ....MICU#3204
Dyer
TN Dyer ....GRWT#9409
Dyersburg 1st
TN Dyersburg ....GRWT#9410

--==<<E>>==--

E T Allen
AR Ashdown ....GRAR#1307
East Point
AL Cullman........................SERD#0206
Eastlake
OK Oklahoma City ....MSRR#6205
Ebenezer
IL Chicago.........................MINC#5203
IL Thompsonville..............MICO#5105
TN Mason...........................GRWT#9303
TN Mercer..........................GRWT#9206
TN Whitwell ....SETG#2110
Ebenezer Hall
IL Buncombe......................MICO#5106
Ebina Shion No Oka
JA 243-0422.......................MSJA#8311
Edgefield
AL Stevenson ....SERD#0813
Eidson Chapel
AL Holly Pond ....SERD#0207
El Camino
FL Miami ....SEGR#0310
El Paso 1st
TX El Paso ....MSDC#8704
El Rebano
CO Antioquia ....MSAN#8905
El Redil
GA Lawrenceville ....SETG#2149
Elk Creek
MO West Plains ....GRMI#4304
Elm River
IL Cisne ....MINC#5107
Elmira Chapel
TX Longview ....MSTR#8111
Elora
TN Elora.............................TNCO#7111
Emaus
CO Buenaventura...............MSCA#8219
Enon
MS Ackerman ....SEGR#0707
Ephesus
KY Harned ....MICU#3205

Erin
MS Union...........................SEGR#0601
TN Erin ....TNNA#7310

--==<<F>>==--

Fairfield
IL Fairfield ....MINC#5108
Fairview
KY Bremen ....MICU#3504
TN Afton............................SEET#2204
Faith
AL Cullman........................SEHO#0213
MI St Clair Shores ....MINC#5501
OK Tulsa............................MSRR#6201
TN Bartlett ....GRWT#9308
Faith Fellowship
TN Lenoir City...................SEET#2319
Faith-Hopewell
AR Batesville ....GRAR#1502
Falling Water
TN Hixson..........................SETG#2111
Falls Chapel
AR Lockesburg ....GRAR#1308
Fayetteville
TN Fayetteville...................TNCO#7112
Fellowship
AR Camden........................GRAR#1309
AR Mountain Home..........GRAR#1505
Fiducia
TN Prospect........................TNCO#7113
Filipos
CO Cali ....MSCA#8211
First Hispanic
FL Tampa ....SEGR#0307
Flat Lick
KY Herndon ....MICO#3606
Flint Springs
TN Cleveland.....................SETG#2112
Flintville
TN Flintville......................TNCO#7115
Florence 1st
AL Florence........................SEHO#0506
Fomby
AR Ashdown ....GRAR#1310
Forrest Avenue
AL Gadsden........................SEGR#0403
Fort Smith
AR Fort Smith ....GRAR#1406
Franklin
TN Franklin........................TNCO#7116
Fredonia
KY Fredonia.......................MICO#3608
Freeport
TX Freeport........................MSTR#8103
Freedom
KY Harned ....MICU#3207
Fullerton
IL Farmer City ....MINC#5404
Fulton
TN South Fulton................GRWT#9412

--==<<G>>==--

Gadsden
AL Gadsden........................SEGR#0402
Garfield
KY Garfield........................MICU#3208
Gasper River
KY Auburn.........................MICU#3306
Gass Memorial
TN Greeneville...................SEET#2205

ALPHABETICAL INDEX OF CHURCHES CONTINUED

Georgetown
  IL Georgetown .... MINC#5204
Germantown
  TN Germantown .... GRWT#9310
Getsemani
  CO El Cerrito .... MSCA#8210
Gilead
  IL Simpson .... MICO#5110
Gill's Chapel
  KY Guthrie .... MICU#3307
Glasgow
  KY Glasgow .... MICU#3108
Gleason
  TN Gleason .... GRWT#9111
Glencoe
  AL Glencoe .... SEGR#0404
Glory Church of Jesus Christ
  GA Duluth .... SETG#2144
Good Hope
  KY Campbellsville .... MICU#3109
Good Prospect
  IL Trilla .... MINC#5205
Good Spring
  KY Fredonia .... MICO#3609
  TN Dukedom .... GRWT#9112
Goodlettsville
  TN Goodlettsville .... TNNA#7328
Goosepond
  AL Scottsboro .... SERD#0803
Goshen
  TN Winchester .... TNMU#7214
Grace
  AR Fayetteville .... GRAR#1405
  CA San Francisco .... MSDC#8510
  MI Lincoln Park .... MINC#5502
  TN Franklin .... TNCO#7145
Grace Community
  AL Millbrook .... SEGR#0407
Green Hill
  TN Bell Buckle .... TNCO#7118
Green Ridge
  KY Lewisburg .... MICU#3308
Greeneville
  TN Greeneville .... SEET#2206
Greenfield
  MO Greenfield .... GRMI#4104
Greens Chapel
  AL Cleveland .... SEGR#0208
Greensburg
  KY Greensburg .... MICU#3110
Greenville
  KY Greenville .... MICU#3505
Groverton
  MS Morton .... SEGR#0602
Gum Creek
  TN Winchester .... TNMU#7215
Gum Springs
  AR Dardanelle .... GRAR#1206
  AR Searcy .... GRAR#1205
Gurley
  AL Gurley .... SERD#0804

--=<<H>>=--

Halls Creek
  TN Waverly .... TNNA#7313
Happy Home
  MO Conway .... GRMI#4306
Harmony
  MO San Antonio .... GRMI#4203
  TN Winchester .... TNMU#7216
Harpeth Lick

TN College Grove .... TNCO#7119
Harrodsburg
  KY Harrodsburg .... MICU#3111
Heartland
  Lenoir City .... SEET#2306
Heartsong
  KY Louisville .... MICU#3222
Hector
  AR Hector .... GRAR#1207
Heights
  NM Albuquerque .... MSDC#8701
Helena
  AL Helena .... SEGR#0108
Hendersonville
  TN Hendersonville .... TNNA#7340
Hickory Grove
  AL Moulton .... SEHO#0507
Hickory Valley
  TN Sparta .... TNMU#7251
Higashi Koganei
  JA 184-0011 .... MSJA#8301
High Point Community
  KY West Somerset .... MICU#3314
Highland
  KY Paducah .... MICO#3414
Hillsboro
  TN Hillsboro .... TNMU#7217
Hohenwald
  TN Hohenwald .... TNCO#7120
Holly Grove
  AL Princeton .... SERD#0805
  TN Brighton .... GRWT#9304
Homewood
  AL Homewood .... SEGR#0111
Hope
  AL Huntsville .... SERD#0812
  FL Valrico .... SEGR#0308
Hope Korean
  NJ Tinton Falls .... SECE#2131
Hopewell
  AL Bessemer .... SEGR#0101
  KY Canmer .... MICU#3112
  KY Salem .... MICO#3610
  MS Walnut .... GRWT#9207
  MO Lamar .... GRMI#4105
  TN Sharon .... GRWT#9115
Hopkinsville
  KY Hopkinsville .... MICU#3611
Horeb-Central
  CO Antioquia .... MSAN#8915
House of Prayer
  AL Cullman .... SEGR#0214
Houston 1st
  TX Houston .... MSTR#8606
Howell
  TN Fayetteville .... TNCO#7121
Hubbard
  TX Hubbard .... MSRR#8410
Hueytown 1st
  AL Hueytown .... SEGR#0109
Humboldt
  TN Humboldt .... GRWT#9116
Huntsville 1st
  AL Huntsville .... SERD#0806
Hurricane
  AL Rogersville .... SEHO#0508
Hurricane Hill
  TN Newburn .... GRWT#9413

--=<<I>>=--

Ichikawa Grace Mission Point

JA 272-0834 .... MSJA#8314
Immanuel
  FL Dade City .... SEGR#0311
Irvington
  KY Irvington .... MICU#3210
Izumi Mission
  JA 245-0016 .... MSJA#8312

--=<<J>>=--

Jackson 1st
  TN Jackson .... GRWT#9208
Jasper
  TN Jasper .... SETG#2113
Jefferson
  TX Jefferson .... MSTR#8109
Jenkins
  TN Nolensville .... TNCO#7144
Jerusalem
  TN Murfreesboro .... TNMU#7218
Joywood
  TN Murfreesboro .... TNMU#7250

--=<<K>>=--

Kelly's Chapel
  TN Whitwell .... SETG#2120
Kelso
  TN Kelso .... TNCO#7122
Kenton
  TN Kenton .... GRWT#9414
Kibougaoka
  JA 241-0825 .... MSJA#8302
Kingdom
  TN Unionville .... TNCO#7123
Knights Chapel
  IN Petersburg .... MINC#5306
Knoxville
  TN Knoxville .... SEET#2305
Korea 1st
  KO South Korea .... SEET#2221
Korean
  TN Cordova .... GRWT#9322
Korean Living Stone
  GA Duluth .... SETG#2130
Kowloon
  HO Kowloon .... MSHK#8803
Koza
  JA 242-0006 .... MSJA#8303
Kunitachi Nozomi
  JA 186-0002 .... MSJA#8306

--=<<L>>=--

La Rosa De Saron
  CO Antioquia .... MSAN#8911
La Virginia
  CO Risaralda .... MSAN#8913
LaGuardo
  TN Lebanon .... TNMU#7219
Lake Hamilton
  AR Hot Springs .... GRAR#1221
Lake Highlands
  TX Dallas .... MSRR#8411
Lawrenceburg
  TN Lawrenceburg .... TNCO#7124
Lebanon
  TN Jefferson City .... SEET#2207
  TN Lebanon .... TNMU#7220
Lebanon North
  IL Fairfield .... MINC#5113
Lebanon South

IL Galatia .... MINC#5114
Leitchfield
    KY Leitchfield................... MICU#3211
Lewisburg
    KY Lewisburg.................... MICU#3309
Lewisburg 1st
    TN Lewisburg ....TNCO#7125
Lexington 1st
    TN Lexington....................GRWT#9209
Liberty
    KY Campbellsville............. MICU#3116
    KY Murray........................MICO#3406
    TN Clarksville.................. TNNA#7315
    TN McMinnville .... TNMU#7222
Lick Branch
    KY Glasgow...................... MICU#3117
Lincoln 1st
    IL Lincoln .... MINC#5405
Lisman
    KY Clay .... MICO#3613
Little Muddy
    KY Morgantown .... MICU#3310
Livingston 1st
    TN Livingston...................TNMU#7223
Lobb
    MO Independence............. GRMI#4209
Lockesburg
    AR Lockesburg ....GRAR#1311
Locust Grove
    OK Locust Grove............. MSRR#6203
    TN Cunningham................ TNNA#7316
Lone Star
    OK Coalgate.....................MSCH#6105
Longview 1st
    TX Longview ....MSTR#8112
Loudon
    TN Loudon........................ SEET#2307
Louisville 1st
    KY Louisville.................... MICU#3212
Lubbock
    TX Lubbock .... MSDC#8702
LuzD.L.Naciones
    TN McMinnville .... TNMU#7252

--=<<M>>=--

Macau
    MA Andar LMN................MSHK#8804
Macedonia
    KY Dalton......................... MICO#3614
Madison 1st
    TN Madison .... TNNA#7329
Madisonville
    KY Madisonville............... MICO#3615
Magnolia
    KY Magnolia..................... MICU#3214
Manchester
    TN Manchester.................TNMU#7224
Mangum
    OK Mangum .... MSRR#6306
Manizales
    CO Caldas........................MSAN#8914
Mansfield
    MO Mansfield.................... GRMI#4308
Maple Springs
    TN Beech Bluff.................GRWT#9210
Maranatha
    CO Guapi .... MSCA#8220
    TX San Elizario................ MSDC#8706
Margaret Hank
    KY Paducah .... MICO#3415
Mariah

TN Waverly........................ TNNA#7317
Marietta
    AR Charleston................... GRAR#1408
    TN Knoxville .... SEET#2308
Marion 1st
    KY Marion .... MICO#3616
Marlow
    OK Marlow .... MSRR#6305
Mars Hill
    AR Pottsville ....GRAR#1211
Marshall
    MO Marshall..................... GRMI#4210
    TX Marshall ....MSTR#8115
Martin
    TN Martin .... GRWT#9117
Maryville 1st
    TN Maryville..................... SEET#2309
Mason Hall
    TN Kenton........................GRWT#9415
Mata de Sao Joao
    BR Bahia........................... MSJA#8313
Maud
    AL Cherokee .... SEHO#0509
McAdoo
    TN Clarksville.................. TNNA#7318
McCains
    TN Columbia.....................TNCO#7126
McGee Chapel
    OK Broken Bow .... MSCH#6106
McKenzie
    TN McKenzie....................GRWT#9118
McLeod Chapel
    MS Macon......................... SEGR#0708
McMinnville
    TN McMinnville .... TNMU#7225
Medina
    TN Medina .... GRWT#9119
Megumi
    JA 207-0023 .... MSJA#8309
Mercy
    TN Lenoir City.................. SEET#2320
Meridian
    TN Greenfield .... GRWT#9120
Meridianville
    AL Meridianville............... SERD#0808
Mesquite
    TX Mesquite .... MSRR#8412
Milan
    TN Milan...........................GRWT#9121
Milburn Chapel
    KY West Paducah.............. MICO#3416
Mill Creek
    TN Puryear........................GRWT#9122
Mohawk
    TN Mohawk .... SEET#2208
Monroe Chapel
    KY Hardyville................... MICU#3119
Monroe City
    IN Monroe City................. MINC#5307
Monteagle
    TN Monteagle ....TNMU#7227
Montrose
    MO Montrose.................... GRMI#4107
Morella
    TN Kenton........................GRWT#9416
Morgantown
    KY Morgantown .... MICU#3311
Morning Sun
    TN Cordova.......................GRWT#9314
Morningside
    IN Evansville .... MINC#5304
Mt Ararat

TN Union City .... GRWT#9417
Mt Carmel
    AR London........................ GRAR#1212
    KY White Plains .... MICO#3617
    TN Franklin......................TNCO#7127
    TN Huntland .... TNMU#7228
    TN Oliver Springs............. SEET#2310
    TN Somerville................... GRWT#9315
Mt Denson
    TN Springfield.................. TNNA#7319
Mt Gilead
    IL Greenville .... MINC#5406
Mt Hebron
    TN Fayetteville ....TNCO#7128
Mt Hermon
    TN Cookeville...................TNMU#7229
Mt Hester
    AL Cherokee .... SEHO#0510
Mt Hope
    TX Joinerville ....MSTR#8117
Mt Joy
    TN Mount Pleasant ....TNCO#7129
Mt Lebanon
    TN Spring Hill ....TNCO#7130
Mt Liberty
    TN Charlotte .... TNNA#7320
Mt Moriah
    KY Summer Shade............. MICU#3120
    TN Pulaski........................TNCO#7131
Mt Nebo
    TN Iron City......................TNCO#7132
Mt Olive
    AR Melbourne................... GRAR#1517
    KY Big Clifty.................... MICU#3216
    TN Dyer ....GRWT#9418
Mt Olivet
    IN Washington .... MINC#5308
    KY Bowling Green .... MICU#3312
Mt Oval
    IL Norris City................... MINC#5116
Mt Pleasant
    AL Muscle Shoals .... SEHO#0511
    KY Caneyville................... MICU#3217
    KY Sullivan...................... MICO#3618
    TN Afton .... SEET#2209
    TN Mount Pleasant ....TNCO#7133
Mt Sharon
    TN Greenbrier .... TNNA#7321
Mt Sinai
    TN Nashville .... TNNA#7330
Mt Sterling
    IL Brookport .... MICO#5117
Mt Tabor
    TN Murfreesboro .... TNMU#7230
Mt Vernon
    KY Leitchfield................... MICU#3218
    TN Ramer..........................GRWT#9213
    TN Rockvale .... TNMU#7231
Mt View
    TN Dover .... TNNA#7322
Mt Zion
    IL Dongola .... MICO#5118
    KY Glens Fork .... MICU#3121
    KY Philpot .... MICU#3507
    MS Columbus .... SEGR#0709
    MS Falkner....................... GRWT#9214
    TX Greenville .... MSRR#8414
Mu Min
    HO Landau Island............. MSHK#8810
Murfreesboro
    TN Murfreesboro .... TNMU#7232

ALPHABETICAL INDEX OF CHURCHES CONTINUED

--==<<N>>==--

Naruse
   JA 194-0041 .... MSJA#8305
Neal's Chapel
   KY Glasgow....................... MICU#3122
Nebo
   AL Lexington .... SEHO#0512
Needham
   KY Eastview .... MICU#3219
New Beginnings
   TN Memphis .... GRWT#9306
New Bethel
   TN Columbia..................... TNCO#7134
   TN Greeneville.................. SEET#2210
   TN Selmer........................ GRWT#9215
New Bethlehem
   TN Newbern..................... GRWT#9420
New Cypress
   KY Rumsey....................... MICU#3508
New Ebenezer
   TN Troy............................. GRWT#9422
New Hope
   AL Birmingham .... SEGR#0104
   AR Batesville .... GRAR#1510
   IL Yale............................. MINC#5208
   KY Paducah .... MICO#3410
   MO Salem .... GRMI#4309
   TN Lebanon .... TNMU#7233
   TN Madisonville .... SEET#2311
   TN Stewart .... TNNA#7337
   TN Whitwell .... SETG#2115
New Providence
   TN Clarksville.................. TNNA#7305
New Salem
   TN Bethel Springs............. GRWT#9216
   TN Lakeland .... GRWT#9316
   TN Sharon....................... GRWT#9124
Newbern
   TN Newbern..................... GRWT#9419
Newberry
   TX Millsap .... MSRR#8415
North Pleasant Grove
   KY Murray .... MICO#3411
North Point
   HO North Point................. MSHK#8805
North Union
   TN Kenton....................... GRWT#9423
Northminster
   TX San Antonio .... MSTR#8610
Nueva Esperanza
   CO Cali .... MSCA#8221
Nueva Jerusalen
   CO Cali .... MSCA#8222
Nueva Vida
   TX Houston...................... MSTR#8612
Nuevo Empezar.................... GRWT#9324
   TN Memphis

--==<<O>>==--

Oak Forest
   KY Summersville............... MICU#3123
Oak Grove
   KY Benton .... MICO#3412
   MO Springfield .... GRMI#4310
   TN Henderson.................. GRWT#9217
   TN Whitwell .... SETG#2121
   TX Georgetown................. MSTR#8607
Oak Grove Union
   KY Clay .... MICO#3619
Oak Hill

TN Paris .... GRWT#9125
Oak Ridge
   TN Oak Ridge .... SEET#2313
Oakland
   KY Calvert City .... MICO#3413
   TN Telford........................ SEET#2211
Old Mt Bethel
   AL Rogersville .... SEHO#0513
Old Union
   AR Magazine .... GRAR#1409
Old Zion
   TN Sparta........................ TNMU#7234
Oldham Chapel
   AL Ashville .... SEGR#0405
Olive Branch
   MS Olive Branch .... GRWT#9312
Oliver Springs
   TN Oliver Springs............. SEET#2314
Oliver's Chapel
   TN Bradford..................... GRWT#9127
Olivet
   TN Savannah.................... GRWT#9220
Olney
   TX Olney.......................... MSRR#8416
One Way
   NY Flushing..................... SECE#2137
Orange
   MO Aurora....................... GRMI#4108
Our Good
   MD Salisbury................... SETG#2138
Owens Chapel
   TN Winchester .... TNMU#7235
Owensboro
   KY Owensboro .... MICU#3509
Oxford
   AR Oxford........................ GRAR#1511

--==<<P>>==--

Palestine
   AR Palestine..................... GRAR#1103
   TN Lexington................... GRWT#9221
   TN Newbern..................... GRWT#9424
Panki Bok
   OK Eagletown.................. MSCH#6108
Park Terrace
   AL Sheffield .... SEHO#0514
Parsons 1st
   TN Parsons...................... GRWT#9222
Pathway
   TX Burleson..................... MSRR#8418
Pereira
   CO Risaralda................... MSAN#8916
Petersburg
   TN Petersburg .... TNCO#7135
Philadelphia
   TN Limestone .... SEET#2212
Phillipsburg
   MO Phillipsburg............... GRMI#4311
Piedmont
   AL Piedmont .... SEGR#0406
Pierson
   MO Martinville .... GRMI#4312
Pigeon Roost
   OK Atoka .... MSCH#6109
Pilot Knob
   TN Bulls Gap .... SEET#2213
Pine Bluff 1st
   AR Pine Bluff................... GRAR#1104
Pine Hill
   TN McDonald .... SETG#2117
   TX Winnsboro.................. MSTR#8122

Pine Ridge
   AR Grapevine................... GRAR#1105
Pine Tree
   TX Longview .... MSTR#8113
Pineville
   AR Pineville..................... GRAR#1512
Piney Fork
   KY Marion .... MICO#3620
Pleasant Green
   TN Atwood...................... GRWT#9129
Pleasant Grove
   AR Searcy .... GRAR#1214
   IL Annapolis.................... MINC#5210
   MO Knob Noster.............. GRMI#4109
   TN Moscow...................... GRWT#9317
Pleasant Hill
   AL Bessember .... SEGR#0710
   KY Owensboro .... MICU#3510
   TN Chuckey .... SEET#2214
Pleasant Mount
   TN Columbia.................... TNCO#7136
Pleasant Union
   TN Millington .... GRWT#9318
Pleasant Vale
   TN Chuckey .... SEET#2215
Pleasant Valley
   KY Kevil .... MICO#3418
Po Lam
   HO Tseung Kwan O,NT.... MSHK#8808
Point Pleasant
   KY Beaver Dam................ MICU#3313
Popayan
   CO Popayan .... MSCA#8227
Poplar Grove
   KY Sacramento .... MICU#3511
   TN Halls.......................... GRWT#9425
Principe De Paz
   CO Cali .... MSCA#8201
Progress
   LA Pleasant Hill................ MSTR#8123
Prospect United
   TN Cleveland .... SETG#2116
Protemus
   TN Troy........................... GRWT#9426
Providence
   IL Carriers Mills............... MICO#5122
   TN Hartsville................... TNMU#7238
Providence 1st
   KY Providence................. MICO#3621

--==<<Q>>==--

--==<<R>>==--

Radcliff
   KY Radcliff...................... MICU#3220
Ramer
   TN Ramer........................ GRWT#9223
Red Bank
   TN Chattanooga................ SETG#2105
Redeemer
   CA San Francisco.............. MSDC#8512
Renacer
   CO Cali .... MSCA#8225
Richard City
   TN South Pittsburg............. SETG#2118
Richland
   TN Lewisburg .... TNCO#7137
Roca De Salvacion
   AL Birmingham .... SEGR#0115
Rock Creek
   OK Honobia..................... MSCH#6111

ALPHABETICAL INDEX OF CHURCHES CONTINUED

Rockvale
    TN Rockvale ....TNMU#7239
Rocky Glade
    TN Eagleville ....TNMU#7240
Rocky Ridge
    AL Birmingham .... SEGR#0105
Rodney
    AR Jordan........................... GRAR#1513
Roellen
    TN Dyersburg ....GRWT#9428
Rogersville 1st
    AL Rogersville ....SEHO#0517
Rose Creek
    KY Nebo ....MICO#3622
Rose Hill
    AR Monticello....................GRAR#1106
Round Lake
    OK Tupelo..........................MSCH#6112
Round Rock
    TX Round Rock ....MSTR#8611
Rozzell Chapel
    KY Mayfield ....MICO#3419
Russellville
    AR Russellville .... GRAR#1216
Ruth Chapel
    TN Livingston...................TNMU#7241
Rutherford
    TN Rutherford...................GRWT#9429

--==<<S>>==--

Sacramento
    KY Sacramento ....MICU#3512
Sagamino
    JA 228-0004 .... MSJA#8304
Salem
    AR Salem .... GRAR#1514
    KY Greensburg .... MICU#3127
    MS Walnut Grove .... SEGR#0607
    MO Warrensburg...............GRMI#4216
    TN Gadsden ....GRWT#9430
    TN Greeneville...................SEET#2216
Samaria
    CO Cali ....MSCA#8217
San Lucas
    CO Palmira.......................MSCA#8215
San Marcos
    CO Cali ....MSCA#8218
San Pablo
    CO Guacari ....MSCA#8212
Sandy Springs
    TX Whitesboro..................MSRR#8420
Santa Fe
    TN Santa Fe ....TNCO#7138
Savannah 1st
    TN Savannah.....................GRWT#9224
Scottsboro
    AL Scottsboro .... SERD#0809
Searcy
    AR Searcy .... GRAR#1218
Selmer Court Avenue
    TN Selmer.........................GRWT#9225
Seven Springs
    KY Center ....MICU#3128
Sewanee
    TN Sewanee ....TNMU#7242
Seymour
    MO Seymour.....................GRMI#4313
Sharing
    NY Flushing......................SECE#2141
Sharon

TN Sharon.........................GRWT#9130
Shatin
    HO Shatin NT ....MSHK#8807
Shaver
    AR Paris .... GRAR#1413
Shawnee Mound
    MO Chilhowee...................GRMI#4111
Shell Chapel
    AR Pine Bluff....................GRAR#1108
Shepherd/Hills
    TX Austin...........................MSTR#8604
Sherwood
    AR Sherwood .... GRAR#1220
Shibusawa
    JA 259-1321 .... MSJA#8307
Shiloh
    IL Virginia .... MINC#5409
    KY Campbellsville............. MICU#3129
    MS Corinth........................GRWT#9226
    TN Greeneville ....SEET#2217
    TN McKenzie.....................GRWT#9131
    TN Palmyra .... TNNA#7338
    TX Clarksville...................MSTR#8125
    TX Midlothian...................MSRR#8421
Shinar
    IA New London.................MINC#5410
Short Creek
    KY Falls of Rough .... MICU#3221
Sidney
    AR Batesville .... GRAR#1515
Silverdale
    TN Chattanooga ....SETG#2106
Smithville
    TN Smithville....................TNMU#7243
South Pittsburg
    TN South Pittsburg.............SETG#2123
Spring Creek
    AL Montevallo .... SEGR#0113
    MO Dunnegan...................GRMI#4113
Spring Hill
    IL Beecher City .... MINC#5411
Springfield
    AL Rogersville ....SEHO#0515
Springfield 1st
    MO Springfield .... GRMI#4314
St Andrew
    TX Odessa.........................MSDC#8703
St John
    TX Arlington..................... MSRR#8413
St Luke
    TN Madison .... TNNA#7332
    TX Fort Worth................... MSRR#8407
St Mark
    TX Fort Worth.................. MSRR#8408
St Timothy
    TX Bedford .... MSRR#8419
Steam Mill
    MS Union.......................... SEGR#0608
Stevenson
    AL Stevenson .... SERD#0810
Stonegate
    OK Edmond .... MSRR#6307
Stone Oak
    TX San Antonio ....MSTR#8608
Sturgis
    KY Sturgis.........................MICO#3625
Sudanese
    TN Gallatin .... TNNA#7341
Sugar Grove
    KY Marion ....MICO#3626
Suggs Creek

TN Mount Juliet................TNMU#7244
Sulphur Springs
    AR Louann .... GRAR#1315
Sumach
    GA Chatsworth...................SETG#2124
Sumkim Presby
    KO Seoul...........................SEET#2222
Swan
    TN Centerville...................TNCO#7140

--==<<T>>==--

Talbott
    TN Talbott ....SEET#2218
Tao Hsien
    HO Kowloon.....................MSHK#8806
The Connection
    TN Nashville .... TNNA#7335
Trezevant
    TN Trezevant.....................GRWT#9132
Trimble
    TN Trimble........................GRWT#9431
Trimble Camp Ground
    AR Dolph .... GRAR#1504
Trinity
    AR Morrilton..................... GRAR#1219
    TX Fort Worth...................MSRR#8409
Trona
    CA Trona...........................MSDC#8503
Troy
    TN Troy.............................GRWT#9432
Tulua Mission
    CO Tulua ....MSCA#8226
Tusculum
    TN Nashville .... TNNA#7333

--==<<U>>==--

Union
    AL Vance........................... SEGR#0114
    TN Knoxville ....SEET#2315
Union Chapel
    IL Galatia ....MICO#5123
Union City
    TN Union City ....GRWT#9433
Union Grove
    AL Holly Pond .... SERD#0211
    TN Columbia.....................TNCO#7141
Union Hill
    AL Anderson ....SEHO#0516
    TN Brush Creek ....TNMU#7246
Union North
    IL Fairfield ....MINC#5124
United
    IL Norris City...................MINC#5119
Unity
    KY Hardin.........................MICO#3422

--==<<V>>==--

Vaughn's Chapel
    KY Calvert City ....MICO#3423
Village
    IL Norris City...................MICO#5125
Virtue
    TN Knoxville ....SEET#2316

--==<<W>>==--

Walkerville
    AR Magnolia..................... GRAR#1317

ALPHABETICAL INDEX OF CHURCHES CONTINUED

Walnut Grove
  AL New Hope .... SERD#0811
  AR Magazine .... GRAR#1414
  TN Burlison...................... GRWT#9320
Warrensburg
  MO Warrensburg............... GRMI#4115
Watertown
  TN Watertown.................. TNMU#7247
Waverly
  TN Waverly .... TNNA#7339
Waynesboro
  TN Waynesboro .... TNCO#7142
Welti
  AL Cullman....................... SEHO#0212
West Nashville
  TN Nashville .... TNNA#7334
West Point
  TN Columbia.................... TNCO#7143
West Union
  TN Millington .... GRWT#9321
Westside
  NM Rio Rancho .... MSDC#8709
Wheatcroft
  KY Wheatcroft.................. MICO#3627
White Oak Pond
  MO Lebanon .... GRMI#4315
Whitney
  TX Whitney...................... MSRR#8424
Whitwell
  TN Whitwell .... SETG#2122
Willoughby
  TN Bulls Gap .... SEET#2219
Willow Creek
  IL Martinsville .... MINC#5211
Winchester 1st
  TN Winchester .... TNMU#7249
Wisdom
  KY Knob Lick................... MICU#3130
Woodlawn
  KY Paducah .... MICO#3417
Woodward's Chapel
  TN Obion .... GRWT#9434

--==<<X>>==--

Xi Lin
  HO Yuen Long .... MSHK#8809

--==<<Y>>==--

Yao Dao
  HO NT.............................. MSHK#8811
Yorkville
  TN Yorkville..................... GRWT#9435
Young's Chapel
  TN Kingston...................... SEET#2317

--==<<Z>>==--

Zamora
  CO Antioquia .... MSAN#8918
Zion
  TN McKenzie................... GRWT#9133
Zion Valley
  TX Chico.......................... MSRR#8425

LOCATION INDEX OF CHURCHES

The four letter abbreviation indicates the synod and presbytery of which the congregation
is a member. The four digit number indicates the church number.
(See pages 10-13 for abbreviations of presbyteries.)

ALABAMA

AL Alabaster
Alabaster .... SERD#0107
AL Anderson
Union Hill .... SEHO#0516
AL Ashville
Oldham Chapel .... SEGR#0405
AL Bessemer
Hopewell........................ SEGR#0101
Pleasant Hill .... SEGR#0710
AL Birmingham
Crestline........................ SEGR#0102
New Hope .... SEGR#0104
Roca De Salvacion......... SEGR#0115
Rocky Ridge................... SEGR#0105
AL Brownsboro
Big Cove .... SERD#0801
AL Cherokee
Allsboro......................... SEHO#0501
Maud .... SEHO#0509
Mt. Hester .... SEHO#0510
AL Cleveland
Greens Chapel................ SEGR#0208
AL Coker
Coker............................. SEGR#0705
AL Cullman
Baldwin Chapel.............. SEHO#0202
East Point .... SERD#0206
Faith .... SEHO#0213
House of Prayer.............. SEGR#0214
Welti.............................. SEHO#0212
AL Florence
Florence 1st................... SEHO#0506
AL Gadsden
Gadsden......................... SEGR#0402
Forrest Avenue .... SEGR#0403
AL Glencoe
Glencoe .... SEGR#0404
AL Gurley
Gurley .... SERD#0804
AL Helena
Helena .... SEGR#0108
AL Holly Pond
Eidson Chapel .... SERD#0207
Union Grove.................. SERD#0211
AL Homewood
Homewood.....................SEGR#0111
AL Hueytown
Hueytown 1st .... SEGR#0109
AL Huntsville
Christ Church................ SERD#0814
Hope.............................. SERD#0812
Huntsville 1st .... SERD#0806
AL Lexington
Nebo.............................. SEHO#0512
AL Meridianville
Meridianville................. SERD#0808
AL Millbrook
Grace Community .... SEGR#0407
AL Montevallo
Spring Creek .... SEGR#0113
AL Moulton
Hickory Grove .... SEHO#0507
AL Muscle Shoals
Mt. Pleasant................... SEHO#0511
AL New Hope
Walnut Grove .... SERD#0811

AL New Market
Concord.......................... SERD#0802
AL Odenville
Branchville..................... SEGR#0106
AL Piedmont
Piedmont .... SEGR#0406
AL Princeton
Holly Grove .... SERD#0805
AL Reform
Antioch.......................... SEGR#0701
AL Rogersville
Hurricane....................... SEHO#0508
Old Mt Bethel .... SEHO#0513
Rogersville 1st .... SEHO#0517
Springfield..................... SEHO#0515
AL Scottsboro
Goosepond .... SERD#0803
Scottsboro .... SERD#0809
AL Sheffield
Park Terrace .... SEHO#0514
AL Stevenson
Edgefield .... SERD#0813
Stevenson .... SERD#0810
AL Vance
Union.............................. SEGR#0114

ARIZONA

AZ Tucson
Desert Gardens............... MIDC#8705

ARKANSAS

AR Ashdown
E T Allen .... GRAR#1307
Fomby .... GRAR#1310
AR Atkins
Appleton........................ GRAR#1202
AR Batesville
Faith-Hopewell .... GRAR#1502
New Hope .... GRAR#1510
Sidney .... GRAR#1515
AR Ben Lomond
Ben Lomond................... GRAR#1301
AR Booneville
Booneville..................... GRAR#1401
AR Calico Rock
Byron............................. GRAR#1508
Calico Rock................... GRAR#1503
AR Camden
Bethesda........................ GRAR#1302
Camden .... GRAR#1303
Fellowship..................... GRAR#1309
AR Charleston
Marietta......................... GRAR#1408
AR Dardanelle
Gum Springs .... GRAR#1206
AR Dolph
Trimble Camp Ground.. GRAR#1504
AR Dover
Dover............................. GRAR#1203
AR Fayetteville
Grace............................. GRAR#1405
AR Fort Smith
Fort Smith .... GRAR#1406
AR Grapevine
Pine Ridge..................... GRAR#1105
AR Hampton

Camp Ground................. GRAR#1101
AR Hector
Hector............................ GRAR#1207
AR Horatio
Dilworth .... GRAR#1304
AR Hot Springs
Lake Hamilton .... GRAR#1221
AR Jordan
Rodney .... GRAR#1513
AR Little Rock
Arkansas Loving .... GRAR#2135
AR Lockesburg
Falls Chapel .... GRAR#1308
Lockesburg.................... GRAR#1311
AR London
Mt Carmel .... GRAR#1212
AR Louann
Sulphur Springs............. GRAR#1315
AR Magazine
Old Union...................... GRAR#1409
Walnut Grove .... GRAR#1414
AR Magnolia
Walkerville .... GRAR#1317
AR Melbourne
Mt Olive .... GRAR#1517
AR Monticello
Rose Hill .... GRAR#1106
AR Morrilton
Trinity............................ GRAR#1219
AR Mount Pleasant
Barren Fork .... GRAR#1501
AR Mountain Home
Fellowship..................... GRAR#1505
AR Oxford
Oxford........................... GRAR#1511
AR Palestine
Palestine........................ GRAR#1103
AR Paris
Shaver .... GRAR#1413
AR Pine Bluff
Pine Bluff 1st .... GRAR#1104
Shell Chapel.................. GRAR#1108
AR Pineville
Pineville .... GRAR#1512
AR Pottsville
Mars Hill .... GRAR#1211
AR Ratcliff
Caulksville .... GRAR#1402
AR Russellville
Russellville.................... GRAR#1216
AR Salem
Salem............................. GRAR#1514
AR Searcy
Gum Springs .... GRAR#1205
Pleasant Grove .... GRAR#1214
Searcy............................ GRAR#1218
AR Sherwood
Sherwood .... GRAR#1220

BRAZIL

BR Bahia
Mata de Sao Joao .... GRAR#8313

CALIFORNIA

CA San Francisco
Chinese.......................... MSDC#8501

LOCATION INDEX OF CHURCHES CONTINUED

Grace ....MSDC#8510
Redeemer ....MSDC#8512
CA Trona
Trona ....MSDC#8503

COLOMBIA

CO Antioquia
Horeb-Central ....MSAN#8915
El Rebano...................MSAN#8905
La Rosa De Saron ....MSAN#8911
Zamora ....MSAN#8918
CO Buenaventura
Divino Redentor...........MSAN#8206
Emaus...........................MSCA#8219
CO Caldas
Manizales ....MSAN#8914
CO Cali
Betania Mission ....MSCA#8204
Bethel ....MSCA#8205
Central...........................MSCA#8208
Filipos ....MSCA#8211
Nueva Esperanza..........MSCA#8221
Nueva Jerusalen ....MSCA#8222
Principe De Paz.............MSCA#8201
Renacer ....MSCA#8225
Samaria ....MSCA#8217
San Marcos...................MSCA#8218
CO El Cerrito
Getsemani ....MSCA#8210
CO Guacari
San Pablo ....MSCA#8212
CO Guapi
Maranatha ....MSCA#8220
CO Montebello
Caleb Mission ....MSCA#8223
CO Palmira
San Lucas.....................MSCA#8215
CO Popayan
Popayan.......................MSCA#8227
CO Quindio
Armenia.......................MSAN#8903
CO Risaralda
Dosquebradas...............MSAN#8907
La Virginia ....MSCA#8913
Pereira ....MSAN#8916
CO Tulua
Tulua Mission...............MSCA#8226
CO Valle
Cartago........................MSAN#8906

FLORIDA

FL Dade City
Immanuel ....SEGR#0311
FL Lutz
Christ............................SEGR#0303
FL Miami
El Camino ....SEGR#0310
FL Tampa
First Hispanic ....SEGR#0307
FL Valrico
Hope.............................SEGR#0308
FL Wimauma

GEORGIA

GA Chatsworth
Sumach...........................SETG#2124
GA Duluth
Glory Church of Jesus.....SETG#2144
Korean Living Stone.......SETG#2130

GA Lawrenceville
El Redil ....SETG#2149
GA Rydal
Bartow........................SETG#2101

HONG KONG

HO Cheung Chau
Cheung Chau.................MSHK#8801
HO Kowloon
Kowloon.......................MSHK#8803
Tao Hsien ....MSHK#8806
HO Landau Island
Mu Min ....MSHK#8810
HO NT
Yao Dao.......................MSHK#8811
HO North Point
North Point...................MSHK#8805
HO Shatin NT
Shatin ....MSHK#8807
HO Tseung Kwan O NT
Po Lam ....MSHK#8808
HO Yuen Long
Xi Lin...........................MSHK#8809

ILLINOIS

IL Anna
Camp Ground.................MICO#5103
IL Annapolis
Pleasant Grove ....MICO#5210
IL Beecher City
Spring Hill.......................MINC#5411
IL Bethany
Bethany ....MINC#5401
IL Brookport
Mt. Sterling ....MICO#5117
IL Buncombe
Ebenezer Hall.................MICO#5106
IL Burnt Prairie
Burnt Prairie...................MINC#5102
IL Carriers Mills
Providence......................MICO#5122
IL Casey
Casey.............................MINC#5201
IL Chicago
Ebenezer.......................MINC#5203
IL Cisne
Elm River ....MINC#5107
IL Dongola
Mt Zion ....MICO#5118
IL Dundee
Comunidad Cristiana ......MINC#5212
IL Fairfield
Cumberland Chapel ....MINC#5104
Fairfield........................MINC#5108
Lebanon North ....MINC#5113
Union North ....MINC#5124
IL Farmer City
Fullerton.......................MINC#5404
IL Galatia
Lebanon South ....MINC#5114
Union Chapel ....MICO#5123
IL Georgetown
Georgetown....................MINC#5204
IL Greenville
Campground...................MINC#5402
Mt. Gilead ....MINC#5406
IL Lincoln
Lincoln 1st ....MINC#5405
IL Martinsville
Willow Creek ....MINC#5211

IL Norris City
Mt Oval ....MINC#5116
United............................MINC#5119
Village ....MICO#5125
IL Petersburg
Petersburg.......................MINC#5408
IL Simpson
Gilead ....MICO#5110
IL Thompsonville
Ebenezer ....MICO#5105
IL Trilla
Good Prospect.................MINC#5205
IL Virginia
Shiloh ....MINC#5409
IL Yale
New Hope ....MINC#5208

INDIANA

IN Chandler
Chandler ....MICO#5302
IN Evansville
Morningside ....MINC#5304
IN Indianapolis
Christ..............................MINC#5305
IN Monroe City
Monroe City ....MINC#5307
IN Petersburg
Knights Chapel................MINC#5306
IN Washington
Mt Olivet........................MINC#5308

IOWA

IA New London
Shinar ....MINC#5410

JAPAN

JA 184-0011
Higashi Koganei..............MSJA#8301
JA 186-0002
Kunitachi Nozomi...........MSJA#8306
JA 194-0041
Naruse ....MSJA#8305
JA 207-0023
Megumi ....MSJA#8309
JA 228-0004
Sagamino.........................MSJA#8304
JA 228-0818
Den-en Mission...............MSJA#8310
JA 241-0021
Asahi Mission Point ....MSJA#8315
JA 241-0825
Kibougaoka.....................MSJA#8302
JA 242-0006
Koza ....MSJA#8303
JA 243-0422
Ebina Shion No ....MSJA#8311
JA 245-0016
Izumi Mission ....MSJA#8312
JA 259-1321
Sibusawa ....MSJA#8307
JA 272-0834
Ichikawa Grace Mission . MSJA#8314

KENTUCKY

KY Auburn
Auburn............................MICU#3301
Gasper River ....MICU#3306
KY Beaver Dam

LOCATION INDEX OF CHURCHES CONTINUED

Point Pleasant................MICU#3313
KY Benton
   Benton......................MICO#3403
   Oak Grove....................MICO#3412
KY Big Clifty
   Mt Olive......................MICU#3216
KY Bowling Green
   Bowling Green..............MICU#3304
   Mt Olivet..................MICU#3312
KY Bremen
   Brier Creek..................MICU#3503
   Fairview......................MICU#3504
KY Calvert City
   Oakland.........................MICO#3413
   Vaughn's Chapel............MICO#3423
KY Campbellsville
   Campbellsville..............MICO#3104
   Good Hope....................MICU#3109
   Liberty.........................MICU#3116
   Shiloh.........................MICU#3129
KY Caneyville
   Caneyville....................MICU#3201
   Mt Pleasant....................MICU#3217
KY Canmer
   Hopewell......................MICU#3112
KY Center
   Bethel.........................MICU#3102
   Seven Springs.................MICU#3128
KY Clay
   Lisman.......................MICO#3613
   Oak Grove Union...........MICO#3619
KY Dalton
   Macedonia....................MICO#3614
KY Eastview
   Needham......................MICU#3219
KY Edmonton
   Cedar Flat....................MICU#3106
KY Falls of Rough
   Short Creek..................MICU#3221
KY Fredonia
   Fredonia.........................MICO#3608
   Good Spring.................MICO#3609
KY Garfield
   Garfield.........................MICU#3208
KY Glasgow
   Glasgow......................MICU#3108
   Lick Branch..................MICU#3117
   Neal's Chapel.................MICU#3122
KY Glens Fork
   Mt Zion.........................MICU#3121
KY Greensburg
   Greensburg....................MICU#3110
   Salem.........................MICU#3127
KY Greenville
   Greenville....................MICU#3505
KY Guthrie
   Gill's Chapel.................MICU#3307
KY Hardin
   Unity.........................MICO#3422
KY Hardyville
   Monroe Chapel..............MICU#3119
KY Harned
   Ephesus......................MICU#3205
   Freedom......................MICU#3207
KY Harrodsburg
   Bethel #1......................MICU#3103
   Harrodsburg.................MICU#3111
KY Hartford
   Beulah.........................MICU#3501
KY Hawesville
   Dukes.........................MICU#3204
KY Herndon

Flat Lick......................MICO#3606
KY Hopkinsville
   Hopkinsville..................MICO#3611
KY Horse Cave
   Clear Point....................MICU#3107
KY Hudson
   Coyle.........................MICU#3203
KY Irvington
   Clifton Mills..................MICU#3202
   Irvington......................MICU#3210
KY Kevil
   Bethel.........................MICO#3404
   Pleasant Valley..............MICU#3418
KY Knob Lick
   Antioch......................MICU#3101
   Wisdom......................MICU#3130
KY Leitchfield
   Leitchfield....................MICU#3211
   Mt Vernon....................MICU#3218
KY Lewisburg
   Green Ridge..................MICU#3308
   Lewisburg....................MICU#3309
KY Louisville
   Heartsong....................MICU#3222
   Louisville 1st..................MICU#3212
KY Madisonville
   Madisonville.................MICO#3615
KY Magnolia
   Magnolia......................MICU#3214
KY Marion
   Marion First..................MICO#3616
   Piney Fork....................MICO#3620
   Sugar Grove..................MICO#3626
KY Marrowbone
   Casey's Fork..................MICU#3105
KY Mayfield
   Calvary.........................MICO#3405
   Rozzell Chapel..............MICO#3419
KY Morgantown
   Little Muddy.................MICU#3310
   Morgantown..................MICU#3311
KY Murray
   Liberty.........................MICO#3406
   North Pleasant Grove.....MICO#3411
KY Nebo
   Rose Creek..................MICO#3622
KY Owensboro
   Owensboro..................MICU#3509
   Pleasant Hill..................MICU#3510
KY Paducah
   Highland......................MICO#3414
   Margaret Hank..............MICO#3415
   New Hope......................MICO#3410
   Woodlawn....................MICO#3417
KY Philpot
   Mt Zion.........................MICU#3507
KY Providence
   Providence 1st...............MICU#3621
KY Radcliff
   Radcliff.........................MICU#3220
KY Rumsey
   New Cypress.................MICU#3508
KY Russellville
   Bald Knob....................MICU#3302
KY Sacramento
   Poplar Grove.................MICU#3511
   Sacramento...................MICU#3512
KY Salem
   Hopewell......................MICO#3610
KY Sturgis
   Sturgis.........................MICO#3625
KY Sullivan

Mt. Pleasant..................MICO#3618
KY Summer Shade
   Mt Moriah....................MICU#3120
KY Summersville
   Oak Forest....................MICU#3123
KY Water Valley
   Bayou de Chien.............MICU#3401
KY West Paducah
   Milburn Chapel..............MICU#3416
KY West Somerset
   High Point....................MICU#3314
KY Wheatcroft
   Wheatcroft....................MICO#3627
KY White Plains
   Mt Carmel....................MICO#3617

KOREA

KO Seoul
   Korea 1st......................SEET#2221
   Sumkim Presby..............SEET#2222

LOUISANA

LA Pleasant Hill
   Progress......................MSTR#8123
LA Quitman
   Antioch......................MSTR#8101

MACAU, PORTUGUESE PROVINCE

MA Andar LMN
   Macau.........................MSHK#8804

MASSACHUSETTS

MA Malden
   Casa De Fe....................SEET#2220

MARYLAND

MD Salisbury
   Our Good......................SETG#2138

MICHIGAN

MI Lincoln Park
   Grace.........................MINC#5502
MI St Clair Shores
   Faith.........................MINC#5501

MISSISSIPPI

MS Ackerman
   Enon.........................SEGR#0707
MS Cedarbluff
   Cairo.........................SEGR#0704
MS Columbus
   Beersheba....................SEGR#0702
   Columbus....................SEGR#0706
   Mt Zion.........................SEGR#0709
MS Corinth
   Shiloh.........................GRWT#9226
MS Falkner
   Mt Zion.........................GRWT#9214
MS Macon
   McLeod Chapel.............SEGR#0708
MS Morton
   Groverton....................SEGR#0602
MS Olive Branch
   Olive Branch................GRWT#9312
MS Union

Erin............................ SEGR#0601
Steam Mill..................... SEGR#0608
MS Walnut
Hopewell.................... GRWT#9207
MS Walnut Grove
Salem........................ SEGR#0607

MISSOURI

MO Aurora
Orange....................... GRMI#4108
MO Chilhowee
Shawnee Mound.......... GRMI#4111
MO Conway
Happy Home .... GRMI#4306
MO Dunnegan
Spring Creek .... GRMI#4113
MO Greenfield
Greenfield................... GRMI#4104
MO Independence
Lobb........................... GRMI#4209
MO Knob Noster
Pleasant Grove .... GRMI#4109
MO Lamar
Hopewell.................... GRMI#4105
MO Lebanon
White Oak Pond........... GRMI#4315
MO Mansfield
Mansfield.................... GRMI#4308
MO Marshall
Marshall .... GRMI#4210
MO Martinville
Pierson....................... GRMI#4312
MO Montrose
Montrose..................... GRMI#4107
MO Phillipsburg
Phillipsburg................ GRMI#4311
MO Salem
New Hope .... GRMI#4309
MO San Antonio
Harmony .... GRMI#4203
MO Seymour
Seymour...................... GRMI#4313
MO Springfield
Oak Grove................... GRMI#4310
Springfield 1st............. GRMI#4314
MO Warrensburg
Salem......................... GRMI#4216
Warrensburg .... GRMI#4115
MO Wentworth
Bethel......................... GRMI#4102
MO West Plains
Elk Creek .... GRMI#4304

NEW JERSEY

NJ Tinton Falls
Hope Korean .... SECE#2131

NEW MEXICO

NM Albuquerque
Heights....................... MSDC#8701
NM Rio Rancho
Westside .... MSDC#8709

NEW YORK

NY Flushing
One Way....................... SECE#2137
Sharing........................ SECE#2141

OKLAHOMA

OK Ada
Covenant .... MSRR#6304
OK Atoka
Pigeon Roost .... MSCH#6109
OK Broken Bow
McGee Chapel .... MSCH#6106
OK Burns Flat
Burns Flat.................... MSRR#6301
OK Clinton
Clinton........................ MSRR#6302
OK Coalgate
Coal Creek .... MSCH#6102
Lone Star...................... MSCH#6105
OK Eagletown
Panki Bok.................... MSCH#6108
OK Edmond
Stone Gate................... MSRR#6307
OK Honobia
Rock Creek................... MSCH#6111
OK Locust Grove
Locust Grove................ MSRR#6203
OK Mangum
Mangum .... MSRR#6306
OK Marlow
Marlow........................ MSRR#6305
OK Oklahoma City
Eastlake .... MSRR#6205
OK Tulsa
Faith .... MSRR#6201
OK Tupelo
Round Lake .... MSCH#6112

PENNSYLVANIA

PA Bridgeport
Bridgeport .... MICU#3131

TENNESSEE

TN Afton
Fairview .... SEET#2204
Mt Pleasant................... SEET#2209
TN Algood
Algood......................... TNMU#7201
TN Atoka
Bethel .... GRWT#9301
TN Atwood
Atwood........................ GRWT#9101
Pleasant Green .... GRWT#9129
TN Bartlett
Faith .... GRWT#9308
TN Beech Bluff
Maple Springs .... GRWT#9210
TN Beechgrove
Beech Grove................. TNMU#7204
TN Bell Buckle
Green Hill.................... TNCO#7118
TN Belvidere
Belvidere...................... TNMU#7205
TN Bethel Springs
New Salem.................... GRWT#9216
TN Bethpage
Dry Fork...................... TNNA#7309
TN Bolivar
Bolivar......................... GRWT#9202
TN Boonshill
Boonshill...................... TNCO#7106
TN Bradford
Bradford .... GRWT#9104
Oliver's Chapel............ GRWT#9127

TN Brentwood
Brenthaven .... TNNA#7331
TN Brighton
Holly Grove .... GRWT#9304
TN Brunswick
Brunswick .... GRWT#9302
TN Brush Creek
Union Hill .... TNMU#7246
TN Bulls Gap
Pilot Knob .... SEET#2213
Willoughby................... SEET#2219
TN Burlison
Walnut Grove .... GRWT#9320
TN Camden
Camden .... GRWT#9105
TN Cane Ridge
Cane Ridge .... TNNA#7326
TN Centerville
Swan........................... TNCO#7140
TN Chapel Hill
Chapel Hill .... TNCO#7109
TN Charlotte
Charlotte...................... TNNA#7303
Mt Liberty .... TNNA#7320
TN Chattanooga
Chattanooga 1st.............. SETG#2104
Cornerstone Community TNNA#2107
Red Bank...................... SETG#2105
Silverdale .... SETG#2106
TN Chuckey
Pleasant Hill................. SEET#2214
Pleasant Vale .... SEET#2215
TN Clarksville
Bethel .... TNNA#7302
Calvary .... TNNA#7342
Clarksville .... TNNA#7304
Liberty........................ TNNA#7315
McAdoo .... TNNA#7318
New Providence............ TNNA#7305
TN Cleveland
Charleston .... SETG#2102
Cleveland .... SETG#2108
Flint Springs................ SETG#2112
Prospect United............. SETG#2116
TN College Grove
Harpeth Lick .... TNCO#7119
TN Columbia
Columbia 1st................. TNCO#7110
McCains....................... TNCO#7126
New Bethel................... TNCO#7134
Pleasant Mount.............. TNCO#7136
Union Grove.................. TNCO#7141
West Point .... TNCO#7143
TN Cookeville
Cookeville 1st .... TNMU#7210
Dry Valley .... TNMU#7213
Mt Hermon................... TNMU#7229
TN Cordova
Korean......................... GRWT#9322
Morning Sun .... GRWT#9314
TN Cowan
Cowan .... TNMU#7211
TN Cunningham
Locust Grove................ TNNA#7316
TN Decaturville
Camp Ground................ GRWT#9204
TN Dickson
Dickson .... TNNA#7308
TN Dover
Mt View...................... TNNA#7322
TN Dresden
Dresden....................... GRWT#9110

TN Dukedom
   Good Springs .... GRWT#9112
TN Dyer
   Bells Chapel .... GRWT#9403
   Dyer.............................. GRWT#9409
   Mt Olive .... GRWT#9418
TN Dyersburg
   Dyersburg 1st .... GRWT#9410
   Roellen .... GRWT#9428
TN Eagleville
   Rocky Glade .... TNMU#7240
TN Elora
   Elora .... TNCO#7111
TN Erin
   Arlington .... TNNA#7311
   Camp Ground .... TNNA#7312
   Erin .... TNNA#7310
TN Fall Branch
   Bethesda .... SEET#2201
TN Faulkner
   Mt Zion .... GRWT#9214
TN Fayetteville
   Fayetteville .... TNCO#7112
   Howell .... TNCO#7121
   Mt Hebron .... TNCO#7128
TN Flintville
   Flintville .... TNCO#7115
TN Franklin
   Belleview .... TNCO#7104
   Franklin .... TNCO#7116
   Grace .... TNCO#7145
   Mt Carmel .... TNCO#7127
TN Friendship
   Bethesda .... GRWT#9404
TN Gadsden
   Salem .... GRWT#9430
TN Gallatin
   Sudanese .... TNNA#7341
TN Germantown
   Germantown .... GRWT#9310
TN Gleason
   Gleason .... GRWT#9111
TN Goodlettsville
   Goodlettsville .... GRWT#7328
TN Greenbrier
   Mt Sharon .... TNNA#7321
TN Greeneville
   Cedar Hill .... SEET#2202
   Gass Memorial .... SEET#2205
   Greeneville .... SEET#2206
   New Bethel .... SEET#2210
   Salem .... SEET#2216
   Shiloh .... SEET#2217
TN Greenfield
   Meridian .... GRWT#9120
TN Halls
   Poplar Grove .... GRWT#9425
TN Hartsville
   Providence .... TNMU#7238
TN Henderson
   Oak Grove .... GRWT#9217
TN Hendersonville
   Beech .... TNNA#7301
   Hendersonville .... TNNA#7340
TN Hillsboro
   Hillsboro .... TNMU#7217
TN Hixson
   Falling Water .... SETG#2111
TN Hohenwald
   Hohenwald .... TNCO#7120
TN Hollow Rock
   Barren Springs .... GRWT#9102

TN Humboldt
   Double Springs .... GRWT#9109
   Humboldt .... GRWT#9116
TN Huntland
   Mt Carmel .... TNMU#7228
TN Iron City
   Mt Nebo .... TNCO#7132
TN Jackson
   Claybrook .... GRWT#9205
   Jackson 1st .... GRWT#9208
TN Jasper
   Jasper .... SETG#2113
TN Jefferson City
   Lebanon .... SEET#2207
TN Kelso
   Kelso .... TNCO#7122
TN Kenton
   Kenton .... GRWT#9414
   Mason Hall .... GRWT#9415
   Morella .... GRWT#9416
   North Union .... GRWT#9423
TN Kingston
   Young's Chapel .... SEET#2317
TN Knoxville
   Beaver Creek .... SEET#2301
   Knoxville .... SEET#2305
   Marietta .... SEET#2308
   Union .... SEET#2315
   Virtue .... SEET#2316
TN Lakeland
   New Salem .... GRWT#9316
TN Lavinia
   Cool Springs CC .... GRWT#9107
TN Lawrenceburg
   Lawrenceburg .... TNCO#7124
TN Lebanon
   LaGuardo .... TNMU#7219
   Lebanon .... TNMU#7220
   New Hope .... TNMU#7233
TN Lenoir City
   Faith Fellowship .... SEET#2319
   Heartland .... SEET#2306
   Mercy .... SEET#2320
TN Lewisburg
   Lewisburg 1st .... TNCO#7125
   Richland .... TNCO#7137
TN Lexington
   Lexington 1st .... GRWT#9209
   Palestine .... GRWT#9221
TN Limestone
   Philadelphia .... SEET#2212
TN Livingston
   Livingston 1st .... TNMU#7223
   Ruth Chapel .... TNMU#7241
TN Loudon
   Loudon .... SEET#2307
TN Madison
   Cristo Vive .... TNNA#7314
   Madison 1st .... TNNA#7329
   St Luke .... TNNA#7332
TN Madisonville
   Corntassel .... SEET#2304
   New Hope .... SEET#2311
TN Manchester
   Manchester .... TNMU#7224
TN Martin
   Martin .... GRWT#9117
TN Maryville
   Clark's Grove .... SEET#2302
   Maryville 1st .... SEET#2309
TN Mason
   Ebenezer .... GRWT#9303

TN McDonald
   Pine Hill .... SETG#2117
TN McEwen
   Cumberland Valley .... TNNA#7307
TN McKenzie
   McKenzie .... GRWT#9118
   Shiloh .... GRWT#9131
   Zion .... GRWT#9133
TN McMinnville
   Bates Hill .... TNMU#7203
   Blues Hill .... TNMU#7207
   Dibrell .... TNMU#7212
   Liberty .... TNMU#7222
   LuzD.L.Naciones .... TNMU#7252
   McMinnville .... TNMU#7225
TN Medina
   Medina .... GRWT#9119
TN Memphis
   Colonial .... GRWT#9305
   New Beginnings .... GRWT#9306
   Nuevo Empezar .... GRWT#9324
TN Mercer
   Ebenezer .... GRWT#9206
TN Milan
   Milan .... GRWT#9121
TN Millington
   Pleasant Union .... GRWT#9318
   West Union .... GRWT#9321
TN Mohawk
   Mohawk .... SEET#2208
TN Monteagle
   Monteagle .... TNMU#7227
TN Morristown
   Dover .... SEET#2203
TN Moscow
   Pleasant Grove .... SEET#9317
TN Mount Juliet
   Suggs Creek .... TNMU#7244
TN Mount Pleasant
   Mt Joy .... TNCO#7129
   Mt Pleasant .... TNCO#7133
TN Mt Juliet
   Cloyd's .... TNMU#7208
TN Mulberry
   Champ .... TNCO#7108
TN Murfreesboro
   Jerusalem .... TNMU#7218
   Joywood .... TNMU#7250
   Mt Tabor .... TNMU#7230
   Murfreesboro .... TNMU#7232
TN Nashville
   Brush Hill .... TNNA#7325
   Donelson .... TNNA#7327
   Mt Sinai .... TNNA#7330
   The Connection .... TNNA#7335
   Tusculum .... TNNA#7333
   West Nashville .... TNNA#7334
TN Newbern
   Hurricane Hill .... GRWT#9413
   New Bethlehem .... GRWT#9420
   Newbern .... GRWT#9419
   Palestine .... GRWT#9424
TN Nolensville
   Jenkins .... TNCO#7144
TN Oak Ridge
   Oak Ridge .... SEET#2313
TN Obion
   Cloverdale .... GRWT#9407
   Woodward's Chapel .... GRWT#9434
TN Oliver Springs
   Mt Carmel .... SEET#2310
   Oliver Springs .... SEET#2314

LOCATION INDEX OF CHURCHES CONTINUED

TN Palmyra
   Shiloh .... TNNA#7338
TN Paris
   Oak Hill...................... GRWT#9125
TN Parsons
   Parsons 1st .... GRWT#9222
TN Petersburg
   Petersburg..................... TNCO#7135
TN Portland
   Boiling Springs .... TNCO#3303
TN Prospect
   Fiducia........................... TNCO#7113
TN Pulaski
   Mt Moriah .... TNCO#7131
TN Puryear
   Mill Creek .... GRWT#9122
TN Ramer
   Mt Vernon .... GRWT#9213
   Ramer............................ GRWT#9223
TN Rockvale
   Mt Vernon .... TNMU#7231
   Rockvale .... TNMU#7239
TN Rutherford
   Rutherford .... GRWT#9429
TN Santa Fe
   Santa Fe........................ TNCO#7138
TN Savannah
   Olivet............................ GRWT#9220
   Savannah 1st .... GRWT#9224
TN Selmer
   New Bethel.................... GRWT#9215
   Selmer Court Avenue .... GRWT#9225
TN Sewanee
   Sewanee .... TNMU#7242
TN Sharon
   Hopewell....................... GRWT#9115
   New Salem .... GRWT#9124
   Sharon .... GRWT#9130
TN Smithville
   Banks............................ TNMU#7202
   Smithville..................... TNMU#7243
TN Somerville
   Mt Carmel .... GRWT#9315
TN South Fulton
   Fulton .... GRWT#9412
TN South Pittsburg
   Richard City .... SETG#2118
   South Pittsburg............. SETG#2123
TN Sparta
   Hickory Valley .... SETG#7251
   Old Zion .... TNMU#7234
TN Spring Hill
   Ash Hill........................ TNCO#7101
   Mt Lebanon.................. TNCO#7130
TN Springfield
   Mt Denson.................... TNNA#7319
TN Stewart
   New Hope .... TNNA#7337
TN Talbott
   Talbott .... SEET#2218
TN Telford
   Oakland......................... SEET#2211
TN Trenton
   Concord......................... GRWT#9106
   Davidson Chapel........... GRWT#9108
TN Trezevant
   Trezevant...................... GRWT#9132
TN Trimble
   Cool Springs........... GCGRWT#9408
   Trimble......................... GRWT#9431
TN Troy
   New Ebenezer .... GRWT#9422

   Protemus .... GRWT#9426
   Troy.............................. GRWT#9432
TN Union City
   Antioch Union.............. GRWT#9401
   Beech............................ GRWT#9402
   Bethlehem .... GRWT#9405
   Mt Ararat...................... GRWT#9417
   Union City.................... GRWT#9433
TN Unionville
   Kingdom .... TNCO#7123
TN Watertown
   Commerce .... TNMU#7209
   Watertown .... TNMU#7247
TN Waverly
   Concord......................... TNNA#7306
   Halls Creek................... TNNA#7313
   Mariah.......................... TNNA#7317
   Waverly .... TNNA#7339
TN Waynesboro
   Waynesboro................... TNCO#7142
TN Whitwell
   Cedar Springs................ SETG#2119
   Ebenezer....................... SETG#2110
   Kelly's Chapel .... SETG#2120
   New Hope .... SETG#2115
   Oak Grove..................... SETG#2121
   Whitwell....................... SETG#2122
TN Winchester
   Goshen .... TNMU#7214
   Gum Creek .... TNMU#7215
   Harmony .... TNMU#7216
   Owens Chapel .... TNMU#7235
   Winchester 1st.............. TNMU#7249
TN Yorkville
   Yorkville....................... GRWT#9435

TEXAS

TX Arlington
   St John.......................... MSRR#8413
TX Austin
   Austin 1st .... MSTR#8601
   Shepherd/Hills.............. MSTR#8604
TX Bedford
   St Timothy.................... MSRR#8419
TX Bertram
   Bertram......................... MSTR#8605
TX Burleson
   Pathway......................... MSRR#8418
TX Chico
   Zion Valley .... MSRR#8425
TX Clarksville
   Shiloh .... MSTR#8125
TX Daingerfield
   Daingerfield................... MSTR#8106
TX Dallas
   Lake Higlands .... MSRR#8411
TX Denton
   Denton .... MSRR#8404
TX El Paso
   El Paso 1st.................... MSDC#8704
TX Fort Worth
   St Luke......................... MSRR#8407
   St Mark......................... MSRR#8408
   Trinity........................... MSRR#8409
TX Freeport
   Freeport......................... MSTR#8103
TX Georgetown
   Oak Grove..................... MSTR#8607
TX Greenville
   Mt Zion .... MSRR#8414
TX Houston

   Houston 1st .... MSTR#8606
   Nueva Vida.................... MSTR#8612
TX Hubbard
   Hubbard......................... MSRR#8410
TX Jefferson
   Jefferson....................... MSTR#8109
TX Joinerville
   Mt Hope........................ MSTR#8117
TX Longview
   Elmira Chapel .... MSTR#8111
   Longview 1st................. MSTR#8112
   Pine Tree .... MSTR#8113
TX Lubbock
   Lubbock .... MSDC#8702
TX Marshall
   Marshall .... MSTR#8115
TX Mesquite
   Mesquite .... MSRR#8412
TX Midlothian
   Shiloh .... MSRR#8421
TX Millsap
   Newberry....................... MSRR#8415
TX Odessa
   St Andrew..................... MSDC#8703
TX Olney
   Olney............................. MSRR#8416
TX Round Rock
   Round Rock .... MSTR#8611
TX San Antonio
   Northminster .... MSTR#8610
   Stone Oak..................... MSTR#8608
TX San Elizario
   Maranatha .... MSDC#8706
TX Troup
   Concord......................... MSTR#8104
TX Whitesboro
   Sandy Springs .... MSRR#8420
TX Whitney
   Whitney......................... MSRR#8424
TX Winnsboro
   Pine Hill .... MSTR#8122

CUMBERLAND PRESBYTERIAN CHURCH IN AMERICA
Denominational Center
226 Church Street, NW, Huntsville, AL 35801
(256)536-7481 OR FAX (256)536-7482
cpcaga@aol.com

Moderator of the General Assembly:
Elder Lewis Leon Cole, Jr., PO Box 335, Warren, MI 48090
(248)770-1540   llcole1951@yahoo.com

Vice-Moderator of the General Assembly:
Reverend Anthony Hollis, 1100 Gateway Avenue, Apt 200, Chattanooga, TN 37402
(423)645-3277   anthony_hollis@att.net

Administrative Director of the Cumberland Presbyterian Church in America:
Reverend Doctor G. Lynne Herring, 3244 Vicksburg SW, Decatur, AL 35603
(256)536-7481(w)   (256)355-7677(h)   cpcaga@aol.com

Stated Clerk of the General Assembly:
Elder Craig A. White, 134 McEntire Lane SW A36, Decatur, AL 35603
(256)565-5751   white8@bellsouth.net

Engrossing Clerk of the General Assembly:
Reverend Lela Fencher, 620 Live Oak Circle, Fairfield, AL 35064, (205)780-4913
(205)789-3913

Church Paper: *THE CUMBERLAND FLAG*
Editor: Reverend Doctor G. Lynne Herring, 3244 Vicksburg SW, Decatur, AL 35603
(256)536-7481(w)   (256)355-7677(h)   cpcaga@aol.com

SYNODS - PRESBYTERIES - STATED CLERKS

Alabama Synod - Elder Vanessa Midgett, 118 Thunderbird Drive, Harvest, AL 35749
1. Birmingham Presbytery - Rev. Teresa Paige, 228 S Park Road, Birmingham, AL 35211
    (205)706-9057   tcpaige12@yahoo.com
2. Florence Presbytery - Rev. Dr. Laurentis Barnett, 118 Ivyridge Road, Madison, AL 35758
    (256)489-6246
3. Huntsville Presbytery - Rev. Dr. Theodis Acklin, 3415 Mastin Lake Road, Huntsville, AL 35810
    (256)945-7216
4. South Alabama Presbytery - Elder Minnie McMillan, 54 Riverview Avenue, Selma, AL 36701
    (334)875-9617   mmcmillan@ccal.edu
5. Tennessee Valley Presbytery - Rev. Critis Fletcher, 68 Mattie Street, Russellville, AL 35654
    (256)332-6325   gepolar@bellsouth.net
6. Tuscaloosa Presbytery - Rev. Jacqueline Lang, 904 35th Avenue, Tuscaloosa, AL 35401
    (205)292-1048

Kentucky Synod - Elder Leon Cole, Jr., PO Box 335, Warren, MI 48090
1. Cleveland, Ohio Presbytery - Elder Greg Scruggs, 1117 Mt Vernon Blvd, Cleveland Heights, OH 44112
    (216)645-9584   gsagi57@yahoo.com
2. Ohio Valley Presbytery - Elder Sharon Combs, PO Box 122, Sturgis, KY 42459
    (270)860-4175   scombs1@bellsouth.net
3. Purchase Presbytery - Elder Sherell Sparks, 79 Paraadise Lane, Metropolis, IL 62960
    (618)203-2799   relld2000@yahoo.com

Tennessee Synod - Rev. Anthony Hollis, 1100 Gateway Avenue Apt 200, Chattanooga, TN 37402
1. Elk River Presbytery - Elder Jacquelyn Cooper, 4705 Indian Summer Drive, Nashville, TN 37207
    (615)440-3010   jmcooper12@comcast.net
2. Hiwassee Presbytery - Elder Stephine Martin, 205 North Point Road, Sweetwater, TN 37874
    (423)486-7633   stephanie.nicole@yahoo.com
3. New Hopewell Presbytery - Elder Cecelia Bowden, PO Box 661, Huntington, TN 38344
    (731)9864266

Texas Synod - Rev.Robert E Thomas, 1017 N Englewood, Tyler, TX 76643
1. Angelina Presbytery - Elder Tom Jones, 739 County Road 4720, Troup, TX 75789
    (972)285-0642   tjones1239@aol.com
2. Brazos River Presbytery - Elder Joy Wallace, 541 Glen Arbor Drive, Dallas, TX 75241
    (214)415-8734
3. East Texas Presbytery - Rev. Kay Ward Creed, PO Box 1316, Henderson, TX 75653
    (903)657-7169

INDEX

Camp Grounds 24
Center Offices C
Chaplains, Alphabetical Roll of..15
Churches
    Alphabetical Roll of..143
    Location by State or Country 150
Clerks of Synods and Presbyteries, Alphabetical Roll of 10
Cumberland Presbyterian Church in America, Directory of Officers..159
Cumberland Presbyterians Serving Outside the United States 21
Directories of Churches by Presbyteries
    Andes (MSAN) 27
    Arkansas (GRAR) 30
    Cauca Valley (MSCA) 36
    Choctaw (MSCH) 39
    Columbia (TNCO) 40
    Covenant (MICO) 44
    Cumberland (MICU) 49
    Cumberland East Coast (SEEC) 56
    del Cristo (MSDC) 57
    East Tennessee (SEET) 60
    Grace (SEGR) 65
    Hong Kong (MSHK) 70
    Hope (SEHO) 72
    Japan (MSJA) 74
    Missouri (GRMI) 77
    Murfreesboro (TNMU) 80
    Nashville (TNNA) 85
    North Central (MINC) 90
    Red River (MSRR) 94
    Robert Donnell (SERD) 98
    Tennessee-Georgia (SETG) 100
    Trinity (MSTR) 104
    West Tennessee (GRWT) 107
General Assembly Officers and Members of Agencies 1
Ministers
    Alphabetical Roll of..117
    Gained or Lost in 2014..14
    Memorial Roll of Ministers in 2014 16
    Ordained in 2014..14
Mission Probes..22
Moderators, Living 9
New Church Developments 22
Priority Goals i
Provisional Churches 23
Summary of Statistics of Presbyteries by Synods..26
Symbols, Explanation of..25
Synods and Presbyteries
    Abbreviations of..10
    Clerks of..10
Vision of Ministry i

www.ingramcontent.com/pod-product-compliance
Lightning Source LLC
Chambersburg PA
CBHW080935040426
42443CB00015B/3416